Students At Risk

M. Lee Manning
Old Dominion University

Leroy G. Baruth
Appalachian State University

Allyn and Bacon
Boston • London • Toronto • Sydney • Tokyo • Singapore

To my wife, Marianne, for her commitment to family and education; my daughter, Jennifer, who offered insightful comments; my son, Michael, who strives for excellence in all he does; and their grandmothers, Margaret and Annie, who for many years have been a positive influence on our lives.

MLM

To my wife, Carmella, for her many years of educating at-risk students; and my daughters—Seana, Kelly, and Katey—for the many lessons they taught me.

LGB

Series Editor: Virginia Lanigan
Editorial Assistant: Nicole DePalma
Cover Administrator: Suzanne Harbison
Composition Buyer: Linda Cox
Manufacturing Buyer: Louise Richardson
Marketing Manager: Ellen Mann
Editorial-Production Service: Spectrum Publisher Services, Inc.
Production Administrator: Ann Greenberger

Copyright © 1995 by Allyn & Bacon
A Simon & Schuster Company
Needham Heights, Massachusetts 02194

Library of Congress Cataloging-in-Publication Data

Manning, M. Lee
    Students at risk / M. Lee Manning, Leroy G. Baruth.
       p. cm.
    Includes bibliographical references and index.
    ISBN 0-205-15464-6
    1. Socially handicapped children—Education—United States.
  2. Problem children—Education—United States. I. Baruth, Leroy G.
  II. Title.
  LC4091.M29 1994
  371.96′7′0973—dc20   93-50125
                                                                          CIP

Printed in the United States of America

10 9 8 7 6 5 4 3 2 1   98 97 96 95 94

Contents

Preface

The late 1980s and early 1990s ushered in an interest in addressing at-risk conditions—a surge of journal articles on at-risk conditions, a plethora of at-risk programs being implemented nationwide, and an increased recognition that professional educators have a responsibility to address the needs of at-risk children and adolescents. While educators have long sought to provide all children and adolescents with appropriate educational experiences, identifying and assessing at-risk children and adolescents are relatively recent efforts, perhaps due to increased numbers of at-risk learners or to educators accepting greater responsibility toward learners that need specialized services.

It is not surprising that at-risk learners and appropriate education programs and efforts are receiving considerable attention. Many questions have arisen with respect to at-risk learners: What designating term aptly describes at-risk learners? What professionals are responsible for addressing the needs of at-risk learners? How can learners' at-risk conditions be addressed? How do school practices contribute to at-risk learners' conditions? What can be done to ensure fairness in testing and assessment procedures? How can at-risk learners' strengths be measured objectively? These selected questions represent only a few reasons for the current interest in at-risk learners. Regardless of how educators answer these questions, the strengths and weaknesses of at-risk children and adolescents must be addressed by caring, competent, and concerned educators. To do otherwise would be a failure to meet one's professional responsibilities and also will contribute to many learners not meeting their full potentials.

Several problems will continue to place youth in jeopardy in the twenty first century: the school dropout rate, teenage pregnancy, substance abuse, anxiety disorders, delinquency and violence, poverty, and a host of other conditions and behaviors. *Students At Risk* is designed for professionals such as university professors teaching courses in at-risk education, public and private school educators working daily with at-risk learners, and human service specialists addressing specialized needs.

Basic Premises

The basic premises of *Students At Risk* include 1) at-risk children and adolescents deserve educators' and human service professionals' attention; 2) at-risk conditions and behaviors can be identified and their potential for harming children's and adolescents' present and future well-being can be assessed; 3) at-risk children and adolescents can be provided effective programs and efforts designed to address specific conditions and behaviors; and 4) at-risk children and adolescents need objective identification and assessment procedures. Regarding the latter, this book strongly urges educators to strive for objective and valid identifications and assessments. Children and adolescents differ—a condition devastating to one learner may be a motivating factor to another. For example, one learner growing up in poverty might have his or her chances of educational success greatly diminished, while another might perceive education as a means out of poverty. All educators know of children and adolescents who have overcome serious at-risk conditions and situations or who have perceived a reason to stop engaging in at-risk behaviors and then went on to reach extraordinary heights, either in personal achievements or contributions to mankind.

Organization of the Book

Students At Risk contains three parts consisting of 10 chapters and an Epilogue. Each part provides a foundation for the next part and allows the reader to progress through a logical organization.

Part I, the Introduction, introduces the book and makes readers aware of at-risk learners' problems and also proposes that professionals working with at-risk children and adolescents are responsible for identifying at-risk conditions and for addressing their students' needs. Chapter 1 explains the various at-risk conditions and their potentially harmful effects on children, adolescents, and society. Chapter 2 suggests methods, techniques, and checklists for identifying and assessing at-risk conditions and behaviors.

Part II, At-Risk Conditions, takes a more detailed look at at-risk conditions and provides examples of successful programs. Chapters 3, 4, and 5, respectively, examine school, societal, and personal conditions. For example, Chapter 3 looks at school conditions such as overexpectations, inappropriate curricular and organization patterns, and ineffective teaching practices. Chapter 4 looks at conditions such as drugs, eating disorders, and AIDS, and Chapter 5 focuses on suicides, exceptionalities, and shyness and withdrawal, just to name a few topics.

Part III, The School's Response, examines classroom procedures, alternative learning environments, the involvement of parents and families, and exemplary programs designed to address school and societal conditions. Chapter 6 examines the school curriculum, organization, and management. Chapter 7, a key chapter for addressing the needs of at-risk learners, proposes that these learners need alternative learning environments. Chapter 8 maintains that the involvement of parents and families in at-risk learners' education is an essential for programs and efforts to achieve maximum potential. Chapters 9 and 10 focus on programs and efforts addressing school conditions and societal and personal conditions, respectively. Finally, the Epilogue provides hope for at-risk students and proposes the necessity for the future being a prime time for responsive action.

Special Learning Features

Students At Risk has several pedagogical features designed to assist the reader. Each clarifies and enlivens the text and, the authors hope, motivates readers to think about material and to take planned and deliberate action to help at-risk children and adolescents.

- *Probing Directions:* Located at the beginning of each chapter, the probing directions feature provides readers with a brief overview of topics to be covered in the chapter.
- *Case Studies:* Case studies are given in all chapters and located near related material. They provide a scenario involving professionals and other concerned people working to address a particular problem.
- *Suggested Activities:* Located throughout selected chapters, the suggested activities sections provide readers with examples of at-risk programs that have promise for specific conditions and behaviors.
- *Activities:* This feature, located throughout the text, provides readers with activities that require either first-hand involvement with at-risk children and adolescents or opportunities to learn more about working with these learners.
- *Reviewing What You Have Read:* This feature, located at the end of each chapter, provides a brief check-up for readers to review valuable information and to refocus on the main points addressed in the chapter.
- *For Additional Information:* Also located at the end of the chapter, this feature provides readers with an annotated listing of current journal articles, books, and other information about working with at-risk children and adolescents.
- *Appendix:* A comprehensive appendix provides names and addresses of many foundations, corporations, and resource centers that provide valuable information and various forms of assistance.

About the Authors

The authors bring considerable expertise, first-hand experience, and interest to *Students At Risk*. One author brings years of experience in educational curriculum and instruction and first-hand experiences working daily with at-risk students on both the elementary and secondary levels. The other author brings a counseling background and first-hand experiences working with at-risk learners in counseling situations. Both are genuinely interested in helping at-risk children and adolescents. *Students At Risk* reflects both education and counseling perspectives that substantiate the authors' beliefs that identifying, assessing, and helping at-risk learners should be team efforts reflecting collaborative relationships.

M. Lee Manning teaches in the Department of Educational Curriculum and Instruction, Darden College of Education, Old Dominion University, Norfolk, Virginia. He has taught a number of grade levels, working with at-risk children and adolescents in a lower socioeconomic school. His current interests include at-risk learners, effective middle school practices, and multicultural education. He has coauthored three books and has authored or coauthored more than 100 articles and book reviews in such journals as *Phi Delta Kappan, Childhood Education, NASSP Bulletin, Action in Teacher Education,* and *The Clearing House.*

Leroy G. Baruth, a proven and respected counselor, administrator, and writer serves as department chairperson in the Department of Human Development and Psychological Counseling, Reich College of Education, Appalachian State University, Boone, North Carolina. He has published many journal articles and authored or coauthored 17 books. In addition to his extensive research and writing, he has worked with and counseled at-risk children and adolescents in school and clinical settings. Like the first author, he has public school experience with school-age children and adolescents, which has allowed him to make the transition from research and theory to practical application.

Acknowledgments

The authors wish to offer their appreciation to Betty Levin of the Department of Educational Curriculum and Instruction, Darden College of Education, Old Dominion University, for her willingness to help whenever needed and for excellent typing and computer assistance and expertise; Jennifer Dotson and Michelle Neil for the preparation of the Instructor's Manual that accompanies this book; Virginia Lanigan, Series Editor, for her patience, advice, and editorial assistance; and Nicole DePalma, Series Editorial Assistant, for her kindness and assistance whenever the authors called Allyn and Bacon.

Also, they wish to thank the professionals in the field who reviewed this manuscript and provided valuable comments and suggestions: Jan McCarthy, University of South Florida; Eugene Eubanks, University of Missouri–Kansas City; and Carol Anne Pierson, University of Central Arkansas.

MLM
LGB

Part I

Introduction

Chapter 1
At-Risk Students and Programs

Chapter 2
Identification and Assessment

1

At-Risk Students and Programs

Outline

Overview

Probing Directions

A Word of Caution

At-Risk Students
Defining Who Is and Who Is Not at Risk
Demographic Characteristics

The Term "At-Risk"

At-Risk Conditions
Etiology: School, Social, and Personal
Specific Conditions

At-Risk Programs
Rationale
A Brief Historical Overview
Prerequisites

Selected Types of At-Risk Programs
Compensatory
Other Programs Addressing Specific Conditions

Overview

The number of children and adolescents who are at risk today and the potential consequences of these learners being at risk are causes for educators' immediate concern and attention. There are many indicators of children and adolescents being at risk: They are dropping out of school without hope of future education or gainful employment; they are becoming parents and/or victims of sexually transmitted diseases; they are becoming addicted to drugs and alcohol; they are becoming lower achievers at all educational levels; and they are living in poverty, often with little hope of breaking out of poverty's confines. The list is virtually endless. Educators have a threefold responsibility to: 1) understand at-risk students, whether they are elementary, middle, or secondary learners; 2) to know at-risk conditions and their consequences; 3) and to know established and proven at-risk programs designed to meet individual learner's needs. Designed for both prospective and practicing educators, this chapter looks at the challenge of understanding and assisting at-risk learners, and at the schools' role in addressing learners' at-risk conditions.

Probing Directions

This chapter on at-risk children and adolescents does the following:

1. Examines whether children and adolescents are at risk and when potentially dangerous conditions warrant educators' attention.
2. Examines demographic characteristics of at-risk children and adolescents.

3. Provides a succinct overview of the at-risk conditions addressed in this text.
4. Defines "at-risk programs" and provides a brief historical overview of the effort to help at-risk learners.
5. Examines several types or categories of at-risk programs.
6. Examines the various roles of the school in addressing the needs of at-risk children and adolescents.
7. Lists and describes several suggested resources, books, and journals that interested readers may consult.

A Word of Caution

Before beginning our discussion on at-risk students, it is important to note that learners of all grade levels deserve individual attention. One child living in poverty may be at risk; another may not. Some low achievers may lack the ability to learn, while others may be merely unmotivated or preoccupied with some other at-risk condition, such as being pregnant or having an addiction to drugs. Some painfully shy learners might be at risk, even though others may deal adequately with their shyness. An essential point warrants consideration—very few assumptions about at-risk learners and conditions can be made with certainty. Learners and their at-risk conditions must be considered individually, and programs that meet individual needs must be provided.

A consideration of cultural and gender differences does not imply that such differences are at-risk conditions or indicators. However, when educators identify at-risk learners and plan appropriate educational experiences, all factors and differences warrant consideration. For example, being a female African-American does not make one at risk. But if this adolescent has reading difficulties and attends a school that primarily addresses the needs of middle-class, majority-culture males and fails to recognize cultural and gender issues, the female adolescent's chances of becoming at risk might increase. Thus, the dangers of assumptions, stereotypes, and labeling are emphasized throughout this text. Doing otherwise shortchanges at-risk learners and has the potential for contributing to the learner's at-risk conditions or behaviors.

At-Risk Students

An understanding of "who is and who is not at risk" is necessary prior to determining the most appropriate educational experiences for a child. The nature of at-risk conditions often makes determinations difficult. This section shows the difficulty in determining who is at risk and who is not, and then looks at age, gender, cultural, and geographic characteristics. Although educators need to understand the many differences among learners, it is again important to point out that gender and cultural differences should not be considered at-risk conditions. Chapter 2 examines signs and characteristics that indicate a propensity toward being at risk in more detail.

Defining Who Is and Who Is Not at Risk

Educators during the past ten years have begun to use the term "at risk" to describe a particular category of students. Although the meaning of the term has never been precise and varies among educators and situations, Slavin (1989), referring only to academically at-risk learners, defines "at risk" as referring to students who, on the basis of several risk factors, are unlikely to graduate from high school. Slavin is certainly correct in his definition and in his suggestion to address the academic needs of these learners, yet educators will also be confronted with children and adolescents who have other at-risk conditions and factors. For example, educators will be responsible for working with students who are at risk due to health problems, substance use, disabilities, socioeconomic status (SES), attempted suicides, and other behaviors such as experimenting with drugs and sexual activity.

This book addresses students' academic needs, as well as looks at children and adolescents with other at-risk conditions and behaviors. The rationale for such an approach is that while many students are at risk academically, others engage in at-risk behaviors (such as those just mentioned) that make them academically at risk or at least increase the odds of learners not meeting their educational potential. Professional educators have a responsibility to children and adolescents who do not know or are unwilling to admit the dangers associated with substance use, sexual experimentation, and suicidal behavior. Therefore, this broad use of "at risk" challenges educators to understand the identifying characteristics of perhaps several at-risk conditions and to be knowledgeable of many programs and efforts designed to address specific at-risk conditions.

Sometimes, determining when students are at risk can be a difficult task. The many developmental occurrences, changes in family structures, pressures and pitfalls of school, and societal pressures undoubtedly place children and adolescents at risk. Walker (1991) aptly summarized the situation:

> *Every student is at risk for some reason. We cannot wait until a student is labeled as such to intervene; rather, we must plan for the success of all students. (p. 112)*

Likewise, two students may be experiencing similar situations and might be at risk, while other students experiencing the same at-risk conditions might be functioning adequately. Most educators can recall situations in which divorce and family breakup negatively affected some students, while other students dealt capably with the situation.

The authors stand by their statement that making assumptions requires considerable caution; thus, three fairly conclusive assumptions can be reached. They are as follows:

1. All children and adolescents are at risk at some time.
2. At-risk conditions affect children and adolescents in different ways and might not affect some children and adolescents at all.
3. Educators must use great caution when determining who is and who is not at risk.

The educator's challenge lies with determining whether and when at-risk conditions should be addressed. This appears to be a simple decision—educators without doubt always have a professional and ethical responsibility to address at-risk conditions. However, at-risk conditions do not always have clear-cut, defined lines. As previously mentioned, conditions that place some students at risk may not affect other students—the key is to decide *when a student is at risk*. For example, for some learners, being quiet and shy is an at-risk condition, while for others it is simply a personal characteristic. The quiet, shy learner may not be at risk until school assignments require social interaction or speaking in front of the group. Likewise, a decline in academic achievement due to loss of student interest or lack of motivation might be temporary in some cases and a serious at-risk indicator in others. Except for showing signs of concern and encouragement, the former situation might be best ignored. However, a serious at-risk indicator, such as suicidal thoughts, calls for decisive and immediate attention. Educators' responsibilities include being able to determine when conditions are temporary and best not addressed, and when conditions are of a more serious nature.

If a specific condition places a student at risk, the educator certainly has the professional responsibility to take immediate and appropriate action. Educators must also take appropriate action any time serious or life-threatening behaviors are recognized.

Demographic Characteristics

Determining demographic characteristics depends on the at-risk condition being considered; however, some general conclusions can be reached. As with other characteristics, educators must carefully avoid stereotyping learners. In this discussion of demographic characteristics, careful attention, whenever possible, will be given to informing readers of a specific at-risk condition.

Increasing numbers of 10- to 14-year-olds are experimenting with drugs, alcohol, and sex, at-risk behaviors that have potentially serious consequences. Adolescents, long thought to be the most vibrant and indestructible age group, are actually quite vulnerable due to their tendency to engage in at-risk behaviors. The majority of adolescent deaths result from motor vehicle accidents, suicide, and homicide rather than physical diseases. In fact, one report suggested that one-fourth of 10- to 18-year-olds are in a high-risk group, and one-half are at higher than normal risk. Another population of the 10- to 18-year-old age group are at serious risk due to circumstances not under their control (i.e., poverty, broken homes, disease, physical impairment, mental stress, and homelessness) (Office of Technology Assessment, 1991). Some at-risk conditions affect boys more than girls and vice versa. For example, both boys and girls die in automobile accidents, yet the majority of the responsibility of teenage pregnancy falls on the girl. Edelman (1989) reported that each year 1 million teenage girls get pregnant, and two-thirds of these are not African-American, are not poor, and do not live in inner cities. Female adolescents are obviously the only adolescents at risk of pregnancy; they are also more likely than males to be the victims of rape or sexual abuse. In addition, they are more likely to report distress and to attempt suicide than males. Male adolescents (especially older males) are more likely than females to die as a result of accidental injuries, homicide, or suicide, and to be victims of robbery and assault (Office of Technology Assessment, 1991).

Third, cultural and ethnic differences can be found in at-risk conditions. Emphatically speaking, a student should not be labeled "at risk" simply on the basis of cultural and ethnic characteristics. It is important that cultural and ethnic differences are considered to be strengths, enriching the culture of the United States. However, perhaps due to racism, stereotypical perceptions, and discrimination, some culturally diverse groups experience increased propensity toward being at risk than their Anglo-American counterparts. Further, educators have a professional and ethical responsibility to avoid stereotypes and preconceived expectations for achievement and behavior. Although one child or adolescent in a cultural group may be at risk, many others may not be. Evidence focusing on the propensity of culturally diverse groups toward being at risk, particularly from health perspectives, include:

Anglo- and African-Americans are about equally reported to be limited in a major activity due to a chronic condition.

African-American males experience a degree of double jeopardy, being more likely than Anglo-American males to die as a result of homicide.

African- and Hispanic-American females have high adolescent pregnancy and birth rates.

African-American adolescents account for 36% of the 13- to 19-year-olds with AIDS.

Native American adolescents are at high risk for a number of health problems, including alcohol abuse, motor vehicle accidents, mental health problems, substance use, pregnancy, and periodontal problems (Office of Technology Assessment, 1991).

The Term "At Risk"

The use of "at risk" to describe learners is often controversial and deserves serious consideration from caring and concerned educators. The at-risk label can convey a negative connotation and has the potential to be an obstacle to addressing learners' conditions. Some educators feel the negative nature of the term "at risk" calls for its replacement by a more positive term. Other descriptive terms also have come under intense scrutiny; for example, "culturally diverse" is taking precedence over "minority," and the term "exceptional" is being used rather than some of the terms with a more negative connotation, such as "retarded" or "cripple."

Although concern and controversy continue to surround the term, there is little concrete evidence to indicate with any degree of certainty what future labels might be. Therefore, suggesting another term would be speculative at best and might limit the future of at-risk learners. For example, at-risk learners are in danger of failing to meet their potential in some way, whether by committing suicide, being involved in drug or sexual experimentation, being academically slow, or presenting other at-risk conditions. Since those conditions have the potential for serious consequences, perhaps "at risk" should be continued since it conveys a sense of urgency.

Another related and potentially dangerous practice is labeling children and adolescents. Experienced educators realize how labels can affect a student throughout his or her school years and often on into their later lives. A child or adolescent categorized as a behavior problem can carry the label for years, regardless of whether learning difficulties have been overcome or if behavior has changed from negative to positive. Labeling a student as at risk can have far-reaching consequences for future educational achievement and behavior patterns.

Activity 1-1

Design a survey to determine at-risk conditions that *might* be more powerful for young females and culturally diverse groups. Maintain objectivity—be careful not to assume that a difference *is* an at-risk condition. Also, design your survey in such a manner that results are not based on stereotypes, preconceived judgments, and unsubstantiated opinion.

Activity 1-2

Consider the term "at risk" and then prepare a list of pros and cons concerning its appropriateness. Is the term too negative? What term do you suggest to describe these children and adolescents that would not have a stigmatizing effect?

Educators categorizing learners as at risk should consider the following points. First, learners should be carefully and objectively evaluated to determine whether they really are at risk. Second, applying the at-risk label should be done *only* when it is for the educational welfare of the learner. Third, the effects of the label on the self-concept deserve major consideration. Any negative feelings conveyed by the "at-risk" label should be countered with positive experiences, successful educational accomplishments, and other measures to improve the self-concept of the student.

The issue of whether "at risk" conveys a negative connotation needs to be resolved. Crucial questions include: What effects does the term "at risk" convey? What other term might be more appropriate yet, at the same time, not downplay the urgency of addressing these learners' needs? Is there a more objective term and what steps can educators take to convince other educators to adopt the preferred term? These questions will have to be answered in the twenty-first century. In the meantime, educators must recognize the possible dangers associated with the term and devise an agenda to counter any negative effects.

At-Risk Conditions

Etiology: School, Social, and Personal

Although educators' real challenges lie in identifying at-risk learners and providing an appropriate remediation program, determining the cause of at-risk conditions can be helpful and can contribute to the selection of the at-risk program. First, *school conditions* might actually be creating at-risk conditions: inappropriate instruction, competitive learning environments, ability grouping, and hostile classroom environments are just a few ways schools contribute to problems faced by at-risk learners. Second, at-risk characteristics can result from *societal factors* such as children and adolescents being rushed to engage in adult behaviors and consumer habits. Also, the American society's tendency to be racist and sexist and to discriminate against culturally diverse groups, females, and children and adolescents with disabilities contribute to learners being at risk. Third, *personal causes* might include lower self-concepts, lower ability, a lack of motivation, and a decision to experiment with drugs and alcohol.

Also, as Case Study 1-1 shows, some students are at risk due to a combination of factors. For example, a student might have low intellectual ability, a history of lower academic achievement, a poor self-concept, a life-style of poverty, and may attend an inner-city school. In such a situation, finding a cause might prove difficult. However, getting to know the at-risk learner and speculating on the underlying conditions and causes that make the learner at risk may help in the development or the selection of an at-risk program.

Case Study 1-1: Teresa—A Case of Multiple Causes

Teresa, a 12-year-old Hispanic-American girl, entered Clear View Middle School about 6 weeks after the school year has started. Her parents worked odd jobs when and where they could find manual labor. Teresa's teachers and principal immediately noticed her at-risk indicators. She was one of four children of migrant status, living in poverty, and, although she did not bring her school records, all indications suggested that she had a reading problem and was functioning several grade levels behind the average. Her teacher quickly recognized a number of at-risk indicators, felt Teresa needed additional, specialized resources, and consulted the principal, Mrs. Santiago.

Mrs. Santiago, Teresa's teacher, and several resource and remedial teachers met to formulate a plan for helping Teresa. First, the group decided to make sure Teresa really was at risk before taking any decisive action. Committee members knew Teresa had only been at the school for several weeks, they had not received her school records, and they knew the dangers associated with using assumptions to label a learner. The group decided that considering the available information, Teresa was an at-risk learner. She was a lower achiever, poor, and had several indications of a lower self-concept. Sufficient multiple causes could be determined to decide with certainty that Teresa needed special help. The group planned a methodical agenda:

- Teresa was to be tested by the school psychologist, using the most objective, culture-free test available.
- A conference with Teresa's parents and family members was to be requested.
- Coordinated approaches of administrators, teachers, resource and remedial specialists, and social service agencies were to be used.

- Educational programs designed to address Teresa's needs were to be planned.
- Periodic evaluation to determine the effectiveness of the education plan was to be carried out.

The teachers decided Teresa was a unique case. They had worked with at-risk students before, but never one who had so many at-risk conditions. Although labeling should be avoided whenever possible, placing an at-risk label on Teresa was especially difficult because she has a wide variety of conditions, any of which could have serious consequences. Initial steps were taken—Teresa was identified as an at-risk learner and a plan was developed to help her.

Specific Conditions

Lower Achievers

Underachievement or failing to achieve at one's potential is a common problem facing both at-risk students and their educators. It is a well-publicized fact that American students often fall short in their academic achievement and that, in some cases, they fare poorly in comparisons with students in Japan and other industrialized nations (More bad news . . . , 1991). Perceptive educators have always monitored their students' progress; however, educators working with at-risk students may have a heavier burden with the identification and planning of appropriate learning experiences.

The number of students falling behind by one or more grade levels in school provides disturbing and convincing evidence that educators should identify lower achievers at the earliest possible time. For example, in 1985, 26.6% of 9-year-old males and 21.4% of females were one or more grade levels behind in school. The percentages rise as children grow older: 31.7% of 13-year-old males and 24.0% of females were falling behind. By age 15, the percentages were 30.3% and 25.2%, respectively. Although these percentages represent a composite of all Anglo-, African-, and Hispanic-American groups, the percentages grow more serious when considering only culturally diverse groups (Children's Defense Fund, 1988).

The consequences of lower achievement or failing to achieve at one's potential can have serious repercussions on students' present attitudes toward education and on their future career aspirations. First, failure often leads to additional failure or the expectation to fail. Once students are labeled (either by their teachers or themselves), the tasks of catching up and achieving at expected levels are difficult tasks. Being promoted to the next grade level often means additional frustration and failure. Second, lower achievement often leads to a lower self-concept, which only worsens the situation. Third, lower achievement results in less ambitious career plans and in an increased likelihood of dropping out of school altogether. Also, once students are functioning below grade level, the tendency to fall further behind increases with each additional grade. Both the student and the nation as a whole suffer when students fail to achieve at their academic potential.

School Dropouts

Considerable controversy and confusion have clouded the term "dropout." What is a dropout? What methods should be used to calculate dropout rates? Several problems surface when considering dropouts. First, students may be defined as dropouts when they leave school for reasons other than promotion, transfer, graduation, or death. Another definition includes students older than compulsory school age who leave school of their own volition, or a student who leaves school for any reason other than death (Barber & McClellan, 1987). Second, school districts do not calculate dropout rates using the same procedure. Some districts compute dropout rates annually rather than according to how many starting freshmen actually receive diplomas 4 years later. Such a policy can show a dropout rate of 15% when the rate is closer to 50%. Even with these lingering questions, the seriousness of the dropout problem can be seen in the nation's lost productivity and also in the tragic waste of young lives (Hahn, 1987).

The number of dropouts and the number of students who are at risk of dropping out are disturbing for the nation as a whole. During 1988, 4.3 million students older than age 14 (11%) dropped out of school. Of this number, 3.5 million were Anglo-American, 700,000 were African-American, and 100,000 were Hispanic (U.S. Bureau of the Census, 1990). Male dropouts outnumbered female dropouts. For example, 16% of the males between the ages of 18 and 19 were dropouts, while only 12% of females in this age group had dropped out. Geographic information shows differences among cities and regions. Dropout rates in Boston, Chicago, Los Angeles, and Detroit rank among the highest; in fact, dropout rates were twice as high in the larger cities than in smaller cities. Among the geographic regions, states in the Southwest experienced the highest dropout rate (21%), the Northeast had 18%, the Southeast had 11%, and the Northwest had 9%. The Midwest, the area with the most homogeneous student population, has the lowest rates in the nation (Hahn, 1987).

The consequences of dropping out are disturbing for the individual and for society as a whole. Each year's class of high school dropouts costs $296 billion in lost productivity and foregone taxes during the course of their lifetime. The unemployment rate for dropouts is more than 25%, and of those who can find employment, two-thirds earn only minimum wage. Culturally diverse dropouts fare in the job market even worse (Muha &

Cole, 1991). Although dropouts face a bleak and uncertain economic future, other problems are also apparent, such as loss of self-esteem, a sense of failure or inability to achieve, lack of opportunities (economic and others) throughout one's life, and perhaps a lack of self-satisfaction with one's job due to boring, unfulfilling jobs.

Teenage Pregnancy

Recent increases in sexual activity, pregnancies, and abortions indicate that adolescents, and often children, increasingly participate in at-risk behaviors. In fact, teenagers under the age of 15 are 15 times more likely to give birth than their peers in other Western nations (Buie, 1987). Also, about half of American teenagers are sexually active by the time they leave high school, and one in four young women have experienced a pregnancy (Kenny, 1987). Barth, Middleton, and Wagman (1989) summarized the evidence on youth pregnancy:

- Teenage pregnancy remains the major reason for students leaving school.
- By the age of 15, 6.6% of females and 17.5% of male teenagers have had intercourse.
- More than half of America's high school students report having had intercourse.
- Sexually active adolescents do not use contraception consistently or effectively, and almost 20% of all teens have an unintended pregnancy.

Several factors have contributed to the growing recognition of the severity of the teenage pregnancy problem. First, reports during the 1970s and 1980s stated that sexual activity and pregnancy among high school students cannot be considered "deviant" (Kenny, 1987, p. 728). Second, Title IX of the Education Amendments of 1972, which protects students in federally funded education programs against discrimination on the grounds of pregnancy or parenthood, allows pregnant students and young parents to remain in school (Kenny, 1987).

The consequences of teenage pregnancy can be harsh in social, economic, and educational costs. At-risk behaviors resulting in teenage pregnancy lead disproportionately to the birth of low-weight babies who are vulnerable to a variety of poor outcomes. Initial hospital care for low-birthweight infants averages $20,000. Total lifetime medical costs for low-birthweight babies average $400,000. Of unmarried teens who give birth, 73% will be on welfare within 4 years (Carnegie Council on Adolescent Development, 1989). As these figures indicate, the direct costs of teenage childbearing (i.e., health care and welfare costs) tend to be borne by society as a whole. One estimate claims that it cost $18,130 a year to support a 15-year-old mother and her baby. The teen pregnancy problem is compounded by the likelihood that pregnant teenagers will withdraw from school. As many as 40% of girls drop out of school due to pregnancy or marriage. Girls who are not pregnant when they withdraw from school often become unwed mothers afterward, which makes their entry into the workplace more difficult than dropouts without children (McClelland, 1987).

Tobacco, Alcohol, and Other Drugs

Experimenting with alcohol, tobacco, and other drugs increases children's and especially adolescents' propensity toward being at risk. A two fold problem results. First, these are actually at-risk behaviors; and second, engaging in these behaviors can contribute to other at-risk tendencies or behaviors such as teenage pregnancy, health problems, or withdrawing from school. Whether caused by wanting to act more mature, peer pressure, or conforming to societal expectations (i.e., television commercials implying that happy, successful people drink alcohol), the tobacco, alcohol, and drug problem undoubtedly represents a serious at-risk threat to young people. Another disturbing problem is the young ages at which children begin to experiment with dangerous substances.

Adolescents often underestimate the dangers of using alcohol and have expressed their belief that alcohol is the most prevalent drug problem among American students. In a survey of students, one-third reported that they had five or more alcoholic drinks on at least one occasion in the previous 2 weeks. Likewise, another survey found that 11.8% of 12- to 17-year-olds had smoked cigarettes in the past month. To the question of whether these children and adolescents had ever smoked cigarettes, 42.3% answered in the affirmative. The use of alcohol and tobacco by adolescents living at home appears to be far greater than the use of illicit drugs (Office of Technology Assessment, 1991). Table 1-1 provides the percentages and ages using marijuana, alcohol, and cigarettes.

Table 1-2 provides the percentages of students that are using marijuana, alcohol, and cigarettes.

TABLE 1-1 Percentages Using Marijuana, Alcohol, and Cigarettes

Ages (years)	Marijuana (%)	Alcohol (%)	Cigarettes (%)
12–13	2	10	3
14–15	8	23	10
16–17	23	45	30

Adapted from Children's Defense Fund. (1988). *Making the middle grades work*. Washington, DC: Author.

TABLE 1-2 Percentages of Middle Grades Students Experimenting with Drugs

Grade	Inhalants	Cocaine	Heroin	Stimulants	Tranquilizers
6	2.1	0.2	0.2	0.7	0.6
7 to 8	3.8	0.8	0.2	3.9	1.6

Adapted from Children's Defense Fund. (1988). *Making the middle grades work*. Washington, DC: Author.

Delinquency, Hate Crimes, Gangs, and Criminal Behaviors

Violence in American society is an all-too-common occurrence. Muggings, beatings, knifings, and shootings characterize some environments, and by the age of 8, some children are hardened, insensitive, and distant. Nicholson, Stephens, Elder, and Leavitt (1985) summarized the situation when they wrote, "The level of violent crime perpetuated by juveniles in our society is three times greater today than it was in 1960" (p. 494). Evidence of juvenile delinquency in the lives of many children and adolescents include the following:

- Approximately 28,200 students are physically attacked in America's secondary schools each month.
- Almost 8% of middle and high school students missed at least 1 day of school per month because they were afraid to go to school.
- Estimates of the annual cost of crime, including vandalism, run from about $50 million to $600 million. The best estimate of the yearly replacement and repair costs due to crime is about $200 million (Greenbaum & Turner, 1989; Hranitz & Eddowes, 1990).

In recent years, youth 18 years of age and younger have accounted for about 20% of all violent crime arrests in the United States, 44% of all serious property arrests, and 39% of overall serious crime arrests. Chronic youthful offenders commit many more crimes than do chronic adult offenders—an average of 36 per year for juveniles and 12 per year for adults (Vander Zanden, 1989). In 1988, there were 1.6 million arrests of adolescents and, in 1987, about 700,000 adolescents were confined to public or private juvenile facilities. In recent years, the number of adolescents confined to correctional facilities has been increasing; however, this increase might result from adolescents being confined for minor offenses rather than serious offenses (Office of Technology Assessment, 1991).

Also disturbing is that children and adolescents are twice as likely as adults to be victims of crime. One survey found that from 1982 to 1984, youth 12 to 19 years of age were the victims of 1.8 million violent crimes and

3.7 million thefts per year. About one-third of all violent crimes against younger teenagers and 83% of the thefts occur at school. Older teenagers are victims of 14% of the violent crime and 42% of the thefts at school (Vander Zanden, 1989). It is important to note that adolescents (especially those who are African-American and male) in the United States are more likely to be victims of violent crimes than individuals from other age groups. Violence by adolescents and by individuals from other age groups is a major cause of death among young people (Office of Technology Assessment, 1991).

Juvenile delinquency refers to antisocial and lawbreaking activities that are reported to authorities and to antisocial behavior, which does not get reported. One survey of nearly 1400 male and female teenagers indicated that 80% or more had participated in some form of delinquent behavior such as drinking, theft, truancy, destruction of property, assault, gang fighting, carrying a concealed weapon, and using false identification (Seifert & Hoffnung, 1991).

Gangs, another problem contributing to children and adolescents being at risk, cross cultural and geographic boundaries. Unlike gangs in the past, which formed for social acceptance, today's gangs are motivated by violence, extortion, intimidation, and illegal trafficking of drugs and weapons. Gangs today are better organized, remain active longer, have access to sophisticated weapons, and are much more mobile. Also, gangs are not just a big-city or inner-city problem. Gang members cross all cultural and geographic boundaries. Mid-size and small cities are being affected as well as some suburban and rural areas. Since younger gang members and most potential gang members attend school, schools have become a prime recruiting grounds. Turf is often staked out, drugs and weapons are sold, and extortion occurs (Today's gangs cross cultural . . . , 1992). One can readily see how children and adolescents can be placed at risk when gangs market drugs and weapons at school and make extortion demands of students as they walk to and from school.

Hate crimes also increasingly make children and adolescents at risk. Hate crimes can include words and deeds motivated by negative feelings and opinions about a victim's race, ethnicity, religion, and sexual preference. The incidence of hate crimes is currently soaring at record-breaking rates throughout the nation. Hate crimes may seem different from other assaults only in terms of their motivation; however, some characteristics of hate crimes are relatively rare in other crimes of violence. Characteristics of hate crimes include:

1. Perpetrators of the hate crime and the victim may be total strangers, in contrast to most assault crimes where the two people know each other.
2. Perpetration, rather than engaging in a one-on-one assault, involve more than one perpetrator assaulting a single victim.

3. Perpetrators often attack younger or weaker victims, and often arm themselves, attacking unarmed victims.
4. Perpetrators usually engage in extremely violent crimes and inflict serious injuries.
5. Perpetrators often destroy or damage property, rather than taking something of value.
6. Perpetrators usually fail to gain anything materialistic from the assault.
7. Perpetrators frequently engage in hate crimes at churches, synagogues, mosques, cemeteries, monuments, schools, camps, and in or around the victim's home (Bodinger-deUriarte, 1991).

Causes of hate crimes may be bigotry; the unbearable sense of personal failure leading to the need to avoid self-blame by scapegoating others; the need to feel powerful by subjugating others; the need to feel superior by dehumanizing others; and various other causes resulting from social unease, economic unease, and political unease (Bodinger-deUriarte, 1991).

Poverty and Lower Socioeconomic Conditions
The SES of many children and adolescents in the United States contributes to them being at risk. Although a learner's SES cannot be used as the sole criterion in determining propensity toward being at risk, SES does play a major role in many crucial areas. Lower SES has also been linked with other at-risk factors such as low ability, lack of motivation, or poor health. The SES of significant numbers of children and adolescents should be a cause for alarm.

More than 12 million children in the United States—about one in five children—are poor. Children are about twice as likely to be poor than any other group, including the elderly. Equally bad, the number of poor children in the United States continues to grow. For example, the number of children living in poverty increased by more than 2.2 million from 1979 to 1989 (Children's Defense Fund, 1991).

Poverty often takes a more severe toll on culturally diverse children and adolescents and adds to the likelihood of these groups being at risk. The estimated proportion and number of adolescents affected include more than one out of four U.S. adolescents overall (8.4 million); two out of four African-Americans, Hispanic-Americans, and Native Americans; and one out of three Asian-American adolescents (Office of Technology Assessment, 1991). For some groups, the percentages affected by poverty are increasing. For example, in 1989, the number of African-Americans in poverty increased by 14.1% while the number of Hispanics grew by 69.6%. Even worse, the Asian-American numbers living in poverty increased to 123% (Children's Defense Fund, 1991).

The family structure can be either a cause of the lower SES or can contribute to the problem. Children and adolescents in female-headed families are five times as likely to be poor than those in married-couple families. Poverty rates in families headed by women are very high regardless of race or ethnic group; for example, 63% for African-Americans, 64% for Hispanic-Americans, and 42% for Anglo-Americans. Slightly more than half of all poor children now live in female-headed families. Simply blaming the poverty problem on female-headed families is too simplistic and ignores the social and economic struggles that two-parent families increasingly face. Nearly 5 million poor children lived in married-couple families in 1989. Even if there were not any families headed by females in this country, the United States would still have the highest poverty rate of all industrialized nations (Children's Defense Fund, 1991).

The consequences of poverty can be devastating to developing children and adolescents. From the earliest years of childhood, poverty places its victims at higher risks. For example,

- Poor children are less likely to receive the key building blocks of early development, such as adequate nutrition, decent medical care, a safe and secure environment, and access to early childhood development programs to supplement learning opportunities in the home.
- Poor children are far more likely to be hungry.
- Poor children are far more likely to fall behind in school; for example, 16-year-olds who have lived at least half their lives in poverty are twice as likely to have repeated at least one grade as those whose families have never been poor.
- Poor teenagers are four times more likely than nonpoor teens to have below-average basic academic skills.
- Poor teenagers, regardless of their race, are nearly three times more likely to drop out of school than nonpoor teenagers.
- Teenage women who are poor and who have below-average basic skills, regardless of their race, are five and one-half times more likely to have children than nonpoor teenage women with average or better basic skills (Children's Defense Fund, 1991).

In summary, the challenge of educating children of poverty has long been recognized as difficult. Many of these children and adolescents perform poorly on academic tasks. Likewise, the school, serving large numbers of these children and adolescents, faces a variety of problems that pose barriers to providing high-quality education such as high rates of mobility among learners' families, a high prevalence of severe emotional and behavioral problems among students, large numbers of students with limited

English proficiency, low staff morale, and inadequate facilities and resources (Knapp & Shields, 1990).

Exceptionalities

PL 94-142 (Education for All Handicapped Children Act of 1975) mandated that children with disabilities be educated in the least restrictive environment and required that children's and adolescents' disabilities be addressed to the fullest extent of the law. However, students' disabilities still may place them at risk and, in some cases, may continue to contribute to their problems. It is important to note that the term exceptionality does not include only disabilities; the term should also include the gifted and talented children or adolescents who do not meet their potential or, in some cases, fail outright in academic, vocational, social, or other pursuits. That is, a learner may be gifted and talented, but still not excel.

Table 1-3 provides a listing of disabilities and the percentage for each. It is important to note that the categories are those identified by PL 94-142 and to remember that the right column refers to the percentages of the disabled population rather than the general school population.

Suicides

Suicide ranks today as the second or third leading cause of death among industrialized nations of the world. In the United States, the teenage suicide rate has tripled during the past 30 years. In fact, suicide currently accounts for more than 5000 deaths or nearly 20% of all the deaths each year among

TABLE 1-3 Disabling Conditions

Disability	Total	
	Number	Percentage
Learning disability	1,926,097	43.60
Speech or language impairment	1,140,422	25.80
Mental retardation	664,424	15.00
Emotional disturbance	384,680	8.70
Multiple disabilities	99,416	2.20
Hard of hearing and deaf	66,761	1.50
Orthopedic impairment	58,328	1.30
Other health impairment	52,658	1.20
Visual impairment	27,049	.61
Deaf–blind	1,766	.04
All conditions	4,421,601	100.00

Adapted from Haring, N. G., & McCormick, L. (Eds.). (1990). *Exceptional children and youth.* Columbus, OH: Merrill, p. 20.

young people. Children and young people who attempt suicide tend to be female, by a ratio of four to one, but completed suicides are higher among males. Males typically use active methods such as shooting or hanging, and females commonly use passive methods such as taking poisons or drugs (Strother, 1986). Table 1-4 shows the suicide rates among children and adolescents.

Although Table 1-4 provides disturbing rates, it is also important to remember that reported suicides are greatly outnumbered by unreported suicides, attempted suicides, and other types of self-destructive behavior.

Health

Although children often experience childhood diseases such as chicken pox, mumps, ear infections, measles, and various digestive and respiratory problems, they may be among the healthiest of all people. Compared to adults, they suffer fewer of the illnesses and physical damage that are commonly associated with prolonged exposure to physical and emotional stress and with aging. Still, however, adolescents experience greater health risks than either children or adults. Compared with either groups, adolescents are much more likely to be injured in motor vehicle accidents, to misuse alcohol and other drugs, to become pregnant, and have poor health care and eating habits (Seifert & Hoffnung, 1991).

Often questioned as a legitimate disorder of children, depression is a contemporary and common problem. The consensus today is that depression exists among children and adolescents and that the number of cases may be 2% to 20% of the school-age population. Symptoms may include change in appetite or weight, sleep disturbances, psychomotor problems, loss of interest in usual activities, loss of energy, feelings of worthlessness or excessive guilt, complaints of difficulty concentrating, and thoughts of

TABLE 1-4 Suicide Rates by Sex, Race, and Age Groups, 1989 (Death Rates per 100,000 Population)

	Male		Female	
	Anglo-American	African-American	Anglo-American	African-American
All ages	21.4	12.2	5.2	2.4
Ages 10 to 14	2.2	1.7	.4	*
Ages 15 to 19	19.4	10.3	4.5	2.3

Adapted from U.S. Bureau of the Census. (1990). *Statistical Abstracts of the United States.* Table 125. p. 90. Washington, DC: Author.
*Number too small to compute.

death or suicide. Depression, however, may not always be termed as such and may be cited as a learning disability, hyperactivity, school phobia, somatic complaints, and conduct disorders (Epstein & Cullinan, 1986).

Adolescent health problems that contribute to the propensity to being at risk include infectious mononucleosis, hepatitis, and sexually transmitted diseases, such as syphilis, gonorrhea, genital warts, genital herpes, chlamydia, and AIDS. Other behaviors that make adolescents at risk and that are discussed in this section on health include nutritional problems, obesity, and an obsession with thinness. Table 1-5 looks at several problems encountered by adolescents.

The consequences of children and adolescents being at risk due to health reasons are readily apparent. First, if a person believes he or she will be perpetually healthy, it can result in that person not taking reasonable care of his or her body or taking unnecessary risks that can result in injury or death. Second, Seifert and Hoffnung (1991) maintained that inadequate nutrition can interfere with a teenager's ability to concentrate at school and to engage in peer-related activities. Third, an obsession with thinness can result in serious health problems and even death. Fourth, the consequences of casual sexual relationships may include pregnancy or sexually transmitted diseases. Fifth, tobacco use and drug and alcohol abuse, topics to be addressed in another section, represent major health problems that either make students at risk or worsen their chances of overcoming at-risk conditions.

An easily recognizable consequence of health problems is the number of days lost from school (and the resulting loss of instructional time) due to acute health conditions. For example, in 1987, males lost 320 days and females lost 359 days per year per 100 children, ages 6 to 16. Health conditions preventing school attendance included infective and parasitic problems, respiratory conditions, digestive system conditions, and injuries. It is interesting to note, however, that the number of days lost due to health conditions has dropped steadily from 1962 to 1987 (U.S. Bureau of the Census, 1990).

TABLE 1-5 Types of Problems Encountered By Adolescents and Available Estimates of Prevalence

- Acute physical illness (all at one point or another)
- Serious chronic physical problem (5% to 10%)
- AIDS and other sexually transmitted diseases (STDs)
- Pregnancy (1 million per year) and parenting (490,000 per year)
- Mental health—diagnosable disorders (18% to 22%); subjective distress (25%)
- Substance abuse (depends on substance and measure of frequency of use)

Adapted from Office of Technology Assessment, (1991). *Adolescent Health* (brochure).

At-Risk Programs

Rationale

Providing a rationale for at-risk programs is probably among the easiest tasks associated with the movement to address the needs of at-risk children and adolescents. First, professional educators can readily see the need to help at-risk students and to accept responsibility for planning, designing, implementing, and evaluating programs. Second, legally and ethically, educators are also responsible for helping at-risk children and adolescents meet their maximum potential.

A Brief Historical Overview

One cannot extend an examination of at-risk children and adolescents too far into history. The term "at-risk" is a relatively new term, perhaps fueled by the 1983 publication of *A Nation at Risk*, which declared the United States to be at risk (Brandt, 1990). Although growing in number and severity, conditions now placed under the umbrella term "at risk" have actually been around for years. All educators recall lower achievers, school dropouts, substance abusers, suicidal students, and learners discriminated against due to their gender, culture, or exceptionality. Recently, however, children and adolescents experiencing these conditions and behaviors have been assigned the at-risk label—at risk of reaching a goal that, ordinarily, would have been attainable. Presently, more specific terms (i.e., school dropouts) are used when necessary to pinpoint problems and to plan appropriate educational programs.

Prerequisites

Successful at-risk programs require educators to take several steps in the beginning in order to gain support and to provide the best possible programs for children and adolescents in need. Although considering these steps will contribute to program effectiveness, other factors that reflect a district's individual needs and resources probably need to be taken into account. These factors are as follows:

1. Establish a task force at the district level to complete an assessment study to determine the school's response to at-risk learners. The task force should include people from all segments of the community (i.e., parents, teachers, students, staff members, community agencies, and business leaders) and should help create a strong commitment to help at-risk children and adolescents.

2. Complete an assessment program of the district's policies, procedures, practices, and programs to determine conditions that improve or exacerbate the problems of at-risk students.
3. Identify potential resources and options at the building, school district, and community levels to assist at-risk populations and to reduce their propensity toward being at-risk.
4. Assess and determine requirements in terms of time and expense in terms of changes in policies, procedures, and school climate.
5. Devise an assessment plan to evaluate the effectiveness of at-risk programs (McLaughlin & Vacha, 1992).

Selected Types of At-Risk Programs

Nearly everyone agrees that conventional teaching methods are less effective for these young people and that conditions in their homes and communities do not support school learning. Some researchers report that some poor children seem to require more explicit instruction than middle-class children, but others warn about the negative consequences of tracking. Most experts advise that at-risk students have the same rights to valued cultural knowledge. How can we respond appropriately to students who have special needs without treating them differently from others? Practicing educators must consider all the issues and, against devastating odds and with limited resource, make the best possible decisions (Brandt, 1990).

At-risk programs basically fall into two major groups: 1) Compensatory or academic programs such as Chapter 1, Head Start, Follow Through, and Special Education; and 2) programs addressing specific at-risk conditions such as alcohol and drug programs, efforts to curb teenage pregnancy, and programs designed to lessen violent and criminal behaviors. It is important to note that many programs do not fall neatly into these two groups. Some overlap and others do not seem to fall into either group. This introductory section on types of at-risk programs provides a cursory look at at-risk programs rather than providing a comprehensive examination. Many programs focusing on a wide array of at-risk programs will be described in Chapter 9 on school conditions and Chapter 10 on personal and social conditions.

Compensatory

Compensatory education is an effort by schools to provide special instruction for students whose out-of-school lives are considered to be so different from that of most students that they are at a disadvantage in the regular school program. The types of deficiencies most often addressed involve economic and social deprivation associated with poverty, family instability, and other social conditions that hinder education (Myers & Myers, 1990).

Compensatory programs seek to improve educational experiences for economically disadvantaged students. Proponents of compensatory programs believe remedial programs and special activities can compensate for the disadvantages experienced by students and can result in more effective learning and increased academic achievement. The Elementary and Secondary Education Act (PL89-10) passed in 1965 provided $1 billion in Title 1 (now called Chapter 1) funds to supplement and improve the education of economically disadvantaged children. By 1988, Chapter 1 expenditures exceeded $4 billion per year and other federal compensatory funds added more than $2 billion more (Ornstein & Levine, 1989). Chapter 1 had a very well-defined purpose—to increase the reading and mathematics achievement of low-achieving students within schools with concentrations of students from low SES (Slavin, 1989).

Compensatory programs usually provide remedial instruction, special activities, and supplemental services intended to make instruction for disadvantaged students more effective and to produce greater achievement. These efforts include early childhood education programs for high-risk students; family intervention programs; bilingual education; special guidance and counseling; tutoring services; and dropout programs (Myers & Myers, 1990). Other compensatory programs from preschool to higher education focus on reducing class size and providing remedial programs, special personnel, enrichment experiences, personnel training, additional school personnel, and school desegregation (Ornstein & Levine, 1989).

Five principal service delivery models have been used under Chapter 1 funding:

- *Pullout:* Students are taken out of their homeroom classes for 30- to 40-minute periods, during which time they receive remedial instruction in a subject that has been causing them difficulty.
- *In-class:* The teachers and usually a teacher's assistant work with eligible students within the regular classroom setting.
- *Add-on:* Teachers provide services outside the regular classroom, as in summer school or afterschool programs.
- *Replacement:* This involves pacing Chapter 1 students in self-contained classes in which they receive most or all of their instruction.
- *Schoolwide projects:* Programs in which all students in a high poverty group have special educational experiences (Slavin, 1989).

Other related compensatory programs include Head Start, a federal program for students from age 3 to school entry; Follow Through, a program designed to maintain the successes of students in Head Start by building

---

Activity 1-3

Contact a school to determine which, if any, at-risk programs are provided to its students. Label these programs as academic, drug education, suicide prevention, and so forth. Then, make a list of at least two other programs the school could try.

---

services for low-income students in the early elementary grades; and intervention services, a continuum of services for students with disabilities. Other efforts have included methods (i.e., ability grouping) once thought to work and to produce academic achievement being replaced by alternative models and learning environments with which at-risk learners can better relate (Slavin, 1989).

Other Programs Addressing Specific Conditions

Other at-risk programs address specific conditions such as efforts designed to address the needs of suicidal students, substance abusers, and learners with lower self-concepts. Note, however, that these at-risk programs usually include some emphasis on learning the basic skills. For example, a self-concept program naturally has as its primary emphasis improving the learner's self-concept; however, enhancing one's feelings of competency probably, and certainly should, include improving one's chances of being successful in school. Likewise, programs aimed at substance abusers and potential school dropouts also need a focus on basic skills such as reading, mathematics, and writing. Chapters 9 and 10 of this text provide names and descriptions of selected at-risk programs designed for specific at-risk conditions. Then, after each discussion, the authors included a list of characteristics of programs that effectively meet the needs of children and adolescents. Also, the "For Additional Information" sections of Chapters 9 and 10 and other selected chapters provide other sources of at-risk programs and efforts.

The Role of the School

The school's role in helping at-risk learners lies in several broad areas. They are as follows:

Identification and assessment
Providing alternative learning environments
Coordinating K–12 approaches and social service agencies' efforts
Working to engage parents and families
Evaluating school effectiveness

Rather than limiting roles and responsibilities to these five areas, it should be understood that many other roles can and should be included in the effort to help at-risk children and adolescents.

Identification and Assessment

One of schools' primary roles is to identify at-risk children and adolescents, and then to carefully assess the extent of at-risk conditions. All school personnel (i.e., administrators, teachers, various resource and remedial specialists, counselors, psychologists, and social service agencies) should be involved in this identification process that is responsible for helping at-risk children and adolescents. The plight facing many at-risk students is too great for one person to identify and address. Often, commercial diagnostic tests are not available to assist in the identification of at-risk learners. In these cases, educators must rely on appropriate checklists to determine "who is and who is not at risk." Checklists for each at-risk condition and behavior discussed in this text appear in Chapter 2.

A point related to the schools' identification role is identifying and assessing for at-risk conditions should not contribute to or make learners at risk. For example, educators in the past have used identification and assessment procedures that may have failed to recognize learners' special intelligences or their gender, cultural, and developmental differences. Through inaccurate or biased results, tests may have been the actual reason or cause for students being at risk.

Providing Alternative Learning Environments

Curricular, organizational, instructional, and management practices used with most children and adolescents are simply inappropriate for at-risk learners (Brandt, 1990). The curriculum may be irrelevant, instructional approaches may foster competition, organizational approaches may require tracking or ability grouping, and management practices may be inflexible. In other words, all students may be expected to learn in ways similar to learners who typically succeed in U.S. schools. Such an assumption can be

---

Activity 1-4

List at least five testing and assessment instruments, the addresses of the publishers, and the limitations and advantages of each. Also, suggest several sources (perhaps resources) educators can consult to determine whether testing and assessment instruments are appropriate for at-risk learners.

a serious error and can lead to teachers' approaches being incompatible with learners' perspectives or styles of learning.

At-risk children and adolescents who find traditional educational experiences difficult or impossible may benefit from an alternative learning environment, a major premise of this book. Alternative learning environments include cooperative learning, grouping patterns other than ability grouping, individualized instruction, classroom management practices promoting harmony over control, and learning opportunities where educators and students agree on a contract specifying individual educational goals and the means to accomplish these goals.

Major prerequisites to providing successful alternative learning environments include recognizing that some at-risk students do not respond to traditional approaches and accepting responsibility for providing more compatible educational experiences. Both prerequisites require a change of thinking from the mind-set that all students learn in the same manner and that schools should address the needs of the majority.

Coordinating K–12 Approaches and Social Service Agencies' Efforts

Identifying and helping at-risk learners is simply too monumental a task for teachers working in isolation. Although the classroom teacher might be among the first to detect possible at-risk conditions, teachers should not be considered solely responsible for addressing needs in areas in which they might or might not be qualified. Efforts to help at-risk learners should include professionals who have special expertise in working with special conditions or behaviors. Two aspects warrant consideration for effective coordinated efforts to become a reality.

First, efforts must be K–12 approaches that reflect developmental differences and in which educators below and above the learners' grade level provide input and make suggestions. For example, a sixth grader with a reading problem benefits when the teacher works with the fourth- and fifth-grade teachers to learn what worked best in the past and with the seventh- and eighth-grade teacher to learn what content and skills will be needed in those higher grades. Coordinated practices should be commonplace in all schools and at all levels; however, in actual practice, such integrated efforts are often the exception rather than the rule.

Second, coordinated efforts should include other teachers, remedial and resource educators, counselors and school psychologists, and social service agencies. Only then will all available areas of expertise be tapped. Most educators readily recognize the benefits of taking advantage of other sources of professional talent within the school, but few teachers recognize social service agencies' responsibilities to school-age learners and the special assistance these organizations can provide. The availability of social service organizations, of course, depends on the quantity and quality of social services in a particular community. Thus, providing a complete listing of agencies and organizations would be impossible in this text. Educators of at-risk learners do, however, have a responsibility to the profession and to their learners to seek professional assistance outside the school whenever possible.

Working to Engage Parents and Families

Educators working with at-risk children and adolescents need to understand and accept the school's role of engaging parents and families in all aspects of the education program. Unfortunately, at-risk learners often do not benefit from a close working relationship between educators and parents. Reasons for engaging parents in the educative process, causes for parents' reluctance, and practical ways of involving parents in the education of at-risk learners can be identified.

Reasons for involving parents in the education process include the positive relationship existing between parent involvement and school achievement, increased student attendance, positive parent–learner communication, improved student attitudes and behavior, and more parent–community support (Chavkin, 1989). Another reason includes parents providing information and insights that may not be clear to teachers and administrators. Also, educators who understand parents' perspectives and concerns usually better understand at-risk learners and their problems. Finally, children and adolescents who see their parents actively involved in educational efforts may be more inclined to give their best effort in school and to cooperate than when educators work alone.

Parents are sometimes reluctant to become involved in their children's education. Reasons for this hesitation include:

1. Parents may be unwilling to admit their children or adolescents are at risk.
2. Parents may not understand their role in helping their children and adolescents in school.
3. Parents may have negative school expectations and, therefore, feel uncomfortable dealing with educators' expectations.
4. Parents may feel unable to offer worthwhile help or advice working with the problems or behaviors they really do not understand.
5. Parents may feel addressing at-risk learners' conditions is the school's responsibility—educators are trained to work with at-risk students and should accept the responsibilities.

Activity 1-5
Devise a five-point plan for engaging parents and families in the education of their at-risk learners. Include in your plan a sample letter requesting parents' and families' support and involvement. Why might parents and families be reluctant to become involved in their children's education? What suggestions can you offer to address this reluctance?

Regardless of the reasons for failing to become active participants in learners' education, parents should be involved and their advice sought whenever possible. As discussed in greater detail in Chapter 8, educators can engage parents by visiting in the home, asking for help and advice, providing opportunities for direct involvement in classroom activities, requesting participation on advisory councils, and, in fact, making any effort that brings the parent into the classroom or involves parents in their children's education.

Evaluating School Effectiveness

Evaluating school effectiveness, another crucial role of the school, requires conscientious, methodical approaches and should be undertaken with a specific, clear-cut purpose. Several reasons document the need to evaluate the schools' effectiveness, and several points should underlie all evaluation. Evaluation, although sometimes painful and threatening, should be a positive, constructive process that focuses on strengths and seeks to detect weakness.

Undoubtedly, evaluation is a necessary component of any teaching effort. Educators need to document their effectiveness, pinpoint needed changes, and learn how at-risk learners can be most effectively helped. In addition, evaluation is often needed for documentation purposes—the effectiveness of programs need to be demonstrated and, perhaps, justified for future funding. The school's evaluative efforts should include questions such as: Are at-risk children and adolescents being helped? Are there learners becoming "less" at risk? Have at-risk behaviors been reduced? Are learners progressing to a point that the at-risk label can be dropped?

Several points underlie all evaluative efforts. First, evaluation should not be undertaken just for the sake of evaluation. Instead, evaluation should provide educators with a sense of success in working with at-risk learners and should provide the basis for changes in educational programs. Second, evaluation should include the efforts of a number of people, such as educators, parents, administrators, and even at-risk learners themselves. Evaluative reports that document a program's effectiveness and serve as a basis for

---

Activity 1-6

Design a survey to assess schools' effectiveness in serving at-risk children and adolescents. Focus on efforts such as identification, methods, curriculum, resources, school environment, and guidance efforts. Be sure the survey assesses the degree to which the school takes a "total school approach," which includes the efforts of all school professionals.

---

program decisions should reflect more than one perspective. For example, an aspect of an at-risk program may be considered highly effective by a teacher, yet may receive a low grade by parents, or vice versa. Third, evaluating the school's effectiveness in helping at-risk learners must include a number of aspects such as administrators' and teachers' efforts, materials, identification and assessment procedures, effectiveness of specific efforts, and as previously mentioned, the degree to which students are becoming less at risk.

The mind-set adopted toward evaluating school efforts will be a crucial point. Evaluation should be seen as a means of improving efforts and overall programs and, generally speaking, as a positive and constructive process rather than as a means to find fault and condemn efforts. In other words, professional educators should perceive the school's evaluative role as an opportunity to build on strengths and to identify weaknesses rather than as a negative and faultfinding process to be feared. Until educators adopt such a mind-set, evaluation will play a minor constructive role in the process of helping at-risk children and adolescents.

Case Study 1-2 looks at a school's response when the educators decided at-risk students' problems needed to be addressed and shows how the team approach included a number of professionals and parents and how they were selected.

Case Study 1-2: A School's Response

Smithville School was a K–8 school in a semirural area. The teachers were conscientious, motivated, and respected in the neighborhood, but the school had a substantial number of at-risk learners, especially in grades 5 to 8. At-risk conditions included high dropout rates, a large number of low achieving students, some indicators of drug use, and a few (yet increasing number) pregnant eighth graders. Generally speaking, the educators at the school recognized the growing problem and reached two conclusions. First, curricular content and instructional methods used more than a decade ago needed to be changed to meet the needs of at-risk learners. Second, the school needed to take immediate, decisive action.

A committee was formed consisting of the principal, selected teachers from K to 4 and 5 to 8, resource and remedial specialists, a representative from the social service agency, a school psychologist, a counselor, and several families of children experiencing at-risk conditions. After several meetings to decide on strategies, the committee decided to meet to address learners' needs. The agenda included a wide array of topics such as:

1. Preparing a statement of commitment that emphasized care, concern, and commitment
2. Deciding on a means to determine who was at risk and who was not at risk to avoid unnecessary labeling
3. Deciding on diagnostic testing instruments that were as culture-, class-, and gender-free as possible
4. Committing to accept that traditional course content and teaching-learning methods were not appropriate for the children being taught and accepting the fact that alternative learning environments might be necessary to address the needs of at-risk learners
5. Emphasizing a coordinated approach of educators, parents, family members, and social service specialists
6. Providing an objective evaluation system designed to assess children's progress and to determine curricular and instructional changes to be made
7. Committing to seek the expertise and assistance of teachers in lower grades as well as higher grades, so that one group could provide input about learners and the other group, respectively, could provide suggestions on curricular content that would prepare learners for the higher grades.

The principal approved of the progress being made and insisted on regularly scheduled meetings to determine progress and overall welfare of at-risk learners. The group knew this task would take time, patience, and effort. Dramatic progress would not be easy. Still, the school personnel took an active stand to help at-risk learners and committed to continuing the effort to help at-risk learners.

At-Risk Children's and Adolescents' Effects on Other Learners

Do at-risk children and adolescents have a negative effect on those learners who are not at risk or does the diversity of at-risk learners actually contribute positively to the educational environment? Considerable discussion has revolved around this issue. The way educators feel about this issue undoubtedly affects their perception of learners as well as their commitment to learners and the educational experiences they receive.

One argument suggests that the diversity of at-risk learners does indeed contribute to the overall school program. Just as not all people in a community share similar characteristics, not all learners in a school are alike. In essence, the argument holds that learners benefit from the diversity (i.e., strengths, weaknesses, special gifts, differences, and shortcomings). All learners can benefit from knowing a learner whose at-risk conditions are overshadowed by certain strengths or the learner's intense motivation, determination, and perseverance under difficult circumstances. Such diversity is the essence of humanity and contributes to the school being a microcosm of the overall society.

Another argument, not quite so democratic and humanitarian, disagrees and, in fact, suggests that at-risk learners pose outright dangers to other learners, provide poor role models and negative peer pressure, take time and resources (financial and otherwise) away from other learners, and add a "bad element" to the overall educational environment. It is true that a person does not have to look far to find at-risk learners who are violent, and do, indeed, place other learners in danger. Young students or students affected by peer pressure might be influenced by these learners. The misbehaving learner takes an inordinate amount of the teacher's time and energy and also disturbs other learners who really want to learn. "Slow learners" might hold back other learners and prevent them from progressing at a faster pace. In fact, these slow learners might actually contribute to other learners being placed at risk (i.e., faster learners who are held back or bored with the rate at which the teacher is progressing).

It will likely be best to look at each at-risk learner individually to determine whether the at-risk condition negatively influences other learners' chances of school success or if violent tendencies place other learners in a dangerous situation. For legal, ethical, and professional reasons, such individual determinations are probably the rule anyway. Students with tendencies toward violence should be removed from the general school population, perhaps, and placed in an alternative school in which special attention and care can be provided. A similar rule may apply to learners using drugs and alcohol; other learners should not be confined to classrooms where illegal substances are being used. Slow learners (who are neither harmful or using drugs and alcohol) should be allowed to remain in regular classrooms with special help being provided by educators, special educators, and counselors. Both slow learners and other learners can benefit from being placed in the same classroom as long as both groups receive educational experiences that are developmentally and academically appropriate. All learners benefit when slow and fast learners are grouped together in the same classroom; however, both slow and fast learners need educators who ensure that slow learners are challenged yet not frustrated and that fast learners are not held back and bored.

This issue will probably never be settled to the satisfaction of all learners, educators, and parents. Progress, however, can be made toward a more satisfactory resolution when educators consider individual situations to determine the effects at-risk learners have on other learners, consider the most effective environment for all learners, and engage in deliberate, objective follow-up to determine whether placement decisions for at-risk learners are jeopardizing other learners' chances of school success.

Case Study 1-3 looks at how one principal responded when school board members asked for a response to parents' questions.

Case Study 1-3: At-Risk Learners and Other Learners in School Together

Some parents had discussed with school board members the possibility of at-risk learners "taking away" from other learners. The concern went something as follows:

> *Teachers are taking too much time with those at-risk learners. Classes are smaller, they have more materials and, in some cases, even special programs. We are concerned. Our children in the regular classrooms do not get such treatment. Nothing equal about this situation! Our children are being shortchanged and being penalized for being good students and for staying out of trouble.*

A couple of school board members began thinking, and one said, "Their concerns do sound reasonable." Using appropriate channels, the board asked the principal to appear in a closed session of the board meeting to address the legitimacy of the parents' concerns. Then, an ad hoc committee would report back to the parents.

Mr. Falicov, the principal, planned his response and prepared for questions. This might become a controversial issue, he thought, "I need to handle this carefully. I definitely do not want the board to consider this as a serious issue." He outlined his major points:

I. Responsibility
   A. Legally
   B. Professionally
   C. Ethically
II. Addressing At-Risk Learners' Needs
   A. Smaller classes

      1. Rationale
      2. State mandates
      3. Funding sources
   B. Materials
      1. Address specific needs
      2. Available to other learners
      3. Provided by philanthropic foundations and professional associations
   C. Other Students
      1. Their needs being met—not penalized
      2. All state mandates met
      3. Financing from different sources
      4. Closely monitored for signs of at-risk behavior
III. Publicity and Information Dissemination Campaign
   A. Need to make parents more aware of schools' responsibility for at-risk learners
   B. Explain how at-risk programs and other programs complement one another
   C. Explain how all students benefit from diversity and schools' efforts to help at-risk learners
   D. Explain the need for closer communication between the board and the school
   E. Help parents and community realize the moral and legal necessity to provide programs for at-risk children and adolescents
      1. Newspaper articles
      2. "Town Session" meetings sponsored by the school
      3. Speakers for community organizations

Mr. Falicov marked his outline "ROUGH DRAFT." He knew this was only a start and that he would need to refine his thoughts and comments. This meeting had the potential for affecting future attitudes (as well as funding) of at-risk programs.

Activity 1-7

Write a position paper outlining your thoughts on the effects of at-risk learners on the child or adolescent who is not at risk. Include issues such as poor role models, outright dangers, the time and resources given to at-risk learners, and any other points you feel should be mentioned.

Challenging Educators to Improve the Lives of At-Risk Children and Adolescents

The premise of this text is to challenge and motivate educators to address the needs of at-risk children and adolescents. Meeting this challenge requires educators to form an awareness of at-risk learners and their conditions; learn indicators that suggest possible at-risk conditions to be addressed; and provide alternative curricular content and instructional approaches. These challenges cannot be taken lightly or half-heartedly. Unmet personal potential, that is, the American society being laden with unemployment and welfare, calls for an immediate response to meet at-risk learners' needs. This text calls for awareness, shows how to identify, and suggests effective at-risk programs.

The degree of success reached in helping at-risk learners will depend a great deal on the educators' motivation to help at-risk learners. Some teachers say, "I was not trained to teach at-risk learners, I was trained in English or mathematics." Such teachers would be unlikely candidates to work successfully with at-risk learners. Regardless of the grade level or the subject area for which a teacher was trained, teachers who are effective and successful with at-risk learners accept the challenge to help *all* learners rather than just those who are academically successful. Likewise, these educators see it as their responsibility to address substance abuse and other at-risk conditions. As previously stated, the challenge cannot be taken lightly. The consequences for children, adolescents, and American society are too great for educators to neglect.

Activity 1-8
Prepare a futuristic paper on at-risk learners and the educators who address their needs. How will contemporary issues be addressed? What new issues will challenge at-risk learners and their educators? Consider present "moods" and "mind-sets" toward education, at-risk learners, and their educators.

Reviewing What You Have Read About At-Risk Students

1. Slavin (1989) defines _____ as students who, on the basis of several risk factors, are unlikely to graduate from high school.
2. Educators considering age, gender, cultural, and ethnic characteristics must carefully avoid _____ learners.

3. The mortality among adolescents usually results from _____
_____ , _____ , and _____
rather than physical diseases.

4. It is important to state that _____ should be considered as strengths, providing enrichment to the United States; however,
perhaps due to racism and discrimination over the years, some culturally
diverse groups experience greater at-risk problems than their Anglo-
American counterparts.

5. _____ experience a degree of double jeopardy, be-
ing more likely than Anglo-American males to die as a result of homicide.

6. _____ adolescents are at high risk for a number of
health problems, alcohol abuse, motor vehicle accidents, mental health
problems, substance use, pregnancy, and periodontal problems (Office of
Technology Assessment, 1991).

7. Adolescents often underestimate the dangers of using _____
_____ and have expressed their belief that alcohol is the most prevalent
drug problem among U.S. students.

8. _____ is an effort by schools to provide special
instruction for students whose out-of-school lives are considered to be so
different from that of most students that they are at a disadvantage in the
regular school program.

9. _____ is an example of a federal compensatory
program for students from age 3 to school entry and is designed to increase
chances of later school success.

10. The term "at risk" is a relatively new term, perhaps fueled by the 1983
publication of _____ , which declared the United
States to be at risk.

11. _____ is a contemporary and common problem
that often affects children and may include changes in appetite or weight,
sleep disturbances, psychomotor problems, loss of interest in usual activities, loss of energy, feelings of worthlessness or excessive guilt, complaints
of difficulty to concentrate, and thoughts of death or suicide.

12. _____ ranks today as the second or third leading
cause of death among industrialized nations of the world and, in the United
States, the rate has tripled during the past 30 years.

13. Children and adolescents in _____ are five times
as likely to be poor than those in married-couple families.

14. _____ can include obscene messages against eth-
nic, racial, and religious groups; the mocking of sexual preferences; verbal
abuse and threats; and, generally speaking, words and deeds motivated by
negative feelings and opinions about a victim's race, ethnicity, religion, and
sexual preference.

15. _____ are another problem causing some children and adolescents to be at risk across cultural and geographic boundaries, and are motivated by violence, extortion, intimidation, and illegal trafficking of drugs and weapons.

Answer Key: 1. academically at-risk learners; **2.** stereotyping; **3.** motor vehicle accidents, suicide, homicide; **4.** cultural and ethnic differences; **5.** African-American males; **6.** Native American; **7.** alcohol; **8.** Compensatory education; **9.** Head Start; **10.** *A Nation at Risk*; **11.** depression; **12.** suicide; **13.** female-headed families; **14.** hate crimes; **15.** gangs

Summary

The movement to identify and address the needs of at-risk children and adolescents is well under way. For many years, learners sometimes attended school with little hope of ever graduating, while others used drugs, alcohol, or harbored suicidal thoughts. Regardless of the condition, these students were at risk of not achieving in school or in other areas such as health or lower self-concepts. Educators working with at-risk learners now realize that appropriate action can be taken. Learners' at-risk indicators can be identified and programs can be provided that address individual at-risk conditions. Successful programs require educators who recognize at-risk conditions, have a commitment to help these students meet their potential, and have the ability to design appropriate programs. The possibilities for at-risk learners look bright. Educators are better trained to detect at-risk indicators and to provide appropriate at-risk programs. A knowledge base in the professional literature has increased in both quantity and quality, and in most educational circles. Further, an enthusiastic commitment to design at-risk programs that address the needs of at-risk children and adolescents has been made.

For Additional Information on At-Risk Students

Bodinger-deUriarte, C. (1991, December). Hate crime: The rise of hate crime on school campus. *Research Bulletin* (10), 1–6. Bodinger-deUriarte examines hate crimes, their characteristics, and the crucial role of schools in fighting the problem.

Children's Defense Fund. (1992). *The state of America's children.* Washington, DC: Author. This CDF publication takes a comprehensive look at health, child care, family income, housing, education, and children in the streets.

Educational Leadership. (December 1992/January 1993). This special issue on students at risk explores a variety of topics such as preventing early school failure, avoiding suspension, supporting victims of child abuse, HIV students, and crack-affected learners.

Equity and Excellence. (1991, Fall). The theme issue of this excellent journal focused on "Students At Risk in Our Schools" and examined issues such as defining dropouts, school resources for at-risk youth, school reform for at-risk students, and low achieving students.

McLaughlin, T. F, & Vacha, E. F. (1992). The at-risk student: A proposal for action. *Journal of Instructional Psychology, 19*(1), 66–67. These two authors briefly provide characteristics of at-risk learners and offer suggestions for districts beginning programs.

Martinet, K. (1993). Youth gangs: A spreading problem. *Momentum, 24*(2), 68D72. Martinet examines this national problem, the reasons for gangs, and possible solutions.

Reed, S., & Sautter, R. C. (1990). Children of poverty: The status of 12 million young Americans. *Phi Delta Kappan, 71*(10), K1–K12. Reed and Sautter, in this special report in the *Kappan*, examine who children in poverty are, the impact they have on schools, and what schools can do to help children of poverty.

Scales, P. C. (1991). *A portrait of young adolescents in the 1990s: Implications for promoting healthy growth and development*. University of North Carolina–Chapel Hill: Center for Early Adolescence. Scales takes a comprehensive look at health status and social health of young people and also discusses programs, policies, and approaches.

Slavin, R. E., Karweit, N. L., & Madden, N. A. (1989). *Effective programs for students at-risk*. Boston: Allyn and Bacon. This text contains 12 edited readings and focuses on issues such as students, classroom programs, and programs at the various grade levels.

U.S. Department of Education. (1990). *A profile of the American eighth grader*. Washington, DC: Author. As the title implies, this comprehensive government publication examines eighth graders, their in-school and out-of-school experiences, and their preparations for high school.

2

Identification and Assessment

Outline

Overview

Probing Directions

Identifying At-Risk Students
  The School's Responsibility
  Identifying Children and Adolescents in Crisis

Identifying Specific At-Risk Conditions and Indicators
  Lower Achievers
  School Dropouts
  Exceptionalities
  Teenage Pregnancy
  Alcohol, Tobacco, and Other Drugs
  Juvenile Delinquency and Criminal Behaviors
  Poverty and Lower Socioeconomic Status
  Suicides
  Health Problems
  Risky Behaviors

All Children and Adolescents Are At Risk at Some Time
  The Risk in Being Average
  Passing Through Developmental Stages

Overview

Educators play a significant role in the identification of at-risk children and adolescents. Without caring educators trained to recognize potential problems, at-risk children and adolescents might become casualties of the school systems. The classroom teacher may be among the first to recognize and report students with potential problems, but all educators are professionally responsible for identifying at-risk learners. This chapter focuses on at-risk conditions and their respective indicators, and also emphasizes the necessity of coordinated efforts among professionals to identify at-risk children and adolescents.

Probing Directions

This chapter on identifying at-risk children and adolescents does the following:

1. Encourages educators to accept responsibility for identifying at-risk children and adolescents.
2. Emphasizes the need for accurately and objectively making identification and assessment decisions.
3. Defines a "crisis" and offers identifying characteristics that suggest a child or adolescent is experiencing a crisis.
4. Provides, whenever possible, names of instruments, assessment devices, and checklists designed to identify at-risk children and adolescents.
5. Offers the theory that all children and adolescents might be at-risk at some time in their lives.
6. Shows the importance of coordinating efforts among administrators, teachers, counselors, school nurses, social service referral agencies, and parents to identify at-risk children and adolescents.
7. Informs readers of sources of additional information on identifying at-risk children and adolescents.

Identifying At-Risk Students

Identification of at-risk students, whether elementary, middle school, or secondary, requires educators' acceptance of responsibility, commitment to objectivity, and knowledge of at-risk indicators. Educators accept this responsibility either because job descriptions require identification and reporting or because they have genuine desires to help individual students in need. Early intervention might be the factor that determines whether an at-risk condition significantly affects a learner's future and overall well-being. Identification of potential at-risk problems and intervention before problems grow more acute requires educators to recognize identifying characteristics and the benefits of early intervention.

The School's Responsibility

Educators during the 1990s and beyond undoubtedly will be expected to identify students demonstrating at-risk behaviors. Such an expectation is reasonable because educators might recognize potential problems that parents and others might not recognize or be willing to admit. Likewise, the professional preparation that educators receive will contribute to their being able to detect characteristics or conditions. This responsibility also includes the imperative to consider students individually and objectively. For example, a student who has particular indicators (perhaps withdrawal) might be at risk whereas another student demonstrating the identical behavior might not be. The task of educators is to identify students in need while simultaneously avoiding labeling those students who are not at risk. Likewise, decisions regarding a student's propensity toward being at risk should never be based on racial, ethnic, or gender factors.

Identifying Children and Adolescents in Crisis

A "crisis" is any event or experience that demands higher levels of coping skills than one is presently able or knows how to perform (Exline, 1993, p. 13). Crisis may be manifested through physical, psychological, and social symptoms, each having identifiable characteristics. Physical symptoms may include headaches, stomachaches, vomiting, diarrhea, and wetting or soil-

---

Activity 2-1

Respond to the proposal that schools are responsible for the identification of at-risk children and adolescents. Focus on such issues as identification, at-risk programs, and assessment. Also, consider where the school's responsibility ends and social service agencies roles begin.

ing of clothes. Psychological symptoms may include increased irritability, quarreling, lower tolerance, temper tantrums, clinging behavior, and exaggerated fears. Social symptoms may include withdrawal from peers and activities, decreased energy, self-rejecting talk, sarcasm, belittling or increased teasing of others, increased lying, and talking of bizarre or exaggerated stories as if they were true (Exline, 1993).

Identifying Specific At-Risk Conditions and Indicators

Lower Achievers

Educators can readily see evidence of low academic achievement and also pinpoint identifying characteristics of at-risk learners. The National Assessment of Educational Progress (NAEP) found that the average 9-year-old and the average 17-year-old in 1988 had significantly higher reading performance than their counterparts in 1971; however, the overall increases were relatively small, and the performance of 13-year-olds has remained essentially unchanged since 1971. Also, the gains achieved by 9-year-olds between 1971 and 1980 and the average achievement levels in 1984 and 1988 were slightly lower than the level obtained in 1980. Mathematics achievement showed only minor changes. For example, the performance of 9- and 13-year-olds increased by only a moderate amount. In contrast, the scores of 17-year-olds have shown a net decline since 1973, although improvements since 1982 appear to be stable (Linn & Dunbar, 1990).

Educators of at-risk children and adolescents and, in fact, educators of all students have reason for concern: Learners in most states test below grade level and some states well below grade level; the mathematical skills of most high school seniors are limited to the eighth-grade level; and only 5% of the 12th graders tested showed sufficient skills to be capable of college mathematics (More bad news . . . , 1991).

Not surprising, homeless children also experience lower academic achievement. Landers (1989) reported that researchers for Advocates for Children of New York found children of homeless families performed poorly in school and also had more erratic attendance records than children living in more established homes. Educators identifying children with the potential for lower academic achievement should not assume all homeless children are at risk; however, learners being homeless should be a possible identifying characteristic.

Educators working with at-risk students have significant responsibilities in the identification of lower achievers and the provision of appropriate educational experiences. Knowing the characteristics and behaviors of students who either function below grade level or who are at-risk of failure will be a first step in addressing educational needs.

Lower Achievers: At-Risk Indicators to Recognize

1. Achieving one or more grade levels behind
2. Achieving below one's potential regardless of grade-level performance
3. Failing to demonstrate motivation or interest in schoolwork or in academically related activities
4. Failing to complete homework, classwork, and projects on time
5. Demonstrating "ups and downs" or periods of low and high academic achievement without a plausible reason for the difference
6. Being homeless, either temporarily or for an extended period

School Dropouts

Educators identifying at-risk children and adolescents find that dropouts give fairly specific reasons for withdrawing from school. Determining why students withdraw from school can help educators identify other students at risk of withdrawing. Rather than being able to pinpoint one single factor, a number of identifying factors can suggest a potential dropout. Likewise, the notable differences between reasons offered by males and females suggests a consideration of the diversity among the genders. Also, it is interesting to note the considerable differences and similarities among students, teachers, and social scientists as to why students drop out of school.

Students' Reasons for Dropping Out
Reasons males often cite include poor school performance, suspension, marriage, and wanting to earn money. Females cited reasons such as marriage and pregnancy, school factors, and economic reasons (Muha & Cole, 1991). Other reasons given for dropping out included poor academic performance, dislike of school, alienation from peers, or the need to help the family financially (Hahn, 1987). Other reasons students give for dropping out include poor teachers and boring classes, family problems, language-related problems, personal problems, low self-esteem, drugs, disruptive behavior, truancy, and academic failure (Balch, 1989).

Teachers' Reasons for Students Dropping Out
Teachers' responses in a study to determine reasons for students dropping out included psychological immaturity, rebelliousness, single-parent family, lack of self-responsibility, rigid personality, behavior problems, excessive absenteeism, authoritarian personalities, working mother, shyness, short

attention spans, few school contacts, low reading levels, and social isolation (Fitzgerald, 1990).

Social Scientists' Reasons for Students Dropping Out
Social scientists have identified 10 major risk factors indicating students might drop out of school: behind in grade level and older than classmates; poor academic performance; dislike of school; detention and suspension; pregnancy; welfare recipients and members of single-parent homes; the attractiveness of work or military service; undiagnosed learning disabilities and emotional problems; and language difficulties (Hahn, 1987).

Without a doubt, educators are in a prime position to identify potential dropouts. Selected characteristics that indicate a propensity toward being at risk include low basic skills test performances, low grades, below grade-level achievement, failure to complete assigned work, failure of parents to monitor and encourage academic achievement, and failure to perceive the relevance of academic accomplishment to the world of work (McLaughlin & Vacha, 1992).

Students most likely to have poor grades in the eighth grade and to have dropped out by the tenth grade include:

- Students from single-parent families, who are over age for the peer group and frequently changed schools
- Students whose parents who did not participate in school activities, never asked them about school, and held low expectations for them
- Students who repeated an earlier grade, had histories of poor grades in mathematics and reading, or who did little homework
- Students who often came to school unprepared for schoolwork, cut classes frequently, and were frequently tardy or absent
- Students considered passive, frequently disruptive, inattentive, and underachieving
- Students from schools with large minority enrollments (Young adolescents at risk, 1993).

Understanding the self-perceptions of school dropouts provides another means of identifying learners with the potential for dropping out of school. Because students at risk do not perform academically, educators often assume they are lazy and unmotivated. However, these students may view themselves as defeated or needing assistance schools do not provide. Likewise, these students often need specific subject matter assistance and desire personal and warm relationships with teachers and peers. At-risk learners who may appear discouraged and perhaps defeated often want to do well in school and are willing to accept assistance and direction from caring educators. They need more individual assistance and personal contact than many of their peers. Perceptive educators can sometimes identify potential dropouts by pinpointing feelings of defeat or feelings of needing personal attention (Ruff, 1993).

While parents might not recognize (or might not want to admit) at-risk indicators, educators who know reasons for other students dropping out can develop a profile of characteristics or indicators to look for in other students.

School Dropouts: At-Risk Indicators to Recognize

1. Low self-esteem
2. Psychological immaturity
3. Rebelliousness and aggressive behavior
4. Single-parent family
5. Behavior problems
6. Excessive absences
7. Low academic achievement
8. Compulsive behavior
9. Low reading levels
10. Short attention span
11. Social isolation, lack of friends, and few school contacts
12. Lack of participation in extracurricular activities
13. Retained in elementary or middle school
14. Low teacher morale

Adapted from Fitzgerald, J. (1990). Students at risk: Are secondary teachers able to identify potential school dropouts? *Education, 111*(2), 227.

Exceptionalities

Exceptional children and adolescents may fall into several categories: learning disabled, mentally impaired, emotionally disturbed, hearing or speech impaired, orthopedically impaired, visually impaired and several other or multiple conditions. Although PL 94-142, The Education for All Handicapped Children Act of 1975, theoretically provides for these learners' needs, in reality, many of these children and adolescents continue to be at risk, especially since exceptionalities can bring on other at-risk conditions. Educators are challenged to identify exceptional youngsters and any special at-risk conditions they face.

Identifying and assessing students with exceptionalities often leads to labeling, a practice with many ill effects. Labeling learners has such potentially harmful effects that educators assigning labels to children may be placing children and adolescents at great risk. Although educators have the learner's interest and educational welfare at stake, labeling learners as "slow" or "disabled" can sometimes cause irreparable harm, not only during school programs, but throughout entire lives. Educators should be cognizant of this practice and should know when labeling is in the learner's best interest.

Disadvantages of labeling children and adolescents include:

- Learners labeled as disabled or exceptional may be permanently stigmatized, rejected, or denied opportunities for full development.
- Learners labeled as mentally retarded or the equivalent may be assigned to inferior educational programs in schools or placed in institutions without the benefit of legal protection.
- Large numbers of culturally diverse learners are inaccurately classified as mentally disabled on the basis of scores earned on inappropriate tests (Biehler & Snowman, 1990).

Case Study 2-1 illustrates the dangers of labeling learners and also shows how both students' and teachers' perceptions can be affected by placing learners in categories.

Case Study 2-1: The Dangers of Labeling

Mrs. Washburne, principal of Washington Middle School, was looking through student permanent records when she saw several disturbing labels: "behaviorally maladjusted," "slow learner," "retarded," "below average," "gifted," "troublemaker," "unmotivated," "emotionally disturbed," and other labels. She realized the dangers of labeling: Teachers often expect too little, sometimes they expect too much, learners are often placed in wrong groups, and learners' entire lives might be affected by labels placed on them in elementary school. Another concern was that such labeling had the potential for being both unprofessional and unethical. She admitted to herself that while labeling learners had the potential for helping, the practice should be limited to only those cases when learners were clearly helped.

Mrs. Washburne knew that her professional responsibilities required her to address the situation: First, teachers should be made aware of the dangers of labeling; second, through in-service opportunities, she would encourage teachers to think about labeling and alternatives; third, teachers would be encouraged to make diagnoses using the most objective and reliable means; and fourth, teachers should assign a label only when the diagnosis is accurate and in the learner's best interest.

When, then, if ever, should learners be labeled? Students should be given a label only when placing a label on the learner is in the student's best interest and when the learner's condition can be professionally documented

---

Activity 2-2

Propose a plan whereby the damaging effects of labeling can be eliminated or at least reduced. Include in your plan when, if such a time exists, educators *should* label learners.

---

with substantial objective data. The label should serve a meaningful purpose and should provide a basis for assisting the overall educational progress of the learner. Even when this is the case, educators have a moral, ethical, and professional responsibility to assess learners periodically, to diagnose accurately, to follow all due process procedures, and to ensure that learners are placed in other groups or classes if the disabling or exceptional conditions change.

As previously stated, exceptionalities also include gifted and talented learners who may be at risk, of failing to achieve in their areas of giftedness. The educator has an equal responsibility to identify and assess gifted learners and to help them achieve their levels of potential, regardless of the area of giftedness. Characteristics of giftedness and high levels of creativity include: generating a large number of ideas or solutions to problems and questions; expressing opinions, sometimes radical and spirited in disagreement; displaying a good deal of intellectual playfulness, and fantasizing; accepting disorder; being unafraid of being different; relying more on own evaluations than on those of others; and displaying humor, playfulness, and relaxation in creative products (Wolf, 1990).

The consequences of failing to address children's and adolescents' exceptionalities can be severe and long lasting: lost potential, both for the individual and the nation; misbehavior problems that might be misunderstood by educators; a loss of self-esteem—an important factor influencing both academic achievement and social behavior; and outright failure resulting in low achievement and school dropouts.

Exceptionalities: At-Risk Indicators to Recognize

1. One or more disabling conditions requiring the professional attention of school personnel
2. Lower academic achievement or reduced socialization clearly resulting from disabling conditions
3. Learners who, for one reason or another, are not having their needs met in accordance with legal mandates
4. Labels that may miscategorize learners or may not be in their best educational interests
5. Learners who do not participate in school-related activities to the point disabling conditions allow

Teenage Pregnancy

The adolescent tendency to experiment with sexual activity at increasingly younger ages has resulted in a rising incidence of teenage pregnancy. Rather than "blaming the victim" or perceiving teenage pregnancy as a societal problem, educators' professional responsibilities include identifying pregnant school girls and, if possible, identifying students at risk of getting pregnant. In a more idealistic setting, schools would have significant, caring adults with whom young girls could confide, ask questions, voice concerns, and seek advice before the pregnancy occurs. In our more realistic world, schools often do not (or, perhaps for legal reasons or time constraints, cannot) provide these significant adult relationships.

Educators and counselors are in prime positions to identify pregnant students and students at risk of getting pregnant, and to counsel pregnant teenagers. Whether the young girl admits the pregnancy or it becomes obvious to the teacher or counselor, the first identification often comes from the school. Of the several identifiers for being at risk, the one standing out the most is young girls perceiving a bleak future. Educators need to watch closely for school girls who perceive little or no future or those whose future appears to be centered totally on a boy.

Many parents might not be aware of the most obvious signs of teenage pregnancy or they might be unwilling to admit their daughter is either pregnant or is risking pregnancy. In such cases, educators might be the first to try to help the girl or convince her to confide in her parents or other significant family members.

Educators of at-risk students are likely to find interesting the relationship between sexual activity and academic success. In a study of girls ages 12 to 17, sexual activity was found to be more prevalent among females with lower grades. While 37% of students with overall grades between C and F were reported to be sexually active, only 21% of students in the B+ to A range were sexually active (McClelland, 1987). Although lower academic achievement does not always indicate a student is sexually active, it can serve as an indicator that can be considered along with other factors.

Teenage Pregnancy: At-Risk Indicators to Recognize

1. Physical indicators of pregnancy such as unexplained weight gain and abdominal growth
2. Emotional indicators of pregnancy such as crying, undue anxiety, irritableness, and mood swings
3. Explicit knowledge of sexual relations
4. Unusual curiosity about sex or "what happens when one is pregnant"
5. Inordinate concern with pregnancy, adoption, abortion, or becoming a mother
6. Other females in the family being pregnant as teenagers

Alcohol, Tobacco, and Other Drugs

Although the use of marijuana, alcohol, and cigarettes is the most prevalent indicators, educators need to look for other drugs such as (listed in descending order of use) stimulants, inhalants, cocaine, hallucinogens, tranquilizers, and sedatives. Johnston, O'Malley, and Bachman (1986) in their study for the National Institute on Drug Abuse found evidence that middle grade students also use drugs. Therefore, just as secondary school educators have a responsibility to identify at-risk adolescents experimenting with tobacco, alcohol, and other drugs, educators in elementary and middle schools should also watch for at-risk indicators such as males and older students. That is, students are more likely to experiment during later adolescent years than early adolescent years. The high proportion of young people who have tried any illegal drug (61%) by their senior year continues to grow substantially. Males are more likely than females to use most illegal drugs at all ages. For example, about twice as many high school males (6.9%) as females smoke marijuana on a daily basis (Atwater, 1988).

Whether tobacco, alcohol, or an illicit drug, the consequences of experimenting or daily use can be severe and either constitutes at-risk behavior or contributes to at-risk conditions. Death, health problems, automobile accidents, school failure, loss of self-esteem, and criminal records are just a few of the many problems resulting from drug abuse. Drug abuse can also contribute to or complicate pregnancy. In 1989, 11% of all babies born had some trace of drugs in their systems; this number is three times as high as 1985 (Viadero, 1989). Educators, working with at-risk or potential at-risk learners, have a responsibility to look for indicators of tobacco, alcohol, and illicit drug use.

Selected characteristics that are warning signs of alcohol abuse include a decline in grades, switching of friends, emotional highs and lows, defiance of rules and regulations, becoming secretive, loss of energy, withdrawal from school functions, changes in physical hygiene, being late or absent, and obvious behaviors such as slurred speech, an unsteady walk, the smell of alcohol, and becoming unusually agitated in class (Horton, 1992).

Alcohol, Tobacco, and Other Drugs: At-Risk Indicators to Recognize

1. Erratic behavior, unexpected outbursts of behavior, and emotional "ups and downs"
2. Knowledge of alcohol, drugs, and drug paraphernalia
3. Loss of motivation or interest in school
4. Long absences from school or home
5. Poor muscle coordination
6. Sleepiness
7. Restless and talkative
8. Sharp drop in school performance

Juvenile Delinquency and Criminal Behaviors

The consequences of juvenile delinquency are many. First, the victims suffer injuries, loss of self-esteem, and theft as well as being afraid to attend school. Second, the actual person doing the delinquent behavior can face any number of negative possibilities. Third, school systems and taxpayers must pay for vandalism and additional security needed to protect school property.

Educators often consider juvenile delinquents to be the responsibility of law enforcement officers, a societal problem with which educators should not have to deal. Although one can present a logical argument for educators believing juvenile delinquency is a societal and law enforcement issue, another argument suggests educators can and should play a major role in identifying delinquent activities. In fact, educators are in a prime position to detect indicators that suggest delinquent behavior, and although educators should not be expected to perform law enforcement roles, they are held responsible for students' safety and overall welfare. Therefore, knowing the characteristics and identifiers that suggest a propensity toward being at risk of violence or criminal activity can contribute to a safe school setting for all learners.

Research shows that family situation, friendships, and personality are associated with delinquency. More specific identifiers of delinquency include a poor parent–child relationship characterized by hostility, lack of affection, and underinvolvement; overly harsh and authoritarian methods of discipline; a high degree of family conflict and disorganization; and the presence of a parent with a personality disturbance and a criminal history (Sarafino & Armstrong, 1986; Seifert & Hoffnung, 1991).

Although educators should not be accountable for juvenile delinquents' criminal behaviors at home or at school, they can watch for indicators to suggest that a student is at-risk of delinquent behaviors. Also, it is important to look for these indicators in relation to other behaviors such as missing school, school failure, and experimenting with alcohol and drugs.

Juvenile Delinquency and Criminal Behaviors: At-Risk Indicators to Recognize

1. Open hostility toward authority—school, parents and family, and law enforcement
2. Excessive wealth for the family's SES
3. Association with gangs or older individuals known for delinquent behavior
4. Vandalism, minor or major, committed against school property
5. Knowledge of methods associated with crime and juvenile delinquency: threats, blackmail, stealing, extortion, criminal sexual conduct, fighting, and so forth

Poverty and Lower Socioeconomic Status

Every year, large numbers of families become poor because of divorce, separation, unemployment, or temporary disability. As previously mentioned, poverty cannot automatically be assumed to be an at-risk condition; however, perceptive educators teaching or counseling children and adolescents whose parents are experiencing any of the four just listed problems, should consider these factors as possible at-risk indicators.

For many of these families, the length of the stay in poverty is brief, but some families suffer longer spells of poverty because of prolonged physical disability, lack of job skills and experience, extended periods of unemployment related to recessions in the national or local economy, reemployment at lower wages when the local economy loses higher paying jobs, or other factors. Other families are formed in poverty. These families generally fare worse and have greater needs than families who become poor. They include large numbers of single-parent families formed outside of marriage; a surprising number of young two-parent families who cannot earn enough from employment to escape poverty; and many families formed by immigrant parents who arrive in the United States with few financial assets and little education. Families formed in poverty tend to have fewer economic, personal, and social resources and to experience longer spells of poverty than other poor families (National Center for Children in Poverty, 1990). Learners with such home situations should be given special consideration to determine whether these circumstances are contributing to their propensity to be at risk.

The challenge of educating the children of poverty has long been recognized as a difficult one. Other indicators include performing poorly on academic tasks; typical problems resulting from schools serving large numbers of at-risk children; high rates of mobility among students' families; a high incidence of severe emotional or behavioral problems among students; large numbers of students with limited proficiency in English; low staff morale; and inadequate facilities and resources (Knapp & Shields, 1990).

Poverty and Lower Socioeconomic Status: At-Risk Indicators to Recognize

1. Outward signs of poverty: old and disheveled clothes, being unclean, and having excessive body odors; other basic necessities of life not being met
2. Hunger; fatigue from lack of sleep; lack of motivation, listlessness
3. Apparent lack of health care and evidence of poor health: fatigue, dizziness, anxiety problems, irritability, headaches, ear infections, frequent colds, unwanted weight loss, inability to concentrate, and increased school absenteeism

4. Unable to pay for school-related items such as lunches, textbook materials, paper and pencils, class photographs, or expenditures for field trips
5. Living with single-parent females or males who provide sole economic support

Suicides

Suicides among children and adolescents may result from an "insolvable problem" in which children harbor feelings of being trapped or incapacitated. Educators can look for several indicators of the insolvable problem: 1) a problem beyond the child's ability to resolve that is deeply rooted and long-standing in the life of the entire family; 2) limitation by the parents of alternative solutions to only one possibility that is undesirable to the child; 3) a problem situation in which every resolution creates a new problem; and 4) a family problem that is disguised from the entire family, which brings pressure to bear on the child to deal with the problem alone (Orbach, 1986; Thompson & Rudolph, 1988).

Specific reasons for suicides that educators can identify may include failing a class at school, depression, lack of supportive friendships, anxiety, unhappiness, family instability, and, especially among adolescents, the loss of a boyfriend or girlfriend or an unwanted pregnancy. Genetics may also play a factor in the decision to commit suicide. The closer the genetic relation to someone who has committed suicide, the more likely an individual is to commit suicide. Remember that the decision to commit suicide is complex and probably has culminated from a number of interrelated factors (Santrock, 1990).

Potential suicides resulting from depression among children and adolescents can often be identified through the Beck Depression Inventory (BDI) (Beck, Ward, Mendelson, Mock, & Erbaugh, 1961) and the Child Depression Inventory (CDI) (Kovacs, 1981). The former, the BDI, is used with adolescents and uses 21 items to provide a depression score. The CDI is used with children ages 8 to 17 (Ponterotto, Pace, & Kavan, 1989). Once educators suspect depression is a problem, these instruments can assist in determining whether suicide may be a possibility.

Interviewing children and adolescents who appear to be suicidal is another useful method of determining potential suicides. For example, students in an interview might reveal anger either at a person or an institution, might have extreme negative feelings toward oneself, or generally speaking, provide evidence of being emotionally upset. Other feelings that might be revealed in the interview include feelings of helplessness or being unable to cope with parents', teachers', peers', or one's own expectations. An interview can provide considerable insight into a child's or adolescent's intentions, and it can have a positive side effect: Interviews can show the child or adolescent that someone cares and has sufficient interest to take the time to conduct the interview.

Case Study 2-2 looks at one school's experience with a student suicide and how it responded.

Case Study 2-2: Suicide Postvention

The faculty at Raines High School had its worst nightmare come true: 16-year-old Jim G. committed suicide. While the administrators, teachers, counselors, and other staff members had planned a postvention program for dealing with suicide, no one ever thought the plan would have to be implemented.

Mrs. Smith remarked, "Why didn't we recognize the situation? We should have known—Jim had so many of the characteristics—a preoccupation with death in music, his parents' divorce and his relocation only a year ago, his declining grades and lack of interest in school, and his withdrawal from his friends. Still, where did he get the gun?"

While the school and the students suffered from the initial shock, the educators were putting their postvention plans into operation. They had been trained to work as a team, had participated in several in-service programs, and had notified community and social service agencies of the suicide. Likewise, the media had been notified and encouraged to report accurate information, to check with Jim's family to avoid misrepresentations, and to avoid making Jim into a hero.

Other aspects of the postvention plan included communicating honestly concerning the death, maintaining the school schedule to the extent possible, and deciding on a plan for the following month: the day of the funeral, the activities in which Jim would have participated (very few in his case), the grief experienced by the students (and the faculty), and deciding whether a special service was needed to provide a sense of finality. The faculty knew that some research suggested a service should not be held; however they also knew that having a service would provide a sense of closure.

The educators at Raines High School faced the situation and knew that the next several months would not be easy, but they also felt comfort in knowing that they had a postvention plan for the next several months.

Educators identifying suicidal students have several roles: establishing policies and procedures for preventing a suicide; making sure all faculty and staff members recognize the warning signs; having an accountable referral system; working with social service and other agencies; and having a postvention plan when a suicide actually occurs.

Suicides: At-Risk Indicators to Recognize

1. Direct suicide threats or comments
2. A previous suicide attempt, no matter how minor
3. Preoccupation with death
4. Loss of a family member, pet, or boy/girl friend through death, abandonment, breakup
5. Family disruptions such as unemployment, serious illness, relocation, divorce
6. Disturbances in sleeping and eating habits and in personal hygiene
7. Declining grades and lack of interest in school or hobbies
8. Drastic changes in behavior patterns, such as a quiet, shy person becoming extremely gregarious
9. Feelings of gloom, helplessness, and hopelessness
10. Withdrawal from family members and friends and feelings of alienation
11. Giving away prized possessions
12. Series of "accidents" or impulsive, risk-taking behaviors: drug or alcohol abuse, disregard for personal safety, taking dangerous dares

Adapted from *Living with 10–15 year olds: A parent education curriculum.* (1982). Carrboro, NC: The Center for Early Adolescence.

Health Problems

Although most people assume children experience the various childhood diseases, for some reason many people consider adolescence to be a healthy and safe period of life. However, the Office of Technology Assessment's (1991) study of adolescent health stated:

> *The conventional wisdom that American adolescents as a group are so healthy that they do not require health and related services is not justified.*
> *(p. 6)*

Many adolescents and children at increasingly younger ages experience nutritional problems, obesity, and an obsession with thinness. These problems might be associated with tendencies to consume fast foods, with adolescents' belief that their health will remain forever, or with society's preoccupation with thinness. Regardless of the cause, many children and adolescents place themselves in at-risk situations that may have serious health and educational consequences.

Adolescents (and increasingly children) have the highest prevalence of unsatisfactory nutritional status of all age groups. Educators knowledgeable of learners' food habits can look for several at-risk identifiers: increased tendency to skip meals (especially breakfast and lunch), snacking (usually candies), consumption of fast foods, and dieting. Food dependence and obesity, other identifying characteristics, frequently place young people in at-risk situations. About 15% of today's teenagers are significantly overweight; being overweight might result from a biologically inherited tendency to be overweight, childhood diet, family attitudes and habits toward food, or lack of exercise. Obesity can have devastating effects on children's and adolescents' overall identity development and sense of self as an attractive person. In some cases, obesity can lead to isolation and can severely limit social opportunities (Seifert & Hoffnung, 1991).

Society's obsession with thinness as the ideal and dominant cultural standard for feminine beauty has led to significant numbers of teenagers being obsessed with being thin. Perceptive educators might be among the first to notice anxiety disorders such as obsessive dietary habits and might be able to respond before learners place their body in serious harm. An extreme form of this quest to be thin is anorexia nervosa, a psychological and physical disturbance in which the teenager starves herself (95% of anorexics are females), exercises compulsively, and develops an unrealistic view of her body. Many anorexics also suffer from bulimia, a disorder in which they eat large amounts of food and then vomit so as not to gain weight. The causes and treatment of these disorders are complex, and between 10% and 20% of youngsters who do not receive professional help die of starvation and its consequences (Seifert & Hoffnung, 1991). Table 2-1 provides educators with several distinct signs or characteristics that are indicators of anorexia nervosa (Atwater, 1988).

Bulimia is closely related to yet also differs from anorexia nervosa. Whereas the aim of the anorexic is to lose weight, the bulimic tries to eat without gaining weight. The bulimic experiences eating sprees or binges, accompanied by an awareness that the eating pattern is abnormal, a fear of not being able to stop eating, and the depressed mood and self-disparaging thoughts that follow eating binges. Then, the person self-induces vomiting so weight will not be gained. Educators should look for young people about 18 years of age who are experiencing unhappy times, mostly girls in middle and upper SES, individuals showing an inordinate concern about their weight and appearance, and frequent weight fluctuations (Atwater, 1988).

Other at-risk indicators include lack of health insurance (one out of seven adolescents or 4.6 million); lack of Medicaid among poor adolescents (one out of three poor adolescents); lack of parental availability to accompany adolescents for health services (the parents of 60% of adolescents work

TABLE 2-1   Signs of Anorexia Nervosa

- Tends to occur during early and mid-adolescence, commonly at 14 or 15 years of age
- Nine to 10 times more common for girls than boys
- More common among all-girl families
- Overweight for age and height
- Intelligent and makes good grades
- Conscientious and perfectionistic
- Teased about her weight, either by peers or adults becomes meticulous about counting calories, what she eats, and how she eats
- Hides or throws food away when pressured by parents to eat
- Emotional problems resulting from growing up in strict families in many cases
- Model child, quiet and obedient, yet lacks a firm sense of personal identity and autonomy
- Suffers from a disturbed body image, so does not realize she is getting seriously thin
- Denies illness and is uninterested in or resistant to treatment and, in severe cases, starvation and even death may occur

full-time); and geographic factors (i.e., estimated numbers indicate that one-third of adolescents live in rural communities) (Office of Technology Assessment, 1991).

Perceptive educators will want to look for conditions or indicators that might suggest students' health habits make them at risk.

Health and Health-Related Factors: At-Risk Indicators to Recognize

1. Depression, sadness, and loneliness
2. Eating disorders such as obesity and/or an obsession with slimness
3. Changes in appetite, weight, or sleeping patterns
4. Evidence of a sexually transmitted disease
5. One or more acute physical illnesses
6. Signs of substance (alcohol, tobacco, and drugs) use or abuse
7. Obvious signs of poverty
8. Substantial numbers of days missed from school

Simply because a learner demonstrates particular characteristics or behaviors does not automatically imply a propensity toward being at risk. While all at-risk identifiers should be recognized and monitored, educators must use caution to avoid mislabeling learners as being at risk when they are really not. Case Study 2-3 considers whether a 9-year-old boy should be labeled as at risk.

Case Study 2-3: Is Matt an At-Risk Child?

Matt, a 9-year-old African-American boy, puzzles his teachers and counselor. He demonstrates several at-risk behaviors yet appears to function normally in most social and academic situations. His at-risk indicators include being shy and a little withdrawn, being placed in a less difficult reading class, and being from a family in which children have a history of dropping out of school. Matt's teachers and counselors wonder whether they should intervene or if they are placing too much emphasis on a few isolated factors.

One perceptive educator in the school urged the counselor and educator to take a cautious approach to labeling Matt as an at-risk student. She reminded the others that Matt's cultural background should be appreciated yet decisions should reflect objectivity and a consideration of a variety of factors. Likewise, each behavior (i.e., withdrawal and shyness and being in a less difficult reading class) should be considered yet should not be determining factors.

A professional decision was reached not to label Matt as being at risk. Both the teachers and counselors agreed to monitor Matt's at-risk behaviors closely to see if conditions grew more severe or if he began to fail academically or became more withdrawn. If Matt becomes overly withdrawn to the point at which he does not have friends or if he falls farther behind in reading, then appropriate action might include additional remedial work, counseling intervention, meeting with his parents, and planning a concerted school effort to address his needs.

Risky Behaviors

Risky or dangerous behaviors are other at-risk conditions facing children and adolescents and can often be identified by perceptive and caring educators. While adolescents have relatively low mortality rates, danger continues to exist. The leading causes of death among adolescents differ somewhat from those of other age groups. For example, adolescents are more likely than younger and older Americans to die of injuries resulting from accidents, suicide, and homicide.

Activity 2-3

Compile a list of factors or conditions that underlie all at-risk conditions (e.g., low self-concepts). Propose how programs can address a specific at-risk condition *and* the underlying conditions in your list.

Activity 2-4

Make a list of conditions that make all or most learners at risk at some time. Offer a rationale for each condition you provide. How can educators most effectively detect which learners are affected by at-risk conditions and which are not?

Risky Behaviors: At-Risk Indicators to Recognize

1. *Family problems:* high levels of stress or conflict; physical, sexual, or emotional abuse
2. *Recreational problems:* lack of opportunities to engage in attractive, satisfying, and healthful recreational activities
3. *Nutrition and fitness problems:* nutritional and fitness problems such as mineral deficiencies, imbalanced diets, and obesity
4. *Chronic physical illness:* acute physical problems and respiratory illnesses, the leading causes of school-loss days
5. *Dental and oral problems:* problems resulting from the transition from childhood to adolescence and from increasing personal responsibility for oral hygiene
6. *AIDS and other sexually transmitted diseases:* at risk of pregnancy and various diseases
7. *Mental health problems:* feelings of sadness, depression, and hopelessness (Office of Technology Assessment, 1991).

The belief that many learners are at risk at one time or another becomes clear when educators consider the Office of Technology Assessment's conclusions regarding health problems, injuries, and accidents. Also, the fact that youngsters might be at risk at some times and not at risk at other times challenges professionals to make objective identification and assessment decisions. An adolescent living in an urban, poverty-ridden area might be more at risk of homicide or drug-related injury than an adolescent living in a rural areas whose daily use of firearms might result in an accident. Likewise, a child or adolescent might suffer an acute illness during one period of life yet be healthy during the remainder. The educator's responsibility with this issue includes being able to identify when children or adolescents are at risk and when they are not.

All Children and Adolescents Are At Risk at Some Time

An author once spoke with a 13-year-old girl about the various at-risk conditions affecting some learners in her age group and in her school. She asked what at-risk conditions were, and the author listed four or five. She perceptively responded, "*All* learners are at risk at some time!" This young girl had a keen recognition of learners that educators often overlook. This section explains how all learners can be at risk at various points in their lives and not be at risk at others. The following quote illustrates the diversity among at-risk youth:

> *At-risk youth cannot be stereotyped by color, age, economic level or family situation. They belong to all races. They include infants, children, and teens. They come from two-parent and single-parent families, some rich, some poor. Some at-risk youth live in the suburbs, others on farms and in cities (National Catholic Education Association, 1993, p. 4).*

The challenge is for perceptive educators to understand children and adolescents, to recognize the identifying characteristics or signals of specific at-risk conditions, and to determine with some degree of accuracy when an at-risk condition affects children and adolescents.

In an article titled "The Camouflaged At-Risk Student: White and Wealthy," Metz (1993) proposes that many adolescents who "have it all" (p. 40) are also at risk. Metz maintains that her years of working with at-risk adolescents prompts the following risks to which the white and wealthy are particularly vulnerable:

- Depression and suicide
- Alcohol and substance abuse
- Pregnancy and abortion
- AIDS and venereal disease
- Acquaintance and date rape
- Anxiety and stress
- Boredom and loneliness
- Cynicism
- Low self-esteem
- Eating disorders (Metz, 1993).

Metz's article reinforces the point that stereotypical generalizations cannot be used for identifying at-risk youth. Believing the learner living in poverty-ridden conditions is at risk while the wealthy learner living the so-called "good life" is not at risk fails to recognize the need for objective identification procedures.

The Risk in Being Average

Some educators working to challenge brighter students and reacting to disorderly students sometimes overlook average or ordinary children. Clearly, students of all ages and abilities can be at risk and average children do, indeed, function in at-risk situations when their teachers focus time and energy only on bright high achievers and on misbehaving students. A nationwide study of K–12 schools revealed factors linked to making children and adolescents at risk such as changes in personal health, family stability, school performance, peer relations, participation in activities, and overall self-esteem. Another study focusing only on rural students concluded rural students fared worse than nonrural students in some areas such as low self-esteem, substance abuse, depression, suicide attempts, child abuse, poverty, sexual activity, and in situations with alcoholic parents, or students who are migrants (Wylie, 1992). These factors can be considered when identifying and assessing at-risk conditions.

Passing Through Developmental Stages

Children and adolescents passing through the various developmental stages face a number of tasks and challenges that can result in at-risk conditions. Young people might develop at-risk conditions when forming new friendships, developing unfamiliar physical skills, growing toward independence, and developing appropriate sex roles. Identifying characteristics include learners having difficulty making new friends, feeling awkward in physical education class, and subsequently experiencing low self-concepts. These students sometimes engage in at-risk behaviors to compensate for feelings of frustration and inadequacy.

Early and Late Maturers

Educators should watch for early or late maturing rates, both of which have the potential to make students at risk. Santrock (1990) reported that early maturing boys felt more positive about themselves than their later developing peers. Similar but not as strong findings were reported for early maturing girls. Other findings showing how early and later maturing can affect young people include:

1. Early maturing boys had a higher level of self-esteem than middle or late maturing boys in the seventh grade, but significant differences did not exist in the ninth and tenth grades.
2. Early maturers were less satisfied with their bodies than were late maturers, and early maturers expressed dissatisfaction with their weight.
3. Early maturing girls reported being more popular and dated more than late maturing girls.
4. Early maturing girls appear to have more independence than late maturing girls.

5. Early maturing girls were less likely to have good grades and scored lower on achievement tests than their peers (Santrock, 1990).

Perceptive educators can readily recognize how developing early or late can affect self-concept, one's perception of the body and weight, an adolescent's pursuit of independence, and a learner's degree of academic achievement can result in an at-risk condition. A preoccupation with oneself naturally develops during development. While not an at-risk condition in and of itself, this preoccupation can lead to at-risk conditions. Constantly examining and comparing physical and social characteristics with others of similar age results in a continued look at height, weight, and related differences. Youngsters with overt differences may be the only ones to notice such differences, which can play a significant role in determining their self-concept. These differing characteristics also influence learners' opinions of their ability to interact socially. To pinpoint a student's propensity toward being at risk, educators should consider each case individually. First, being an early or late maturer might affect one student yet not have any significant effect on another. Second, an early or late maturing student might be at risk in one area at one time yet may not demonstrate any signs of being at risk at another time.

Peer Pressure

Educators identifying potential at-risk learners often consider learners' friends and the extent to which peer pressure affects relationships and behaviors. Peers are without doubt a major source of influence in the decisions reached by children and adolescents. Children and adolescents becoming involved with drugs, alcohol, smoking, and sexual activity (Elkind, 1981; Postman, 1983) provide evidence of the desire to conform to peer norms. Davis, Weener, and Shute (1977) feel that the peer group is often the primary reference source for attitudes, values, and behavior and serves as a mechanism for decision making. Their research also indicates that children with positive outlooks and attitudes toward their environment—for example, teachers, school, and other students—will more likely respond positively to peer pressure.

Educators need to accept the fact that peer pressure will always influence youngsters' behavior, attire, and speech. An excellent example of students wanting to dress similarly was evident in a sixth-grade classroom where 22 of 24 students wore blue-and-white cloth shoes. While wearing blue-and-white shoes did not constitute an at-risk condition, the possibility existed that learners would participate in other less desirable behaviors to satisfy peers. In addition, educators should remember that attempts to compete with peers are usually futile; peer pressure remains a vital part of the socialization process and a healthy self-concept still serves as the best anti-dote to negative peer pressure. For example, a teacher who works with a drug prevention program recently remarked that a healthy self-concept was one of the most effective means of preventing and combatting drug abuse (Manning & Allen, 1987).

In closing, the issue of "all learners being at risk at some time" calls for professional recognition and proper action. All learners may be at risk at some time in their school lives, but professionals should avoid placing a permanent at-risk label on learners when, in actuality, they might be at risk for only a brief time. The educator's challenge is to be able to determine if and when learners are at risk and to decide on appropriate programs to address the condition.

Coordinating Professionals' and Parents' Efforts

Identification of at-risk children and adolescents should include a coordinated effort by administrators, classroom teachers, school nurses, social service agencies, and parents. The nature and severity of at-risk learners' problems are too serious to leave to chance or only to classroom teachers. Although the teacher might be among the first to identify a potential at-risk condition, other professionals should also accept responsibility for identification and for working with teachers toward common goals. School personnel should be well-acquainted with social service agencies that can provide services of a specialized nature. Likewise, parents and families should play major roles, both as sources of identification and as partners in helping at-risk children and adolescents.

The roles and responsibilities of school personnel, social service agencies, and parents might include, but are not limited to, the following:

Administrators

- Provide leadership in the effort to identify at-risk children and adolescents, especially in coordinating the efforts of all professionals.
- Communicate effectively among teachers, social service agencies, and parents regarding identification of at-risk learners.
- Provide school personnel with appropriate in-service activities on identifying and working with at-risk children and adolescents.
- Insist on objectivity and accuracy in identification procedures to avoid labeling or to minimize its effects.

Classroom Teachers

- Maintain constant observation for indicators of at-risk conditions.

- Make appropriate referrals in a timely and professional manner based on accurate, factual, and objective information.
- Communicate with parents and families and request their input and assistance in the identification of at-risk children and adolescents.
- Insist on coordinated approaches and shared efforts from all school personnel in the identification of at-risk children and adolescents.

Guidance Counselors

- Understand the unique developmental needs of at-risk children and adolescents and how development might contribute to at-risk conditions.
- Know appropriate individual and group counseling strategies that work with at-risk children and adolescents and with culturally diverse learners.
- Know appropriate tests and assessment instruments for making objective and accurate identification decisions.
- Suggest to teachers and/or students appropriate strategies to eliminate or reduce the at-risk conditions and provide counseling to individual students addressing their respective at-risk conditions.

School Nurses

- Provide teachers and students with factual knowledge about at-risk conditions such as teenage pregnancy, alcohol and drug abuse, and other health concerns.
- Assist with the identification process by helping classroom teachers decide who should and who should not be considered at risk.
- Meet with at-risk children and adolescents to convey the health implications of their behaviors or conditions.
- Suggest the point when the school's role should end and more specialized medical expertise and treatment should begin.

Social Service Agencies

- Serve as a resource agency to provide expertise and services not available in the school setting.
- Serve as an impetus to influence community and home standards (i.e., poverty situations in the home), which educators are powerless to change.
- Monitor progress away from school or situations where school officials lack jurisdiction.
- Provide educators with information about home and family conditions that otherwise would not be known.

Parents and Families

- Provide assistance in the identification of at-risk children and adolescents by providing information and insight on the child or adolescent in the home environment.
- Provide support and encouragement for educator's efforts and programs.
- Take advantage of the powerful influence of immediate and extended families (especially with regard to culturally diverse children and adolescents).
- Change home and family situations that might be contributing to the at-risk condition (i.e., older brothers and sisters experimenting with drugs).

Activity 2-5

Devise a "coordination plan" for coordinating the efforts of administrators, teachers, counselors, school health personnel, social service agencies, and parents. Develop clear and concise roles and responsibilities for each (in addition to the roles suggested in the text). Also, include a clear rationale for such coordinated efforts.

Reviewing What You Have Read About Identification and Assessment

1. The _____ may be among the first to recognize and report students with potential problems; however, all educators are professionally responsible for identifying at-risk learners.

2. The _____ sampled the academic achievement of 9-, 13-, and 17-year-olds and concluded that many students were either low achievers or not achieving to their potential.

3. Considerable controversy and confusion have clouded the term _____ _____ ; for example, what methods should be used to calculate rates and reasons for the at-risk condition.

4. _____ remains the major reason that students withdraw from school.

5. Evidence and surveys indicate that _____ is the most prevalent drug problem among U.S. adolescents.

6. _____ refers to antisocial and lawbreaking activities that are reported to authorities and to antisocial behavior that does not get reported.

7. More than 12 million children in the United States—about one in five children—live in _____ .

8. A significant problem associated with identifying and assessing students with exceptionalities is the potentially harmful effects of _____ _____ .

9. _____ ranks today as the second or third leading cause of death among industrialized nations of the world; in fact, the rate in the United States has tripled during the past 30 years.

10. Society's obsession with thinness as the ideal has led to significant numbers of teenagers having _____ , a psychological and physical disturbance in which the teenager starves herself, exercises compulsively, and develops an unrealistic view of her body.

11. Barriers contributing to children and adolescents being at risk include lack of _____ (one out of seven adolescents or 4.6 million) and lack of _____ among poor adolescents (one out of three poor adolescents).

12. _____ may be at risk due to lowered self-concepts, poor perceptions of body and weight, and dangerous pursuits of independence.

13. Many anorexics also suffer from _____ , a disorder in which they eat large amounts of food and then vomit so as not to gain weight.

14. The needs of learners with _____ such as being learning disabled, mentally disabled, or emotionally disturbed were supposedly addressed in PL 94-142, the Education for All Handicapped Children Act of 1975.

15. A correlation between teenage pregnancy and _____ suggests that students' school achievement and their perception of their future affect sexual activity and their propensity toward getting pregnant.

Answer Key: 1. classroom teacher; **2.** National Assessment of Educational Progress (NAEP); **3.** "dropout"; **4.** Teenage pregnancy; **5.** alcohol; **6.** Juvenile delinquency; **7.** poverty; **8.** labeling; **9.** Suicide; **10.** anorexia nervosa; **11.** health; insurance; **12.** Early and late maturers; **13.** bulimia; **14.** exceptionalities; **15.** academic success

Summary

Identifying at-risk children and adolescents will continue to be a major responsibility of elementary and secondary school educators and human resources professionals into the twenty-first century. These professionals can be more accurate with their identification procedures if they know the signs and indicators that suggest specific at-risk conditions. Likewise, educators should maintain objectivity to avoid assigning labels that will impede learners' progress. Responsibility and accountability for identifying at-risk children and adolescents will continue to increase; however, responsible educators with a knowledge of at-risk conditions and with the ability to identify at-risk learners will be prepared to accept these professional roles.

For Additional Information on Identification and Assessment

Adolescent health. (1991). Congress of the United States: Office of Technology Assessment. This government publication on adolescent health uses detailed charts, tables, and a comprehensive discussion to explain the problems being faced by many adolescents.

Brandt, R. S. (Ed.). (1990). *Readings from educational leadership: Students at risk.* Alexandria, VA: Association for Supervision and Curriculum Development. This collection of articles focuses on at-risk learners, exemplary programs, what administrators and teachers can do, dropout programs, poor students, effective schools, teaching thinking, and bilingual programs.

Carnegie Council on Adolescent Development. (1992). *Fateful choices: Healthy youth for the 21st century.* Waldorf, MD: Author. This book reports statistics about the physical, mental, and emotional health of American youth and makes recommendations regarding the promotion of adolescent health.

Checklist for Identifying the Potential Dropout. *California Curriculum News Report.* (1986, October). Sacramento: California State Department of Education. This 19-item checklist identifies potential dropouts by having the user make decisions concerning "Vulnerable to Dropping Out" and "Favorable to Completing School."

Children's Defense Fund. (1991). *Child poverty in America.* Washington, DC: Author. This publication uses many tables and charts to examine poverty in America and says that poverty can be eliminated by the year 2000.

Dropout Prevention Survey. (1985, May). Pontiac, MI: Oakland County Schools. This survey looks at 23 factors and conditions related to students dropping out and then identifies the source (i.e., school, home, community) of the condition.

Kenny, A. M. (1987). Teen pregnancy: An issue for schools. *Phi Delta Kappan, 68*(10), 728–736. This article suggests that the teen pregnancy problem is increasingly becoming a problem for the schools and reviews the kinds of programs that schools have adopted.

Muha, D. G., & Cole, C. (1991). Dropout prevention and group counseling: A review of the literature. *The High School Journal, 74*(2), 76–79. These authors look at the dropout problem and the reasons for students dropping out, and suggest group counseling for potential dropouts.

Ruff, T. P. (1993). Middle school students at-risk: What do we do with the most vulnerable children in American education? *Middle School Journal, 24*(5), 10–12.

Ruff suggests methods of identifying potential dropouts and also offers suggestions for establishing local programs.

Theriot, R., & Bruce, B. (1988). Teenage pregnancy: A family life curriculum. *Childhood Education, 64*(5), 276–279. Theriot and Bruce propose a family curriculum for sixth, seventh, and eighth graders in an attempt to acquaint teenagers with topics such as self-esteem, decision making, and responsible sexual behavior.

Thornburg, K. R., Hoffman, S., & Remeika, C. (1991). Youth at risk; society at risk. *The Elementary School Journal, 91*, 199–208. These authors maintain that many children and youth today are at risk and also suggest new roles and responsibilities for schools.

Wylie, V. L. (1992). The risk in being average. *Middle School Journal, 23*(4), 33–35. Wylie makes an excellent point that educators have probably suspected but usually have not addressed: Many children and adolescents are at risk because they are average and are ignored by educators who feel responsible for challenging the bright and for dealing with misbehaving students.

Part II

At-Risk Conditions

3

School Conditions

Overview

To suggest that school conditions may contribute to children's and adolescents' propensity toward being at risk may seem oxymoronic to some readers. However, educational conditions do, indeed, contribute to learners feeling frustrated or feeling inadequate to cope with and succeed in school environments, and perhaps, even increases their chances of dropping out of school. Too often, teaching-learning practices address the needs of middle-class Anglo-Americans (and in some cases, only boys) and fail to address the needs of learners who may not fit the educational mold some educators expect. These learners may have motivational levels, learning styles, ability levels, or personal educational perspectives that are incompatible with the expectations and practices of educational institutions. Another condition that can contribute to students being at risk is referred to as the "hidden curriculum," which can affect students through expectations and beliefs conveyed in a more subtle manner. Placement in a school that expects homogeneity or adaptation can often result in students becoming at-risk casualties. This chapter looks at school conditions that may contribute to placing children and adolescents at-risk and also proposes that schools should accept responsibility for eliminating or at least reducing ineffective, inappropriate practices.

Probing Directions

This chapter on school conditions does the following:

1. Examines the school's role in accepting responsibility for reducing at-risk conditions.
2. Explores how the overexpectations and underexpectations of educators can jeopardize learners' chances of educational success.
3. Shows how curricular experiences and organizational patterns may contribute to learners' being at risk.

4. Shows how teaching and management practices may contribute to learners being at risk.
5. Explains the importance of examining the teaching-learning practices from multicultural perspectives.
6. Shows how the schools' "hidden curriculum" may contribute to learners' propensities for being at risk.
7. Suggests other sources of information that focus on recognizing and improving school conditions.

The School's Role in Reducing At-Risk Conditions

Schools have long been thought of as institutions that help and nurture students, that build on strengths and remediate weaknesses, that address different learning styles, and, generally speaking, that help students to realize their potential by providing motivation and exploring ability. Although some educators undoubtedly address these and other aspects, other educators, perhaps unknowingly, fail to meet these lofty goals and may contribute to the educational downfall of some learners.

Educators at all school levels should accept responsibility for recognizing and evaluating school conditions that contribute to students being at risk. Such a professional responsibility includes an adequate response to address these conditions. Prerequisite to the actual response, however, is the need for educators to recognize that school conditions, long thought to contribute to students' intellectual growth and overall well-being, might actually contribute to learners being at risk.

Once educators have recognized and accepted the fact that some school conditions contribute to children and adolescents being at risk, an agenda must be planned to respond to the conditions. Evaluational instruments and methods such as questionnaires, checklists, and student interviews may be used to determine conditions that need to be addressed. Such conditions include children's and adolescents' learning styles, teacher-learning-evaluation practices, gender and cultural perspectives toward education, and, in particular, motivation and educational success. To this end, the mind-set that all students need to be college-bound, highly motivated high-achievers needs to be examined. A more realistic belief is to accept that tremendous diversity exists among students and that this diversity is enriching to both the school and society. Likewise, schools have a responsibility to meet the needs of all learners rather than just a select group thought to be destined for educational success.

The remainder of this chapter examines how school practices contribute to students being at risk. Conditions examined will include expecting too much and too little from learners as well as curricular, organizational, teaching, and management practices that place learners in at-risk situations. In addition, the school's "hidden curriculum" and how it may detrimentally affect children and adolescents, both educationally and in more personal dimensions, will be explained.

The School as the Culprit

To be candid, commonly accepted educational practices may either be the cause of or contribute to at-risk learners' problems. In an attempt to plan educational experiences for a large number of learners with varied abilities, educators often—consciously or unconsciously—plan for students in the middle and subsequently do not serve the faster or slower learners or students at risk of other conditions. Schools can be stressful, boring, danger- ous, and, generally speaking, harmful to at-risk students' cognitive, social, and overall growth. Consider the following:

> *Schools can indeed be punishing settings for at-risk students. Students report that teachers do not understand them, the work is too difficult or boring, they fear for their physical safety, they cannot complete homework assignments, they do not or cannot participate in extracurricular or social activities, and they get little or no support from home. At-risk students are avoiders—they avoid school because it is too demanding, frightening, or punishing. Viewing events from the perspective of these students, perhaps it is surprising that they stay in school as long as they do (Crist, 1991, p. 37).*

Other conditions that indicate the school might be the culprit in at-risk students' lives include the current national obsession with testing and as- sessment (to be examined later in more detail); the violence in U.S. schools; homogeneous grouping, which segregates learners according to ability, gen- der, or race; and the emphasis on competition, which separates learners into winners and losers.

Case Study 3-1 looks at how a perceptive counselor took action to eliminate a school's practices that contributed to students being at risk.

Case Study 3-1: An Elementary School Examines Its Practices

Mrs. Smithfield, a school counselor, had been considering a question for several months: Are school practices and policies actually contrib- uting to students being at risk? Feeling this question needed considera- tion and study, she took her concern to a faculty meeting. A committee was formed and challenged to develop a broad list of areas to deter- mine the extent to which the school actually contributed to children being at risk. Several weeks later, the committee suggested a more intensive examination of several possible areas: grading and promotional practices; achievement expectations; behavior policies; equal treatment of all learners; parental involvement in terms of activities and expectations; overemphasis on academic achievement; instruction focused on only one intelligence at the expense of other areas; organizational practices (i.e., homogeneous ability grouping); segregation of cultures and sexes; classroom management practices, such as giving too much or too little work; assignments that are too difficult or too easy; overemphasis on testing and overreliance on test scores; and negative verbal environments (i.e., sarcasm). Next, the committee decided to divide these broad areas into questions on a checklist to determine whether the school actually contributed to children's propensities toward being at risk.

Skeptics questioned why the school would contribute to students being at risk.

"Unconsciously," one committee member replied, "We do not consciously contribute, but in some ways, schools are to blame for students being at risk and in some cases, they make matters worse."

This elementary school had begun one of the most important steps a school can undertake to help at-risk children—they were examining their own practices and policies.

Challenges for educators include realizing when their curricular and instructional practices result in problems for at-risk learners and determining appropriate actions. Several steps might be necessary to accomplish this goal. First, educators need to accept the fact that proven and carefully planned educational experiences might actually place students in academic or some other type of jeopardy. Second, educators need to draw a fine line between appropriate and inappropriate practices and accept the fact that practices which contribute to the success of one student might be devastating to another. For example, competition has long been the standard in U.S. schools. Rather than encourage students to work cooperatively or to help each other learn, educators have encouraged competition among learners. For some learners, competition became the motivating force; for others, competing with peers contributed to divisiveness and actually resulted in students "giving up." Third, educators need to understand individual students, how they learn, their goals and frustrations, and what educational practices will contribute to their academic and overall success.

Attitudes toward at-risk students and the educational programs designed to address their needs represent another area in which the school can be the culprit. Whereas most educators believe all children and adolescents should have the most effective educational programs, some educators harbor negative feelings, blame at-risk learners for their problems, feel re-

Successful Program: Reading Strategically

The educators in the Montgomery County, Maryland, public school system recognized that one of education's most stubborn problems is how to teach unsuccessful students to read. Traditional skills-based discovery learning programs did not work with many unsuccessful readers.

These educators responded with a program called "Students Achieving Independent Reading" or SAIL. The program's goal was to help students become successful independent readers and learners as soon as possible. To achieve this, the team established a strategy based program that emphasized the whole reading process. SAIL became an implementation strategy for a meaning-based, integrated language arts curriculum. To promote understanding of the reading process, the model taught strategies by emphasizing a reading process:

- *Getting ready to read:*
    Setting personal goals

Understanding the reading process
- *Before reading:*
    Establishing a purpose for reading
    Deciding how to process the text
- *While reading:*
    Choosing and using a monitoring strategy
    Choosing and using a problem-solving strategy
- *After reading:*
    Choosing and using an appropriate evaluation strategy

Actual classroom strategies included a positive reading environment; teachers reading orally daily; students reading whole discourse daily; teachers providing silent reading times; and opportunities for high-risk students to select and use appropriate strategies while reading independently (Bergman & Schuder, 1992/1993).

sources and time spent on at-risk learners take away from other learners, and feel the responsibility for at-risk learners lies with social service agencies and other professionals specifically trained to work with at-risk children and adolescents. Such opinions without doubt add to the seemingly punishing practices of many schools and also add to the problems faced by at-risk learners.

Activity 3-1

Prepare a survey to assess the degree to which the school is a culprit. For example, after a number of school visits, make a list of school expectations and practices that actually make learners at risk or increase at-risk conditions. Be sure your survey includes (but is not limited to) curriculum content, organizational classroom management, and the overall school environment.

Overexpectations and Underexpectations

Overexpectations

Educators, parents, and the general public often clamor for schools to have high expectations and rigid academic achievements and to use taxpayers' dollars wisely. Such attitudes, though perhaps well meaning, can in some cases actually place students at risk. Pushing learners to achieve without regard to individual ability and without understanding cultural orientations toward motivation can result in frustration, a lower self-concept, and giving up altogether. Failing to assess learners' actual abilities may also result in overexpectations. Students, both low and high achievers, may be placed in competitive situations where they see themselves as unable to compete or as outright failures. Closely related to such practices is the tendency to rush children and adolescents into adulthood. Rather than allowing children to be children, adults often expect children to dress like adults, perform tasks like adults, and act and behave in an adult fashion.

The old adages of hard work, determination, and perseverance have long been respected in U.S. school systems. These adages, however, can have negative effects on learners: feelings of failure, feelings of not belonging, giving up, and a host of medical and psychosocial problems resulting from stress. All children and adolescents should be pushed to achieve at their maximum potential; however, perceptive educators recognize the fine line between meeting one's maximum potential and expecting the learner to achieve at levels of frustration. While the former results in learners experiencing challenges and successful academic achievements, the latter can result in frustration and failure. Expecting overachievement and having high standards have been perceived as lofty educational goals for some time. Ironically, although students need adequate and developmentally appropriate educational challenges, the "overexpectation" mindset can actually result in failure and in other at-risk conditions.

Underexpectations

Underexpectations, equally as serious as overexpectations, plague some U.S. schools and place learners in at-risk situations by allowing learners to achieve at a level below their potential. The seventh-grade girl who has the ability to achieve at high levels might be unmotivated and might demonstrate satisfactory achievement that is actually far from her potential. Even this learner who is not in danger of failing can be considered at risk because her potential has not been recognized; she hasn't been challenged to the limit of her ability. Educators have the twofold responsibility and challenge of recognizing learners' potentials and taking action to provide intellectually and developmentally appropriate educational experiences.

Successful Program: The Milliken II Program

Based on the work of James Comer, the Milliken II program in Prince George's County, Maryland, combines classroom, school, and home elements in a coordinated attempt to improve academic achievement through fostering high expectations. The program builds in parental involvement, team planning, a positive social and academic environment, and the adaptation of the school system's curriculum to meet specific student needs. Other aspects include reduced staff-to-student ratios, extra instructional materials, and computer labs. The results of the Milliken II program include schools gains on the California Achievement Test of almost two to one, compared to the district as a whole (Murphy, 1988).

Too often, educators fall into the trap of stereotyping learners. For example, educators make a serious error when they assume that culturally diverse learners or lower socioeconomic groups are going to fail or score lower on standardized tests or other academic tasks. Because of disadvantaged backgrounds, teachers may think "We shouldn't place too much stress on those learners." Other errors might include harboring lower expectations for girls in the areas of science and mathematics. Such thinking constitutes a serious mistake and fails to recognize individuality and potential among all people, regardless of culture, gender, or social class.

Guidelines for Avoiding Overexpectations and Underexpectations

What, then, can educators do to avoid expecting over- or under-achievement, rewarding mediocrity, or perpetuating the ideas that some learners are at risk *only* because of their culture, gender, or socioeconomic class? Some guidelines are given next; however, it is important for educators to consider individual students and related factors.

1. Insist all students achieve at their maximum potential, being careful to avoid both overexpectations and underexpectations. Such a practice requires knowing individual students, their motivation records, their aspirations, and their frustration levels.

2. Avoid basing academic and social expectations on cultural, gender, or socioeconomic stereotypes. For example, educators need to avoid assuming that all Asian-Americans are hardworking and intellectually bright, that all disadvantaged children and adolescents have learning problems, and that girls do not perform well in science courses.

3. Avoid using a middle-class, Anglo-American mindset as the standard for determining learners' ability and motivation levels. Social classes and cultural groups demonstrate motivation and achievement in various ways. For example, some cultures such as Native-Americans and Hispanic-Americans prefer not to stand out among their peers (Baruth & Manning, 1992).

4. Administer diagnostic tests and assessment instruments that are as culture- and gender-free as possible. Suggested testing instruments include the Cattell Culture-Fair Intelligence Test and the System of Multicultural Pluralistic Assessment (Lonner & Ibrahim, 1989).

5. Work with parents, school psychologists, guidance counselors, and other teachers to determine learners' ability and motivation levels as well as other strengths and weaknesses.

6. Understand the concept of multiple intelligences (Blythe & Gardner, 1990; Gardner, 1987; Walters & Gardner, 1985) and plan teaching-learning experiences that address more than one intelligence, for example, the boy who shows little ability in reading yet shows potential in spatial relationships.

Successful Program: Project KARE (Keeping At-Risk Enrolled)

The KARE program provides accelerated instruction through a computer-assisted instructional plan. Focusing on middle school and high school students, Project KARE considers several criteria when selecting participants: teacher recommendations, one grade level of retention, achievement test scores, attendance, attitude, discipline, and student and parental commitment. KARE's overall objective includes providing students a chance to advance two grade levels in one academic year and to rejoin their appropriate age peers.

The program currently operates in three middle schools and one high school. Each site consists of 30 students and two specially trained teachers. Two block classes are held each day with 15 students and two teachers in each 3-hour block.

Middle school students are provided accelerated instruction in mathematics and language arts/reading.

Students receive counseling three times a week. For the remainder of the day, students attend heterogeneously grouped classes for all other subjects.

High school students spend three periods a day in the program with two KARE teachers. The courses offered include computer-assisted competency-based alternatives to traditional English, mathematics, science, and social studies. Students also benefit from a counseling component. Students progress at their own pace and units are awarded on completion of the identified course requirements. As a means of reaching promotion and graduation standards, the program carefully monitors attendance, discipline, and self-esteem and assists students improve in these areas (Lee, 1992). For more information, contact Sharon Lee, Anderson School District, P.O. Box 439, Anderson, South Carolina, 29622.

Activity 3-2

Give several examples of learners experiencing teachers' overexpectations or underexpectations. How did these expectations affect learners, their motivation, their self-concept, and their overall school success? Suggest several measures to avoid overexpectations and underexpectations.

Case Study 3-2 focuses on overexpectations and looks at Jon, a boy under considerable pressure to succeed.

Case Study 3-2: Jon, A Case of Overexpectations

Jon, a 13-year-old middle school student, played in the band, played on the basketball team, and was a member of the "High Achievers." Although everything seemed like a dream come true, Jon was actually an at-risk student. His parents, especially his father, pressured him constantly to be a high achiever, his teachers gave him higher level work, and he was tough on himself when he did not reach his and their expectations. While Jon was bright and was an overachiever, he did not have the intellectual capacities to sustain high academic achievement. He felt considerable stress and its related conditions as he tried to please his parents and teachers.

One of his more perceptive teachers recognized Jon's plight and talked with the principal and guidance counselor. "What can we do to help Jon," she asked. "He is under tremendous pressure to achieve at high levels—everyone expects so much from him!" The teacher, principal, and guidance counselor decided to take a team approach to help Jon. They would speak with Jon's parents to explain that although Jon was bright and overachieved in many ways, he was under considerable pressure. Such stress and pressure was detrimental to Jon and could have additional unwanted consequences in the future. Likewise, they decided to talk with Jon's teachers, the faculty sponsor of the "High Achievers," and his basketball coach. Whereas Jon should be encouraged to achieve, they explained that expectations from all should take on a more realistic perspective. The team also decided to keep an eye on Jon and meet again in several weeks to assess Jon's progress and "state of mind."

In summary, teachers demanding both "too much" or "not enough" place students at risk of failure, loss of self-esteem, and frustration. To avoid either pitfall and the accompanying detrimental conditions requires determining actual ability levels and the provision of an educational program that builds on strengths and remediates weaknesses.

Successful Program: Raising Expectations

Meadowbrook Middle School in Orlando, Florida, identified a group of at-risk learners with the following characteristics and placed them in the Meadowbrook program: high absenteeism, excessive number of discipline referrals, two or more years older than classmates, poor grades, low stanine scores on standardized tests, and parents who did not complete high school. Believing students should be challenged, the program provided an atmosphere of academic challenge and an expectation for achievement. All students were expected to participate at all times. Teachers constantly called students' names and challenged them to provide answers to a wide range of questions and to affirm or challenge other students' responses. Also, teachers consistently dealt with discipline problems, assisted students with difficult materials, and responded to students not paying attention.

Several conclusions can be reached from the Meadowbrook program:

1. Students who do not perform successfully in a traditional classroom will not perform substantially better within a smaller class setting.

2. Academically at-risk students may be found in every classroom and will benefit from the use of alternative teaching strategies.

3. Demanding that students meet higher standards, not lower ones, improves students' productivity and self-esteem.

4. Teaching students to act responsibly by holding them immediately accountable for their actions and allowing them to solve their own problems prepares them for coping with life outside the classroom.

5. Empowering students to realize their true potential through a variety of activities (i.e., academic, artistic, physical, social, and community service) provides lasting effects.

6. Administrative commitment is critical to the concept of creating successful learners from the early planning stages through implementation and evaluation.

7. Involving parents of academically at-risk students, and providing educational experiences for them as well, provides support for the students (Taylor & Reeves, 1993).

Inappropriate Curricular Practices

In a survey of problems facing American education, respondents listed "poor curriculum/poor standards" as the fifth most serious problem with which educators had to deal (Elam, Rose, & Gallup, 1992). Some controversy might surround the general public's definition or perspective of "curriculum" as well as its basis for assigning curriculum such low marks; however, assuming the validity of this opinion, curriculum in U.S. schools may be even worse for at-risk learners who often fail to see how school expectations relate to their personal lives. For example, a learner in a lower socioeconomic urban school might fail to realize how education will improve one's life especially in areas with high unemployment and high crime rates. Educators need to examine objectively the school curriculum and decide how educational experiences can most effectively address at-risk learners' needs and weaknesses.

The school's curriculum or the courses taught and the educational experiences provided can contribute to children and adolescents being at risk: curricular experiences without relevance to "real life," curricular goals with narrow views of educational success, subject matter selected for whole classes rather than an individual's growth and development levels, and a curriculum designed to isolate unsuccessful students rather than help all learners develop successfully to their maximum potential. Curricular experiences should build strengths, remediate weaknesses, and address learners' interests; however, curricular experiences too often place learners into groups of achievers and nonachievers or, in some cases, into the college-bound, the general education track, and educational failures. This latter group might be at-risk learners who were not successful with the school curriculum or who had other at-risk conditions that were made more acute by an unresponsive curriculum.

Relevance

Learners are usually most successful when educational experiences relate to their personal and career aspirations and generally have relevance to their everyday lives. Concerned with relevance, Dewey wrote 60 years ago:

> *From the standpoint of the child, the great waste in school comes from his inability to utilize the experiences he gets outside of school in any complete and free way; while, on the other hand, he is unable to apply in daily life what he is learning at school. (Dewey, 1956, p. 75)*

Learners with higher aptitudes, higher motivational levels, and powerful family support might be able to deal with abstract learning or perceive relevance to a curriculum that expects long-term commitment. On the other hand, at-risk learners might need educational experiences that contribute to more immediate financial stability rather than working to achieve some future unattainable goal. Still, educators providing a curriculum relevant for at-risk learners should not "water down" the curriculum or add to learners' problems by having lower expectations and fewer demands for excellence in learning pursuits. At-risk learners must be able to see how curricula experiences have the potential for improving their lives. For example, the 16-year-old boy with a reading deficit who has strengths with numbers and spatial relationships might become even more at risk when forced to study Shakespeare's plays. The key is to consider each individual learner and respective at-risk conditions and then plan a curriculum with which learners can relate and build on for future educational success.

Orientations Toward Success

For too long, many schools have provided curricular experiences designed to address a narrow view of what it means to be "educationally successful." Successful learners, sometimes thought to learn regardless of the school's efforts or shortcomings, are often from higher socioeconomic groups, are highly motivated, generally perceive schools as successful places, and have parents and families who emphasize education. All educators, however, can attest to the growing numbers of children and adolescents who do not fall into these categories. Students without economic advantages and with poor self-concepts often fail in school, do not feel schools provide for their needs, and do not view schools as places that invite success. These situations require schools to change their orientations as to what actually constitutes success. Without doubt, learners aspiring successfully to teach, to be an accountant, and to practice medicine or law can be counted among the school's successes. Realistically speaking, however, many children and adolescents do not fall into these groups and are often perceived as doing less well or are considered to be among the school's failures. Orientations toward or perceptions of success need to be examined and eventually changed to reflect students' individual needs. Rather than considering only professional careers as successful, orientations of what constitutes school success must also include other financially lucrative and personally rewarding occupations such as automobile mechanics, heating and air conditioning specialists, and other jobs traditionally termed "blue collar." The accomplishment of such goals requires that schools provide at-risk learners with appropriate educational experiences and also view the education of these learners to be as important as that of students demonstrating more traditional and accepted orientations toward success.

Activity 3-3
Explain how "orientations toward success" actually affect one's educational successes. Show how definitions of success vary among cultures and genders. Tell the dangers of middle-class Anglo-American educators expecting similar success orientations from all students, regardless of cultural, gender, or social class backgrounds.

Developmentally Inappropriate Subject Matter

For too many decades, educators planned instructional experiences for whole classes. Mrs. Taylor taught a group of 11-year-old and a few 12-year-old sixth graders and assumed that all learners had similar learning rates, developmental levels, and motivation. While such practices undoubtedly had detrimental effects on low- and high-ability students, the overall achievement and self-concept of at-risk learners suffered even more. The at-risk learners in Mrs. Taylor's class may have been the slow learners who increasingly fell behind academically or they may have been the intellectually bright and motivated who sat bored and unchallenged. In either situation, potential and talent were wasted because the teacher designed educational experiences for the whole class rather than considering individual needs, abilities, and aspirations.

Curricular Experiences Contributing to Achievers/Nonachievers and Winners/Losers

Through difficult curricular material, standards that are too high, and rigid grading practices, schools too often intentionally "force out" academically weak and unmotivated students. The competitive nature of schools, whether in academics or athletics, results in some learners being rewarded for exceeding and others falling increasingly behind. Some elite preparatory schools (where students elect to attend or their parents select for them) might feel their responsibilities include determining which students are qualified or unqualified for institutions of higher education. However, while public schools should have high expectations, these schools have neither the right nor the responsibility to "force out" or make students feel like winners and losers.

Still other schools unintentionally cause students either to fail or not perform at their highest potential levels. For example, while schools claim to provide equal opportunity, one can easily see evidence indicating that not all school programs are equal and not all students are educated equally. Poverty and socioeconomic conditions often determine which programs schools can offer; however, in some cases, school programs appear to lack the will, determination, and commitment to provide appropriate educational experiences.

Whereas the fact that some schools are not able to afford educational materials and resources might be unavoidable, another potential obstacle, the school's "hidden curriculum," could also contribute to students becoming at risk. A school's hidden curriculum, which can be intentional or unintentional, also influences student progress and places students in privileged or at-risk situations. While some aspects of the curriculum are readily discernible to children and adolescents attending a school, other aspects are more subtle and might be equally influential. For example, one does not have difficulty determining whether culturally diverse people are addressed honestly and adequately in textbooks and other curricular materials. One can also ascertain with relative ease whether tracking and ability grouping have resulted in all culturally diverse people or lower class students being segregated or relegated to second-class status. There is, however, another equally important curriculum, one that has a powerful influence on children and adolescents.

Referring to the hidden curriculum, Jarolimek and Foster (1989) wrote:

The hidden curriculum is pervasive in a classroom and school and reflects the attitudes of the teacher, the administration, and the children. Without saying so directly, the teacher, through a combination of circumstances, conveys to the children much about the expectations and values that are prized. Through the hidden curriculum, children learn the extent to which life at school suits them and their needs. Lessons learned through informal interaction with other children may condition a child's social skills and human relationships for a lifetime. Children learn, often without being told, which models of behavior are highlighted for emulation. They learn which behavior is likely to gain favor and which is not. They know a great deal about how the teacher feels toward social issues, groups, and individuals, and, again, without ever having been told explicitly (p. 65).

One might logically expect the school curriculum to address learners' physical, academic, and social needs, especially since a major purpose of schools is to prepare children and adolescents for an ever-changing world. Such expectations, however, do not always become reality. In fact, the curriculum may hold even worse consequences for at-risk learners. Perceptive educators periodically assess the curriculum for its relevance, for its capacity to nurture, for its developmental appropriateness, and for its less visible or hidden potential to affect learners and their future.

Inappropriate Organizational Patterns

School organizational patterns can also contribute to children and adolescents being at risk. Every day students are labeled, grouped, and categorized according to test scores and teachers' perceptions of motivation, ability, and achievement. Learners may be placed in classes that are too difficult or too easy, resulting in either frustration or boredom. While organizational patterns create frustration or stifle academic and social growth, learners either become at risk or leave school altogether. Organizational patterns can shortchange learners and actually contribute to the seriousness of their at-risk conditions.

Ability Grouping

Educators often group students for instructional purposes on the basis of test scores, previous grades, teacher recommendations, and other supposedly objective information. The basic rationale for grouping students is to narrow the abilities range, thus providing teachers with a homogeneous group that is supposedly easier to teach. Two dangers inherent to any grouping process are placing students in the wrong group and having an organizational pattern that segregates students by race or social class. The dangers of grouping students by ability and achievement have been adequately documented (Manning & Lucking, 1990). Emphatically stated, whether considering race, social class, gender, or at-risk condition, organizational patterns should not result in segregation or in some students being educated by inferior teachers or in inferior schools, while other students receive preferential treatment. Organizational patterns should result in a student population representative of the entire school population and, if possible, the composition of the community at large.

The possibility that ability grouping may result in a form of segregation should warrant educators' attention and concern. Ability-grouping patterns often parallel students' nonacademic characteristics, such as race or ethnic background, socioeconomic class, or personal appearance. Lower socioeconomic status and minority learners often find themselves placed in lower ability groups, whereas students from the higher socioeconomic strata are often placed in the higher ability groups. These patterns of grouping appear to be related to ethnicity and socioeconomic standing, rather than purely academic abilities and achievement levels (Riccio, 1985).

Sendor (1989) reported on the *Montgomery v. Starkville Municipal Separate School District* case, which grappled with the thorny issue of grouping students by achievement. The policy grouped elementary and secondary students into classes within each grade level according to achievement, and kept the students in these groups for the entire school day. The National Association for the Advancement of Colored People filed a complaint with the Office of Civil Rights (OCR) saying that the school officials used student grouping as a subtle technique to maintain racially segregated schools. While the OCR did not order an end to achievement grouping, it did recommend four changes: 1) Only objective data should be used for placing students; 2) students should be retested frequently; 3) the curriculum should help lower achieving students to improve performance; and 4) teachers should receive training in the remedial instruction necessary to help low-achieving learners.

Research on ability grouping (Manning & Lucking, 1990) also indicates that teachers interact differently with students in the various ability groups (Harp, 1989; Hiebert, 1983). Students in higher groups may be "chartered" (Gamoran, 1986, p. 185) to learn more, regardless of material taught. Hiebert (1983) studied teacher behavior in homogeneously grouped reading classes and concluded that lower ability students spent more time on decoding tasks while higher ability students worked on word meaning. Similarly, the lower ability students participated in oral reading activities while higher ability groups read silently (Harp, 1989). Another study revealed that teachers' evaluative comments with higher ability learners became lengthier, more elaborate, and more positive over the school year. In contrast, teachers progressively described lower ability students in briefer and more pejorative terms (Berliner, 1986). Other advantages of being placed in higher ability groups include the fact that students work in environments more conducive to academic skills; have more opportunities to demonstrate competence; and practice more autonomous, self-disciplined modes of learning (Grant & Rotenberg, 1986).

The implications of ability grouping include the following: Students feel academically and socially inferior; academic achievement does not increase and in some cases actually decreases; the self-concept of lower ability learners decreases; teachers react differently with various ability groups; and students are often segregated by culture, race, and social class (Manning & Lucking, 1990). These consequences, which are sufficiently serious to warrant educators' attention, are even more serious for at-risk learners who already may have low self-concepts, lower academic achievement, and receive unequal treatment from the teacher.

The Dangers of Labeling

Labeling learners has such potentially harmful effects that educators who assign labels may be placing children and adolescents at great risk. As discussed in Chapter 2, although such educators probably have the learners interest and educational welfare at stake, labeling learners as "handicapped," slow," or "disabled" can sometimes cause irreparable harm, not only during school, but throughout their entire lives. Educators should be cognizant of the disadvantages of labeling, and should know when the practice is or is not in the learner's best interest.

Activity 3-4

Review research and scholarly opinions on the dangers of ability grouping. Write a position paper explaining how teachers can group students in more humane, positive organizational patterns.

When, if ever, should learners be labeled? Students should be given a label when, and only when, placing a label on the learner represents the student's best interest, and when the learner's condition can be professionally documented with substantial objective data. The label should serve a meaningful purpose and should provide a basis for assisting the learner's overall educational progress. Even when this is the case, educators have a moral, ethical, and professional responsibility to assess learners periodically, to diagnose accurately, to follow all due-process procedures, and to ensure that learners are placed in other groups or classes if the handicapped or exceptional conditions change (Baruth & Manning, 1992).

Lockstep Graded System

The lockstep graded system, more commonly referred to as graded schools, places learners in a particular grade based on their chronological age, i.e., six-year-olds are in the first grade, eight-year-olds are in the third grade, and so forth. Proponents claim that this graded system has several basic features such as recognizing chronological age as the primary, if not the only, determiner of grade placement; having an identified body of skills, knowledge, and appreciations; placing students in a sequence of 12 or 13 positions called "grades"; having textbooks that provide scope and sequence for a specific grade; providing a sequence based on yearly, quarterly, or semester promotions; and allowing for various organizational structures, which commonly accommodate the elementary, middle, and high schools.

For more than a century, the graded school has been a major organizational pattern, especially in the elementary school, providing U.S. schools with a means of educating large numbers of students (at least theoretically). In reality, however, many learners, both fast and slow, experience considerable frustration from either being bored or struggling to keep up, respectively.

It has been long recognized that graded schools do not meet the needs of all learners; however, at-risk students may be in an even more precocious situation when forced to conform to the expectations of graded schools. Depending on the at-risk condition, graded organizational patterns can contribute to learners' propensity toward being at risk or, in some cases, be the actual cause of an at-risk condition. Perceptive teachers plan individual programs for learners that reduce the pressure on students to progress too fast or too slow, but, in many cases, learners either become at risk or have their at-risk conditions made more acute by being locked into a particular grade level.

The nongraded school represents one means of reducing the disadvantages of the graded school. In a nongraded school, learners are positioned, accepted, and supported at their maturity levels and progress at their own rates of development. Although such an organizational pattern requires teachers to be more specific about objectives, materials, and procedures, it provides learners with opportunities to be successful, motivated, and challenged. Likewise, children and adolescents experience greater continuity in learning experiences.

Elementary, middle, and secondary schools need to examine their organizational patterns to determine whether grouping, labeling, and graded classrooms contribute to students' being at risk. The school and class organization can contribute to several at-risk conditions such as academic problems, lower self-concept, behavior problems, and a lack of adequate socialization, to name just a few conditions or problems. An examination of organizational patterns can improve the educational environment and academic achievement of all students, but the benefits for at-risk children and adolescents may be even greater.

Ineffective Teaching Practices

As with curricular and organizational practices, teaching practices can also contribute to children and adolescents being at risk. Teaching practices such as an overreliance on group instruction, lecture approaches, and worksheets rather than more individual approaches, which actively involve students in their learning, often contribute to students' lack of school success.

Large Group Instruction

Large group instruction, that is, occasions when information, perhaps introductory in nature, can be conveyed to a number of learners at once, obviously has its place in classrooms. Providing large group instruction can be both useful and successful. For learning to be most productive, individual students need to be considered. Do students' learning styles coincide with large group techniques? Will some learners benefit more from sharing thoughts in small group sessions? Do some students need more time to process information cognitively and to ask questions and clarify thoughts? Perceptive educators understand the advantages and limitations of large group instruction and also recognize how learners, especially at-risk learners, might or might not benefit from such instructional situations.

Overreliance on Lecture Methods

Another school condition, the lecture method, has been a popular teaching tool for many years. The assumption was made that the lecture was the most efficient means of conveying information to a group of students. Although both advantages and disadvantages can be listed for this teaching method, educators who use the lecture approach should carefully determine its effects on at-risk learners.

Advantages of the lecture method include the following: Information can be conveyed to a large number of students at one time; relevantly significant amounts of information can be conveyed in a short time; and an effective lecturer can hold listeners' attention and inspire and motivate them to excel in a given endeavor.

The following are some of the disadvantages of the lecture method: The lecturer or the material may be boring; lectures may be disorganized and listeners may lose interest; listeners may have difficulty following lectures and taking notes; lectures depend primarily on the auditory mode; lectures usually fail to engage or involve students; and the success of the lecturer depends on the lecturer's ability to speak, persuade, and explain content materials.

Without doubt, educators should be wary of using the lecture method with less-than-successful learners. At-risk learners might be preoccupied with personal problems such as suicidal thoughts or a possible pregnancy; might be unable to listen effectively for long periods of time; might not have the cognitive capacity to process large amounts of information; or might be under the influence of alcohol or drugs, which does not contribute to effective listening. Educators choosing to adopt the lecture method with at-risk learners need to consider the nature of the at-risk condition, work to involve listeners as much as possible, learn the techniques of effective lecturing, learn to develop rapport with the listening audience, and realize the limitations of the approach, especially with students who for one or more reasons might be at risk of failing or not achieving at their highest potential.

The Monotonous Routine of Worksheets

Anyone acquainted with schools today probably agrees that educational experiences in most schools at all levels include an abundance of worksheets or workbooks. Likewise, the proliferation of worksheets and workbooks appears to have created a lucrative financial market. Whether worksheets help or hinder learning has yet to be decided. Extreme examples of learners completing worksheets all day or young children facing only paper and pencil tasks undoubtedly serve little genuine educational purpose.

Without doubt, students need applicational opportunities and, in some cases, providing each student with a worksheet might be the most effective instructional means. The practice of exploring a concept and then allowing learners to practice or apply the concept appears educationally appropriate for some learners—but certainly not all. Teachers relying on worksheets are making several, perhaps unconfirmed, assumptions. Depending on the individual teaching situation, assumptions may include the following: All students learn most efficiently doing paper and pencil tasks; worksheets are the best means of providing opportunities for application; learners have the reading and writing ability to be successful; and students have the motivation to work alone toward completing the assignment. These assumptions may hold true in some cases. Bright and motivated students and students under strict teacher control might experience personal rewards by completing worksheets.

An overdependence on worksheets, however, can place some learners in at-risk situations that can jeopardize their educational achievements, both present and future. At-risk learners, depending on their condition, may have learning styles incompatible with worksheets, may lack the motivation to complete assignments, may not see the relevance of worksheets, may lack the reading and writing skills necessary to experience success, and may learn more efficiently from hands-on activities. In other words, a learner interested in air conditioning work might benefit more from working with a master craftsman than completing worksheets on installation procedures.

Other Teacher Practices and Behaviors

The research on effective teaching has pointed out that the teaching act can be divided into areas such as planning, instruction, management, communication, and attitude. All teachers need these skills, especially those working with at-risk learners. While these five broad areas provide valuable direction, research has identified even more specific behaviors that contribute to academic achievement. However, readers who are either visiting schools or already working in schools can readily attest to the fact that not all teachers demonstrate effective teaching behaviors. Specific practices and behaviors that can make at-risk conditions more acute include teachers being unorganized; not preventing problems from occurring; expecting some students to achieve while having low expectations for others; assigning seatwork that is too easy or too difficult; failing to encourage positive behavior; and not using time productively.

Sometimes the mindset of teachers working with at-risk learners may be one of defeat, frustration, and an expectation that their efforts, although well intentioned, will be insufficient to make the change needed in a learner's life. "Carl already has a serious self-concept problem due to his reading problems—should I really insist on his meeting the required reading expectations?" "Susan is going to get pregnant and drop out of school no matter what I do!" "These students have failed too long—there is not much hope for them." Such thinking often means teachers demonstrate less positive teaching behaviors, have lower expectations of learners, and generally feel their work has little or no real purpose.

Effective teaching of at-risk children and adolescents begins with a sound knowledge of the effective teaching research, a commitment to the effective teaching behaviors such that they become a part of teachers' everyday routine, and an understanding of the at-risk conditions that jeopardize the educational futures of many learners. School conditions should contribute to the success of youngsters rather than contributing to their failure.

Ineffective Management Practices

Management practices can be defined in several ways. First, management has traditionally been thought of as a teacher's behavior management practices. Such a perspective included rules and regulations and, of course, the consequences for disobeying the rules. A second and more contemporary definition of management takes a broader perspective and includes behavior management practices and other management-related items such as transitions from one subject area to another; the actual moving of students from one location in the school to another; distribution of workbooks and other materials; and keeping up with homework assignments; and personal belongings. Either perspective of management can create additional difficulties for at-risk learners. Commonly accepted behavioral expectations that work well for most students might place at-risk learners in even greater jeopardy. Likewise, at-risk students might need a break between classes, might need more time to stretch and get ready for the next class, and might need more or less flexibility in the classroom routine.

Management practices, as with curricular experiences, organizational patterns, and teaching practices, can make students at risk or actually worsen existing at-risk conditions. School-wide management systems and teacher behavior expectations often do not work with at-risk students, just as they do not always work with culturally diverse learners. What school and teacher expectations and policies might especially compound the problems of at-risk children and adolescents? This section examines school conditions and management policies and shows how classroom management practices that have proven satisfactory with other students can affect at-risk children and adolescents.

1. Students' concepts of sharing and working with others are often misunderstood, that is, some cultures place tremendous emphasis on sharing, cooperation, and collaboration while other cultures emphasize private ownership, working independently, and competition (Sanders, 1987).

2. Some students are not accustomed to the many rules and behavior expectations that are accepted norms in many U.S. schools. For example, Native American children grow up with few rules and consequences for certain behaviors (Sanders, 1987).

3. Curricular and instructional experiences that are too easy or too difficult and not based on learners' developmental levels can lead to both learning

and behavior problems. The boy who is clearly at risk due to his reading problem will not benefit when forced to struggle through *Beowolf*, an instructional experience he cannot do and cannot see any possible use for knowing. In all too many cases, students placed in such situations act out to get attention or to show their frustration.

4. Some at-risk learners' do not understand or identify with certain behavior expectations such as older teenage boys and girls being required to sit in small desks throughout the entire school day. For example, the 17-year-old boy with two part-time jobs who is supporting himself financially should not be treated like a sixth grader. Likewise, the 15-year-old mother should be allowed more freedom and flexibility than a sixth grader.

5. Some educational activities require too little involvement or active work for older students. Older students sitting for long periods of time feel uncomfortable and frustrated when they could be actively involved in school shop, home arts, automobile mechanics, building construction, or a wealth of other possibilities that would allow at-risk students to perceive school as a worthwhile place for all learners.

6. Teachers often misunderstand students' actions or behaviors, especially with culturally diverse students. Teachers, often middle-class Anglo-Americans, might misunderstand cultural and individual characteristics such as the fact that some children and adolescents look away when they are spoken to by a person of authority. The situation mentioned in the next paragraph aptly summarizes how a misunderstanding can lead to future confusion. According to Smith (1981), the cultural tendency of African-Americans to look away or to do something else while conversing often concerns Anglo-American counselors who interpret such behavior as indicative of "sullenness, lack of interest, or fear" (p. 155). Smith cites the incident of an African-American female adolescent who was sent to the principal's office for her "insolent behavior." The adolescent explained:

> *Mrs. X asked all of us to come over to the side of the pool so that she could show us how to do the backstroke. I went over with the rest of the girls. Then Mrs. X started yelling at me because she said that I wasn't paying attention to her because she said that I wasn't looking directly at her. I told her I was paying attention to her (throughout the conversation, the student kept her head down, averting the principal's eyes) and then she said that she wanted me to face her and look her squarely in the eye like the rest of the girls (who were all white). So I did. The next thing I knew she was telling me to get out of the pool—that she didn't like the way I was looking at her. So that's why I am here (p. 155).*

Some students' at-risk conditions grow more acute because of teacher ineptitude or lack of ability to work with students with problems. Teachers

---

Activity 3-5

Visit several elementary, middle level, or secondary classrooms to observe teachers providing educational experiences. Make a list of ineffective practices or those procedures that do not "work" or do not contribute to students' achievement. Offer an explanation as to why teachers continue with teaching-learning experiences that do not work or are, in some cases, blatantly harmful.

---

often contribute to behavior problems through insensitivity to student individuality, inappropriate expectations for students that become self-fulfilling prophecies of misbehavior, lack of ability to provide appropriate management and instruction, and preoccupations with irrelevant tasks and routines (Cullinan & Epstein, 1990).

The inability to address at-risk students' behavior problems can lead to teacher frustration and other behavior problems. Power struggles (e.g., a teacher orders a student to do something and the student refuses) can lead to a "power of wills" in which neither the teacher nor the student wins. The teacher may have the order obeyed, yet little in the form of a positive learning experience resulted from the incident. The frustrated student may make it a goal to aggravate the teacher or might drop out of school. Most teachers can manage the "good" students through encouragement and positive reinforcement; however, teachers need more than the minimum expertise when working with at-risk children and adolescents.

Case Study 3-3 provides an example of a teacher reflecting on her own classroom practices.

Case Study 3-3: Mrs. Miller Reflects on Her Classroom Practices

Mrs. Miller, a seventh-grade teacher, wondered why she had so many at-risk students: Some don't care, others can't learn, Jason might be using drugs with his older brother, Sally may drop out like her older sister—why do I have so many at-risk students? Mrs. Miller, a perceptive teacher, questioned whether she might be contributing to learners' at-risk conditions. She certainly never meant to, but maybe her teaching practices, her curricula, her classroom management policies, and her attitudes toward the learner and toward teaching actually might add to learners' problems.

Mrs. Miller decided to make a rough list; then she would try to check each item to determine the extent to which it contributed to learners being at risk.

1. Do I provide curricula experiences that
   a. reflect learners' development and learning levels?
   b. address learners' weaknesses and build on strengths?
   c. provide adequate "expectations"?
   d. nurture rather than weed out learners?
2. Do I provide organizational experiences that
   a. avoid labeling of students and the potentially disastrous consequences?
   b. provide continuous learning and progress?
   c. promote grouping of learners, without regard to culture, gender, or academic achievement?
   d. allow alternative learning environments such as cooperative learning?
3. Do I provide teaching practices that
   a. encourage small group and individual instruction?
   b. rely on methods other than lecture and worksheets such as small group discussions, independent study, and experience approaches?
   c. meet the educational needs of various cultures, social class, and both sexes?
   d. contribute to learners feeling psychologically safe, secure, and at ease?
4. Do I provide classroom management practices and policies that
   a. reflect the special and specific needs of at-risk learners?
   b. reflect an understanding of culturally diverse learners such as the Native American concept of sharing?
   c. demonstrate fairness and respect for all learners?
   d. contribute to effective use of time and a respect for productive use of time?

Mrs. Miller realized her list was only a representative beginning, but from this start, she could continue to add items and she could begin to evaluate her teaching and learning practices.

Inadequate Equal Access

The principle of equal access to all school experiences and programs holds that all students have equal opportunity to participate in education experiences offered during each grade level. Instructional practices that hinder students from participating in extracurricular activities and prevent students from participating in the most advanced curricular levels have the potential to contribute to children and adolescents being at risk. Numerous examples can be found of the equal access concept being violated in schools today: First, an eighth-grade girl "tried out" for cheerleading with more than a hundred other girls, even though only 14 would be selected. While she memorized the cheers, learned the jumps, and gave four days to the pursuit, the girl was not chosen. The school completely failed to provide equal access to more than 86 girls, including the girl who practiced diligently to become a member of the team.

A second situation, just as serious as the first, involved another seventh-grade girl "trying out" for the school play. She remained after school and faithfully participated in the tryouts. Again, nearly a hundred students tried out for the 11 parts, yet this time, even worse odds faced female would-be participants: Of the 11 parts, the teachers only needed 4 girls! Not only did the school violate the concept of equal access to participating in the play, girls faced even more difficult obstacles to equal access.

Third, another school required seventh-grade students to choose between art, music, and band. A young learner, showing talent and interest in both art and music, faced a difficult decision because the school schedule did not allow students to participate in all three areas or even two areas (Manning, 1993).

The possibilities associated with providing equal access for all learners greatly outweigh educators' efforts. For example, learners feeling anonymous in large schools begin to feel known and recognized; learners with low self-esteem, resulting from being denied participation, experience increased self-worth; and students realize the advantages of equal access and the disadvantages inherent with competing for a limited number of participatory opportunities. Equal access possibilities can become a reality when educators take definite steps to ensure that all students have equal access to all school programs and activities.

One middle school principal, talking about cheerleading teams, assured parents that all students would have an opportunity to participate. "We have ten cheerleading teams," she said. "If more girls want to join a team, then we will begin additional teams." The school offered similar commitments to volleyball, soccer, and other sports.

Another time, teachers announced the opportunity to participate in a play. All students participated—some had speaking roles, others sang as a group; however, everyone who wanted to be on on stage had the opportunity in some honest capacity. Other possibilities the school suggested included having more than one play or perhaps having a series of one-act plays scheduled over a weekend or even several weekends.

Homogeneous ability grouping also violates the equal access concept. First, students should not be tracked according to ethnicity, gender, general ability, primary language, or handicap. Second, instruction should be organized around knowledge central to the curriculum rather than around a sequence of skills so that students who vary in skill level can study common areas of knowledge together. Third, grouping by skill level for remedial or accelerated learning should be defined on the basis of valid, specific instructional purposes. Fourth, other practices contributing to equal access include involving students in their own learning, recognizing individual variability in learning, utilizing a variety of classroom organizational patterns (such as large and small group, independent learning, peer tutoring, and cooperative learning), utilizing educational technology, stressing active learning, emphasizing higher order thinking skills, and employing school schedules that maximize flexibility (California State Department of Education, 1987).

Reviewing What You Have Read About School Conditions

1. Too often, teaching-learning practices address the needs of _____ _____ (and, in some cases, only boys) and fail to address the needs of learners who may not fit the educational mold some educators expect.

2. In a survey of problems facing American education, respondents listed "_____" as the fifth most serious problem with which educators had to deal.

3. Students, both low and high achievers, may be placed in _____ _____ where learners see themselves as unable to compete or as outright failures.

4. _____ , equally as serious as overexpectations, often plague some U.S. schools and place learners in at-risk situations by allowing learners to achieve at a level below their potential.

5. A school's "_____" may include sexism, lack of trust, racism, and classism; may be intentional or unintentional; and may place students in privileged or at-risk situations.

6. Students should be _____ when, and only when, such a practice is in the student's best interest, and when the learner's condition can be professionally documented with substantial objective data.

7. The _____ , more commonly referred to as graded schools, places learners in a particular grade based on their chronological age, that is, six-year-olds are in the first grade, eight-year-olds are in the third grade, and so forth.

8. The _____ is one means of reducing the disadvantages of the graded school. In a nongraded school, learners are positioned, accepted, and supported at their maturity levels and progress at their own rates of development.

9. Two dangers inherent to any _____ are those of placing students in the wrong group and having an organization pattern that segregates students by race or social class.

10. _____ should include a consideration of students' concepts of sharing, their views of competition and cooperation, and their cultural perceptions of rules and regulations.

Answer Key: 1. middle-class Anglo-Americans; **2.** poor curriculum/poor standards; **3.** competitive situations; **4.** Underexpectations; **5.** hidden curriculum; **6.** labeled; **7.** lockstep graded system; **8.** nongraded school; **9.** ability grouping process; **10.** Management practices.

Summary

Nearly all contemporary schools advocate that their school curriculum, instructor, organization, and management practices address children's and adolescents' individual needs and should contribute to overall physical, academic, and social growth. Philosophy statements espouse these convictions and most educators verbally support this belief. However, in actual practice, school conditions do not always contribute to student growth. In fact, just the opposite occurs—school conditions often frustrate, under challenge or over challenge learners, create obstacles to school success and personal self-concept, and in some cases unintentionally encourage students to drop out of school. School conditions for at-risk learners may be even more threatening. While successful students may be able to deal with school conditions that are not conducive to learning, these same conditions may compound at-risk students' problems. The educator's role includes identifying school conditions causing problems and then taking an active stance to change or improve the situation.

For Additional Information on School Conditions

Association for Supervision and Curriculum Development. 1250 N. Pitt Street. Alexandria, VA 22314-1403. ASCD provides workshops, seminars, a journal, books and monographs on developing humane and effective teaching practices.

Charles, C. M. (1992). *Building classroom discipline*. White Plains, NY: Longman. Charles, in this new edition of his excellent text, includes a chapter on "The Management of Students at Risk." Charles defines at-risk students, looks at the problems of culturally diverse learners, and offers suggestions for educators.

Growing up is risky business and schools are not to blame. (1993). Bloomington, IN: Phi Delta Kappa. This Phi Delta Kappa report examines children's and adolescents' physical, psychological, educational, personal, and social problems; offers an opinion on who or what may have been responsible; and tells what schools are doing to address the problems.

Institute for Motivational Development, 200 West 22nd Street, Suite 235, Lombard, IL 60148; (708)627-5000. This institute provides information and workshops on motivation and various factors affecting motivation and personal development.

Manning, M. L., & Lucking, R. (1990). Ability grouping: Realities and alternatives. *Childhood Education, 66,* 254–258. These two authors tell how ability grouping affects academic achievement, self-concepts, teacher behaviors, and culturally diverse students. Alternatives to ability grouping are also given.

NASSP Bulletin. (Winter, 1991). Programming for at-risk students (special issue). The *NASSP Bulletin* examines such topics as how school policies affect dropout rates, helping students with the transition from elementary to high school, and effective suicide prevention programs.

Pecaut, L. S. (1991). Why can't Johnny learn? *Principal, 70*(4), 29–30. Pecaut believes learning problems have many causes and encourages educators to use the correct label when determining appropriate educational programs.

4

Societal Conditions

Overview

Schools at all levels during the 1990s and beyond increasingly will be expected to accept responsibility for societal at-risk conditions. Two issues quickly surface when discussing the school's role in addressing societal at-risk conditions. First, some educators may argue that their responsibility ends when the school day ends. Still others accept responsibility only for "educational problems" and negate any responsibility for the societal problems children and adolescents bring to school. Second, the close relationship between personal and societal conditions often makes it difficult or impossible to distinguish between the two; for example, eating disorders and drug abuse can be classified as both personal and societal. Both issues lead some educators to argue that the school is not at fault and, thus, should focus only on its traditional roles of addressing intellectual development and improving academic achievement. The problem with such thinking is that students cannot achieve academically and socially if they are abusing alcohol and drugs, are concerned about being pregnant, or are suffering from an eating disorder. One can easily understand how these and similar conditions can hamper school efforts and can lead to other at-risk conditions. This chapter examines societal at-risk conditions, encourages educators to accept responsibility for addressing societal conditions, and shows how schools can address societal at-risk conditions.

Probing Directions

This chapter on societal conditions does the following:

1. Explains the close connection between societal and personal conditions that contribute to children and adolescents being at risk.
2. Encourages educators to accept responsibility for helping learners deal with at-risk conditions not normally considered to be the school's responsibility.
3. Explains the school's role in addressing societal at-risk conditions such as substance use and abuse, teenage pregnancy, AIDS and other sexually transmitted diseases (STDs), and eating disorders.
4. Explains how parents, the media, and schools pressure children and adolescents "to grow up too fast."
5. Explains how societal conditions such as poverty and unemployment, single-parent homes, and racism contribute to learners being at risk and work as barriers to overcoming at-risk conditions.
6. Shows how educators can make a commitment, determine the school's roles, and take appropriate action.
7. Provides additional sources of information on organizations and references that address societal at-risk conditions.

Societal Conditions Contributing to At-Risk Conditions

One can justifiably argue that the close connection between societal and personal at-risk conditions makes differentiation difficult at best. It takes only one example to illustrate the rationale for this argument: Does the school dropout problem result from personal reasons such as lack of motivation, from social reasons such as poverty leading to the need for employment, or from some complex combination? Also, in some cases, some personal at-risk problems may be made more acute by social problems. For example, a teenager trying to avoid alcohol may feel considerable pressure from peers and the media to use alcohol. An adolescent might feel that the use of alcohol is necessary to maintain friendships or to be accepted by a particular, significant group. The anorexic girl may feel society demands perfection and slimness, whereas another feels obligated to be active sexually because her or his friends believe such activity to be widespread.

Successful Program: Huffman Middle School

The faculty and administration at Huffman Middle School in Birmingham, Alabama, decided to address the growing drug problem in their school. An anonymous survey revealed a third of the students used tobacco and experimented with alcohol. This needs assessment helped to convince skeptical faculty members that a problem really did exist. Huffman's drug education program, called RAIDers (Resisting Actions Involving Drugs), began with a more disciplined environment: a dress code enforced with vigor, increased expectations for student behavior, a written drug policy shared with all students and their families, and training of teachers in types of drugs and drug use by staff from local drug-treatment centers. Parents assumed important roles, formed an advisory council, promoted drug awareness, shared information on children's activities, and started a 24-hour Telephone-a-Parent line for children who wanted to discuss problems. The school's health curriculum focused on drugs and their physical and psychological effects and also dealt with problems and pressures leading to drug use as well as conflict-resolution techniques. Huffman invited churches, hospitals, and community groups to take an active role in the RAIDers program. Churches held drug programs and neighborhood businesses belonged to a RAIDers WATCH patrol. These merchants observed students leaving school and checked for smoking, drinking, and other signs of trouble. All stores agreed not to sell tobacco or alcohol to students.

Huffman recognized its drug problem and began a comprehensive program that resulted in success. In fact, in four years no Huffman Middle School student has been suspended for smoking or other drug use (Hereford, 1993).

One can also argue that it really does not matter whether causes are personal or social, because either way the school is not the culprit and, therefore, does not have to accept responsibility for addressing societal at-risk conditions. Such opinions, while argued persuasively, negate the importance of the school's role in helping students meet their fullest potential. Admittedly, the school may not be responsible for many problems such as poverty, but caring and perceptive educators still accept the responsibility of addressing societal at-risk conditions. Educators' acceptance of responsibility can be seen in responsive programs aimed at addressing substance abuse, teenage pregnancy, AIDS and other STDs, and eating disorders. The mindset that students are responsible for their own destiny and that schools' responsibilities do not extend to these conditions only makes schools' efforts more likely to fail or at least not meet desired expectations.

Case Study 4-1 looks at how educators addressed the needs of Susan, an at-risk 14-year-old.

Case Study 4-1: Susan, An At-Risk Student

Susan, an intelligent 14-year-old, makes high grades, demonstrates potential in both art and music, and shows considerable leadership ability, yet her teachers are concerned that she might be well on the way to becoming an at-risk student.

Her eighth-grade teacher explains, "Susan is growing up too fast—she dresses and acts like older students—and appears to be experimenting with tobacco, alcohol, and possibly drugs. She spends a lot of time with her older boyfriend who might also be at risk of using drugs."

A colleague asked a difficult question: "That is a true picture of Susan and she might indeed be at risk even though she is an excellent student in my class, but where does our responsibility end? I do my best from eight to three, but if Susan has problems, then she will have to deal with them. Those things you mention are not our responsibility and perhaps not any of our business."

The principal, Dr. Hall, responded that while she could understand both viewpoints she felt Susan's future educational progress might be at stake. "If she is engaging in substance abuse, and possibly experimenting sexually, she is an at-risk student. We need to take appropriate action."

The principal requested a time to meet with Susan's parents, her teachers, and the counselor. They would ask the parents if they had noticed any changes. Rather than making accusations based on hearsay, the counselor would carefully talk with Susan to determine *if* a problem existed. If a problem did exist that would interfere with her academic and social progress, then the counselor would be asked to propose a plan, subject to the suggestions and recommendations of others involved.

The group felt that while the potential problem had not been settled, concrete and positive steps had been taken. Likewise, the school was accepting responsibility for at-risk conditions it did not create yet had the potential to affect educational progress.

Successful Program: Browning Middle School

Browning Middle School in Browning, Montana, has a drug education curriculum that crosses subject areas and includes drug and alcohol information, values clarification, conflict-resolution skills, and the building of self-esteem. Actual teaching plans reflect these areas and help students learn the dangers of drugs and the alternatives to alcohol in coping with disappointment, anger, and stress. In addition, Montana's Bureau of Indian Affairs funds a DARE (Drug Awareness Resistance Education) program at the school, which focuses on helping children who are experiencing peer pressure to try drugs. Browning worked to form alliances with the community; for example, it joined forces with the Blackfeet Tribal Business Council to introduce a sobriety rodeo. Rodeos had often been sponsored by liquor and tobacco companies and had been big party days. The alliance arranged to hold a rodeo at which alcohol was not served or advertised. Tobacco was not advertised either. Also, the school sought ongoing ways to involve parents such as by hosting potluck dinners and family night basketball games. Teachers received training in understanding the needs of students and parents from drug-abusing families. Also, grants and district funding helped provide additional training to keep all staff current on drug education research and curriculum. Browning also recognizes the power of positive role models—a tutoring program matches students with good study skills with those in need of help (Hereford, 1993).

Activity 4-1

Survey several schools to determine their efforts to address societal conditions contributing to students being at risk. For example, some people suggest that teenage pregnancy, AIDS, and eating disorders are societal problems rather than school problems. Others maintain "problems are problems" and schools must react appropriately. In practice, determine whether schools are addressing societal conditions.

Other Societal Conditions

As perceptive readers realize, distinguishing between school and societal differences can be a difficult task at best, since the relationships and connections between schools and society are so complex and intricate. For example, some could argue that the at-risk conditions discussed in Case Study 4-1 could result from schools' reflections of societal mores, expectations, and pressures. Several at-risk conditions are more a reflection of the society than the school, although one cannot hold schools blameless if conscientious attempts are not made to reduce the at-risk condition. Other societal conditions that contribute to students being at risk include rushing children to grow up too fast; poverty, unemployment, lower socioeconomic classes, and lack of equal opportunity; and single-parent homes. This section examines several societal conditions and shows how they can affect at-risk learners.

The Rush to Grow Up Too Fast

The disappearance of childhood, which is becoming increasingly visible in American society, has serious implications for children, adolescents, parents, and educators. One can easily see that adult behavior, dress, concerns, and stresses increasingly dominate the childhood years. The problem is a reflection of contemporary society's apparent urge to rush children through childhood. Although a solution is possible, total commitment from parents, educators, and others interested in children is necessary to avoid placing learners at risk.

Children are being rushed into becoming adults because adults' lives have changed. The effects of a decade of social upheaval among adults, that is, exploding divorce rates, decline of parental and institutional authority, widespread acceptance of living together, and the swift media reflection of these trends, began to trickle down to the childhood years. Specifically, the number of children affected by divorce grows daily, resulting in an increased number of single-parent homes. Such changes, along with the increased employment of mothers and the general breakdown in family life, weakened the protective membrane once separating children from the adult world (Winn, 1983).

Many contemporary parents want their children and adolescents integrated into the adult world early, often causing problems, stress, and confusion. Such a mindset toward hurrying children to grow up early all too often results in learners being pushed to be miniachievers rather than permitted to be children. Although parents have traditionally taken pride in their children's achievements, many contemporary parents burden children with expectations and anxieties that result in a loss of the childhood years. Parents have also shortened the childhood years by pressuring children to achieve early in competitive team sports, academics, or social interaction:

> *There is no room today for the "late bloomer," the children who come into their own later in life rather than earlier. . . . Children have to achieve success early or they are regarded as losers (Elkind, 1981, p. 17).*

Many schools, by becoming increasingly industrialized and product oriented, have also contributed to the disappearance of childhood. For example, Elkind (1981) cites evidence such as textbooks standardized on a national level, machine-scored testing, rigid-age grouping, and tightly sequenced curriculum and teaching. Ten years later, Elkind (1993) reiterated his concern that the disappearance of the childhood years contributed to children being at risk. Similarly, Manning and Manning (1981) write of schools' "assaults" on childhood: Rampant testing, homogeneous grouping, worksheets, fragmentation of subject areas, an inordinate amount of drill, and undue sitting and listening have a negative impact on childhood.

Some situations in which children are forced to grow up too fast result from youngsters being latch-key children. The term "latch-key children" evolved from the fact that house keys often hang around their necks and when they leave school they come home to an empty house and are often expected to perform household duties or take care of younger siblings until a parent arrives home. Problems experienced by latch-key children include loneliness, fear, watching too much television, and peer pressure that can contribute to at-risk behaviors.

Poverty, Unemployment, and the Social Class System

Students living in poverty and economically disadvantaged neighborhoods are undoubtedly more at risk than students living in middle- and upper-class communities. Such a statement is not meant to imply that all students living in poverty are at risk; many students from economically disadvantaged situations demonstrate a powerful motivation to rise above their economic plight. However, the often-dismal effects of poverty, parents' low educational attainments, racism, and sometimes discrimination toward the

---

Activity 4-2
Visit several schools to observe evidence of children growing up too fast. Begin a chart divided into three categories: behavior, dress, and language. List examples under each group. Then offer several ways the school can respond to or help the youngsters.

lower classes make rising above one's plight difficult or even impossible. In such cases, poverty can be devastating in terms of attitude toward school, success orientations, motivation to excel, and academic achievement. In fact, elementary and secondary schools have been generally ineffective in responding to economically disadvantaged students, either due to a lack of power to initiate significant change or because schools, generally speaking, have been unable to provide teaching-learning experiences that have proved effective for economically disadvantaged learners.

The American social class system is now generally understood to consist of three broad classes: working, middle, and upper. It is well known that there is a strong relationship between social class and educational achievement in America. Traditionally, lower-class students have not performed as well as middle- and upper-class students. Most social scientists believe that populations can be classified according to social class groups, which differ in their economic, social, and political interests and characteristics: upper class, upper middle class, lower middle class, upper lower class, and lower class. Individuals very high in occupational prestige, amount of education, income, and housing value have a high socioeconomic status (SES); they are viewed by others as upper-class persons and are influential and powerful in their communities. Conversely, persons low in SES are viewed as lower class. They do not generally exert much power or influence.

Successful Program: Nonschooled Immigrant Children

Morse (1990), a migrant education specialist, believes that nonschooled immigrant children face difficult challenges. These children might speak little or no English, might not be literate in their own languages, and might experience difficulty as they confront U.S. schools. Such difficulties can make children at risk; however, schools can focus efforts to help in several directions. First, on entering school, children can be provided a buddy to assist in understanding the school and its functions. Second, goal setting should occur that recognizes the long-term educational needs of the child and the maximum cooperation of the parents. Third, if the child lacks literacy, the school should determine the practicality of teaching the children first-language literacy. Fourth, the needs of parents and families should be considered and, whenever possible, addressed by the school. Educational approaches with previously nonschooled immigrant children can include developmental learning approaches, the use of manipulative objects, high interest materials, experiential learning, multisensory teaching experiences, whole language, and cooperative learning. An essential element of all successful programs is making sure learners feel their cultural backgrounds—their language, family, and background—are respected (Morse, 1990).

Activity 4-3
How can schools help children and adolescents living in poverty? Educators often feel helpless because they cannot provide financial assistance or help families move out of poverty areas. Still, other means may be available to help these children and adolescents. List four or five ways educators can help learners living in poverty.

In recent years, a number of observers have also identified an underclass group within the working class. The underclass generally resembles the lower class, but as the term implies, many of its members are the third or fourth generation of a family to live in poverty and are dependent on public assistance to sustain a relatively meager existence. Usually concentrated in the inner core slums of cities or in deteriorated rural poverty areas, members of the underclass frequently have little or no hope that their economic and social situation will ever improve.

Income and poverty status are also closely associated with family structure. For example, the increase in single-parent families headed by low-income females has been large. As poverty rates among two-parent families and among the elderly substantially declined during the past three decades, the proportion of the poverty population that lives in female-headed families correspondingly increased. This phenomenon, frequently referred to as the "feminization" of poverty, was marked by an increase from 20% in 1960 to 43% in 1985 in the percentage of poor white children being raised in female-headed households. The comparable increase for poor African-American children was from 29% to 78% (Ornstein & Levine, 1989).

Lower-class or underclass learners often do not succeed in middle- and upper-class schools. Reasons for low achievement might include:

1. *Inappropriate curriculum and instruction:* Curriculum materials and instructional approaches frequently assume that students are familiar with vocabulary and concepts to which lower-class students have had little or no exposure.
2. *Differences between parental and school reinforcement of learning experiences and norms:* Lower-class parents typically use physical punishment when their children actively misbehave or do not follow instructions. Schools, on the other hand, tend to stress the middle-class approach, which emphasizes internalization of norms through feelings of shame and guilt.
3. *Lack of previous success in school:* Lack of academic success in the school not only detracts from learning more difficult material later, but also damages a student's perception that he or she is a capable learner who has a chance to succeed in school and later life.

4. *Difficulty of teaching conditions in lower-class schools:* As lower-class students fall further behind academically and as both teachers and students experience frustration and discouragement, behavior problems increase in the classroom and teachers find it still more difficult to provide a productive learning environment.

5. *Differences in teacher/student backgrounds:* Teachers with middle-class backgrounds may experience particular difficulties in understanding and motivating their disadvantaged pupils.

6. *Teacher perceptions of student inadequacy:* Based on low levels of achievement in their classrooms, many teachers in lower-class schools reach the conclusion that large numbers of their students do not have the experiences and ability to succeed in school.

7. *Ineffective homogeneous ability grouping:* Educators faced with large groups of low achievers frequently address the problem by setting them apart in separate classes or subgroups in which instruction can proceed at a slower pace without detracting from the performance of high achievers.

8. *Low standards of performance:* The end result of this series of problems is that by the time low-achieving, lower-class students reach the upper elementary grades or the high school, they are required to accomplish very little—low performance has become acceptable to their teachers (From Ornstein, Allen C., & Levine, David U. *Foundations of Education*, Fifth Edition. Copyright © 1993 by Houghton Mifflin Company. Used with permission.).

Inner City Schools

Inner city learners face a wealth of problems that reflect their daily lives and have the potential to make them at risk: low academic achievement; high dropout rates; lack of motivation to achieve; few successful role models; little support from parents, extended family members or primary caregivers; poor study habits; and an orientation toward life that encourages living in poorer housing areas and maintaining one's status in lower socioeconomic levels rather than studying and taking advantage of education as means of improving oneself educationally and socioeconomically. Many of these learners come to school from urban and public housing areas and are not prepared for the challenges of education. Similarly, their primary caregivers, whether immediate parents, relatives, older siblings, or unrelated adults, have grown up in similar conditions and often failed to take advantage of educational opportunities. The loss in human potential to individual boys and girls is tremendous: lost opportunities, lost wages, unfulfilled societal contributions, and untapped human potential.

Rather than providing "more of the same experiences," these learners need at-risk approaches that research indicates are effective with low-achieving inner city students. Also, efforts should provide parents and extended family members with knowledge, skills, and parenting behaviors that contribute to children's academic achievement and provide teachers with knowledge of instructional techniques that have proven successful with inner city learners. Learners, parents, and teachers should work collaboratively to address low-achieving learners' academic achievement, self-esteem, overall commitment to schoolwork, and aspirations for future educational attainment. Specific needs of inner city learners need to be addressed:

- Low academic achievement
- Low self-esteem
- Feelings of little control over their lives
- Inappropriate behavior at school and in the community
- Lacking a vision for the future (except for a continuance of low SES and living in public housing)
- Placing little value on school success
- Lacking long-term goals
- Little motivation to succeed in school endeavors
- Erratic and inconsistent attendance records.

The plight of many inner city learners affects not only the learners themselves but also communities, states, and the nation. While their needs are diverse, their academic achievement represents a potential to meet a cross section of needs. Such an attempt is long overdue; many inner city children view low SES and problems associated with inner city life as "givens"—a way to live and a way of survival when inner city schools fail to meet learners' academic needs.

At-risk programs designed to meet the needs of inner city learners should strive to improve learners' daily grades, report card grades, and standardized test scores. Likewise, improving academic achievement should increase the likelihood of at-risk learners' staying in school rather than dropping out when the law allows, and also should improve attitudes toward school and future educational aspirations. Whereas increasing academic achievement is the major need, other needs that have a major effect on learners' academic achievement should also be addressed. These needs include increasing motivation, school attendance, improving self-esteem, improving behavior and attitudes, completing homework, developing effective study habits, and, as a whole, developing a success orientation.

Successful Program: Jackie Robinson Middle School

In a move to transform their inner city school, the children and adults at Jackie Robinson Middle School in New Haven, Connecticut, committed to becoming a community of students, teachers, parents, administrators, paraprofessionals, neighborhood residents, and representatives of social service agencies. These educators had a number of goals for their students, but one of their prime goals was to keep students on track, both academically and socially. Considerable thought went into not letting these students fall prey to the pitfalls of inner city living. While the school is based on James Comer's school development concept (discussed in greater detail in Chapter 10), the concept still allowed the educators sufficient flexibility to make decisions they thought best for the children at Jackie Robinson Middle School.

Comer's inner city schools do not have major delinquency problems or incidents of violence. Efforts focus on instilling large measures of self-esteem and self-confidence. The students who felt better about themselves and their abilities often experienced higher academic achievement and positive social interaction. Comer proposed that children who feel attached and close to adults would also experience higher academic achievement.

Jackie Robinson Middle School has a number of programs designed to help students experience social and academic success:

- A "Body Shop" where learners can ask questions and receive guidance on sex and physical problems related to growing up.
- An afterschool Homework Club, where adults help students with homework problems.
- SPACES, a program that teaches middle school learners how to use technology such as computers and video cameras.
- Drug counseling teams consisting of parents and teachers helping students threatened by drugs.
- A Bereavement Group to help children deal with personal tragedies (Elliot, 1992).

Calling for a legislative agenda for children at risk, Chafel (1990) proposed a number of steps designed to address the broad developmental needs of children in poverty:

- Infants born at low birthweight, prematurely or with handicaps should be provided more forms of effective prenatal care.
- Children suffering from poor health, malnutrition, and correctable physical defects should be nurtured through better child health services and an extension of Medicare services.

- Children growing up hungry or without adequate shelter should be assisted through expansion of women's, infants', and children's programs and provision of affordable housing.
- Children growing up without adequate guidance from their parents can be helped by comprehensive and intensive programs that link families with a broad array of social and family support services that respond flexibly to a wide variety of needs.
- Children who are at risk of school failure can be nurtured though high-quality preschool intervention programs that provide intellectual stimulation and the opportunity to learn language and socialization skills.
- Children who grow up in low-income families can be helped by high-quality, low-cost child care (Chafel, 1990).

Successful Program: Summerbridge

Summerbridge is a tuition-free, minority-based "workshop in education" (Irvine, 1992, p. 20) that takes a comprehensive approach to meeting the needs of high-potential middle school youth. The intensive six-week summer program, conducted at San Francisco University High School, focuses on after-school classes, counseling, advocacy, student learning skills, enrichment, the building of self-concepts, and understanding choices and opportunities. In essence, this program seeks to prepare students for the academic high school.

Summerbridge, located in urban San Francisco, works to meet the needs of inner city youth:

> The character of the student body reflects our belief that all students are at risk and need rigorous preparation and support for success. The student body, 75 percent of color, mirrors the rich socioeconomic and ethnic diversity of our urban community (Irvine, 1992, p. 20).

Summerbridge brings together different people in a safe and respectful atmosphere that encourages risk taking and exploration of personal potential. Based on the belief that educational excellence must be for all people, Summerbridge is a comprehensive program that stresses leadership, adventure, advisement, advocacy, and a rigorous academic program. The program empowers students through scholarship, workshops, and field trips. For example, eighth graders travel to City Hall to solve a creative assignment in which they work on fictitious yet complicated bureaucratic assignments.

Summerbridge reaches out to students of color (p. 23) and students from lower socioeconomic backgrounds. As the demographics of our society change, the school-aged population will shift to include many more students of color and lower socioeconomic groups (Irvine, 1992).

Single-Parent Families

It is imperative to make clear at the outset that single-parent families do not always constitute an at-risk condition. Just as many two-parent families contribute to children and adolescents being at risk, many single-parent families provide supportive and helpful home situations. Sometimes, but certainly not always, other at-risk conditions accompany single-parents homes, that is, in many situations, females may do less well financially, which further contributes to children and adolescents being at risk.

According to Thompson and Rudolph (1988), children need warm, loving, and stable home environments in order to grow and develop in a healthy manner. Years ago, children lived in large and stable extended families. Fathers worked, mothers worked in the home, and an unmarried aunt or uncle often lived near the family. Grandparents lived in close proximity to provide an extra sense of closeness. There were many loving and significant adults around when a child needed to talk or needed to be with someone. In today's more complex society, home and family life are not as simple: Grandparents may live miles away, aunts and uncles may pursue their own interests, and fathers and mothers may work long hours to provide financial security. A majority of mothers of school-age children work to help support the family, yet many mothers continue to accept major responsibility for care of the home. Likewise, the steadily increasing incidence of divorce in families during the past few years has resulted in single parents assuming the roles of mother and father more frequently, doubling the burden on the single parent and leaving little time for parenting (Thompson & Rudolph, 1988).

The following figures show the increasing number of single-parent families in the United States (U.S. Bureau of the Census, 1991):

- In 1989, 616,000 children under the age of 18 lived only with a male head of the household.
- In 1989, 6,519,000 children under the age of 18 lived only with a female head of the household.

Table 4-1 shows the breakdown of several cultures and illustrates the seriousness of the situation facing some African- and Hispanic-American families.

Remembering the point made at the outset that many children and adolescents thrive successfully in single-parent homes, how might such a home situation constitute an at-risk condition? Single-parent families might

- have fewer financial resources to provide experiences that contribute to personal, social, and academic growth.
- have less time to spend together since one parent has to assume total responsibility for household responsibilities and parenting roles.

TABLE 4-1 Children Under 18 Years Old, by Presence of Parents, 1989

	Number (1,000)	Mother Only	Father Only	Neither Parent
All races	63,282	14,608	2,016	46,658
Anglo-American	50,895	8,585	1,577	40,733
African-American	9,543	5,516	358	3,669
Hispanic-American	7,121	1,938	239	4,944

Compiled from U.S. Bureau of the Census, *Statistical abstracts of the United States, 1992* (112th ed., p. 54). Washington, DC: U.S. Government Printing Office, Table 68.

- result in children and adolescents being unsupervised after the school day ends.
- result in children feeling responsible for the breakup of the family.
- fail to provide developmentally appropriate sex role modeling.
- fail to provide an adequate sense of "family" or "belonging."
- be unable to provide assistance with homework and participation in school functions.

Some educators might say, "Divorce and other single-parent living arrangements are societal problems. What can educators do?" While schools cannot be held responsible for learners living in single-parent homes, it is possible for educators to understand changing family structures and the problems and concerns of learners from single-parent homes, and to realize how home and family life affect personal, social, and academic growth. An emotionally distraught learner might be unable to listen attentively, to perform at one's potential, and to participate successfully in social experiences. While educators cannot add surrogate parenting roles to their many other responsibilities, they do need to understand how family situations can affect learners and need to accept responsibility for helping children and adolescents from single-family homes whenever possible.

Delinquency and Criminal Activity

One can open nearly any newspaper and see evidence of children and adolescents increasingly engaging in criminal behaviors. Learners are at risk of being involved in criminal activities or being a victim of such activities. Once confined only to large urban schools in low socioeconomic areas, school violence continues to expand into other schools in what were once thought of as safe neighborhoods.

At one time, schools were thought to be a haven of safety, a place where learners were safe from the realities of street life and from guns and revenge.

Yet, *Newsweek* (Nordland, 1992) reports that today's schools are different places:

> *Guns are as familiar as bookbags. . . .*
>
> *. . . kids with guns are becoming small angels of death.*
>
> *. . . guns have become the leading cause of death among older teenage boys—white and black—in America (p. 22).*
>
> *Gun violence is on the rise in schools all over America. . . .*
>
> *. . . one student in five reports carrying a weapon of some kind and about one student in 20, or 5.3 percent, reports carrying a gun (p. 25).*

It does not take scholarly expertise to realize how violence can affect children and adolescents and contribute to their being at risk of becoming either a participant or a victim. A child or adolescent engaging in delinquent behavior for profit, for revenge, or for other reasons obviously is not placing a priority on learning and academic achievement. These learners are undoubtedly placing themselves and others in at-risk situations. Perhaps worse, however, is the boy or girl who attends school to learn, to obey rules and meet expectations, and to perform to the best of one's abilities and becomes a victim or, at least, experiences considerable anxiety and stress, which interfere with learning and one's chances of school success.

Maintaining that "Children are the real victims of violence," Hranitz and Eddowes (1990, p. 5) list poor grades, low motivation, and weak long-term goals as evidence of learners experiencing difficulty due to violence. Likewise, violence contributes to other risk factors such as early sexual activities and teenage pregnancy. For example, teenage mothers often have more behavior problems such as running away, fighting, stealing, smoking, or other behaviors resulting in teacher or school action.

Hranitz and Eddowes (1990) suggest the following:

- Federal and state legislation must be aimed at strengthening the family.
- Families must have access to adequate food and decent housing.
- Programs providing support systems for families must be expanded.
- School and community agencies must cooperate in providing appropriate activities for children and adolescents.

Newsweek (Salholz, et al., 1992) suggests that teachers, principals, and parents can work together to help curb school violence:

- Teacher training needs to prepare instructors to deal with disruptive students and to break up fights *before* they escalate into murder.
- Schools need to identify fight-prone kids when they're young and introduce them to nonviolent alternatives.
- Schools need more adults on campus to provide supervision.

- Communities should conduct programs to teach parents how to handle and store guns.

In summary, while educators should not be called on to deal with criminal behaviors in schools and on playgrounds, the sad reality is that educators do face these problems and their consequences. No longer isolated to urban, low socioeconomic areas, these problems are extending to the suburbs and to rural areas and affect elementary and middle school learners as well as secondary school students. Increasingly, students are being placed at risk, resulting in loss of academic potential, loneliness and social isolation, and an outright fear of attending school. Educators cannot be expected to handle the problem single-handed; however, perceptive educators might consider ways of involving parents, teacher organizations, and community agencies in an effort to reduce the effects of crime and violence.

Successful Program: James P. B. Duffy School No. 12

James P. B. Duffy School, an urban elementary school, transformed chaos into harmony when the principal and staff replaced their disciplinary policy of traditional roles with the "ten commandments of behavior" (Wager, 1992/1993, p. 34). Before taking drastic action, the school experienced considerable violence: older children terrorizing younger ones, extortion, fist-fights, adults being run over with bicycles, and conflicts between racial groups.

The educators at this school took powerful action and announced the ten commandments:

1. No weapons—real or toy.
2. No pushing, tripping, hitting, or fighting.
3. No swearing.
4. No threatening.
5. No insulting others.
6. Stay where adults are in charge.
7. No class disruption or refusal to follow adult direction.
8. Respect things that belong to others (no stealing, extorting, destroying).
9. Do not touch fire alarms; do not bring matches.
10. No alcoholic beverages, drugs, or cigarettes.

Next, the educators established the procedures:

1. At the first infraction, the teacher counsels the student and informs a parent.
2. On the second infraction, the teacher hand delivers a referral to the Climate Committee.
3. A date is set, usually within 24 hours, for parent, child, and teacher to appear at a hearing.

The school also initiated a system of rewards: short movies on Friday afternoons, three weeks of sequential good behavior resulted in a full-length movie with popcorn; Good Citizen Badges for deserving students, and attendance at a Good Citizen's Banquet for students receiving an A in citizenship on four successive report cards (Wager, 1992/1993).

Activity 4-4

Make a list of commonly held stereotypical beliefs about boys and girls (for example, "Boys should not cry" or "Girls giggle a lot"). Then, observe the girls and boys in your class to test the validity of your list. Next, have the boys and girls make a similar list, and have a discussion of the differences between girls and boys. How might an educator's expectation of girls or boys affect actual teaching situations?

Sexism and Gender Stereotyping

Gender can be defined as a term that describes differences in masculinity and femininity—the thoughts, feelings, and behavior identified as either male or female (Gollnick & Chinn, 1990). Although many similarities exist between males and females, differences also exist that educators should recognize and to which they should offer an appropriate response. Likewise, in addition to addressing differences and similarities, educators should also seek to clarify stereotypical beliefs about males and females.

What are some differences between males and females?

1. Beginning at about 10 years of age, girls excel at verbal tasks; beginning in early adolescence, boys excel at mathematical tasks; between 10 and 12, boys begin to excel on visual/spatial tasks.
2. Concerning socialization and affiliation, there are no differences between the sexes.
3. Concerning activity level, there are no differences between the sexes.
4. Beginning around age 2, boys are more verbally and physically aggressive (Gollnick & Chinn, 1990).

Stereotyping defines male and female roles in a narrow fashion, and defines behaviors for the two sexes as quite different from one another. Gender stereotypes are instilled and perpetuated by television, children's literature, and adult expectations of sex-specific behaviors of boys and girls. While some progress has been made toward more objective perceptions of sex and gender roles, some stereotypical images continue to impede the progress of females (and, in many cases, males):

1. Males and females are too often portrayed in traditional and rigid roles, for example, careers such as doctors and nurses, or men as breadwinners and women as housekeepers.
2. Magazines and newspaper sections are often directed at one audience, for example, women's sections that include articles on fashion, food, and social events.

3. Textbooks often portray boys involved with important activities, while girls are playing with dolls and giving tea parties.
4. In print and nonprint media, men are found in about six times as many different occupations as women (Gollnick & Chinn, 1990).

While the negative results of gender stereotyping are too numerous to list, educators who are working to help children and adolescents can readily see the importance of addressing gender concerns. The challenge is actually twofold: Educators' efforts must include not only gender differences and cultural differences, but also the intricate relationship between the two (Baruth & Manning, 1992).

Racism, Discrimination, Prejudice, and Lack of Opportunity

Some indications suggest that the most blatant forms of racism, discrimination, and prejudice have lessened during the last couple of decades. Culturally diverse people have made significant strides due to the integration of schools, efforts directed at equal housing opportunities, affirmative action programs, the Voting Rights Act, and other civil rights legislation. While these improvements represent noteworthy and commendable progress, one can certainly not assume that racism, discrimination, and prejudice no longer exist. These conditions continue to exist and to impede, often in more covert or subtle forms, the progress of culturally diverse students and also females. These conditions place some students at risk (i.e., the girl who is ignored in science classes) and sometimes make other conditions more acute (i.e., the African-American boy who has his minor reading problem made worse by a teacher who believes culture and socioeconomic status determine achievement levels).

Often defined as the domination of one social or ethnic group by another, racist individuals have used an ideological system to justify the discrimination of some racial groups against others. The evidence of racism toward culturally diverse groups in the United States is all too evident: African-Americans have faced discrimination in housing, employment, schooling, and in various other areas, despite civil rights legislation. Hispanics have been exploited as migrant farmworkers, Asian-Americans were excluded as immigrants into the United States during the early 1900s, and Native Americans had their land taken and were placed on reservations (Lum, 1986).

Racism continues to be a major force that affects the attitudes and behavior of children today. Racism is such a strongly negative emotional experience that culturally diverse students' attention may be diverted from academic pursuits and toward responding to racism in unconstructive ways. Educators sometimes do not respond because they feel unable to change students' experiences or because such actions take away from academic subject areas. Educators who fail to respond to racism send signals to students that racism is either acceptable or a trivial issue. Since failure to counteract racism has two damaging consequences, educators have a responsibility to respond appropriately (Pollard, 1989).

Lum (1986) described racism as

1. the belief that there are well-defined and distinctive races among human beings
2. the belief that racial mixing lowers biological quality
3. the belief in the mental and physical superiority of some races over others
4. the belief that racial groups have distinct racial cultures to the extent that some races are naturally prone to criminality, sexual looseness, or dishonest business practices
5. the belief that certain races have temperamental dispositions, which is a form of stereotyping
6. the belief that the superior races should rule and dominate inferior races (pp. 129–130).

Whether by overt racism, such as the Ku Klux Klan's acts of violence and hatred, or the more covert forms of racism and discrimination often found in employment and housing, African-Americans and other minorities continue to experience inequities and inequalities. Although the overt acts and Jim Crow attitudes are not as visible as they were several decades ago, racial injustices continue to affect minorities' progress and well-being. Educators of all cultures may have to deal with problems resulting from these realities in the United States, and may have to sort through their own personal biases and long-held cultural beliefs (Baruth & Manning, 1992).

Unequal opportunities, both subtle and blatant, which result from racism and discrimination undoubtedly place or contribute to children and adolescents being at risk. Racist and discriminatory beliefs such as believing all African-American learners are slow and academically inferior and believing all Asian-Americans are intellectually superior and high achievers impede the progress of both culturally diverse groups. While the former might be underchallenged, the latter might be overchallenged and placed under undue stress to achieve. Some learners might be blatantly informed that they are inferior, mediocre, or superior; however, other children and adolescents might suffer from more subtle forms of discrimination such as being placed in lower ability groups, being subject to an overdependence on drill and worksheets rather than more creative, problem-solving approaches.

Other examples may include culturally diverse learners being *perceived* as at risk (when they are really not) and then being placed in industrial or trades courses rather than more academically oriented classes.

The U.S. society in some aspects is again becoming segregated. The so-called "white flight" to avoid inner city living and, in some cases, to avoid integration and forced bussing has resulted in yet another form of segregation, *de facto* segregation that, although not sanctioned by law, has had similar consequences—races and socioeconomic groups are educated separately and, all too often, unequally. Considerable differences exist between expenditures per pupil in more affluent districts and financially less stable inner city schools. Students in both districts may be at risk, either of not having equal educational opportunity or not having adequate opportunities to get to know various cultures and social classes.

Another lens for viewing this predicament is the polarization of social classes. For example, many successful African-Americans have moved to the suburbs and now have their children attend schools with higher expenditures per pupil and better records of academic achievement. Similarly, some lower-class Anglo-Americans have been "left behind" in the white flight. Being uneducated, untrained, and unable (or unwilling) to flee to the suburbs, these people remain in urban neighborhoods. Rather than being only racially segregated, such an example constitutes social class segregation, a form of segregation often just as insidious as deliberate racism and discrimination. Other societal ills that contribute to students' social and academic problems include social isolation, a lack of positive African-American male role models in highly populated urban areas, and inner city schools that often fail to respond to the unique needs of its urban dwellers. Such societal ills undoubtedly contribute to children and adolescents being at risk, and once learners are labeled as being at risk, pose barriers to educators trying to lessen the at-risk conditions.

In summary, learners, especially those who are culturally diverse and at lower socioeconomic levels, have their social and academic achievement as well as their overall opportunities limited by societal conditions such as the aforementioned living in poverty; living in overcrowded, crime-ridden, and drug-infested neighborhoods, lack of proper medical care; attending schools where segregation, intentional or unintentional, continues to limit opportunities; and living in areas where learners' preschool or early educational experiences do not contribute to academic success.

It is ironic that the nations and its schools that purport equal opportunity for all children and adolescents actually contribute to some learners being at risk. Some educators might feel a responsibility or moral obligation to change or revise societal attitudes. Other educators might not feel responsible for societal ills or might feel powerless to control or influence societal conditions and people's attitudes. (These views toward schools' roles are usually termed "revisionist" and "traditionalist," respectively, and are discussed in more detail next.)

The School's Role in Addressing Societal Conditions

Philosophical Positions

Throughout history, educators have argued such issues as society's effects on schools and vice versa, whether schools should teach the status quo or whether schools should take deliberate action to improve or "revise" society. Philosophical camps have taken positions for both stances and have fought vigorously to promote their perspectives, often at the expense of students' overall welfare. This section looks at two philosophical interpretations of the functions of schools and suggests, rather emphatically, that regardless of the philosophical position adopted, schools still have the responsibility to help students, especially at-risk students, whose educational progress is being hampered by societal conditions.

Growing recognition during the past few decades of the strong relationship between social class and school achievement has led to a fundamental disagreement between those who support the traditional view of the role and function of schools in our society and those who accept one or another variation of what is frequently called the revisionist view.

The traditional view perceives the educational system as established and, to a substantial degree, functioning successfully to provide economically disadvantaged students with meaningful opportunities for social and economic advancement. Revisionists, by way of contrast, believe that the schools fail to provide most disadvantaged students with a meaningful chance to succeed in society. Many revisionists also believe that schools are not even designed to accomplish this purpose, but instead are actually established and operated to perpetuate the disadvantages of lower-class students from one generation to the next.

The revisionist contends that the upper middle class has successfully operated to enhance its own power and prestige relative to lower-class and minority groups, both immigrants and native-born Americans. By controlling the schools, the elite groups admitted few poor and minority youth into high school academic programs and institutions of higher learning; they channeled this "underclass" into second-rate secondary schools, third-rate community colleges, and fourth-rate jobs. Many of the revisionists and critical theorists also believe that the educational system has been set up specifically to produce disciplined workers at the bottom of the class structure. This is accomplished in part by having the school emphasize discipline in lower-class schools or classrooms, just as the lower-class family and the factory labor system also emphasize external discipline (Ornstein & Levine, 1989).

The traditional point of view, while it acknowledges the relationships among social class, educational achievement, and success in the economic system, emphasizes the opportunities that exist for lower-class students to improve their status and the data indicating that many lower-class youth do experience social mobility through the schools and other social institutions. Most traditionalists believe that our educational and economic institutions provide opportunity for lower-class students to advance within a larger system that balances stress on excellence with provision of opportunity to succeed for those who start out disadvantaged.

The traditional view admits that schools serve as a screening device to sort different individuals into different jobs. But this screening process is not fundamentally based on race, ethnic origin, or income, as the revisionists contend. Along with recognizing marked differences in individual abilities, the traditional view recognizes that certain qualities lead to success in school and asserts that these are related to qualities that make the individual more productive on the job. Although these correlations may be imperfect, competitive firms can use this information and offer the better jobs to individuals who complete more schooling and do well in school. Put another way, the better educated get the better jobs because they have been made more productive by the schools (Ornstein & Levine, 1989).

One does not have to look far to see evidence of schools being a reflection of the society at large: Equal opportunity in society requires equal opportunity in schools, too; one's constitutional rights in society extend to schools; and the push to understand and address the sexism and racism that plagues U.S. society has extended to educational institutions. Such examples are positive and will undoubtedly contribute to the overall welfare of all races and both sexes. However, not all of society's reflections on schools have been positive. For example, the drug problem in U.S. society is devastating some schools; sexual permissiveness has engaged younger and younger girls until the problem now dramatically affects many schools, including, unfortunately, middle schools; and the crime and violence, once plaguing only inner cities and other high crime areas, now plagues many high schools. Whereas these factors affect all learners, they might have even harsher effects on at-risk learners who already have other problems. For example, the 14-year-old girl whose top priority is to have friends might engage in at-risk behaviors, such as sexual activity and substance abuse, that she otherwise would not have tried. While readers can think of many other examples, the powerful relationship between society and schools has been made clear. Whether educators subscribe to revisionist or traditional positions, perceptive educators realize that they have a major responsibility to help all learners achieve at their highest potential. Educators' responsibilities with at-risk learners may be even greater, especially since social conditions that do not dramatically affect so-called "normal" youngsters may have devastating effects on learners already diagnosed as at risk.

The School's Role

Regardless of whether educators subscribe to revisionist or traditionalist perspectives, or some intermediate model, their role in improving at-risk learners' chances of success should take three directions: Make a commitment, develop appropriate strategies, and evaluate efforts to determine progress and the need to revise strategies.

The first step in reducing society's ill effects on at-risk learners is to make an overall school commitment (i.e, all teachers, all staff, and all administrators committing to work as a *team*) to address societal problems that reduce at-risk learners' chances of school and personal success. Such a commitment is not an easy task and should not be taken lightly. Societal conditions such as poverty, racism, sexism, being from lower social classes, and violence are difficult problems to overcome. Changing racist and sexist attitudes is not done as easily as changing grouping approaches or instructional styles. Educators need to base commitments on the mindset that efforts must be continuing and will often be frustrating, yet also must be considered worthwhile to all learners and, especially, learners at risk of academic, social, or other failure.

The second step is to develop appropriate strategies to address specific problems. For example, educators must pose the strategic question of "What societal conditions can we realistically address?" A committee formed of administrators, staff members, teachers, parents, students, and community members can consider such a question. While a few conscientious brainstorming sessions could provide excellent starting points, other means of identifying societal conditions such as checklists, surveys, and questionnaires deserve consideration and eventual use. It will be important to compare perceptions such as teachers' and students' opinions of what could be done to make school experiences more successful.

Once the effects of societal conditions have been clearly identified, then an agenda can be developed for reducing their effects and, subsequently, improving students' chances of educational and social success. For example, few would question that sexism has a fairly strong grip on U.S. society. Admittedly, federal and state legislation as well as a better informed populace have reduced sexism in the workplace, in salaries earned, and opportunities for economic and career advancement. Still, however, informed citizens cannot say that sexism does not pose a problem to the society and

---

Successful Program: One-on-One

In an attempt to address the needs of at-risk learners, the educators at Jarrett Junior High in Springfield, Missouri, implemented a program based on the premise that at-risk learners experiencing academic and attendance problems needed "significant others" (Hereford, 1993, p. 12). Volunteers were recruited among the faculty of 35 to "adopt" a student. All slots filled quickly. Some teachers requested specific students while others asked for random assignments. Each teacher met with his or her student at least once a week during the teacher's conference period to discuss personal and school-related happenings in the student's life. Southwestern Bell offered a $500 grant for teachers to use for their adopted student's birthday, holiday gift, for taking the child to dinner, or for whatever the teacher thought was best for the child. The teachers did a variety of things to let the students know an adult cared for them.

The results were gratifying: Both grades and attendance improved. However, the program had benefits beyond those anticipated. Almost none of these students had discipline referrals, and faculty felt good about the program and the positive effects on at-risk youngsters (Hereford, 1993).

---

its schools. Once the committee has made a firm commitment and has determined "sexism" as an area to address, specific strategies can be planned such as the following: Are boys and girls treated equally? Are expectations for both sexes equal in degree of challenge? Do textbooks, library materials (both print and nonprint media), and instructional materials reflect females in active and positive roles? Do teachers direct more questions to boys than girls? Are more boys selected for offices and leadership roles than girls? This representative list is only a beginning and should be expanded by a concerned and perceptive committee. Then, appropriate action should be taken to correct any situation that impedes the progress of either sex.

The third step is to develop comprehensive and objective evaluative criteria to determine success and future directions to address. Evaluation should be as objective as possible and should elicit responses and opinions from a number of sources, including the students for whom the efforts were designed and implemented. Evaluative efforts should be correctly written to elicit specific opinions and designed in such a manner that the evaluative instrument can be a basis for the future agenda.

Overall, educators addressing societal conditions will likely see better results and subsequently feel more successful when only one or two (perhaps the most severe) conditions are addressed at a time. Addressing a

---

Activity 4-5
Write a position paper on the role of schools in U.S. society. Specifically, should schools adopt traditional roles (teach what exists) or adopt revisionist roles (teach what should be)? Why is the selected role important? How does this philosophical position actually affect learners?

---

number of societal conditions simultaneously might be overwhelming and might take a toll on both educators and at-risk learners.

Case Study 4-2 looks at a school faculty that decided to take a stand toward reducing societal at-risk factors.

Case Study 4-2: A School's Agenda to Address Societal At-Risk Factors

P.S. 190, a high school, had experienced considerable racial problems: Anglo-American students ignoring Black History week; racial graffiti written on school property; several fights and disagreements with racial overtones; and reports that both races were afraid to attend school. The racial discord was taking a toll on both the school and its students. Achievement was dropping, truancy and drug use were increasing, violence was becoming a common occurrence, and, generally speaking, P.S. 190 had lost its "intellectual purpose."

"The problem is not just us," Mr. Duncan stated, "it is indicative of the entire society."

"While this is true," one teacher stated, "we still need to take action—too many of our students are being placed in at-risk situations. If there is anything we can do, we need to!"

This conversation and the educators' concerns resulted in a committee being formed with an equal number of blacks and whites. The committee was charged with the responsibility of addressing the societal problem (actually their main concern rested with P.S. 190) of racism and racial discord. Committee membership consisted of educators, students, parents, and community people. Committee members knew their task would not be easy. They would have to define the problem, plan and implement strategies, and evaluate efforts. Students identified as being most at risk due to racial strife would receive extra attention such as small and large group counseling in their areas of special need. Changing racial attitudes would take understanding and patience. Genuine improvements would take time, but initial efforts had been started.

Reviewing What You Have Read About Societal Conditions

1. A review of the literature on the _____ indicates that the childhood years are filled with adult behavior, dress, concerns, and stresses.

2. Many schools, by becoming increasingly _____ , have contributed to the disappearance of childhood.

3. _____ can be devastating in terms of attitude toward school, success orientations, motivation to excel, and academic achievement.

4. _____ groups often experience a type of double jeopardy due to culture, socioeconomic class, or the complex interaction between the two.

5. The phenomenon, _____ , increased from 20% in 1960 to 43% in 1985 in the percentage of poor white children being raised in female-headed households.

6. _____ might have fewer financial resources to provide experiences that contribute to personal, social, and academic growth and have less time to spend together since one parent has to assume total responsibility for household responsibilities and parenting roles.

7. _____ defines male and female roles in a narrow fashion, and defines behaviors for the two sexes as quite different from one another.

8. Once confined only to large urban schools in low socioeconomic areas, _____ continues to expand into other schools in what were once thought of as safe neighborhoods.

9. _____ perceives the educational system as established and, to a substantial degree, functioning successfully to provide economically disadvantaged students with meaningful opportunities for social and economic advancement.

10. The _____ contends that the upper middle class has successfully operated to enhance its own power and prestige relative to lower-class and minority groups, both immigrants and native-born Americans.

11. _____ , such as rampant testing, homogeneous grouping, worksheets, fragmentation of subject areas, an inordinate amount of drill, and undue sitting and listening, have a negative impact on childhood.

12. The first step in reducing society's ill effects on at-risk learners is to make an _____ to address societal problems that reduce at-risk learners' chances of school and personal success.

13. The so-called white flight to avoid inner city living and, in some cases, to avoid integration and forced bussing has resulted in yet another form of segregation, _____ , that, although not sanctioned by law, still separates races and socioeconomic groups and all too often educates unequally.

14. Racism and sexism may be either _____ the former being blatant and obvious such as acts by racist or sexist remarks written on walls and the latter being subtle racism or sexist actions such as housing or job discrimination.

Answer Key: **1.** disappearance of childhood; **2.** industrialized and product oriented; **3.** Poverty; **4.** Culturally diverse; **5.** "feminization" of poverty; **6.** Single-parent families; **7.** Gender or sex stereotyping; **8.** school violence; **9.** Traditional view; **10.** revisionist view; **11.** "Assaults" on childhood; **12.** overall school commitment; **13.** *de facto* segregation; **14.** overt or covert.

Summary

Children and adolescents are often placed at risk or have their at-risk conditions made more acute by societal conditions. Living in poverty, growing up too fast, attending schools where violence is all too common, and trying to succeed where racism and sexism limit one's potential can exact a significant toll on children and adolescents. Educators may feel overwhelmed when considering all the conditions that contribute to learners being at risk; however, caring and effective teachers, administrators, and support personnel recognize and accept the responsibility to help learners whenever possible. The task of addressing social conditions can never be considered complete or finished—it is an ongoing helping process that helps learners and shows educators' concern for humanity.

For Additional Information on Societal Conditions

Baruth, L. G., & Manning, M. L. (1992). *Multicultural education of children and adolescents*. Boston: Allyn and Bacon. Baruth and Manning examine in some detail the socioeconomic conditions of selected culturally diverse groups.

Brown, A. J. (1993). Developing leadership among urban youth. *Momentum, 24*(2), 46–27. Brown suggests urban youth need leadership skills and proposes two powerful outreach programs.

Elkind, D. (1993). Whatever happened to childhood? *Momentum, 24*(2), 18–19. Elkind examines various factors that narrow the limits of normality for children, thus denying their differences.

Hranitz, J. R., & Eddowes, E. A. (1990). Violence: A crisis in homes and schools. *Childhood Education, 67,* 4–7. These two authors examine the violence in America's schools and offer suggestions for future directions.

Manning, G., & Manning. M. (1981). Assaults on childhood. *Childhood Education, 58,* 85–87. In an article that will have implications for many years, Manning and Manning examine school practices and methods that they consider to be assaults on the childhood years.

Newsweek (1992, March 9). Kids and guns: A report from America's classroom killing grounds. pp. 22–30. This *Newsweek* article explores the violence spreading through America's schools and offers suggestions for school officials trying to combat the problem.

Personal Characteristics

Outline

Reviewing What You Have Read About Personal Characteristics

Summary

For Additional Information on Personal Characteristics

Overview

Personal or individual characteristics often lead to or increase children's and adolescents' propensity toward being at risk. Whereas some might not consider personal characteristics to be the school's responsibility, more perceptive educators realize that regardless of where the responsibility lies, the result remains the same: At-risk conditions and characteristics deserve to be addressed. Failing to meet one's professional responsibilities can result in learners' at-risk conditions increasing in both number and intensity. This chapter looks at learners' personal characteristics and offers suggestions for educators desiring to reduce personal at-risk conditions.

Probing Directions

This chapter on learners' personal at-risk conditions does the following:

1. Explores personal characteristics that contribute to learners' being at risk.
2. Examines the close and intricate relationship between societal and personal conditions.
3. Explores learners' abilities to see the rewards of long-term commitment.
4. Examines the school's responsibility and role in addressing learners' personal at-risk conditions.
5. Explores the powerful effects of learners' self-concepts on motivation and achievement.
6. Suggests other sources of information such as books and journals.

Personal Conditions Contributing to At-Risk Conditions

Considerable similarity, without doubt, exists between societal and personal conditions. Likewise, a cause-and-effect relationship often results. For instance, substance abuse can result in eating disorders, and, similarly, peer pressure can result in pregnancy and substance abuse. In some situations,

---

Activity 5-1

Give one or two examples, other than those given in the text, that show the close connection between societal and personal conditions. Then write a position statement on whether these conditions are the responsibility of the school. Should the school respond or leave responsibility to society and the family?

---

neither societal nor personal conditions can receive absolute blame for at-risk conditions. The acceptance of responsibility for addressing the at-risk condition can be equally confusing. Some argue that educators should accept responsibility for neither, whereas others advocate addressing both. Although arguments can be made for both perspectives, educators realize that the results of at-risk conditions, regardless of origin, remain the same: Learners are at risk of not becoming all they can be. Therefore, for learners' overall welfare, educators need to take a stand for and help at-risk children and adolescents.

Blaming the Victim

Children and adolescents are often blamed for the problems and conditions that make them at risk. Blaming the victim rather than pinpointing more exact causes results in more acute at-risk consequences: the adolescent boy who cannot read, learners from lower social classes who must struggle financially for the barest necessities, and the pregnant, unmarried girl who needs all the available resources her school can offer.

Several perspectives emerge when considering this issue. First, academically at-risk learners can be placed in double jeopardy when blamed for their reading difficulties or for having low self-concepts. Likewise, the at-risk conditions of overeaters or anorexics might grow more acute when blamed for their conditions. Second, disturbing consequences can follow when children and adolescents living in poverty are blamed for being poor. Why don't those people do something to help themselves? Why don't their parents work to provide a decent standard of living? Such perspectives fail to recognize the conditions and effects of poverty and also fail to convey feelings of empathy and caring needed by at-risk children and adolescents. Third, at-risk learners are often blamed for conditions they "bring on themselves," such as drug and alcohol addiction or conditions resulting from being sexually active. One may argue that at-risk conditions result from behaviors of choice rather than being an inherited or acquired disability: The at-risk learner had a choice and made an unwise decision. Fourth, and related, should society be blamed for some at-risk conditions? Impressionable minds can be greatly influenced by society's rush to encourage young people to grow up too fast, to engage in adult and often dangerous behaviors, and to experiment with drugs, alcohol, tobacco, and sex.

Case Study 5-1: Blaming the Victim

Mrs. Blair, a middle school teacher at P.S. 98 spoke: "Those kids—what makes them that way? Some poor children come to school dirty; others take drugs; several can't speak English; and even fourteen-year-old Susan is pregnant." The tirade continued for three to four minutes. "I don't know what to do—give us some decent, motivated students and we might be able to achieve the results the school board wants."

Several teachers listened and either said nothing or nodded their agreement. One teacher, however, Mrs. Santiago, spoke calmly yet directly to Mrs. Blair: "Blaming the victim does not help. Children should not be blamed for their predicaments. They do not choose to be poor and dirty. Some might have made poor choices to experiment with drugs or sexual activity, but they still need our help and understanding, perhaps even more now."

Later, Mrs. Santiago thought how she could have advanced her points. Even the parents should not be blamed—they were a hardworking lot (at least those who could find employment were). Those who know ways to help their children usually do, and in the case of Susan, her mother, frustrated as she is, is trying to help Susan finish school.

Mrs. Santiago made a list of incidents where the victim is blamed:

1. Placing the blame on causes or conditions rather than looking for solutions to or the effects of the causes or conditions.
2. Harboring lower expectations (behavior, achievement, future aspirations) when learners are blamed for at-risk conditions.
3. Placing blame where blame is unwarranted, that is, in the case of poverty, children should not be blamed for their parents' socioeconomic conditions.
4. Placing blame where learners regret previous behaviors. For example, taking drugs and experimenting with sexual activity are regrettable yet, unfortunately, the consequences cannot be erased.

Mrs. Santiago realized that the "blaming the victim" mindset might be difficult to change. What could be done to help victims, she thought? While she continued to be somewhat pessimistic about the likelihood of Mrs. Blair making significant changes, she thought of several approaches that might help teachers and administrators who blame learners for their predicaments: 1) Help others understand that victims are often unable to improve their socioeconomic status; 2) learners who are victims due to their behavior often regret their decisions and need adult assistance and understandings; and 3) blaming victims for their plight is unprofessional and fails to provide the educational attention learners need.

Mrs. Santiago wondered: How many other teachers, like Mrs. Blair, blame students for at-risk conditions? They may not be as blatant as Mrs. Blair, but their everyday treatment of learners might suggest victims being blamed. How many students have received inadequate educational experiences because teachers blamed them for their conditions? How widespread is the problem? How can the school take comprehensive action to combat this problem that affects so many?

Why is the "blaming the victim" perspective even important to educators of at-risk learners? Educators' mindsets toward at-risk learners significantly influence the enthusiasm, dedication, and commitment brought to projects. For example, educators blaming at-risk learners for their problems are likely to be less motivated and committed to educating learners than educators who feel at-risk learners should not be blamed for their conditions.

For some people, perhaps professionals with little patience or commitment, it is easier to blame victims for conditions than to look for more specific individual, educational, societal, or economic causes. However, the consequences of blaming the victim often extend further than just thinking that learners deserve blame for their at-risk conditions. The practice of blaming the victim has been used to excuse or justify many unjust actions such as poorer quality programs, outdated and irrelevant textbooks and other curricular materials, beliefs that lower ability students cannot learn, and at-risk conditions being addressed with inadequate commitment.

The "blaming the victim" mindset deserves to be addressed in several ways. First, educators should not allow their perspectives to interfere with their ability to plan and implement effective at-risk programs. Second, educators need to offer a personal and professional commitment to at-risk learners, and also understand that children and adolescents can be blamed for their conditions. Third, such efforts should include changing the "blaming the victim" perspective among other educators in the school. Educators should be shown how at-risk conditions might result from the individual's actions, home conditions, societal factors, and even the school itself.

Personal At-Risk Characteristics

Self-Destructive Behaviors, Suicides, and Accidental Deaths

Suicide, the most serious personal problem, may be related or caused by other at-risk conditions. The boy under pressure to achieve, the pregnant 14-year-old, or the teenager abusing drugs may all be potentially suicidal at one time or another. Specific reasons for suicides among young people vary just as they do with other age ranges and may include failing a class, depression, lack of supportive friendships, anxiety, unhappiness, family instability, and especially among adolescents, an unwanted pregnancy or the loss of a boyfriend or girlfriend. Genetics may also play a factor in the decision to commit suicide. The closer the genetic relation to someone who has committed suicide, the more likely an individual will commit suicide. The decision to commit suicide is complex and is probably a culmination of a number of interrelated factors (Santrock, 1990).

Educators working with learners suspected of considering suicide should not lessen their efforts when stressful situations appear to be resolved. In fact, this is the time when the young person might be more likely to commit suicide. Atwater (1988) reports that depressed youth, especially the severely depressed, may take their lives as life conditions begin to improve. When most depressed, they might not have the mental and psychological energy to commit suicide yet when they begin to improve and get their energy back, they act on their underlying problems, hopelessness, and then commit suicide.

Differences can also be found among boys and girls at risk of taking their own lives. One study revealed that stress, a contributing factor to suicides, differs among boys and girls. Females expressed significantly more difficulty dealing with stress than males. They were twice as likely to feel sad and hopeless, and were 60% more likely to have a bleak outlook for the future. The study also showed that youngsters engaging in other risk-taking behaviors, such as sexual involvement and alcohol consumption, were more likely to contemplate suicide (Adcock, Nagy, & Simpson, 1991). Other gender differences include adolescent males being more likely to commit suicide and adolescent girls being more likely to threaten such behaviors (Santrock, 1990).

Accidental deaths, another at-risk condition, are responsible for more deaths to U.S. adolescents than any other cause, representing more than half of all deaths to persons aged 10 to 19. Vehicle-related accidents account for almost three-fourths of accidental deaths among persons aged 10 to 19. Other significant causes of accidental death include drowning and firearms accidents. In fact, one survey revealed that more than 40% of 8th and 10th graders indicated they had used a firearm during the past year; of these, more than 40% had used a gun more than 10 times. Many children and adolescents have accidents that do not result in death but do require visits to a physician. These accidents often result in days missed from school, permanent disability, restricted activity, and other problems, any one of which can be considered an at-risk condition. While comprehensive national data are not available to reveal exact occurrences, available data do indicate sports injuries do occur while playing football, basketball, baseball, and riding bicycles (Office of Technology Assessment, 1991).

Sex and cultural differences can also be seen in accidental deaths. Adolescent males, particularly age 15 to 19, are at higher risk than adolescent females. Anglo-American and Native American males have the highest rates of motor-vehicle–related accidental deaths, many of which involve driving and drinking. Adolescent males appear to be more at risk when driving at night. For example, adolescent drivers do only 20% of their driving at night yet they suffer more than half of their crash fatalities at night. Of these accidents, more than half involve alcohol, and about one-quarter of fatally injured drivers aged 15 to 19 are intoxicated. It appears to take less alcohol to place an adolescent at risk for a serious or fatal accident than to place an adult at risk (Office of Technology Assessment, 1991).

Eating Disorders

As addressed in Chapter 2, eating disorders can place children and adolescents in at-risk conditions. The Office of Technology Assessment (1991) reports that adolescent-specific data on nutrition and physical fitness are limited and are often neglected in favor of adult populations. Available data suggest that most adolescents suffer from some nutritional or fitness problems such as mineral deficiencies, imbalanced diets, and overweight or obesity. Female adolescents and those adolescents who are most actively engaged in fitness and athletic activities are more likely than others to have nutritional problems. Available evidence suggests a tendency toward obesity for African-American females and Mexican-American and Native Americans adolescents of both sexes.

Adolescents tend to have little information about nutrition (including how to interpret food labels and how to interpret nutrition information). Likewise, little evidence suggests current school-based nutrition education efforts affect what adolescents eat. In addition, the family, community, or school may have more control than adolescents over nutrition choices (Office of Technology Assessment, 1991).

Truancy

For one or a number of reasons, some children do not attend school on a regular basis, which places their academic and social progress at risk as well as their attitudes toward school. Learners fall behind, miss vital information, lose interest in school and learning, and may eventually drop out of school altogether. Even for the learner who officially stays in school, progress usually cannot stay on schedule. Reasons for truancy can be any number of factors, over which the school often has little control. Reasons may include parents simply not knowing children and adolescents are missing school, lack of a permanent home in the case of children of immigrant workers or the homeless, or prolonged illnesses. In addition, some learners just do not "like" school and look for reasons to be absent. For example, for some students, school can be an uncomfortable place: The 10th grader who has serious reading problems facing predominantly verbal learning tasks, the large 16-year-old sitting in cramped desks, or the learner skilled with her hands being forced to learn from a book just like the other 30 students in the class.

Some school districts face serious problems with chronic truants, including all of the social and academic problems normally associated with truancy and the loss of state financial aid. One district reported that more than half of its high school students were regularly absent. A chronic truant is defined as a student missing at least 18 days without a valid excuse. Under this definition, 4.1% of students are chronic truants. Similarly, on any given day, 10% of the nation's children and adolescents miss school (Rudd, 1991). While gang violence, another at-risk condition, might contribute to some truancy, there does not appear to be a single major problem that can be

---

Successful Program: Project Success

Project Success focuses on helping at-risk high school students in grades 9 and 10. The program seeks to strengthen the self-esteem and the academic achievement of students with chronic poor attendance, a history of discipline referrals, and poor grades. Identified students are placed in a special ninth-grade program, which provides instruction in English, mathematics, social studies, and science. The students then work in small classes with highly trained teachers to improve their academic achievement, attendance, and attitudes about the value of education. Students participating in the program rejoin their peers for electives, physical education, and all special school activities. Results document increased grade-point ratios, improved attendance, and lower suspension rates (Murphy, 1988).

addressed. For example, one student reported being absent to take a sick relative to the doctor or just to stay at home to return to bed. Efforts to curb the truancy problem include tackling the gang violence problem, making classes more interesting, and giving out home phone numbers for teachers so students can call for help (Rudd, 1991).

Self-Concept

More than two decades ago, William Purkey clarified the relationship between self-concept and social and academic achievement in *Self-Concept and School Achievement* (1970) and also showed educators how to invite students to have a better self-concept in *Inviting School Success* (1984). The powerful impact of learners' self-concept on their academic achievement and social well-being has enormous implications for addressing the needs of at-risk populations.

Sufficient evidence exists to document how the self-concept influences academic achievement cognitive developmental changes (Santrock, 1990) as well as social development and overall social well-being (Manning & Allen, 1987). Representative changes in cognitive development include increases in abstract thought, idealism, organization, language sophistication, logical reasoning, perspective taking, and egocentrism (Santrock, 1990). A learner with a positive self-concept will be more likely to take social chances, make new friends, feel psychologically safe in school, work cooperatively, and generally feel good about social abilities (Manning & Allen, 1987). Children's and adolescents' assessment of themselves influences their outward successes and failures as well as their relationships with others (Atwater, 1988). Learners' success in these academic and social areas depends to a large degree on how well learners think they can succeed at these tasks and also their confidence to try new things or to rely on traditional behavior and thought patterns.

An individual's self-concept continually accumulates experiences that "tell" the individual his or her degree of self-worth. The self-concept consists of everyday happenings, good and bad, that the learner experiences. In fact, school and home experiences, both of which should contribute positively to the self-concept, often do just the opposite and damage the self-concept. The implications of self-concept development for at-risk or potential at-risk learners should never be underestimated. Too many negative experiences can destroy learners' beliefs in themselves, which in all too many cases is what happens to at-risk learners: being constantly told at home what one's abilities do not allow, parents discouraging new pursuits to avoid possible failure, and setting unrealistic goals for children and adolescents. The school can be an equal culprit by grouping learners by ability

---

Activity 5-2
Prepare a list of behaviors or signs learners with low self-concepts often demonstrate. Revise this list into a survey or instrument to identify students with low self-concepts. Last, make a list of practices that might improve learners' self-concepts.

---

so all slow learners stay together all day, by providing constant criticism, and by reprimanding students for their lack of academic abilities.

While educators have enormous responsibilities for helping all students to have healthy self-concepts, the challenge of identifying and helping at-risk learners may be even greater. The at-risk learner, whether at risk due to reading abilities or lower socioeconomic status, may become less at risk when educators address the self-concept. Teachers know that children and adolescents feel better about themselves when they do better in school, and vice versa. However, many learners do not receive the positive reinforcement and positive nurturing attention needed to succeed in school and to feel good about themselves (Canfield, 1990).

All efforts and programs designed to help at-risk children and adolescents should include a component designed to improve the self-concept. Although the self-concept is an at-risk condition in and of itself, it also has tremendous potential to influence other at-risk conditions. For example, adolescents may feel more confident or generally better about themselves when using alcohol or drugs; the chronic truant may become a school dropout because when he stays at home, he feels better about himself; or the speech-impaired child may be reluctant to speak because of fear of others laughing. These three representative examples show the necessity of addressing the self-concept, regardless of the at-risk condition. Helping the self-concept might be a major contributing factor to reducing or perhaps even eliminating the at-risk condition.

Exceptionalities

Children and adolescents with exceptionalities have an increased likelihood of being or becoming at risk. The handicapped learner may experience additional social and academic hurdles while the gifted and talented may be at risk of not achieving one's true potential. Sometimes educators have lower expectations for the handicapped and feel gifted and talented learners will "make it on their own." Both these suppositions seriously shortchange exceptional learners. Educators planning and implementing at-risk programs have a responsibility to both handicapped and gifted learners. Doing otherwise places exceptional learners at even greater risk. Categories of exceptionalities include the following:

1. *sensory handicaps,* including hearing and vision impairments
2. *intellectual deviations,* including giftedness as well as mental retardation
3. *communication disorders,* such as speech and language dysfunction
4. *learning disabilities/minimal brain dysfunction* resulting in learning problems without motor involvement
5. *behavior disorders,* including severe emotional disturbances
6. *physical handicaps and health impairments,* including neurological defects, orthopedic conditions, diseases such as muscular dystrophy and sickle cell anemia, birth defects, developmental disabilities, and autism (Haring & McCormick, 1990).

Whereas all exceptional children and adolescents are probably at risk to some degree, a learner's actual propensity toward being at risk, of course, depends on the degree and frequency of the exceptional conditions. For example, speech handicaps vary widely—the stutterer might be fluent in some situations whereas other situations might result in stress and anxiety. At one time, he or she might be at risk and at other times may not. The educators' role is to identify the degree of frequency of the at-risk condition and plan appropriate educational experiences.

Generally speaking, handicapped youngsters are more at risk than the overall population. Educational and societal expectations and practices leading to segregation of handicapped learners from the general population, lower expectations, and nonaccessibility to all programs and efforts have the potential to place handicapped learners at even greater risk. At-risk programs designed to meet individual needs, to address weaknesses, and to build on strengths lessen the handicapped learner's likelihood of becoming more at risk.

One might question how a gifted and talented learner can be at risk. Remembering that a learner can be both gifted and handicapped, at least two reasons provide educators cause for alarm. First, a gifted and talented learner can also be handicapped, which can limit achievement. Also, being handicapped sometimes brings an accompanying emotional handicap that might further hamper achievement. Second, a gifted and talented learner may for one reason or another be at risk due to an inability to work up to achievement possibilities. For example, a girl gifted in science may be at risk when making B's, which for another child might be a sign of extraordinary achievement. All too often, gifted and talented learners become a neglected group because educators think being gifted guarantees achievement. Such thinking constitutes a serious mistake and places gifted learners at risk.

Cultural and Ethnic Differences

At the outset, it is important to make clear that being a culturally diverse child or adolescent does *not* make a learner at risk. In other words, cultural diversity is not an at-risk condition in and of itself. Racism, discrimination, and prejudice contribute to and intensify problems associated with at-risk conditions such as substance abuse, low achievement, teenage pregnancy, and delinquent behavior. Therefore, educators need to recognize the challenges facing culturally diverse learners, yet not allow stereotypical opinions or self-fulfilling prophecies to influence learners and achievement.

Cultural and ethnic differences should be perceived as positive and as enriching to U.S. society. However, in a predominantly middle-class Anglo-American society, cultural and ethnic differences are sometimes viewed as negatives that need to be remediated or eradicated. Such thinking places culturally different children and adolescents at risk because too often edu-

---

Successful Program: Sheltered English

In Sheltered English classrooms, teachers help Limited English Proficient (LEP) and Fluent English Proficient (FEP) students through the difficult task of learning academic content while mastering a second language. LEP students have not attained minimal proficiency in academic and oral language in English, while FEP students have attained proficiency yet continue to need work. In "sheltering" lessons, teachers incorporate second language acquisition principles with traditional teaching methodology to increase the comprehensibility of the lessons. They also adjust the language demands of the lesson by modifying speech rates and tone, by using context clues, and by relating instruction to students' experiences. Likewise, educators avoid idiomatic expressions such as "clear as a bell." Teachers try to bridge the gap between their own language abilities and their students' listening abilities by preteaching two vocabulary sets: 1) the words necessary to understand the content of the lesson and 2) the words used to explain the lesson.

Sheltered English requires extensive efforts to ensure the mastery of new concepts, even when using the same lesson format repeatedly (taking advantage of its familiarity). Extensive efforts are needed to increase student interaction with content by employing small-group cooperative learning and by minimizing lectures (lectures, when used, need to be well organized and to the point), and study skills need to be emphasized. The seven-step plan for Sheltered English includes 1) preplanning the year by developing themes, 2) the diagnosis, 3) setting the stage, 4) preteaching the two vocabulary sets, 5) the instruction, 6) guided practice, and 7) independent Practice (Watson, Northcutt, & Rydell, 1989).

cators often adopt lower expectations, feel bewildered by cultural differences, and perceive these youngsters through middle-class Anglo-American perspectives. Such thinking can indeed place culturally diverse learners in at-risk situations.

Cultural differences might be misunderstood and might ultimately place culturally diverse children and adolescents in jeopardy. The authors encourage readers to remember that any discussion focusing on the characteristics of culturally diverse children and adolescents risks stereotyping and an overdependence on generalizations. The many intracultural, socioeconomic, geographic, generational, and individual differences among cultural groups contribute to their diversity and to the difficulty of describing individuals in the various cultures. Educators and human resource professionals must carefully avoid considering "differences" to be "deficits" or "at-risk indicators."

Native-Americans

- Honor their elders
- Learn through legends
- Share belongings and possessions
- Place emphasis on immediate and extended family
- Convey humble/cooperative attitude
- Are unconcerned with time
- Expect few rules
- Avoid looking speakers in the eye
- Question which culture to identify with (Sanders, 1987).

African-Americans

- Speak a language that is "worthy" at home but "unworthy" at school
- Avoid looking speakers in the eye
- Seek support from larger families and kinship networks
- Seek extended family support in childrearing
- Exhibit cultural pride
- Face overt and implied racism
- Interrupt speaker with encouraging remarks (Axelson, 1985; Boykin, 1982; Hall, 1981; Pinkney, 1975).

Asian-Americans

- Conform to both Asian and Anglo cultures
- Exhibit quiet, reticent, aloof behaviors
- Exhibit dependent, conforming, obedient behaviors
- Place family welfare over individual desires
- Deal with bilingual background

- Show respect and reverence for elders
- Seek extended family support in childrearing
- Control child behavior (misbehavior reflects on the entire family)
- Place family priority over peers (Axelson, 1985; Lum, 1986; Sue & Sue, 1983).

Hispanic-Americans

- Avoid being set apart from group by being different or excelling
- Distrust Anglo-American professionals
- Exhibit strong commitment to Spanish language
- Stand closer, touch, avoid eye contact
- Respect extended family and kinship networks and companion parents
- Consider males to be biologically superior
- Demonstrate commitment to cultural traditions: "personalismo," "dignidad," "machismo," and "respecto" (Christensen, 1989; Fitzpatrick, 1987; Mirandé,1986).

It is important to mention cultural differences because educators sometimes consider learners only from middle-class Anglo-American perspectives and, therefore, misunderstand learner behavior. Cultural differences should not be considered at-risk conditions. One does not have to look far for examples of how cultural differences affect Anglo-American educators' perceptions: the Native-American girl who "borrows" the tape from the teacher's desk because she feels everyone should share; the Asian-American boy who places family welfare over his personal wishes at school; and the Hispanic-American boy who considers males to be biologically superior. Middle-class Anglo-American educators who misunderstand such behaviors and attitudes may actually consider differences to be at-risk conditions or react in such a manner that learners become at-risk students when, in reality, they are not. Perceptive and caring educators recognize that culturally diverse learners can be at risk (just as majority culture learners) and plan an appropriate remediation plan when the need arises.

Successful Program: Newcomer High School

Newcomer High School in San Francisco, California, provides English instruction for students with limited English proficiency in conjunction with bilingual support in content areas. Students may remain at Newcomer High School up to 2 years. After this time, they must transfer to high schools where teachers and other professionals speak only English (Office of Educational Research and Improvement, 1987b).

It is imperative to reiterate that these cultural differences enrich the United States and do not constitute at-risk indicators. On the other hand, educators who misunderstand cultural differences, believe diversity should be eradicated, and believe all learners should act alike and learn like middle-class Anglo-Americans might actually make culturally diverse learners at risk.

Shyness and Withdrawal

Shyness and withdrawal are attempts to avoid participation in one's surroundings. Specific causes may include fearing a particular situation, fearing failure or criticism, lacking self-confidence, or fearing embarrassment or humiliation. At-risk symptoms and conditions often grow worse since educators (and, too often, parents) ignore shy and withdrawn children because they make little trouble compared to the attention-seeking child (Thompson & Rudolph, 1988).

Approximately 40% of all adults report that they suffer from shyness, which probably results from high levels of anxiety and discomfort in social situations. Shyness can also be a particularly painful experience for children and adolescents and can, without doubt, contribute to their propensity toward being at risk. Trying to overcome shyness while simultaneously struggling to achieve autonomy, competence, and a positive self-esteem can often pose considerable hurdles, which can lead to further shame, doubt, guilt, and loss of self-esteem. In fact, shy children tend to have negative self-images and feel less attractive, less intelligent, and less popular than classmates who are not shy (Seifert & Hoffnung, 1991).

Jerome Kagan, in an interview (Brodkin, 1990), maintained that children's shyness can be temperamental or can result from their environment. He suggested that out of about 100 children randomly selected, about 10 to 15 are born with a temperamental bias toward being shy. Other forms of shyness may result from the child's environment such as stressful home situations in which fighting, marital discord, or abuse occurs. Still another form may result from an overprotective home in which parents do not allow children and adolescents sufficient independence (Brodkin, 1990).

Allowing children or adolescents to be shy for long periods of time or to become withdrawn from parents, friends, and society can result in more severe at-risk conditions. Instead of contributing to being at risk, the withdrawal may actually result *from* an at-risk condition. For example, the boy with a stuttering problem may be excessively quiet and avoid social situations, the pregnant 14-year-old may be burdened with worry and fright, and the substance abuser may be "chemically" shy.

What indications or signs, then, should educators and parents look for? First, one must realize that shyness may not pose a problem unless the

---

Activity 5-3

Make a plan to help a shy or withdrawn child. The plan should include the following:

1. A definition of shyness or being withdrawn (i.e., when is a child shy and withdrawn?)
2. A list of characteristics or behaviors that indicate the child is shy and withdrawn
3. A list of steps to make the child feel more secure
4. A list of people (other teachers, counselors, parents, peers, etc.) who can help the child
5. An assessment plan to determine progress and to provide a means of follow-up

---

condition interferes with socialization or prevents children and adolescents from becoming fully functioning learners. With this thought firmly in mind, indications or signs may include avoiding social situations, not wanting to speak in front of a class, overdependence on teachers and parents, an undue lack of self-confidence, choosing to be alone while others work or play in groups, and, generally speaking, withdrawing from others. As previously mentioned, being shy or withdrawn might also result from any of the at-risk conditions discussed in Chapter 2.

Once educators and parents are convinced a child or adolescent suffers from shyness (not developing socially and academically, being lonely, and a negative self-concept), deliberate and specific action needs to be taken. If shyness results from the environment, educators and parents need to work together to change the school and home environments, respectively. Educators can encourage learners to socialize, to speak in front of the class, and to develop confidence. Likewise, parents can bring other children into the home and encourage the child to cope with stressful situations (Santrock, 1990).

Daydreaming and Lack of Interest or Motivation

Daydreaming, another personal at-risk condition, affects many children and adolescents at one time or another. This is not to imply, however, that all daydreaming places learners at risk. Like many other at-risk conditions, daydreaming becomes a problem when it interferes with student performance. Speaking from a positive viewpoint, student daydreaming can solve academic and personal problems, allow themselves to think creatively, and

---

Successful Program: Diversified Educational Experiences Program (DEEP)

DEEP addresses several problems such as the apathetic learner and the poor attender in grades 9 through 12; however, the program has also been used in grades 6 through 8. DEEP's major goal includes developing an instructional process for secondary school classrooms that allows instructors to create an academic environment emphasizing success for all learners while decreasing hostility to educational institutions. DEEP offers students and instructors as method of implementing an academic classroom that differs from the usual model. Students in the DEEP classroom identify needs, formulate objectives, develop tasks based on these objectives, present group and individual projects based on fulfillment of objectives, receive teacher debriefings following presentation of projects, and participate in their own evaluations. DEEP offers learners in academic subjects alternative ways to create, gather, develop, and display information. Making extensive use of electronic and nonelectronic media, the teacher's role assumes the role of adviser, consultant, and learning systems manager. Students work cooperatively to complete tasks, using community resources whenever possible.

Adapted from Sopris West Incorporated. (1992). *Educational programs that work* (p. C-7) Longmont, CO: Author.

allow a time to engage in higher levels of thinking. The educator's challenge lies with determining when daydreaming becomes an at-risk condition.

Educators can also attest to the number of children and adolescents, who for one or more reasons, constantly need to be motivated. Students often seem to have feelings of ennui and appear to be bored, weary of learning, or discontent with their school experiences. As with daydreaming or other symptoms of boredom, being unmotivated or bored for a short period of time might not be a problem or an at-risk condition. Yet a youngster unmotivated for a long length of time might be experiencing or moving toward an at-risk condition.

The keys to helping unmotivated children and adolescents and preventing a lack of motivation from becoming an at-risk condition include deciding with certainty whether the learner really is unmotivated and, if so, learning the reasons for the lack of motivation. Determining a lack of motivation might not be as easy as it sounds. For example, a learner who appears not to care or be motivated might just be presenting a facade. Likewise, motivation can be defined in cultural perspectives—middle-class Anglo-American perceptions of motivation might differ greatly from those of Na-

---

Activity 5-4

Prepare a motivation plan for at-risk learners in a school you have visited. First, make a list of behaviors that indicate a lack of motivation; second, suggest ways to motivate learners. This plan should include a consideration of individual learners' at-risk conditions, and also the learners' cultural, social class, and gender differences.

---

tive-Americans or Hispanic-Americans. On reaching the decision that a student lacks motivation, educators can attempt to identify causes: School assignments might be too easy or too difficult, the student might not be feeling well or might be preoccupied with personal problems, or other at-risk conditions. A pregnant teenager might be genuinely interested in school and recognize its relevance to her future, yet being pregnant and 15 consumes her emotionally and mentally and leaves little energy for school. Likewise, a boy living in abject poverty might be more interested in a bed, a warm room, and his next meal than historical figures. Educators seeking causes for learners' lack of motivation have a headstart on planning and implementing efforts to increase or restore learners' motivation.

Other problems associated with not giving one's fullest attention to classroom activities, such as attention deficit disorder (ADD) and attention deficit hyperactivity disorder (ADHD), affect about 5% of learners today. Educators nationwide are learning more about these disorders and diagnoses (Rodriguez, 1993). To succeed in school, students must be able to maintain thought and concentration on the lesson being taught. Learners with ADD and ADHD are unable to screen out extraneous and irrelevant stimuli that interfere with the learning process. ADD and ADHD can make children and adolescents at risk and can make other conditions more acute.

The American Psychiatric Association has accepted ADD and ADHD as diagnostic categories. Two types of ADD exist: one associated with hyperactivity and one without. The hyperactivity generally refers to an excess of nonpurposeful motor activity, for example, getting out of one's seat, tapping fingers and feet, asking questions incessantly, often repeating the same question, and an inability to sit or stand still (Mercer, 1990). While medication is available for learners diagnosed as having ADD and ADHD, health caretakers appear to be less prone to rely on medication, developing instead appropriate strategies both at home and school (Rodriguez, 1993).

Underachievement

Children and adolescents who "underachieve" may be categorized as slow learners, learning disabled, ADD, or simply underachievers. Too often, these

TABLE 5-1 Types and Characteristics of Learning Problems

Types	Characteristics
Slow learners	Has difficulty with all subjects; cannot master material beyond a certain level; unable to change academic performance; scores between 75 and 90 on standardized tests; tutoring will not significantly affect academic achievement
Learning disabled	Has at least low average intelligence yet not performing at capacity; usually 6 months behind in primary grades and 18 to 24 months behind in upper elementary grades; may exhibit strong abilities in nonacademic areas; tutoring is most effective treatment
Attention deficit disorder	Unable to organize incoming information because of neurological malfunction; inattentive and distractible; does not remain on task due to inability to deal with environmental stimuli or the opposite may hold true; the child may be so intense that changing focus on attention is impossible
Underachievers	Has ability yet inconsistent in achievement; lacks persistence, obedience to time limits, and functional independence; perhaps a fear of the future—by underachieving, adults tighten monitoring effects and make decisions limiting freedom; need counseling to remove obstacles

Adapted from Pecaut, L. S. (1991). Why can't Johnny learn? *Principal, 70*(4), 29–30.

terms are used interchangeably, which has the potential for mislabeling learners and for providing inappropriate school conditions. Table 5-1 provides the characteristics of four types of underachieving learners. Whereas characteristics of underachievers and learners with learning problems can be listed with some certainty, it is important for educators to consider learners as individuals and to avoid the serious consequences that can result from labeling.

1. *Trust seekers:* Early in their lives, the relationship with their parents was disrupted by divorce, abuse, or other causes. As a result, these children become loners and daydreamers, often preferring playmates much older or younger than themselves.

2. *Approval seekers:* These are students who crave acceptance but are constantly criticized at home. They don't study to learn, but to earn the praise of their parents, teachers, and peers. If they are not constantly praised, they stop trying.

3. *Independence seekers:* These kids often do very well in subjects of interest, at the expense of all others. Possessed with a strong independent streak, they are willing to accept failure to show that they don't need or care about their parents.

4. *Dependence seekers:* The hardest type of underachievers to treat, these students feel that the worse they do in school, the more their parents will notice them. Often coddled at home, they become discipline problems who neither respect authority nor fear a future without a high school diploma (Pecaut, 1991).

Some children and adolescents simply do not achieve at their levels of potential regardless of the teacher's expectations or efforts to motivate. Representative reasons for learner underachieving include the following:

1. Teachers fail to recognize potential, multiple talents, or different intellects.
2. Teachers accept mediocrity and below par work rather than expecting learners to achieve at levels of true potential.
3. Students have other interests or are preoccupied with personal problems.
4. School practices and policies stifle creativity or divergent thinking.
5. Teachers place too much emphasis on one aspect, such as verbal learning, and not enough on other aspects, such as science, art, or music.

Any factor or combination of factors can contribute to underachievement. Often, one cannot pinpoint a single source; parents, teachers, and learners may all share the blame. In any event, learners not achieving at their potential represents a serious loss, both for the learner and for the nation as a whole. Losses may result in a loss of self-esteem, lack of success in later educational efforts, and lack of employment opportunities.

Activity 5-5

Why do schools have underachievers, those learners who have the ability to learn and achieve, yet for some reason, do not achieve? Speak with an underachieving child or adolescent to determine causes for underachievement, then prepare a strategy for helping this learner.

Successful Program: Improving Achievement

Dodge Park Elementary School in Prince George's County, Maryland, used high expectations and a stronger core program to raise students' achievement test scores. The school's first step was to admit the school had a problem. Going public with its standardized test scores, the district provided a breakdown showing that some students trailed others by 25 points. Then the district formed a task force of community leaders and educational experts to study the problem and to offer recommendations. The committee's action plan in- cluded higher academic expectations; a curriculum that challenged par- ticipation and performance of low- achieving students; and programs aimed particularly at improving achievement in mathematics and sci- ence. Results have been dramatic: Third graders scored in the 99th per- centile on mathematics on the Cali- fornia Achievement Test; and third graders overall scored at the 94th percentile. In fact, students in the program outscored others, regard- less of cultural backgrounds (Mur- phy, 1988).

Peer Pressure

Peers represent a powerful and often underestimated source of influence on the social, academic, and overall development and actual behavior and attitudes of children and adolescents. Children and adolescents engaging in at-risk behaviors such as smoking, alcohol abuse, and sexual activity pro- vide clear evidence of how peers can influence another's attitudes and behaviors. In fact, the peer group during early adolescence and adolescence often becomes the primary reference for behavior, values, and decision making. The author visited a sixth-grade class in which 22 of 24 students wore blue-and-white cloth shoes. While wearing similar shoes did not place the students at risk, it did show the desire to dress like other students. Students in the class perhaps did not blatantly pressure one another to wear the same kind of shoes, but it still shows that peer pressure, however subtle, affects students and how they act and dress.

Remember, though, that all peer pressure is not negative; perceptive educators readily recognize that peer pressure can be used to influence positive behavior. For example, peer pressure can be used to encourage academic achievement or to discourage drinking and driving. Also, children and adolescents with positive outlooks and attitudes toward school, home, parents, and peers are more likely to respond positively to peer pressure (Manning & Allen, 1987). The educator's task will be to decide how most effectively to lessen the influence of negative peer pressure, such as missing

---

Activity 5-6

Visit a school to observe middle or secondary school learners. What indications of peer pressure, both subtle and blatant, do you see? Look for examples of positive peer pressure and suggest several ways educators can take advantage of positive peer pressure.

---

school to engage in additional at-risk behaviors, and also how to most effectively use peer pressure to encourage desirable behaviors, such as working cooperatively toward a group goal.

A challenge for educators of at-risk students to address is how to lessen the effects of negative peer pressure on students who are either at risk or potentially at risk. A 12-year-old girl once stated that all students are at risk of giving in to peer pressure. A confident and successful student who feels good about the "self," the school, and the home might be less likely to succumb to peer pressure; however, the at-risk student, who may already feel unsuccessful and unconfident, might be even more at risk of giving in to peers in an attempt to feel accepted or a part of the group.

Conflicts with Self

While "conflicts with self" theoretically can include any of the personal at-risk conditions examined in this chapter, the problem of children and adolescents having conflicts with themselves continues to be sufficiently serious to warrant an examination of the topic. Rather than looking again at conflicts such as suicidal behaviors, truancy, and self-concept, this section focuses on other conflicts such as cheating, carelessness with work and property, excessive tension and anxiety, and perfectionist behavior. It is again important to note that not all seemingly at-risk indications actually make a learner at risk. For example, being a perfectionist might lead one learner to high levels of achievement while destroying another learner's self-perception. Learners need to be considered individually to determine whether "indications" or "signs" actually make the learner at risk.

The American school system, with its emphasis on competition rather than cooperation among learners and its encouragement of high grades, often leads to cheating, another at-risk behavior. Whether learners cheat to improve their grades, impress their friends, or because of undue parental pressure, the result continues to be the same: It is a form of dishonesty and places learners in jeopardy with themselves as well as their parents and teachers. Perceptive educators, rather than only administering harsh punishment, will seek to determine the cause of the cheating. Was the work too hard? Had the learner failed to study? Was the learner succumbing to peer pressure? Such questions and a teacher's understanding of individual situations allow a better understanding of both the reason for cheating and an appropriate remediation plan.

Carelessness in work and property represents another conflict that characterizes many children and adolescents. Both teachers and parents often speak of children and adolescents "forgetting" to complete homework assignments or losing jackets or notebooks. Two problems surface: First, poor grades and lower academic achievement result from incomplete schoolwork and, two, significant adults have to think of consequences or, preferably, methods of teaching young people to be more responsible. In deciding appropriate tactics, lecturing, scolding, preaching, or nagging seldom work (Thompson & Rudolph, 1988). As with teaching other desired behaviors, the learner's individuality must be taken into consideration. Teaching individual responsibility for work, property, and actions should be a major facet of all at-risk programs.

Many learners experience excessive tension and anxiety, a third conflict with self. While a little tension and anxiety may keep a learner's attention and may actually motivate learners, too much tension and anxiety may result in an array of problems: continued restlessness and movement, nail-biting, tics, frequent blinking, rapid breathing, repeated throat clearing, and similar somatic complaints (Thompson & Rudolph, 1988). Teachers, knowingly or unknowingly, control the amount of tension and anxiety in their rooms. Behavior expectations, academic standards, verbal and nonverbal responses, physical mannerisms, and frequency and type of questions all contribute to learners' anxiety levels. Another significant factor, the actual classroom environment, deserves consideration: Is the atmosphere one of fear and pressure? Do learners feel accepted and generally liked? Are students shown the respect that all human beings deserve? Many other questions could be asked to determine the classroom atmosphere; however, teachers realizing the impact and effects of their actions on at-risk learners and how they actually contribute to learners' propensity toward being at risk warrants a clear understanding.

The fourth conflict with self, perfectionist behavior, may be thought by some educators and parents to be a major strength, but the perfectionist behavior of children and adolescents can lead to problems as serious as other at-risk conditions. Being an overachiever in U.S. society is generally looked on favorably, but the price of such behavior and achievement (whether in academics, music, or some other area) often exacts a high price. The straight A student who wanted a 100 average rather than a 96 may turn to drugs and alcohol for relief from anxiety or, on perceiving "self" as a failure, may commit suicide. Teachers and parents need to monitor students' study habits and academic achievement to determine that realistic goals and priorities have been established. Setting high goals can have dual effects: First, the student might excel beyond expectations and, second, the student may constantly feel failure, tension, and frustration. Perceptive teachers need to know individual abilities and goals as well as work with parents to accept children's strengths and weaknesses. All children and adolescents need to be motivated to achieve at their maximum abilities, yet not at the expense of positive mental health and at the risk of becoming an at-risk casualty.

Case Study 5-2: The Effects of a Low Self-Concept

Melvin, a 14-year-old boy, had several at-risk conditions: He was extremely skinny, had a speech problem, wore glasses, and was on the receiving end of many cruel jokes. Often burying himself in science fiction books, he avoided many social situations in which he would be laughed at or ridiculed. Physical education classes were nightmares, especially since he was not as strong and coordinated as the other boys. To make matters worse, he could not swim (which he had to admit in front of his entire physical education class). By the end of the ninth grade, Melvin's self-concept was virtually destroyed. His PE coach and his personal typing teacher were among the first to recognize Melvin's problems, his negative self-concept, and their effects on his academic and social progress.

The two concerned teachers worked with the speech therapist and the guidance counselor to work out a plan to help Melvin. While little could be done about his size, other problems could be addressed. The PE coach encouraged him, praised his efforts, and gave him several pointers in basketball. The communications disorder specialist worked on the worst articulation problems and the counselor met with him once a week to discuss his strengths. Also, the assistant principal, who previously had not known of Melvin, volunteered to tutor him in mathematics for 20 to 30 minutes after school each afternoon. The results of their efforts could not be determined overnight; however, a planned and deliberate attempt had been made. Rather than ignoring Melvin's problems, the school had made a commitment to help an at-risk learner.

Other Conditions Contributing to Personal At-Risk Conditions

Other conditions are of a more intangible nature and often cannot been determined as readily as more obvious characteristics. Educators have a twofold task. First, one cannot assume that students do not have at-risk conditions just because pregnancy or substance abuse is not evident. Second, in determining the more intangible conditions, educators cannot fall into the trap of making erroneous assumptions. For example, assuming a learner is unmotivated or uninterested might ignore gender and cultural perceptions of motivation.

A lack of long-term commitment, an at-risk condition that plagues substantial numbers of children and adolescents, may have several causes. First, learners might be in a developmental stage that allows only daydreaming and short-term thinking—a learner might not be able to understand the reason for learning ninth-grade mathematics needed for later work at the university when he or she cannot think a decade into the future. Second, learners living in homeless situations or only existing day to day in poverty, might, realistically speaking, be more concerned with more immediate concerns such as how to stay warm or from where the next meal will come. Educators might experience difficulty convincing the poverty-stricken urban dwelling boy that studying diligently will have long-term rewards when he sees his unemployed father, and also drug dealers driving new sports cars. Third, inattentiveness, daydreaming, and a lack of motivation might result from a poor attitude toward school, teachers, and learning. As mentioned previously, though, caution should be used in determining motivation because definitions and evidences of motivation differ among sexes, cultural groups and social classes.

Another at-risk condition, families and parents not supporting individual and school efforts, poses a significant problem for both students and educators. While most parents want the best possible advantages for their children and adolescents, it appears that other parents either do not share the concern, do not understand the school's efforts, or do not know appropriate action. It is possible that parents living in dire financial circumstances might have more pressing concerns than their children's educational experiences and achievements.

Some children from single-parent homes might be at risk but reaching such a decision must have clear and specific evidence because one cannot conclude that children from single-parent homes are categorically at risk. In some cases, however, children might be at risk when the single parent has to hold two jobs and struggle to make financial ends meet. Such a lifestyle might leave little emotional and physical energy for childrearing. Still, one cannot assume children are at risk simply on the basis of how many significant adults live or do not live in a household.

The School's Role in Addressing Personal Problems

"The problems belong to the learner, and schools cannot be expected to address all the learner's problems," one might say. One could probably offer a logical defense for such a proposal. However, such thinking fails to recognize the problems at-risk students experience. Educators wanting to nurture, guide, and direct learners' growth have a professional responsibility to provide special assistance to at-risk learners whenever possible.

The first step of educators is to determine if and how schools contribute to children's and adolescents' personal at-risk conditions. A close examination of practices and policies may reveal that schools contribute to or aggravate situations to the point at which students become at risk. Some practices, blatant and easy to recognize, include corporal punishment, placing too much stress and pressure on students to achieve, verbal and physical abuse, adherence to an overly regimented school day, and an overreliance on standardized testing. Other problems might be of a more subtle nature such as nonverbal communication conveying negative feelings, segregation of learners according to ability, and, in some cases, racism and sexism. It is important to note that the conditions that affect at-risk learners may not affect other learners. Therefore, rather than taking a wholesale look at learners and conditions, school policies and practices need to be examined to determine their effects on individual at-risk learners.

Once educators accept the fact that schools can and often do contribute to students' at-risk conditions, the challenge lies in deciding appropriate action to determine specific problems and their extent. Such a determination includes considering school policies and practices, academic objectives, opportunities for socialization, behavior rules and expectations, and grading procedures. Educators may decide to devise a checklist to address the needs of the local school. The tasks of determining how schools contribute to at-risk learners' problems and of determining appropriate action should not be the sole responsibility of the teacher. A team consisting of administrators, teachers, school psychologists, counselors, other special service personnel, parents, and students should work in a coordinated fashion to reach this goal. The various perspectives of educators, parents, and students contribute to determining areas needing to be addressed and also allow for consideration of gender, cultural, and social class perspectives.

A major aspect of the plan will be to evaluate the school's efforts to determine progress as well as areas still needing to be addressed. Evaluation should be as objective as possible and should be a team approach so various perspectives will be considered. In all likelihood, the school's role in addressing personal at-risk conditions will be beneficial in and of itself as educators continue to maintain a deliberate focus on helping at-risk learners and will ensure continued involvement of parents and families in school programs.

Reviewing What You Have Read About Personal Characteristics

1. One study revealed that _____ , a contributing factor to suicides, differ among boys and girls, that is, females expressed significantly more difficulty dealing with this at-risk condition than males.

2. _____ may also play a factor in the decision to commit suicide. The closer the relation to someone who has committed suicide, the more likely an individual will commit suicide.

3. _____ , another at-risk condition, are responsible for more deaths to U.S. adolescents than any other cause, representing more than half of all deaths to persons aged 10 to 19.

4. _____ clarified the relationship between self-concept and social and academic achievement in *Self-Concept and School Achievement* (1970) and also showed educators how to invite students to have a better self-concept in *Inviting School Success* (1984).

5. All efforts and programs designed to help at-risk children and adolescents should include a component designed to improve the _____ .

6. A student's _____ can have a significant effect on perceptions of motivation, long-term commitment, and learning styles.

7. _____ are attempts to avoid participation in one's surroundings. Specific causes may include fearing a particular situation, fearing failure or criticism, lacking self-confidence, or fearing embarrassment or humiliation.

8. _____ include at-risk conditions such as excessive tension and anxiety and carelessness.

9. Some children from _____ might be at risk but reaching such a decision must have clear and specific evidence because one cannot conclude that children from these situations are categorically at risk.

10. Another conflict with self, _____ , may be thought by some educators and parents to be a major strength, but such behavior can lead to serious problems.

11. The American school system, with its emphasis on _____ rather than cooperation among learners and its encouragement of high grades, often leads to cheating, another at-risk behavior.

12. _____ represent a powerful and often underestimated source of influence on the social, academic, and overall development and actual behavior and attitudes of children and adolescents.

Answer Key: 1. stress; **2.** Genetics; **3.** Accidental deaths; **4.** William Purkey; **5.** self-concept; **6.** culture; **7.** Shyness and withdrawal; **8.** Conflicts with self; **9.** single-parent homes; **10.** perfectionist behavior; **11.** competition; **12.** Peers.

Summary

Students' personal characteristics, such as self-destructive behaviors, conflicts with self, exceptionality, cultural differences, and shyness and withdrawal, can contribute significantly to students' propensity toward being at risk. As with other at-risk factors, schools have a responsibility to address these characteristics or conditions whenever possible. At-risk learners are best served when educators work with other professionals and parents rather than addressing problems alone. Such teamwork requires specific identification procedures and carefully planned programs to address individual personal needs, and a genuine commitment to help at-risk learners, regardless of the at-risk condition.

For Additional Information on Personal Characteristics

Adcock, A. G., Nagy, S., & Simpson, J. A. (1991). Selected risk factors in adolescent suicide attempts. *Adolescence, 26,* 817–828. These authors studied depression, attempted suicide, and knowledge of common signs of potential suicide in adolescents. Their study also focused on gender and cultural factors that will be helpful to educators identifying potential at-risk learners.

Alderman, M. K. (1990). Motivation for at-risk students. *Educational Leadership, 48*(1), 27–30. Alderman feels educators should help students take responsibility for their learning and suggests a model for motivating at-risk students.

Alliance for Invitational Education, Room 216, Curry Building, University of North Carolina, Greensboro, North Carolina, 27412. This organization focuses on self-esteem and inviting children and adolescents to feel good about themselves and succeed in school. Also, the group publishes a newsletter and sponsors regional and national conferences.

American Anorexia/Bulimia Association (AA/BA), 418 E. 76 Street, New York, New York, 10021. The AA/BA acts as an information and referral group, offers counseling and organizes self-help groups, maintains a speaker's bureau and small library service, and collects research information.

Canfield, J. (1990). Improving students' self-esteem. *Educational Leadership, 48*(1), 48–50. Canfield proposes a ten-step method to strengthen students' self-esteem and increase their chances in life.

Center for Self-Esteem, P.O. Box 1532, Santa Cruz, California, 95060. This center works to improve self-esteem by sponsoring an annual conference, publishing a newsletter, and distributing various curriculum materials.

Colten, M. E., & Gore, S. (Eds.). (1991). *Adolescent stress: Causes and consequences.* New York: Aldine De Gruyter. These two editors have compiled an excellent text, which, as the title implies, focuses on adolescents and stress. Topics examined include anger, worry, and hurt; conflict and adaptation; psychosocial stress; coping strategies; minority youth; and substance abuse and teenage pregnancy.

International Association of Eating Disorders Professionals, 123 N.W. 13th Street, #206, Boca Raton, Florida, 33432. The IAEDP, consisting of eating disorders counselors and therapists, establishes and develops curricula and provides a public education and information assistance.

McCarty, R. J. (1993). Adolescent suicide: A ministerial response. *Momentum, 24*(2), 61–65. McCarty looks at the facts of suicide, appropriate responses, the suicidal person, and distress signals.

McGeady, M. R. (1993). The runaways. *Momentum, 24*(2), 33–35. McGeady examines the reasons for youth running away from home and tells how schools can help.

NASSP Bulletin. The November 1991 issue of the *NASSP Bulletin* focuses on programming for at-risk students and provides a discussion on prevention, dropout programs, dispute management, career information, and helping students changing schools.

National Committee on Youth Suicide Prevention, 65 Essex Road, Chestnut Hill, Massachusetts, 02167. The NCYCP is a volunteer network of concerned parents, professionals, and government officials. It works to increase public awareness of youth suicide.

Noddings, N. (1991/1992). The gender issue. *Educational Leadership, 49*(4), 65–70. Proposing that the male standard serves as a basis for public and educational policy, Noddings suggests the culture of schools should change to reflect both men's and women's perspectives.

THRIVE, Dept. P., 900 N. Klein, Oklahoma City, Oklahoma, 73106. The THRIVE (Truancy Habits Reduced, Increasing Valuable Education) Center consists of a team of school officials, police, social workers, and representatives from the district attorney's office. This team talks with students to assess their problems before they get into more trouble.

Wright, W. J. (1991/1992). The endangered black male child. *Educational Leadership, 49*(4), 14–16. Wright proposes that a better understanding of the African-American male child is needed and suggests a program designed to help this child from the earliest possible level in school.

Youth Suicide National Center (YSNC), 445 Virginia Avenue, San Mateo, California, 94402. The YSNC develops and disseminates educational materials, provides educational programs and services, reviews current youth suicide prevention programs, and establishes model programs.

Part III

The School's Response

6

Classroom Curriculum, Organization, and Management

Outline

Overview

Probing Directions

A Total School Response

The Question of Responsibility

Curricular Efforts
    Provide Appropriate Curricular Experiences for Individual At-Risk Learners
    Provide Developmentally Appropriate Curricular Experiences
    Provide Relevant Curricular Experiences
    Provide a Student-Centered Curriculum
    Provide Nurturing Experiences for All Learners
    Provide Instruction in the Literacies Needed in U.S. Society
    Provide for Cultural Differences and Exceptionalities

Organizational Efforts
    Provide for All Learners
    Provide Continuous Progress Learning and Individualization
    Provide Appropriate Grouping Strategies

Overview

Long-accepted goals of elementary and secondary schools have been to provide curriculum, organizational, and management practices that address student needs, convey cultural heritages, address academic and social domains, and generally help children and adolescents grow up to be productive citizens. These lofty goals, however, have not always been translated into practice. In fact, schools often, perhaps unconsciously, do just the opposite—children and adolescents are bored or frustrated rather than challenged, fail to see the relevance of schooling to their individual lives, taught competition rather than cooperation for living in a democratic society, and often "weeded-out" rather than nurtured. This chapter examines curricular, organizational, and management practices that help at-risk learners, promote their overall well-being, increase their chances of school success, and reduce the severity of at-risk conditions affecting learners.

Probing Directions

This chapter on curriculum, organizational, and management practices does the following:

1. Shows how carefully planned and well-meaning curriculum, organizational, and management practices may actually make students at risk or contribute to their propensity for being at-risk.

2. Clarifies the school's response—the provision of curriculum, organizational, and management practices designed to reduce at-risk conditions.
3. Suggests curricular efforts that meet and address the individual at-risk conditions of children and adolescents.
4. Examines organizational strategies that promote academic achievement and overall student development.
5. Examines classroom management practices that reflect an understanding of the special needs (such as gender, culture, and social class) of at-risk children and adolescents.
6. Suggests additional sources of information for educators planning responsive curriculum, organization, and management practices designed to reduce at-risk conditions.

A Total School Response

It is essential at the outset to emphasize the importance of taking a total school approach when looking for conditions that might cause or increase at-risk conditions. Examining only one area of the classroom or school, such as organization, to determine the school's effects on at-risk learners will not suffice. Perceptive educators realize the necessity of seeing the "whole picture" rather than the effects of various parts. Curriculum influences organization and management and vice versa, and the complex interaction of the three areas creates even more powerful effects. For example, to determine the school's effects on at-risk learners, one usually cannot look at one aspect and immediately ascertain that the source of the at-risk problem has been pinpointed. Schools are complex enterprises—courses taught, experiences provided, teaching strategies employed, grouping arrangements, and behavior management methods function together to create a situation that either nurtures or limits children's and adolescents' academic and social achievements as well as their overall well-being.

Activity 6-1
Examine the philosophy statements of several schools. What evidence indicates that each school offers a total school response to at-risk learners' needs? For example, does the philosophy statement show the importance of the learner, coordinated efforts of all school personnel, and providing for physical and psychological needs as well as academic achievement? In other words, does the school provide a "total response" or merely haphazard and fragmented efforts?

The Question of Responsibility

Probably even the most caring and concerned educator has wondered "Where does my responsibility end?" Such a question is legitimate and eventually may even contribute to the curricular, organizational, and management experiences at-risk students receive. The genuine acceptance of responsibility calls for educators to consider the responsibilities of the profession and to consider how school curriculum, organization, and management can address at-risk learners' conditions.

One argument holds that educators are responsible for all learners, regardless of their at-risk condition. Learners have a right to a free and public education; therefore, educators are responsible for whomever comes to school. The slow learner, the drug addicted, the violent prone, and the potential dropout are the responsibility of the school and its educators. "When one chooses the education profession, she or he cannot select whom to teach," one might say. Another argument suggests that educators are not responsible for at-risk learners. Educators, except for those trained in special education or exceptional children, receive training to work with so-called "normal" learners. These educators are not prepared to deal with at-risk learners, except perhaps for slow learners. Likewise, "teachers should not have to put up with violent students or those on alcohol or drugs," one might argue. The argument continues that at-risk learners should be helped by special educators, by alternative schools, or by social service agencies.

The authors believe educators *are* responsible for all types of at-risk children and adolescents. Educators do not have the right to "pick and choose" whom they want to teach—all learners deserve effective curricular, organizational, and management experiences. However, realistically speaking, all educators are not trained to work with at-risk learners, especially those with specialized conditions.

What, then, is the answer? Providing at-risk learners with appropriate school curricular, organizational, and management experiences should be a coordinated team effort of the at-risk learner, teachers, social services agencies, and parents. Each person or agency should be assigned a clearly defined role and held accountable for its fulfillment. A framework might include the following:

At-Risk Learner

- Accept responsibility for behavior.
- Cooperate with professionals and parents.
- Attend school and participate in at-risk programs.

Educators

- Provide or arrange for appropriate diagnostic testing to determine specific at-risk condition.

- Work with social service agencies to obtain specialized help.
- Work with parents and families to learn more about learners and to suggest appropriate follow-up at home.
- Coordinate efforts between learners, social service agencies, and parents.

Social Service Agencies

- Provide specialized assistance educators cannot provide.
- Ensure that all legal and ethical guidelines are met.
- Suggest when at-risk conditions warrant involvement of law enforcement personnel.

Parents and Families

- Ensure children and adolescents cooperate with school officials and social service agencies.
- Reinforce schools' and social service agencies' efforts at home and in the community.
- Instill in children and adolescents that parents and families are interested and supportive of the schools' and social service agencies' efforts.

Undoubtedly, such a coordinated effort would be more productive than educators working alone.

Case Study 6-1 looks at two teachers debating who is responsible for at-risk learners.

Case Study 6-1: Two Teachers Debate Responsibility for At-Risk Students

Many teachers, at one time or another, have questioned whether they were trained and employed to provide curricular, organizational, and management experiences for at-risk students. Consider the following comments heard one day:

- "We're spinning our wheels—seems like our work and efforts are all for nothing!"
- "Why do we even have these at-risk students? They should be in an alternative school–that's where they belong."
- "Every year the school expects more and more—now we have to work with those pot-smoking, sexually promiscuous girls—what are we to do?"

Ms. Tyler, a first-year teacher in the school, listened intently but did not engage in the conversation. She could not understand the teachers' reasoning. How could they be so uncaring, so cruel, and so callous?

Several weeks passed and Ms. Tyler listed (for herself, at least) the following reasons why educators should accept responsibility and have more positive attitudes toward at-risk students:

1. Educators have a professional and ethical responsibility to address the needs of all students including at-risk learners, whenever possible, regardless of at-risk conditions.
2. Educators need to perceive at-risk learners in a more realistic light; for example, all at-risk learners are not pot-smoking and sexually promiscuous.
3. Educators cannot negate their responsibility for addressing the needs of at-risk learners; however, assistance can be gained from other valuable resources, for example, parents and families, social service agencies, and other professionals in the school.

Armed with this ammunition, Ms. Tyler planned a verbal attack on the teachers she had overheard. She then decided, however, that such a confrontation would probably serve little worthwhile purpose, but that setting an example might have far more significant effects. She outlined her plan to show responsibility and respect for all students and to address the needs of at-risk learners in an objective and conscientious manner. Her plan included modeling professional behavior at all times; showing genuine respect for all at-risk learners; considering learners as individuals without forming or conveying moral judgments; providing appropriate educational experiences for each respective at-risk condition; working closely with parents and families; involving other school professionals and social service agencies whenever possible; using all available resources in the planning and development of programs; and encouraging, perhaps subtly at first, other teachers to adopt more positive perspectives toward at-risk learners.

Curricular Efforts

Curricular efforts that are responsive to the needs of at-risk children and adolescents reflect the reality that these learners have special needs, aptitudes, and interests. Rather than expecting all learners to fit uniformly into a given curricular mold, responsive curricular experiences recognize strengths and weaknesses, provide meaningful curricular experiences, and prepare students for the challenges of living successfully in a democratic society. This section suggests curricular efforts that contribute to the academic and social success of at-risk learners.

Provide Appropriate Curricular Experiences for Individual At-Risk Learners

The individuality of at-risk learners deserves to be recognized in at least three ways. First, while at-risk learners share many similarities (such as the need for academic and social success, companionships, and positive self-concepts with so-called "normal" learners), it is imperative that educators consider them as needing special curricular experiences. Second, all at-risk learners cannot be "grouped" into one category. Some learners might be at risk of academic failure or social maladjustment; other learners may be at risk due to drug use or sexual experimentation. Third, some children and adolescents are at risk in more than one area. For example, an adolescent's drug use might contribute to sexual activity or academic failure.

Two prerequisites surface when determining appropriate educational experiences for individual at-risk learners. First, educators must be *sure* learners really are at risk. Accurate diagnosis is an absolute essential when planning educational experiences that might determine or greatly influence a learner's future. Second, as previously mentioned, individual learners need curricular experiences that address specific at-risk conditions. For example, a potential school dropout unquestionably needs a specially designed program. Similarly, a bright yet unmotivated 14-year-old girl who risks failure of not reaching her academic potential also deserves an individual program.

Successful Program: Southridge Middle School

Southridge Middle School in Fontana, California, houses sixth, seventh, and eighth grades. Many students are at risk due to their economically disadvantaged status. Southridge addresses students' needs in several ways: (1) a structural design that appeals to students more than the designs of traditional schools; (2) a least restrictive environment providing personalized support for positive decision-making, helping students develop organizational skills, and making special attempts to work with parents; (3) working with students on a one-to-one basis as much as possible; (4) teaching students to deal with educational challenges such as having difficulty taking notes when a teacher speaks too fast; and (5) attempting to eliminate student isolation and labeling of students (Mason, 1993).

Provide Developmentally Appropriate Curricular Experiences

Researchers and writers have suggested for several decades that the school curriculum, instructional practices, and the overall teaching-learning environment should reflect learners' developmental levels. While developmental psychologists have offered insightful theories regarding physical, psychosocial, and intellectual development, the process of translating theories into practice has been somewhat slow, especially beyond the elementary school years (Manning, 1993c). Recognition of development as a basis for curricular experiences and the current emphasis on improving educational experiences for at-risk learners provide evidence that at-risk programs should address physical, psychosocial, and cognitive development.

Selected practices that reflect physical development include implementing activities; deemphasizing skills stressing size, strength, and stamina; avoiding activities involving early and late maturers; emphasizing intramural athletic programs where all students participate; and addressing health and developmental concerns such as puberty, AIDS, and health issues. Selected practices that reflect psychosocial development include providing academic and social clubs; promoting friendships and social interaction involving all students rather than encouraging boy-girl pairings; and providing organizational strategies that allow a sense of belonging such as cooperative learning, cross-cultural grouping, and teacher-student teams. Selected practices that reflect cognitive development include consideration of cognitive readiness levels, left brain/right brain learning, active learning, equal access to curricular programs, flexible scheduling, exploratory programs, and peer-based teaching.

Provide Relevant Curricular Experiences

For curricular experiences to be relevant, the content conveyed and overall curricular experiences must be meaningful to the student. In other words, the student must see how teaching-learning experiences relate to life. At-risk students often see little relevance of curricular experiences to their everyday life and needs and find little or no meaning in current educational institutions or practices (Diem, 1992). Studying American history, working mathematic equations, and learning chemical formulas represent respectable school tasks; however, learners plagued with reading difficulties, truancy problems, alcohol abuse, and other such conditions will hardly find these school tasks relevant to their everyday needs. For example, a student concerned about being pregnant will probably not see the usefulness of photosynthesis or understand the importance of events leading to World War II.

> **Activity 6-2**
> Name at least three curricular topics or school practices that have little or
> no relevance for at-risk learners. Why do schools continue to teach topics
> and engage in practices that learners do not need?

This student might see more usefulness in classes preparing her for the
realities of childbearing. In any event, children and adolescents need to view
schooling as a meaningful and useful activity rather than as an ordeal to
undergo. Such a statement especially holds true for at-risk learners who
might have never felt successful in school or who might feel schooling
serves little useful purpose. Relevance can be a hotly debated topic—content
relevant to one student might not be to another, whereas still other students,
conscientious and motivated, consider all learning relevant. Also, since one
does not know what life will bring or demand, how can one determine the
relevance of educational experiences? Although these are no doubt valid
arguments for all students, at-risk students may especially experience difficulty relating to the school curriculum and overall school experiences. Table
6-1 looks at ways educators can provide relevant curricular content and
experiences.

Provide a Student-Centered Curriculum

The national outcry during the last decade or so has resulted in an emphasis
on and, in some cases, an obsession with academic achievement, the accumulation of knowledge, high test scores, and generally speaking has placed
a high priority on the cognitive aspects of learning. While this emphasis on
academic achievement has attracted considerable attention, it has not gone
without its side effects. In some cases, teachers teach to the test without
regard for creativity and incidental learning; students experience stress-re-
lated ailments; learners fail to see the relevance of school work; and educators often ignore students' needs and interests. Such conditions without
doubt have the potential for placing students at risk or aggravating already
existing at-risk conditions.

Providing a student-centered curriculum that focuses on students'
needs, interests, and developmental levels can reduce many at-risk conditions and can help educators realize that while academic achievement deserves emphasis, the "student" cannot be lost in the teaching-learning
process, especially with at-risk learners. Providing a student-centered curriculum takes thought and commitment to understand individual students,
the teaching-learning process, and what policies and practices promote or

TABLE 6-1   Providing Relevant Curricular Content and Related Efforts

At-Risk Condition	Curricula Content	Related Efforts and Strategies
Truancy/potential school dropout	• Provide student with *reasons* for attending school, i.e., programs designed to meet individual needs and interests	• Seek causes of the problem and offer possible solutions • Follow-up daily by school officials
Teenage pregnancy	• Provide developmentally appropriate sex education (and if allowable, factual information on AIDS and birth control) • Provide instruction in family life matters, i.e., child rearing, health care, and budgeting	• Contact professionals, i.e., school nurse, counselor, and social workers
Drug use (including alcohol and tobacco)	• Provide factual information on drugs and their effects	• Contact professionals, i.e., school nurse, counselor, and social workers • Contact law enforcement agencies for help • Work with parents and families to show a team approach
Juvenile delinquency and criminal behaviors	• Provide factual information on delinquency, criminal behaviors, and their consequences	• Contact proper drug enforcement officials • Provide appropriate counseling services • Ensure the safety of potential victims, both at school and traveling to school
Exceptionalities	• Provide educational experiences that meet exceptional learner's needs	• Seek assistance from experts qualified in the area of exceptionality • Meet all legal aspects of PL 94-142 • Integrate learner into the ongoing activities of the class • Perceive exceptional learners as more alike than different
Health problems	• Provide factual and objective information on health care, fitness, and wellness	• Contact appropriate medical or social service agencies • Keep in school—avoid truancy and dropping out
Potential suicides	• Provide content showing means of handling stress and alternatives to suicides	• Contact suicide referral agencies and specialists • Provide opportunities for social interaction • Seek to learn (and reduce) the reason for suicidal behaviors

reflect student centeredness. Several basics or guidelines for providing a student-centered curriculum include the following:

- A concern with or "centering" on individual student's needs and interests
- An emphasis on the growth of the whole learner—a concern with physical, psychosocial, and cognitive development rather than only subject area domains
- An emphasis on intrinsic motivation so learners can build on previous experiences that interested them
- An opportunity for students to provide input and opinions into content to be studied and methods to be employed
- Cooperative opportunities for parents, teachers, administrators, and special service personnel to work together as a team to determine the best or most effective educational plan for learners
- An emphasis on building habits and skills that actually serve as a part of a greater educational experience
- An emphasis on education as a continuous growth process, without a so-called "ending" point.

Table 6-2 provides a description, examples, and implications of several student-centered curricula.

Provide Nurturing Experiences for All Learners

It is imperative for schools to perceive all learners as having the potential to learn and experience academic achievement to some respectable degree and, then, accept responsibility for helping or nurturing all learners to perform at their best. Looking at school districts' goals and objectives and reading individual school's philosophy statements provide sufficient cause to believe that educators are meeting the needs and interests of all learners. However, educational appearances are often deceiving. In reality, learners are tested, sorted, grouped, helped, nurtured, ignored, and forgotten—depending on abilities, motivation, social class, and all too often the apparent wealth, power, and status of the learner's parents. In fact, at-risk learners often experience a situation of multiple jeopardy: Teachers have low

---

Activity 6-3

Observe in several elementary, middle level, and secondary schools to determine *actual* student-centered educational practices, especially for at-risk learners. Divide an observation sheet into three categories—one for each organization—and list behaviors in the appropriate category. Then offer several other suggestions that would help schools to be more student centered.

TABLE 6-2   Variations of Student-Centered Curricula

Type*	Description*	Examples*	Selected Implications
Activity-centered curriculum	A preplanned curriculum is impossible and cannot relate to the problems of real life. Need purposeful activities tied to learners' needs and interests.	Story projects Field trips Interest centers Dramatizations Group work	Pregnant teenagers learning childcare and family life Tobacco-using learners seeing the consequences of tobacco use Low achievers receiving proper diagnostic testing and remediation Learning of trades and skills
Relevant curriculum	Reflects social change Learners must be motivated and interested in learning tasks that are built on real-life experiences	Individual work Independent inquiry Special topics: Environment Drugs Urban problems	Learners work independently on relevant topics such as automobile mechanics, heating and air conditioning, or building construction Provision of educational experiences useful and practical to everyday life
Hidden curriculum	The informal, covert, obscure dynamics of classrooms and schools that affect learning and achievement	Sexism Racism Student-teacher interactions Teacher expectations Rituals, roles, regularities	Work to reduce prejudices and stereotypical opinions of at-risk learners, especially those who are culturally diverse Work to reduce classism, sexism, and racism Work toward high academic and social expectations for *all* students
Humanistic curriculum	Reaction to the overemphasis on cognitive learning in the late 1950s and early 1960s Advocated personal insights and growth; self-concept crucial to learning and development	Independent study Peer tutoring Community and work experiences Activities promoting meaningful relationships among teachers and students	Students with similar at-risk problems working together Work on self-concept Relate educational experiences to real-life work and community experiences Educators show students care and concern Show concern for *all* students, including at-risk learners
Values-centered curriculum	Stresses values related to personal growth Major focus on the affective domain Should work to help persons become positive and purposeful	Projects to clarify values and feelings Activities to show how values and behavior depend on many factors	Help students clarify feelings toward sexual experimentation, drug use, and criminal beh⌐ ⌐ors Show learners actions have consequences and affect others Provide educational opportunities for positive decision-making and making wise and mature choices

*Adapted from Ornstein and Levine (1989).

Successful Program: MOP—"Meaningful Other Person"

McDonald and Wright (1987) explained their MOP program, which has reduced dropout rates by 50%. Counselors train volunteer faculty in such areas as active listening, open communication, and positive feedback. Then teachers meet with potential dropouts in small groups. In essence, the MOP teacher becomes the potential dropout's school-based guardian angel. This teacher looks for students to provide positive feedback, and when students miss school, the teacher calls the home to check on the student. The program's success has been attributed to student-teacher relationships developed through concern and caring.

Readers who desire additional information should consult McDonald & Wright (1987).

---

academic and social expectations, expect them to get pregnant, be involved in drugs, and drop out of school, just to name a few examples. These expectations have the potential for becoming a fairly sophisticated means of "weeding out" students. Educators often direct bright and motivated children and adolescents toward more academic classes and often with "better" teachers. Lower groups or at-risk learners are placed in "at-risk" classes where expectations might be lower and where academic challenges become fewer and fewer. Such evidence suggests schools operate with a hidden agenda with objectives designed to separate those who can do academic work and those who cannot, or—put more harshly and uncaring—to separate the winners from the losers.

Some educators continue to view schools as the place to "weed out" certain types of students. Such perceived function of schools is the antithesis of what schools should be—caring and nurturing institutions designed to help *all* learners develop to their maximum potential.

How can educators provide nurturing educational experiences for at-risk learners? They must follow these five major directions:

- First and foremost, perceive their roles as nurturers and helpers rather than acting to separate "winners and losers".
- Provide all learners with quality curricular experiences, competent and qualified teachers, and equal access to all educational experiences.
- Pinpoint possible at-risk conditions or the potential for at-risk conditions and providing immediate remediation or help.
- Make all school personnel aware of their professional responsibilities to nurture all students and to implement team approaches whenever possible.
- View at-risk learners and programs to be equally important as programs for other learners, i.e., the gifted and talented.

Activity 6-4

Define "equity" and "equal access" (as mentioned in Chapter 3). Are schools today providing equity and equal access for all learners (including at-risk learners) or are these only jargon and buzz words? Provide specific evidence that equity and equal access are or are not being provided.

While these five directions provide only representative directions, readers wanting to work with and help at-risk learners can think of other means to address individual situations. The important point to be emphasized is that educators should not "weed out" at-risk learners by providing them with low-quality programs and failing to address their needs altogether.

Provide Instruction in the Literacies Needed in U.S. Society

Living cooperatively and socially, earning a living wage, and having the ability to live successfully and independently in a rapidly changing democratic society requires specific "literacies." At one time in history, U.S. schools supposedly addressed these tasks or literacies as part of their many responsibilities. However, many schools have not kept pace with the literacies needed for the 1990s and the twenty-first century. In fact, educators trying to address at-risk conditions face new challenges: AIDS, sexual permissiveness, drug/alcohol abuse, tobacco, misbehaving students, and a host of others problems. Whereas one could argue that schools have accomplished these tasks with "seemingly" bright, nonproblematic students, one could also argue persuasively that schools have not prepared at-risk learners with the literacies needed for social and economic survival. Literacy, at one time, basically meant reading or perhaps both reading and writing. Contemporary definitions of "literacies" include broader perspectives such as social literacy, technological literacy, and economic literacy, just to name selective examples. What literacies, then, do at-risk learners need?

The key to the literacy question lies in the determination of "literacies" or at-risk learners' needs. For example, all at-risk learners need some basic literacies such as reading, writing, mathematics, and social skills; however, other at-risk learners might need technological literacy more than others. As previously stated, educators need to individualize education programs for particular learners. Only when educators undertake individualization will at-risk learners needs be identified and addressed.

Provide for Cultural Differences and Exceptionalities

Cultural differences should be viewed as strengths and as enriching to American society. Similarly, learners with exceptionalities should be considered more alike than different. However, educational practices often fail to reflect the needs of exceptional and culturally different learners, sometimes placing them at risk. In other cases, learners' other at-risk conditions may be exacerbated by their cultural diversity or their exceptionalities. The school curriculum should do the following:

- Help all students understand cultural diversity and exceptionalities.
- Make clear that cultural diversity and exceptionalities are not at-risk conditions in and of themselves.
- Provide experiences that promote cultural diversity and exceptionalities.

It is important to reiterate the twofold nature of being at risk and/or exceptional: A child or adolescent might be considered at risk due to either of these two conditions (however, either assumption could constitute a serious mistake) and also these conditions might contribute to an existing at-risk condition. For example, a low-achieving learner's problems might be compounded if English is not the native language, or a learning disabled student might be more at risk if there is a history of school dropouts in his or her family.

Case Study 6-2: The Relevance of the Curriculum to At-Risk Learners

Susan, Josh, and Jason were three children from a socioeconomically poor family. The sister and two brothers lived with their aunt after the mother killed the father. Susan was the oldest and Josh and Jason were about a year apart. All three had severe reading problems, were several grade levels behind in school, and all were known for their rowdy behavior—not dangerous, just constantly disturbing the class during instructional times.

Their curriculum was basically the same as that of the other students in their class and, in fact, the whole school. Mr. McCant questioned: "What relevance can Susan, Josh, and Jason see in diagramming sentences or in studying Mozart or Gerard Manley Hopkins?" He continued, "Don't get me wrong, these are all important and vital to an educated society, but can Susan, Josh, and Jason really relate to them or see how they are relevant to their lives?"

Most members agreed that a plan to help the three (and many other students like them) needed to be developed. While no one advocated returning to the Dick and Jane books of another generation, there was general agreement that the children in this neighborhood should have relevant curricular experiences. This agenda was established:

1. Define curricular relevance for students like Susan, Josh, and Jason.
2. Determine precise curricular content from which the three could learn and benefit.
3. Determine that regardless of the curricular content, basic skills were being met.
4. Provide appropriate diagnostic and remediation work.
5. Provide a team approach of teachers, school psychologists, administrators, and counselors to prove the most relevant and effective education experiences.

The team did not negate the importance of "good" literary works, civic responsibilities, and proper use of the English language. It was, however, trying to teach these literacies in relevant and meaningful terms.

Organizational Efforts

Provide for All Learners

Schools often place major emphasis (such as financial resources, the most effective teachers, the latest technological resources, and the newest and best material) on the brighter youngsters who succeed in school. Such action may result from educators feeling that the students with the most potential need the best educational resources and teachers. Whether or not this is the case, the consequences of such actions further place learners at risk and can also be considered a form of discrimination, an unequal opportunity, or an inequitable education situation. Also, perhaps unwittingly, an educator's choice of organizational patterns often hurts or reduces learners' chances of school success. For example, homogeneous ability grouping (grouping students by ability or academic achievement) creates an inequitable situation: Learners often become segregated by culture, gender, and socioeconomic status. All too often, middle- and upper-class students are placed in higher ability groups, while lower-class students are placed in low-ability classes (George, 1993; Manning & Lucking, 1990).

Grouping by ability results in at least two problems. First, students might be misplaced—grouping criteria might have been wrong or misinterpreted. Second, evidence (George, 1993; Manning & Lucking, 1990) suggests that with lower ability groups, teachers have lower expectations and dem-

---

Successful Program: Classroom Organization and Management

The Classroom Organization and Management Program (COMP), intended to supplement other professional development activities, provides the necessary skills on which to build other academic and instructional programs. COMP provides teachers with management ideas and materials and involves them in activities directly related to classroom management. The program has three focuses: planning, implementing, and maintaining classroom management skills. Training workshops demonstrate process models that can be implemented in a school's own professional development program. Workshops cover such elements as assessment and problem identification, research-based content presentations (using vignettes, case studies, films, and simulations), and formulation of implementation plans (with emphasis on teacher roles, responsibilities, and tasks). Learning materials include two commercially published books and teacher manuals that cover six modules: organizing the classroom, planning and teaching rules and procedures, managing student work, maintaining positive student behavior, planning and organizing instruction, and conducting instruction and maintaining momentum.

Evaluation studies indicate COMP results in significantly higher gains on achievement tests than students in control classes. Teachers participating in COMP used effective practices to a greater extent and students demonstrated less off-task behavior and fewer inappropriate behaviors.

Adapted from Sopris West, Inc. (1992). *Educational Programs That Work*. Longmont, CO: Author, p. B-1.

onstrate behaviors and attitudes less conducive to student success. In essence, a lower achieving student (yet not officially at risk) might actually become a more acute at-risk case simply by being placed in a lower ability group. In such a situation, rather than school organization promoting the overall well-being of the at-risk learner, the organization acts as the culprit and actually places the learner in more serious jeopardy.

What, then, can educators do to ensure that at-risk students benefit from educational programs just as the upper groups and classes do?

- Perceive at-risk learners and other students with an equally important status. Although objectives for each differ, the ultimate educational goal remains the same for both—to help, promote, and nurture learners to develop to their fullest potential.
- Provide equal resources, both quantity and quality, to at-risk learners that students who are not at risk receive. It is important to note that

while these materials do not have to and, educationally speaking, probably should not be the same, equal access and equity should be the standards by which organizational efforts are evaluated.

- Provide organizational strategies that do not segregate learners according to race, gender, and social class.
- Provide equally qualified teachers for at-risk learners and other learners. Encourage teachers working with at-risk learners to maintain positive teaching behaviors and attitudes and high (yet appropriate) expectations.
- Provide an organizational structure that allows at-risk students to have equal access to special services personnel such as guidance counselors, school psychologists, administrators, speech correctionists, and diagnostic/remediation specialists.

Provide Continuous Progress Learning and Individualization

The graded school system (for example, a certain age learner is placed in a particular grade) has been used in U.S. schools for years. The greatest beneficiary, however, may have been the school system itself. The graded system provided an organizational means for students to progress through the school years—educators knew where students were in the educational system and knew where they would be next. In other words, it provided a fairly easy means of "keeping up" with students. The graded system became even more entrenched when textbooks became graded, testmakers normed standardized tests with grades, and textbook writers designated specific content for particular grades. Anyone acquainted with the graded system

---

Successful Program: McCulloch Middle School

Educators at McCulloch Middle School in Dallas, Texas, realized the problems caused by ability grouping: students ostracized upper-track learners for their ability and achievements, and some upper-track learners deliberately did poorly on tests in order to be moved to lower groups. McCulloch's program, which was designed to address these problems, included educating parents and community members of the plan to move away from ability grouping; meeting educators working in similar size schools that had eliminated ability grouping; and seeking grant funds for an extensive staff development program. The program's impressive results included an improved atmosphere, some faculty members feeling a sense of renewal, and students having more opportunities for learning and socialization (Hereford, 1993).

has probably questioned its usefulness. Just one example is the person who reads on the second-grade level yet, because of age, is assigned to the sixth grade. On the other extreme, there is the bright student doing ninth-grade work who sits bored in the same sixth-grade class.

Many students may have been made at risk by the graded system—for example, the child who could not maintain the progress of classmates or the socially immature ninth grader who turns to alcohol for help in coping with peers' social expectations. Other students may have had their at-risk conditions made more acute by grade placements; for example, a child who can, through struggling and determination, produce respectable academic achievement may be overwhelmed by the work expected in a particular grade.

One organizational plan, the *nongraded* or, as it is sometimes called, the *continuous progress* plan provides at-risk learners and other students with opportunities to progress at their own developmental level and learning rates.

Although programs and definitions vary, the following features are common to most continuous progress programs:

1. Continuous progress allows students to work on their academic level throughout the school year.
2. Identification of skills, knowledges, and appreciations within a content area can be addressed over a varying time period without students having to adhere to a specific length of time.
3. Student placement depends on achievement of skills, knowledges, and appreciations without regard for the number of years in school.
4. Extensive reporting and recordkeeping systems contribute to improved communication between teachers and between teachers and parents.
5. Students have successful experiences rather than failure or retention (Shepherd & Ragan, 1992).

Probably the most effective instruction occurs when students receive personal attention or individualized instruction. Such an organizational approach would achieve the following:

- Assume the philosophy that all children and adolescents are unique and deserve educational experiences that meet their individual needs rather than the class as a whole.
- Assess each student's individual strengths and weaknesses.
- Provide developmentally appropriate instruction designed for each student.
- Assess individual progress and evaluate in terms of the individual potential rather than through comparisons with other students.

One major reason for the effectiveness of individualized instruction is that the teacher can tailor instruction precisely to a student's needs. If the student learns quickly, the teacher can move to other tasks; if not, the teacher can determine the problem, try other methods and materials, or just spend more time on the task.

In the real world providing every student with a teacher is impractical. However, for decades educational innovators have been trying to find ways to get as close as possible to a one-to-one tutoring situation (Slavin, 1988).

Individualized instruction can be conducted in various ways, and each must be carefully considered by the teacher to determine its potential effectiveness with individual learners. Table 6-3 defines several means of individualizing instruction; however, the table should not be considered an exhaustive list.

Provide Appropriate Grouping Strategies

Although options to ability grouping are addressed extensively in Chapter 7, it is imperative that student grouping strategies and patterns at least be mentioned in a section on organization efforts and how they either contribute to students being at risk or contribute to their overall well-being. Briefly, students being placed in groups based on ability and academic achievement might be at risk due to their being assigned to either too high or too low of a group. Also, a student placed in a lower group might improve and excel yet unwary teachers might not move the child to a higher group. Organizational strategies include heterogeneous grouping, regrouping, mastery

TABLE 6-3 Individualizing Instruction

Strategy	Brief Description	For Additional Information
Programmed instruction	Students work on self-instructional materials at their own levels and rates	Slavin (1988a) Biehler & Snowman (1990)
Team-assisted individualization	Students work on individualized self-instructional materials at their own levels and rates	Manning & Lucking (1991)
Peer tutoring	Students several years older work with learners in cross-age tutoring; one student works with a classmate in same-age tutoring	Slavin (1988a)
Computer-assisted instruction	Students use computers to work on tutorial programs, problem-solving programs, and dialogue programs	Biehler & Snowman (1990)

learning, or the Joplin plan—all of which are addressed in the next chapter. At this point, it should suffice to say that the school organization should contribute to learners' academic achievement and their overall well-being.

Provide Teacher Team Approaches

Too often, teachers and specialists work in isolation, which eliminates any possibility of shared expertise or team approaches. An eighth-grade teacher works her students in a "behind closed doors" fashion; she often does not benefit from the expertise of her administrator, the counselor, or the at-risk specialist. In fact, she might be devising programs, planning lessons, and doing other forms of duplication that the at-risk specialist might already have or the counselor might be better prepared to handle. This should not be considered a failing on the part of the teacher—professionals cannot have at their fingertips the skills and expertise of a team of experts.

The organizational structure of the elementary, middle, or secondary school should provide for team approaches. One teacher should never be considered totally responsible for a group of at-risk students. At-risk conditions vary in number and in severity. A teacher may be an expert in working with low achievers yet might be totally inept at identifying potential suicides. A team consisting of administrators, teachers, counselors, school psychologists, speech correctionists, special educators, and special personnel trained to work with at-risk students should provide an integrated and carefully planned approach to work with at-risk learners. Each professional specialist has unique skills and expertise to offer the at-risk learner. It is hoped that the planning of instructional programs for at-risk students will someday resemble the procedure required for exceptional children by PL 94-142.

Provide Flexible Scheduling

Too often in the past, schools adopted a rigid time schedule for each subject area. Students, especially at-risk students, cannot have rigid schedules that fail to recognize developmental characteristics or that eliminate students from particular programs. The typical schedule consists of six to eight periods depending on the length of each period and a time frame of 45 to 60 minutes. The rigidity of such schedules often denies students access to programs and to special teaching-learning efforts. Therefore, flexible scheduling might be an attractive alternative.

Flexible scheduling may take several forms. Flexible scheduling provides for varied-size instructional groups and personalized instruction. While class periods may all be the same length of time, other variations might include number of periods and/or times of day in which instruction will be offered. Another option is revolving schedules, which change the times for each period and rotate the periods during the week for shorter or longer time frames. The varied time frames for each period remain the same with the periods rotating from day to day. Several premises are present in modular scheduling: 1) One day's schedule does not have to be the same as the previous day, 2) class size and length can vary according to the specific subject matter being presented, 3) teachers and content can require different amounts of time, and 4) learners differ in the amount of time required to learn something. Thus, the class size, duration of the class, number of required class meetings, aptitudes and interests of learners, the nature of instruction, the content area, and the outcomes of teaching are all variables affecting modular scheduling (Allen, Splittgerber, & Manning, 1993).

Schedules reflective of the research on learners' developmental characteristics provide for diversity in intellectual abilities, the need for exercise and rest, and the need for educational experiences designed for both cognitive and affective goals. The schedule also provides for extended blocks of uninterrupted time, teacher planning time, integration of subjects, varied lengths of instructional time, and innovation and experimentation with varied time schedules (Arnold, 1991).

Committed to the belief that at-risk students need a flexible schedule, one school developed a master schedule that provided flexible blocks of instructional time for each team of teachers and students. Their schedule fostered flexibility by 1) accommodating activities that required varying lengths of time, 2) minimizing the disruption of pull-out programs, 3) providing opportunities for independent study, 4) contributing to in-depth studies, and 5) providing both individual and group work.

Flexible schedules provide opportunities to investigate a wide range of special interests among at-risk learners and still spend the needed amount of time on content. Various means such as independent study and core programs are other possibilities. Flexible schedules allow adequate time for acquisition of knowledge and variation in activities for extended content requirements and can better accommodate differences in students' attention spans.

Provide Organizational Strategies that Recognize Physical Needs

Advocating that learners must be healthy in order to learn, *Turning Points: Preparing American Youth for the 21st Century* (1989) proposed that the school's responsibility includes providing educational experiences that ensure learners will be able to demonstrate several characteristics: physical and mental fitness, a self-image of competence and strength, and self-understanding. Likewise, the school can work toward ensuring student access to health services and establishing the school as a health-promoting environment.

Children and adolescents, seeking a place among their peers, realize that their physical abilities have a dramatic influence on their social acceptance as well as their self-perceptions. Elementary and secondary schools can provide team play and the practice of physical skills so that everyone will have a chance to participate and be recognized. Avoiding competition during physical activities is of particular importance to early or late developing learners who might experience greater chances of becoming at risk.

First, the tremendous physical diversity among learners provides cause to deemphasize activities that stress the size, strength, and stamina of early and late maturers; to recognize learners' needs for physical exercise and their inability to sit for long periods of time; and to provide school policies and behavior expectations that reflect a need for physical activity. One eighth-grade boy, obviously smaller and generally less mature than the other boys, questioned his development and eventually his self-worth when he could not hit a softball as well as other boys. A few kind words from his physical education teacher had a significant impact during difficult times. The teacher realized that the problem resulted from grouping early and late developing learners together rather than exempting some learners from participation in softball. Providing situations in which early and late maturers would not be forced to compete would lessen the severity of such problems (Manning, 1993c).

Second, boys and girls, with their growing muscles and bones and often disproportionate bodies, become uncomfortable when sitting in desks for long periods of time. One sixth-grade boy who often made trips to the pencil sharpener and trash can admitted that he had difficulty sitting comfortably for long periods of time. Perceptive educators of at-risk learners provide breaks and exercise periods, even something as simple as stretch periods in the classroom. Likewise, learning can be made active such as building and making projects and other learning activities that do not require learners to sit.

Activity 6-5

Prepare a survey to determine the effects of organizational strategies on at-risk learners. For example, do organizational strategies result in students being segregated by culture, gender, social class, or ability? Are equity and equal access being fostered or denied? Are learners sitting for long times in cramped desks? What suggestions can you offer for making organizational strategies more conducive to at-risk learners' needs?

Management Efforts

It is important to note that management includes two separate (yet sometimes overlapping) entities. First, efforts can include actual behavior management of students, i.e., convincing students that their learning and the learning of others require behavior conducive to the educational experience. Certain "ground rules" are necessary for classrooms to be physically and psychologically safe, for learners to be able to learn effectively, and for learning environments to be optimal. Second, management can include the teachers' techniques of managing class routines. This aspect of management includes teachers' procedures for returning graded papers, going from the classroom to the lunchroom, handling transitions from one subject area to another, and other such "routine" matters. These two types without doubt overlap, for example, when a child yells for his or her paper when papers are being returned. This section explores management expectations and techniques and shows their possible effects on at-risk children and adolescents.

Provide for Both Individual and Group Rights and Choices

Providing effective learning environments requires educators to consider individual and group rights and choices. Teachers who expect all students to learn in similar learning environments violate the rights and choices of both individuals and groups. This assertion may be even more important for at-risk learners who might not fit the "educational mold." Some at-risk learners need the safety and security of a group, whereas others might need a degree of separation or security *from* the group. Teachers' responsibilities includes considering whether management expectations contribute to or hinder academic achievement, student behavior, and the overall learning environment.

Providing a teaching-learning environment contributing to learning and academic achievement has been a long-accepted expectation and professional obligation of teachers and administrators. For environments to be effective, proper student behavior is essential—classrooms must be free of disturbances, constant bickering, teacher-student confrontations, and threats offered by either teachers or students. However, such a classroom does not have to meet the once strongly felt belief that "quiet classrooms are good classrooms." Students might be working independently, doing library work, working on projects, or participating in other active opportunities that sometimes result in more noise than traditionally expected. Perceptive educators recognize the difference between noise resulting from worthwhile and productive learning experiences and disturbances resulting from mis-behavior.

Provide for Social Class Differences in Management Perspectives

Other essentials to consider when deciding on appropriate management expectations include recognizing differences in management perspectives, i.e., social class orientations toward proper individual and group behaviors. It is imperative to understand the importance of considering students, especially potentially at-risk learners, as both individuals and as members of a social class. In fact, planning management practices from a middle-class perspective can actually contribute to children and adolescents being at risk.

While this text is based on the most current and objective information, it still remains crucial for educators to understand individual children and adolescents within a social class through conscientious study and firsthand contact. Failing to understand individuals and to consider crucial differences may result in assuming too much social class homogeneity, e.g., all lower or upper social classes sharing identical values, problems, and expectations.

With the previous cautionary remarks firmly in mind, Table 6-4 shows possible differences in the behavior and management expectations of various social classes. Note that social classes are not always separated by distinct lines and, therefore, some overlap may occur.

Educators with experience working with youngsters of various social classes quickly recognize how differences between educators (who are predominantly middle class) and learners of various social classes can lead to management expectations that are either too harsh or too lax. A teacher once asked parents for advice on how to deal with their son's academic and behavior problems. Regardless of whether an academic or behavior issue was being discussed, the parents offered the same response, "Paddle him—

TABLE 6-4 Social Classes and Behavior/Management Expectations

Lower Classes	Middle/Upper Classes
Expects fewer rewards for positive behavior	Expects "something" in return for positive behavior
Expects more yelling, threats, and, in some cases, abusive behavior	Expects more discussion of behavior and its consequences
Expects more punishment of a physical nature	Expects more lack of privileges or being on "restriction"

paddle him often and hard!" This example illustrates the crucial difference in management perspectives. The parent expected (and perhaps the child did, too!) the teacher to inflict corporal punishment. The teacher from a middle-class background and a graduate of a teacher education institution advocating more humane management approaches totally disagreed with the parents' behavior management orientations.

The preceding example, which actually happened in a lower-class school, shows how perspectives on behavior and management can contribute to learners being at risk. First, teachers, though well meaning, need to understand that their management efforts might actually be detrimental to the teaching-learning-management process. Although this text does not advocate corporal punishment, the learner's at-risk propensity might have been increasing steadily because the teacher did not understand the student's or the parents' perspectives. Extreme caution, however, is in order. Taking a parent's advice and using corporal punishment on a youngster might greatly increase the propensity toward being at risk, especially if the learner had academic problems or if the learner simply failed to "learn and behave" like the group. In any event, the chance of injuring a learner physically or psychologically is not worth the risks involved with corporal punishment, even if the parent did offer the suggestion.

Provide Management Practices Proven by Effectiveness Research

Experimental studies and syntheses of research on teaching during recent years have provided specific and descriptive information on effective teaching behaviors. Significant works by such researchers as Joyce (1988), Brophy (1987), Walberg (1988), Porter and Brophy (1988), and Brophy and Good (1986) provide a wealth of research on what effective teachers do. These findings have definite implications for educators working with at-risk students, especially since these researchers contend that a powerful relationship exists between teacher behaviors and student achievement and behavior.

The research on effective teachers and effective teaching behaviors indicates that effective teachers demonstrate specific behaviors such as being well organized; preventing problems from occurring; emphasizing academic achievement; expecting all students to achieve; assigning appropriate seatwork; having a good grasp of the subject matter; monitoring student progress; giving adequate feedback; insisting students accept responsibility for their work; using questions appropriately; encouraging positive behavior; demonstrating strong leadership skills; modeling effective techniques; valuing productive time rather than time on task; employing advance organizers; and understanding the relationship between student achievement and teacher behavior (Joyce, 1988; Brophy, 1987; Walberg, 1988; Porter & Brophy, 1988; Brophy & Good, 1986).

What specific teaching behaviors might particularly help at-risk learners? It is crucial to remember that at-risk students, just as all learners, are unique and must be considered individually. However, it is possible to suggest some representative effective teaching behaviors and their possible positive effects on at-risk students.

- *Being well organized* can prevent breakdowns in class routines, loss of instructional time, and opportunities for at-risk students to lose interest.
- *Emphasizing academic achievement* can encourage at-risk learners to continue to persevere, to improve self-concepts, and to realize the importance of academics.
- *Expecting all students to achieve* can show at-risk learners that although they have at-risk problems or conditions, the teacher continues to have high hopes and expectations for them both academically and socially.
- *Monitoring student progress* can show at-risk students that teachers are genuinely interested, caring, and willing to provide assistance whenever needed.
- *Valuing productive time* can convince at-risk learners of the importance of using time productively and in a way that benefits both the individual and the group.
- *Insisting on students accepting responsibility* can show at-risk learners the importance of accepting responsibility for their work, their behavior, their attitudes, and, generally speaking, for their lives.

Provide Appropriate Class Size, Classroom Space, Materials, and Classroom Climate

Management efforts should be perceived as a broad array of efforts rather than in its narrow or traditional sense of only behavior techniques. Teachers may maintain that they have little control over such tangible items as class size and class space; however, effective teachers make the most of available resources. One teacher in a room with wooden floors, without shades and air conditioning, and virtually without books except the children's outdated textbooks still had a "good" classroom. Although conditions were far from conducive to learning, she made the most of available resources. Likewise, readers can probably think of an opposite example where size, space, and resources were plentiful, yet learning still did not occur, and the students' propensities toward being at risk grew more acute.

Educators working with at-risk learners realize the necessity of appropriately sized classes or groups. Admittedly, teachers may have little control over their class size; however, placing students in heterogeneous groups of two, four, or some combination of less than six or seven can greatly provide a feelings of togetherness, a sense of cooperative spirit, and can allow students to feel more a part of a group. At-risk learners can benefit from small heterogeneous groups in several ways:

1. Students have more opportunities to speak, to work cooperatively, to develop social skills, and to learn the dynamics of group interaction.
2. Students can receive more individual attention than in a group of 30 or more.
3. Students can be grouped according to areas of interests.
4. Students can benefit from peer tutoring, whereby learners help other learners with learning activities.

All students should have adequate space to see and hear without sitting cramped in at desks or in chairs that are too small. Because of grade retention, at-risk learners may be older than most other students in a class. Often, adolescents have to occupy desks and chairs designed for younger learners. Even worse, schools that place a high degree of interest on high achievers and the college-bound may place at-risk students in the least comfortable rooms or in those that are the least conducive to learning and socialization. Sitting in a classroom that is too small for students and equipment, that has too little or too much heat or air conditioning, or that is too close to a noisy part of the school can pose at-risk situations. Classroom space should also provide opportunities for active participation, so students can physically move around classrooms for both physical (i.e., exercise) and social (i.e., cooperative learning groups) reasons.

At-risk students, for maximum learning opportunities, need adequate and developmentally appropriate materials and resources. School districts placing the greatest priority on high achievers sometimes fail to address the needs of at-risk learners. The mind-set of purchasing materials for learners who can use them the most negates the importance of equal access, equal opportunities, and even at-risk learners themselves. A survey should be completed to determine whether at-risk learners have effective, clean, accurate, and current materials and resources. To do otherwise suggests that at-risk learners do not have access to learning opportunities. Questions to ask include the following:

1. Are materials available for all at-risk learners?
2. Are materials developmentally appropriate and geared to the needs, learning levels, and interests of at-risk learners?
3. Do materials contribute to the entire school program or to the education of the whole learner?

4. Do materials correlate with the program of study and the overall curriculum?
5. Are students taught respect for books, materials, resources, and equipment?

Climate can be defined as the beliefs, values, and attitudes shared by teachers, students, administrators, parents, and all other people interested in the school and the success of its programs. Within the climate of an effective school, people feel proud, committed, and achievement generally increases. The ten essentials of school climate are as follows:

1. A supportive, stimulating environment
2. Student-centered teaching
3. Positive expectations
4. Feedback
5. Rewards
6. A sense of family
7. Closeness to parents and community
8. Communication
9. Achievement
10. Trust (Shepherd & Ragan, 1992).

The classroom climate may be described as being relaxed, pleasant, flexible, rigid, autocratic, democratic, repressive, and suppressive (Jarolimek & Foster, 1989).

Teachers often deal with children and adolescents as groups rather than individuals. In doing so, students lose their individuality and thus feel anonymous. For example, a teacher may say "The class should pay close attention to what is being said" or "I need the attention of the class." Students begin to feel or assume that they are being viewed as a group. Another related situation that can pose a problem is when teachers impose management systems without involving students in the process. Allowing students to feel they have input into the management system brings more cooperation and positive relationships. Without such feelings, an adversary relationship results and the smallest issue becomes a major confrontation (Jarolimek & Foster, 1989).

The classroom climate can hold several implications for at-risk children and adolescents. First, at-risk students, perhaps more than other students, need to feel a sense of closeness with at least one significant adult individual—a person in whom the at-risk learner can confide and look to as a significant school adult and as a support person. Second, at-risk learners need a supportive climate in which teachers teach individuals rather than "groups" and convey feelings of acceptance and goodwill. Third, at-risk learners need a school that builds on strengths, focuses attention toward weaknesses, and provides programs that address specific at-risk conditions. However, such a curriculum may be meaningless if the school climate conveys distrust, strict teacher dominance and control, and adversary feelings. Regardless of the school curriculum, organization, and management procedures, it is essential that the school climate convey positive emotional tones and promote human relations.

Provide Students with Positive Consequences of Behavior

At-risk students might perceive school and school-related activities in a negative light. Several events can result in such perceptions: The academically at-risk learner might have experienced years of frustration and failure; the suicidal student may feel schools do not offer any hope; and the student experimenting with a drug habit may feel more chance of punishment than help breaking the habit. The negative overtones often associated with schools prevent students from understanding that consequences of behavior can also be positive.

Students must realize that their misbehavior, whether attention-seeking or based on revenge or feelings of inadequacy, is counterproductive to the overall education process. Students also need to know that turning negative behavior into positive behavior can bring positive consequences. For example, instead of making the student more at risk by punishing negative behaviors, educators should strive to reverse the situation by rewarding positive behavior.

Charles (1992) provides several examples of rewarding positive behaviors:

- *Personal attention from the teacher:* Such attention can include greetings, short talks, compliments, acknowledgments, smiles, and friendly eye contact.
- *Positive notes to parents:* Rather than informing parents only when learners have misbehaved, educators can send a brief note or phone call, positive and complimentary, which can do wonders for both students and parents.
- *Special awards:* Many students respond well to special awards given for high achievement, significant improvement, and so forth.
- *Special privileges:* Special privileges include helping take care of classroom animals or equipment, helping with class materials, or working together with a friend.
- *Material rewards:* Younger students like to receive stickers, badges, and ribbons, while older students like such things as posters, pencils, and rubber stamps.

- *Home rewards:* In collaboration with parents, privileges can be extended to the home, i.e., completing homework can earn extra television time, and reading an extra book can earn a favorite meal (Charles, 1992).

Case Study 6-3 shows how a concerned eighth-grade teacher and a committee examined how organizational and management expectations might contribute to students being at risk.

Case Study 6-3: Educators Consider Organizational and Management Expectations

A large urban middle school, P.S. 72, had its share of the students with at-risk conditions. At a faculty meeting, an eighth-grade teacher questioned why P.S. 72 had so many at-risk learners, and also whether the school, somehow unconsciously, could be making students at risk or in some ways making at-risk conditions worse. A committee was formed to determine how the school might be contributing to students' at-risk conditions. Somewhat startling to some faculty members, the report presented several conclusions:

1. At-risk learners received fewer materials, resources, and innovative programs rather than a more equal distribution.
2. At-risk learners had larger classes and teachers had to teach learners with various at-risk conditions, which forced teachers to address more than one condition, thus limiting learners' progress.
3. At-risk learners were grouped homogeneously (according to ability) throughout the entire school day, and few individualized approaches or continuous progress programs were provided.
4. At-risk learners were subject to the exact same rules and expectations as "normal" learners, regardless of the at-risk condition or social class perspectives.
5. At-risk learners were assigned to smaller rooms with less equipment, which denied their access to equal opportunity.
6. At-risk learners received negative consequences for their misbehaviors while their positive behaviors went unnoticed.

The committee agreed to propose solutions for *each* conclusion. This would not be an easy task, but there was a commitment to change the school to better meet the needs of at-risk learners and, at the very least, not to aggravate at-risk conditions. Although such an effort would require extensive time and effort, the benefit to at-risk learners and the school as a whole should be well worth the effort.

Reviewing What You Have Read About
Curriculum, Organization, and Management

1. A _____ approach is necessary when looking for conditions that might cause or increase at-risk conditions, i.e., examining only one area of the school such as organization patterns will not suffice.

2. Curricular efforts responsive to the needs of at-risk children and adolescents reflect the reality that these learners have special _____ _____ , _____ , and _____ .

3. Researchers and writers have suggested for several decades that the school curriculum, instructional practices, and the overall teaching-learning environment should reflect learners' _____ .

4. For curricular experiences to be _____ , the content conveyed and overall curricular experiences must be meaningful to the student in such a way that students see how learning relates to their lives.

5. The national outcry during the last decade or so has resulted in an emphasis on _____ , the accumulation of knowledge, high test scores, and generally speaking, and has placed high priority on the cognitive aspects of learning.

6. The _____ curriculum includes considering such concerns as individual student's needs and interests and an emphasis on the physical, psychosocial, and intellectual development.

7. Proponents of an _____ curriculum contend that curricular experiences should be purposeful activities tied to learners' needs and interests and should include story projects, field trips, interest centers, dramatizations, and group work.

8. To provide nurturing educational experiences for at-risk learners, educators should first and foremost perceive their roles as _____ rather than as one of separating winners and losers.

9. An important point to remember is that educators should not _____ at-risk learners and then provide them with low-quality programs or fail to address their educational needs.

10. _____ can be defined as the beliefs, values, and attitudes shared by teachers, students, administrators, parents, and all other people interested in the school and the success of its programs.

11. The research on _____ suggests that teachers should be well organized, emphasize academic achievement, and convince at-risk learners of the importance of using time productively and accepting responsibility.

12. Selected practices that reflect _____ include consideration of cognitive readiness levels, active learning, and equal access to curricular programs.

13. Climate can be considered a _____ function because it results from a composite of the interactions and transactions between teachers and students.

14. At-risk learners can benefit from small _____ in several ways: Students have more opportunities to speak, to work cooperatively, to develop social skills, and to learn the dynamics of group interaction.

Answer Key: 1. total school; **2.** needs, aptitudes, and interests; **3.** developmental levels; **4.** relevant; **5.** academic achievement; **6.** student-centered; **7.** activity-centered; **8.** nurturers; **9.** "weed out"; **10.** Climate; **11.** effective teaching; **12.** intellectual development; **13.** management; **14.** heterogeneous groups

Summary

At-risk learners at all levels deserve a total school response: curricular efforts, organizational patterns, and management practices. Changing the curriculum might be of little worth if organizational strategies and management practices limit potential or vice versa. Likewise, all school professionals should feel responsible for at-risk learners. Rather than total responsibility being placed only on classroom teachers, responsibility for at-risk learners should include administrators, school psychologists, counselors, and *all* school professionals. Simply put, the problems and conditions at-risk students face have far too serious consequences to deny them a total school effort and the genuine commitment of all educators.

For Additional Information on Curriculum, Organization, and Management

Charles, C. M. (1992). *Building classroom discipline* (4th ed.). White Plains, NY: Longman. Charles includes a chapter on "The Management of Students at-Risk," a useful examination of how to manage at-risk students.

Diem, R. A. (1992). Dealing with the tip of the iceberg: School responses to at-risk behaviors. *The High School Journal, 75*(2), 119–125. Diem describes a study that took a case study approach to determine intervention strategies such as literacy programs, mentors, school-business partnerships, and school counselor programs.

Manning, M. L., & Baruth, L. G. (1991). Appreciating cultural diversity in the classroom. *Kappa Delta Pi Record, 27*(4), 104–107. Manning and Baruth explore children and adolescents in the Native, African, Hispanic, and Asian-American cultures and provide suggestions for readers wanting a better understanding of culturally diverse learners and their families.

Manning, M. L., & Lucking, R. (1990). Homogeneous ability grouping: Realities and alternatives. *Childhood Education, 66,* 254–258. This article examines the dangers associated with ability grouping and offers several suggestions for grouping learners by ability.

Nardini, M. L., & Antes, R. L. (1991). What strategies are effective with at-risk students? *NASSP Bulletin, 75*(538), 67–72. Nardini and Antes report on a middle school and senior high school study designed to determine effective strategies with at-risk learners.

7

Alternative Learning
Environments

Outline

Overview

Probing Directions

The Need for Alternative Learning Environments

Alternative Learning Environments: Some Considerations
Considering Individual Differences
Considering At-Risk Students' Learning Styles
Considering Multiple Intelligences
Considering Individual and Cultural Perceptions of Motivation
and Success
Considering the Possibility of Extensive Practical Application
Considering Healthy School Environments
Considering the School Culture
Considering Literacy Environments
Considering Academic Survival Skills

Alternative Learning Environments: Strategies
Individualized Instruction
Homogeneous Ability Grouping
Cooperative Learning
Technological Advances

Overview

Previous chapters suggested that schools' curricular practices, organizational strategies, and management practices may actually make learners at risk, may contribute to existing at-risk conditions, or may do little to alleviate learners' at-risk factors. Many schools have tried respectable efforts and programs to help at-risk children and adolescents; unfortunately, some efforts resulted only in cosmetic changes, provided "more of the same" learning experiences, or relied too heavily on traditional learning strategies. This chapter suggests basic considerations when planning alternative programs and defines several specific learning environments that have the potential to address the needs of at-risk learners. Prior to selecting any alternative learning environment, however, educators are encouraged to consider their own students' at-risk conditions to determine the most feasible alternative learning environments.

Probing Directions

This chapter on alternative learning environments does the following:

1. Emphasizes that "more of the same" such as increased amounts of homework, more reports, and more rote memorization may not be the answer to addressing at-risk learners' needs, and, in fact, may be detrimental to at-risk learners academically, behaviorally, and socially.
2. Emphasizes basic considerations to be explored when planning alternative learning environments for at-risk children and adolescents.
3. Suggests alternatives to homogeneous ability grouping, which might have disastrous consequences on academic achievement, self-concepts, and teacher behaviors toward learners.
4. Suggests cooperative learning as a teaching-learning activity, which has the potential for helping at-risk learners both academically and socially.

5. Explores how learners who might be unable to cope with school might respond positively to alternative learning environments.
6. Suggests alternative learning strategies that might better meet the needs of at-risk learners.
7. Suggests special schooling alternatives that are specifically designed for at-risk learners.

The Need for Alternative Learning Environments

As previously mentioned, the "more of the same" philosophy usually will not improve the conditions faced by most at-risk students. Low-achieving students do not need more books to read, papers to write, or more mathematics worksheets to complete. If the students have not already responded to such efforts in the past, "more of the same" probably will not work. Also, for children and adolescents who are sexually active, involved in drugs, or potentially suicidal, additional programs that emphasize scare tactics are unlikely to work. Surely, students involved in any of these three at-risk behaviors must have heard of the dangers involved. Programs will have little effect as long as the child or adolescent feels "such dangers cannot happen to me."

Educators have a responsibility to consider learners' at-risk conditions and characteristics, consider previous efforts and programs (and ascertain their success), and then plan alternative learning environments—those environments that meet at-risk learners' needs rather than dooming them to academic, social, or behavioral failure.

The first and basic step in deciding on an alternative learning environment is to realize and accept that previous efforts, no matter how well intentioned, have not worked and probably will continue to frustrate both learner and teacher. Rather than teachers feeling guilty or incapable of providing effective teaching-learning activities, teachers should view the situation as a new opportunity—an opportunity to think of new, creative, and original approaches. It is important that educators not turn to alternative learning environments out of frustration or because they feel like they have failed at their profession. Alternative learning environments should be viewed with enthusiasm, as a new hope, and as means of changing practices that have not worked. Students should also perceive alternative learning environments as positive rather than as the final means to help them overcome their difficulties, regardless of at-risk conditions. Only when learners and teachers have positive perceptions of alternative learning strategies as well as their efforts will these approaches have a chance of improving the lives of at-risk children and adolescents.

Activity 7-1
Consider your school experiences and schools in which you have observed. Provide several examples of the "more of the same" mentality, i.e., providing learners with more and more work, either for remediation or enrichment. Explain why such practices might be even more devastating to at-risk learners.

Alternative Learning Environments: Some Considerations

A prerequisite to planning alternative learning environments is to bring several basic considerations into focus. These considerations include individual differences, learning styles, multiple intelligences, cultural perceptions of motivation, and the possibility of at-risk learners needing practical application. Perceptive educators realize that these considerations represent an excellent starting point and that many other considerations come into play as educators consider individual at-risk learners and their respective conditions and problems.

Considering Individual Differences

While the previous chapter addressed individual differences, differences in individuals are sufficiently important to mention again. Categorizing all at-risk students as being alike constitutes a serious mistake. Likewise, one makes an equally serious mistake by assuming too much homogeneity among learners with similar at-risk conditions. For example, all of the learners at risk of becoming school dropouts do not have the *same* reason for being at risk. All too often, educators group students by at-risk condition, i.e., pregnant teenagers. But some of these learners may have one at-risk condition—pregnancy—while others may have additional at-risk conditions. The first category are intellectually bright, highly motivated, have supportive families and social networks, and except for pregnancy cannot be considered at risk. Also, as is mentioned later, individual differences can result from a number of factors such as social class, perceptions of motivation, and learning styles.

Considering At-Risk Students' Learning Styles

A steadily increasing body of research suggests that equating learning styles and teaching-learning activities contributes to meeting an individual's unique needs (Dunn & Dunn, 1979; NASSP, 1979; Cornett, 1983; Keefe, 1987,

1990; Stewart, 1990). Learning styles have been defined in several ways. First, Cornett (1983) defined learning styles as consistent patterns of behavior defined in terms of cognitive, affective, and physiological dimensions. To some degree, learning styles indicate how individuals process information and respond to affective, sensory, and environmental dimensions of the instruction process. A second definition came from the NASSP (1979). Learning styles were defined as characteristic cognitive, affective, and physiological behaviors serving as relatively stable indicators of how learners perceive, interact with, and respond to the learning environment. The implications of learning styles, however, extend beyond mere definitions. The various dimensions of learning styles result from genetic coding, personality, development, motivation, and cultural and environmental influences (Keefe, 1990).

Understanding learning styles and recognizing their potential for improving academic achievement will undoubtedly be vital during the 1990s and beyond. Students taught by their preferred learning styles demonstrated higher levels of achievement, showed more interest in subject matter, approved of instructional methods, and wanted other subjects to be taught similarly (Bell, 1986).

Suggestions for teaching strategies reflective of learning styles include the following: Use all types of questions, i.e., ones that request factual information and ones wanting value judgments; use advance organizers in an attempt to relate past and present learning experiences; set clear purposes for learning experiences; use multisensory experiences, i.e., students listening as well as reading; and use a variety of review and reflection strategies (Cornett, 1983).

Considering at-risk students' learning styles holds significant potential for helping these learners and for providing educational experiences that contribute to success rather than leading to frustration and continued failure. A problem for years has been that teachers assumed students all learn alike or in a manner (or style) similar to the teacher. Readers should think about conditions under which they learn or perhaps the environment in which this book is being read. For example, a teacher instructs a class on the Vietnam War, its beginnings, battles, and the United States's eventual pullout. The teacher lectures, shows slides, and perhaps allows students to work in groups. In other words, the teacher teaches in the way he or she learns most effectively. While the class may be mixed both culturally and socioeconomically, the teacher expects all learners, both girls and boys, to learn in the same manner or in this case, to use the same styles. Some students studying an event such as the Vietnam War might want an "overall picture" and then focus on the details; other students learn better when they learn the specific events and then cognitively combine these events into a whole. The teacher expecting all students to learn in the same manner can place students in one or both categories in an at-risk situation.

Understanding learning styles and recognizing their potential for improving academic achievement and overall school productivity will undoubtedly be vital for educators of at-risk learners. Allowing students to learn using their most compatible learning styles also includes a consideration of other factors such as light, time of day, temperature, and whether learners prefer to work alone or in groups. Some students prefer to work in a quiet library situation, while others want a "more comfortable" surrounding with some background noise or perhaps a snack. Similarly, some learners prefer the morning hours, while others learn best during the late night hours. All of these factors deserve consideration especially since many teachers expect all learners to sit in rows and learn the *same* material at the *same* time at the same *rate*. Such expectations are compatible with neither logic nor learning styles and, in fact, may even contribute to learners being at risk.

Educators of at-risk learners will also need to be able to assess an individual student's learning styles. Several assessment instruments provide a means of determining specific styles, while some instruments provide a more comprehensive means of assessing overall styles. Two learning style inventories selected for discussion include the Learning Style Inventory (LSI) (Dunn, Dunn, & Price, 1986) and the NASSP Learning Style Profile (LSP) (Keefe & Monk, 1986). First, the LSI looks at many affective and physiological dimensions of learning styles. Learners taking the LSI complete a 104-item self-report, which identifies learning preferences in four situations: 1) environmental conditions, 2) emotional needs, 3) sociological needs, and 4) physical needs. Second, the NASSP LSP (Keefe & Monk, 1986) diagnoses the learning styles of students in grades 6 through 12. The LSP contains 23 scales representing four higher order factors: cognitive styles, perceptual responses, study, and instructional preferences (the affective and physiological elements) (Keefe & Monk, 1986).

Considering Multiple Intelligences

The theory of multiple intelligences (Walters & Gardner, 1985; Gardner, 1987a; Hatch & Gardner, 1988; Blythe & Gardner, 1990) deserves consideration when planning, implementing, and assessing educational experiences for at-risk children and adolescents. The concept of multiple intelligences holds that learners have various types of intelligence rather than a single intelligence. Hatch and Gardner (1988) explained that a learner might have seven different intelligences: linguistic, musical, logical-mathematical, spatial, bodily kinesthetic, interpersonal, and intrapersonal. Although their theory makes sense for all learners, it might make even more sense for at-risk learners, i.e., all educators working with at-risk learners have known a student weak in linguistic areas yet extremely talented in logical-mathematic areas. Another example might be the learner who has considerable ability in spatial relationships yet neither performs or enjoys music of any type. Multiple intelligences provides an explanation for many at-risk students having enormous talent or abilities in some areas while experiencing difficulty in other areas. The difficulties place them in the at-risk category while, in reality, they have considerable untapped and unused talent.

The concept of multiple intelligences has several implications for educators willing to consider changing educational practices that continue to reflect the belief that learners have one established intelligence. First, educators can address human abilities and talents other than the commonly considered linguistic and logical-mathematical intelligences (Gardner, 1987a). Second, shifts in instructional emphases may be necessary. For example, in a typical classroom relying heavily on linguistic and logical-mathematical symbol systems, at-risk learners have little opportunity to develop other forms of intelligence. Third, multiple intelligences theory challenges the viability of standardized, machine-scored, multiple-choice assessments, which do not allow each intelligence to be measured (Blythe & Gardner, 1990).

The belief that people have more than one intelligence holds considerable promise for at-risk children and adolescents. Many learners, for one or more reasons, simply do not or cannot succeed in schools today. Many examples come to mind (all of which are true): The boy virtually unable to deal or cope with school stays in school just to be able to participate in the band; the boy with a severe reading problem who has an outstanding knowledge of World War II; and the girl totally lacking in interpersonal skills yet who can speak forcefully and persuasively to a large group. Many at-risk students might be "at risk" in areas emphasized by the school yet might appear "normal" to people outside the school. For example, a learner can be a "failure" all day at school, but on leaving school, might be quite proficient in sales, music, interpersonal relations, or physical endeavors. One has to question whether some learners are at risk or are made at risk by school practices and expectations that place emphasis only on one type of intelligence.

Activity 7-2

Think about your own as well as others' special talents and skills. Name several examples of multiple intelligences. Why do you think schools limit their focus to only one or two intelligences? Visit several at-risk programs and make a list of several "intelligences"—then, suggest methods, procedures, and resources which address these "intelligences."

Considering Individual and Cultural Perceptions of Motivation and Success

Educators often view motivation from middle-class Anglo-American perspectives and expect such motivational behaviors toward learning and achievement from learners of other cultures and social class backgrounds. The concept sounds logical and simplistic—motivated learners work hard, complete classwork and homework assignments, offer comments in class, enjoy competition, feel proud of high grades and academic accomplishment, and other such behaviors. In other words, motivation leads to success and vice versa. These behaviors sound conducive to school success and students demonstrating these characteristics usually achieve; however, such thinking fails to consider cultural and social class factors. Ames (1990) maintains that understanding motivation requires consideration of such factors as learners' developmental changes, individual and cultural differences, and the classroom setting itself.

Planning effective at-risk programs requires consideration of individual and cultural perspectives of motivation. Some cultures such as Hispanic-Americans do not like to be singled out for achievement or the lack of achievement. Hispanic-American perspectives hold that when one achieves and receives praise for accomplishments, it should not be at the expense of other learners in the class (Mirandé, 1986; Fitzpatrick, 1987; Christensen, 1989). In essence, while U.S. schools respect motivation and competition, students from Hispanic backgrounds do not always share such feelings. It is essential that educators not view all students through middle-class Anglo-American lenses and subsequently perceive students as unmotivated and at risk of failing. Upon understanding individual and cultural orientations toward motivation, educators can ascertain whether learners are truly at risk or simply do not meet middle-class Anglo-American expectations.

Most educators probably agree that a relationship exists between motivation (even when disagreeing on what constitutes motivation) and achievement. Learners experiencing high achievement in some areas, whether academics, athletics, or in other areas, will probably be motivated to repeat the behaviors leading to success. Likewise, a learner's lack of achievement can result in feelings of helplessness and a corresponding lack of motivation. Before applying Ame's (1990) theories to at-risk learners, one must remember that motivation among at-risk learners varies greatly. The pregnant teenager or the drug-addicted learner might show little motivation toward academic achievement yet show tremendous motivation to learn to care for a baby or to get off drugs, respectively. Also, a learner's propensity toward being at risk may increase when educators label them as at risk. Therefore, educators must use great caution to avoid making learners feel like failures and to avoid students developing feelings of hopelessness and subsequent losses of motivation.

Upon understanding the relationship between motivation and individual differences, what steps can educators take to increase the motivation of at-risk learners? The following suggestions do not represent a comprehensive list; however, it does provide an indication of how educators may respond to at-risk learners:

1. Students need genuine educational and social accomplishments and experiences that provide short-term goals and strategies for making progress toward other goals. In other words, rather than having only successful experiences, learners need to learn how to be successful (Ames, 1990).

2. Students should receive praise for a relevant aspect of a task. For example, when a student receives praise for a neat report yet the actual task is the quality of the report itself, achievement may be even more undermined (Ames, 1990).

3. Educators should view at-risk learners from individual perspectives. Remembering the concept of multiple intelligences, a learner might be at risk and thus give the appearance of little motivation while having considerable "intelligence" in another area of intelligence.

In summary, the many and complex facets of motivation prevent educators from making assumptions without first considering factors that influence or provide indications of motivation.

Considering the Possibility of Extensive Practical Application

Using great caution not to imply "more of the same" for at-risk learners, these learners might need additional practice or hands-on application. Returning to the multiple intelligences concept, an at-risk learner might have special talents in one area and be somewhat lacking in others (just as all learners!). Also, individual differences can play a role—some students might be able to learn a skill merely by reading a chapter or an instruction sheet; others might need a hands-on activity to "go through the motions," such as writing an essay or putting together a terrarium in the proper order.

Upon selection of the alternative learning environment, one should remember that the selected learning strategy might not work for all at-risk learners, just as all learning strategies do not work for all other learners. It is equally important to remember that at-risk learners will not learn in the same way or in the same amount of time.

Activity 7-3
Suggest several ways schools can provide practical experience rather than relying too heavily on paper-and-pencil tasks. Think of an at-risk learner who has many practical skills yet "fails" at schoolwork. How can curricular areas required by state mandates be taught through practical methods and practical application?

Educators have to use extreme caution to avoid giving more drill, more written papers, and more projects. The "more of the same" mind-set in planning learning activities must be carefully avoided. There comes a time when extensive practice or practical application still does not increase one's achievement, whether physical, social, or academic. Perceptive educators who understand at-risk learners can determine when extensive practice and practical application fail to achieve desired results and when "more of the same" activities fail to reach the desired objective.

Case Study 7-1 looks at why Carl experiences difficulty in school and then offers suggestions for addressing his strengths and weaknesses.

Case Study 7-1: Considering Why Carl Cannot Cope in School

Carl, an 11-year-old African-American boy, simply could not cope in school. His academic achievement was low, he was a behavior problem, he appeared to be totally disinterested in school and learning, he could not keep up with his peers, and he was well on his way to becoming what his teacher and counselor labeled a potential school dropout. Carl, however, had his strengths—he was creative in art class, he was well versed in current events (from watching television he said), he was sociable and, in fact, demonstrated strong interpersonal skills.

In a team meeting of Carl's teachers, the school psychologist, and counselor, someone stated, "Maybe we have labeled Carl too soon— maybe we should not have labeled him at all—maybe with a little help in the right direction, he could cope with school and our expectations."

"Perhaps, but what do we need to do first?" asked one of Carl's teachers.

The group immediately began compiling a list to remediate Carl's weaknesses and to build upon his strengths. The list and corresponding strategies went as follows:

Weaknesses

Low academic achievement	Assess using diagnostic remediation procedures; plan instructions on Carl's level
Behavior problems	Pinpoint misbehaviors to be corrected; plan appropriate action using small steps; make Carl aware of consequences, both negative and positive
Disinterested in school	Be *sure* Carl is disinterested (remember cultural differences); learn what motivates him; determine his interests and plan appropriate instruction

Strengths

Creative in art	Provide challenging art experiences; integrate art with basic skills subjects
Well versed in current events	Provide opportunities for Carl to share knowledge with class to build confidence
Strong interpersonal skills	Provide cooperative learning activities and peer-tutoring experiences

The team decided to contact Carl's parents to let them know of the school's plan. This plan would be pursued for a month or six weeks, and then Carl's at-risk conditions would be reassessed and the plan modified, if needed.

One faculty member said, "I like what we have done—we have a plan to help Carl cope with and succeed in school. This is a small beginning, but we had to start somewhere."

Considering Healthy School Environments

Healthy school environments provide opportunities for students to interact, to find meaning in schoolwork and relationships, and to feel a sense of recognition. Strategies to create such environments include the following:

1. *Schools must provide ongoing opportunities for interaction between teachers and students.* Educators of all levels need to interact with students and to make students feel recognized and accepted. Through smaller classes or, more realistically, smaller groups, educators can increase positive interactions with and among students.

2. *Students must be held accountable for their behavior and learning.* Holding students accountable for their behavior shows they are recognized. To ignore a misbehavior or fail to make a student complete an assignment or participate in class activities provides a signal that academic and behavioral expectations are low. Teachers who fail to hold high expectations for at-risk students and who fail to hold them accountable merely perpetuate students' feelings of invisibility.

3. *Each student is recognized.* The need to be recognized is common to all people, and for most at-risk students, this need has been unfulfilled. Healthy school environments provide opportunities for students to be noticed and connected to other human beings in trusting relationships. These relationships require considerable time and energy and are most effectively accomplished through individual, personal experiences with caring adults (Pigford, 1992).

Healthy environments also include positive verbal environments, which have been reported as having particular significance in contributing to the overall development of learners. Negative verbal environments cause learners to feel unworthy, incompetent, or insignificant as a result of what adults say or do. The most obvious examples include screaming at or making fun of children and adolescents or using ethnic slurs. More common adult behaviors may include showing little or no interest in children, speaking discourteously, or dominating verbal exchanges that occur daily. Verbal comments in positive environments are aimed at satisfying learners' psychological needs and making them feel valued. In speaking situations with children and adolescents, adults should focus not only on the content but also on the affective impact of their words. To maximize healthy environments, teachers should use appropriate words to show caring and affection, should speak courteously and listen attentively, should plan spontaneous opportunities to talk with each learner, and should avoid making judgmental comments about learners (Kostelnik, Stein, Whiren, & Soderman, 1988).

Successful Program: STAY (School to Aid Youth)

The STAY program, primarily an elementary school effort, focuses on creating positive attitudes toward school, building self-esteem, and, generally speaking, increasing children's ability to learn. Serving as a pull-out program, STAY serves first-grade learners identified as being at risk during their kindergarten year. Procedures include one-on-one tutoring and small classes for intensive reading and mathematics instruction. The program stresses communication between parents and teachers. Results of a 10-year study revealed that 80% of the STAY learners performed at or above grade level (Peck, 1989).

Considering the School Culture

The school climate, sometimes called the culture, environment, or the atmosphere, includes all the events of the school day and the spirit in which these events occur. More specifically, the school climate includes the cooperativeness of professional staff—from the administrators to the custodial staff. How do these people treat at-risk learners? Are at-risk learners treated with respect, contempt, or simply ignored? Are daily interactions positive? Do learners feel good about school, its teachers, and the overall educational program? Do teachers have positive and caring attitudes toward at-risk learners and do teachers convey these attitudes to all learners? All children and adolescents need a warm, caring, and positive school environment. While all learners undoubtedly need a positive school climate, at-risk children and adolescents might have a more acute need for acceptance, recognition, and special assistance.

School climates often consist of "intangibles"—aspects difficult to pinpoint and, if considered alone, might appear immaterial, i.e., educators meeting all students at the classroom door and offering some kind of positive comment. While difficult to pinpoint, the school climate might be the factor that decides a school's fate. The following questions, while not an exhaustive list, provide an indication of factors to consider when determining school climates:

1. Do teachers treat at-risk learners with respect and genuine concern, both for their educational achievement and for their overall personal and social growth?
2. Do at-risk learners have equal access to the school's resources and materials, just as other learners?
3. Are verbal comments offered in positive and caring matter?
4. Do all professional staff—other teachers, guidance counselors, and administrators—genuinely care about the success of all learners?
5. Do at-risk learners have opportunities to make significant decisions about their daily school routines as well as their future aspirations?

The list could continue for several pages, but a question and two examples make the point clear. Do at-risk children and adolescents learn in a positive environment where all teacher actions and educational experiences demonstrate concern, caring, and respect? All educators can likely remember a class at some stage of their educational experience that was positive, a joy to attend; comments could be offered and questions asked without fear and school conditions and teacher's actions generally contributed to learners' social and academic growth. On a more negative focus, educators can also usually think of an opposite situation where schools demonstrated a methodical, mechanized routine, the teacher appeared cold, uncaring, and unconcerned, and, overall, feelings of distrust and suspicion appeared to surround all educational decisions.

Without doubt, at-risk learners, already experiencing a risk condition, need the former classroom climate where they can trust significant adults, learn in a positive climate, learn to believe in themselves, develop feelings of self-confidence, and feel educators are genuinely interested in helping them in their areas of need.

Considering Literacy Environments

Literacy environments provide learners with opportunities to interact with teachers and other learners. The school environment actually alters the way at-risk learners learn to read, write, and develop higher order thinking skills needed to learn content. Teachers' efforts to build meaningful relationships with at-risk students and motivate them in reading and writing are crucial to learning and development. Many at-risk students' previous experiences in schools and relationships with their teachers have been negative and stressful. They have few role models for literacy and fewer if any meaningful goals or incentives to achieve. No single instructional approach meets the widely diverse needs of all students at risk. By identifying strengths and linking firsthand experiences and background knowledge to reading and writing instruction, teachers provide an academic setting in which at-risk students can be successful and one in which mutual understanding, respect, and trust can flourish (Gentile & McMillan, 1992).

Considering Academic Survival Skills

School success requires students to master a variety of behaviors that technically cannot be classified as academic skills. These behaviors, sometimes called work habits or prerequisites for academic success, facilitate the acquisition of academic knowledge, which increases students' likelihood of educational success. Academic survival skills include attending to the task, following directions, raising one's hand to ask and answer questions, and writing legibly. The converse also holds true; failing to demonstrate these behaviors negatively affects academic achievement and teacher-student interaction (Morgan & Jensen, 1988; McWhirter & McWhirter, 1990).

Educators teaching academic skills offer a significant contribution to at-risk learners who might not know these skills or realize their importance in determining school success. Regardless of students' at-risk condition, the learning of academic survival skills and social skills (such as polite forms of disagreement and expressing one's opinions) can help the learner, both academically and socially.

Successful Program: Creative At-Risk Education

The Del Dios Middle School Creative At-Risk Education (CARE) program in Escondido, California, provides a safe and nurturing alternative educational setting where middle school students who have poor attendance records, are emotionally and/or physically abused, and are behaviorally difficult can succeed. Through this program students experience academic success, develop positive self-esteem, and become respected members of the student body. Statistically, these students will drop out of school, end up on welfare, or through criminal activity, serve time in prison.

The program removes the most demanding and behaviorally difficult students from the regular classroom and places them in a setting that focuses on improving behavior and self-esteem through individual and group counseling. Academic achievement has improved through small class instruction and the development of parent support programs. CARE students work closely with the associated student body (ASB) officers in planning schoolwide activities, providing them experiences in teamwork and leadership. Although the program was primarily developed to serve the students at Del Dios Middle School, students from other Escondido middle schools have been accepted in the program. The program serves 2.5% of the student population at Del Dios and spans a variety of socioeconomic levels ranging from the affluent to the homeless. Thirty-nine percent of the CARE students qualify for the federally funded free or reduced lunch program.

The program provides the opportunity for students to improve academic skills due to smaller class size, and individual assistance allows the student to improve grades as well as attitudes toward school. Individual and group counseling contributes to improved behavior. Problems shared during counseling sessions encompass emotional, physical, and sexual abuse; alcoholism; drug addiction; the manufacture and sale of drugs by parents; neglect; abandonment; and homelessness. Goals of improving self-esteem and developing teamwork skills are met through shared projects with the ASB and through peer counseling sessions. Related goals of assisting dysfunctional families and meeting the basic needs of food and clothing are met through job placement, referral to other agencies, parent support groups, and assistance from community organizations (Kuhns, 1992).

Alternative Learning Environments: Strategies

Alternative learning environments may take many forms: different organizational patterns, curriculum designed to meet individual needs, a management system allowing democratic procedures, or a teaching-learning strategy such as cooperative learning. Alternative learning environments can be within a classroom, within a school, or in a totally different school such as a special school for pregnant teenagers, a school for potential drop-outs, or a school for juvenile delinquents or learners prone to violence. This section looks at selected alternative learning environments and suggests, both theoretically and practically, that at-risk learners need a learning environment in which success becomes the norm rather that the exception.

Individualized Instruction

Individualized instruction probably continues to be the most effective means of instructing learners. Although the term can be defined in various ways, Dawson (1987) has stated that "Individualized instruction means tailoring learning activities to the needs of individualized students" (p. 364). This definition means providing learners an opportunity to work and progress at their own pace and ability. Special learning materials sometimes have to be developed to meet individual needs, interests, or learning styles. Individualized instruction has been criticized as being too time-consuming and allowing students too little direct instruction. Teaching materials consist of self-instructional units, answer sheets, and tests designed for students working in small heterogeneous groups. Students complete their own work and also assist other students who may be having difficulty (Dawson, 1987).

Homogeneous Ability Grouping

The research (Manning & Lucking, 1990) on ability grouping suggests educators should seek viable alternatives to organizing learners according to ability and academic achievement. The implications send a clear message to educators working with at-risk learners: Placing all at-risk learners together for instruction or placing at-risk learners in low-ability groups might seriously impair their chances of overcoming at-risk conditions. Beliefs that homogeneous ability grouping lowers self-concepts and causes psychological damage among lower ability students is evidenced by learners' placed in lower ability groups feeling "dumb." If learners are not at risk, they might become at-risk learners as they develop feelings of defeat and frustration. Even with learners having these feelings, many educators continue to group according to ability and to believe that the practice actually reduces a student's propensity toward being at-risk.

Definitions and Rationale

Ability grouping generally implies grouping students for instructional activities by ability or achievement to create the greatest amount of homogeneity among learners (Slavin, 1987a). The rationale has been that grouping students for instruction decreases the differences among learners' knowledge, skills, developmental stages, and learning rates. Rather than risking too much learner heterogeneity and risking a lesson being too easy or too difficult for some learners, teachers assume that learners can be grouped according to an established criteria, for example, previous ability and achievement, so they all can profit from one lesson (Slavin, 1987b).

Self-Concepts and Attitudes
Proponents of ability grouping argue that the self-concept of low-ability learners suffers when they compete in high-ability groups; therefore, ability grouping improves low-ability learners' self-concepts. Research studies, however, do not support this supposition (Dawson, 1987). In fact, available research suggests that the desirable attitudes and self-concepts of low-ability children may be seriously impaired when homogeneously grouped (Wilson & Schmits, 1978). Evidence also suggests that ability grouping may adversely affect the attitudes, achievement, and opportunities of students in lower ability groups (Riccio, 1985). Students assigned to classes on the basis of ability may experience a stigmatizing effect, which may evoke in students low expectations for both achievement and behavior (Slavin, 1988b). A lower self-concept might already be a problem with at-risk learners. These learners deserve an organizational arrangement that promotes their self-concept and increases their overall chances of school success.

Academic Achievement
Overwhelming evidence indicates that ability grouping does not enhance student achievement in the elementary school (Dawson, 1987; Gamoran, 1986; Slavin, 1987a, Slavin, 1987b). Slavin (1988b) concluded that "overall, the effects of ability grouping cluster closely around zero for students of all achievement levels" (p. 69). Another serious situation results as one considers evidence suggesting that ability grouping may actually reduce achievement levels among average- and low-ability learners (Dawson, 1987).

Teacher Behaviors
Teachers vary their interaction styles and teaching techniques with lower- and upper-ability students, often shortchanging lower ability learners. Specifically, teachers often use challenging and creative teaching techniques with upper-ability groups while using more routine methods (e.g., drill and worksheets) with lower-ability learners. Likewise, some teachers offer short explanations to lower-ability groups yet provide upper-ability groups with more elaborate and thought-provoking explanations. In reality, teachers often prejudge lower-ability students' ability and motivation and, consciously or unconsciously, select teaching-learning experiences and harbor attitudes that have the potential for impeding the progress of lower-ability learners (Manning & Lucking, 1990). At-risk learners need educators who

are caring, concerned, and competent to address at-risk conditions. The evidence examined in this section suggests that homogeneous ability grouping is the antithesis of the organizational structure at-risk learners need.

Multicultural Concerns

The possibility of ability grouping resulting in a form of segregation should warrant educators' attention and concern. Ability grouping patterns often parallel students' nonacademic characteristics such as race or ethnic background, socioeconomic class, or personal appearance. Lower socioeconomic status and minority learners often find themselves placed in lower ability groups. Such practices may be discriminatory since students are segregated along ethnic and social class lines (Dawson, 1987).

Ability Grouping and At-Risk Learners

Educators working with at-risk learners need to avoid grouping their students by ability—perceived or documented. In fact, suggesting an incompatibility between homogeneous ability grouping and appropriate educational experiences for at-risk learners is a serious understatement. Homogeneous ability grouping has too many disadvantages and shortcomings for all learners, especially for learners already experiencing difficulty. At-risk learners need programs that increase academic achievement, efforts that contribute to positive self-concepts, teachers that demonstrate effective teaching techniques and caring attitudes, and organizational patterns that promote harmony among students of varying genders, cultures, and social classes. The evidence just discussed, especially the research of Manning and Lucking (1990), suggests that ability grouping produces just the opposite effects—academic achievement does not increase (and in some cases actually decreases); self-concepts reach new lows; teachers demonstrate behaviors that learners do not need, especially at-risk learners; and, in many cases, learners are segregated by race, culture, or social class. The challenge for educators of at-risk learners is to identify organizational strategies that counteract the disadvantages of ability grouping.

Alternatives to Ability Grouping

The overwhelming evidence indicating that ability grouping fails to improve students' academic achievement and simultaneously damages slower learners' self-concepts illustrates the need for alternatives to this organizational practice. While this assertion holds true for all learners, it may be particularly true for at-risk learners. The following list, while neither definitive nor exhaustive, offers several alternative organizational approaches that have the potential for addressing at-risk learners' needs.

1. *Heterogeneous grouping:* Classes and groups of students can be organized with a mixture of learners of all ability levels. In contrast to homogeneous

ability grouping, this organization allows students to experience learners of all abilities, ethnicity, and socioeconomic status. Teachers using such an organization pattern have the responsibility to adapt learning environments to meet the needs of individual students. Relating instruction and materials to individual needs eliminates the categorical labeling process that accompanies homogeneous ability grouping (Riccio, 1985).

2. *Regrouping by subject area:* This grouping arrangement allows learners to remain in heterogeneous groups most of the day and then "regroup" within the class for selected subjects, for example, reading and mathematics (Slavin, 1987b). Such an organization allows learners to know and socialize with students of other ability levels, socioeconomic classes, and ethnic backgrounds, but it also provides ability groups within subskills for selected subject areas. When properly implemented, regrouping has three advantages: 1) Students stay in heterogeneous groups most of the day, thus reducing the labeling effect; 2) students are grouped on the basis of their ability in a particular subject rather than overall achievement; and 3) elementary regrouping plans tend to be more flexible than ability-grouped classes because changing students for a class or two is less disruptive than changing basic class assignments (Slavin, 1988b).

3. *Joplin plan:* Actually a form of regrouping, this plan assigns students to heterogeneous groups for the major portion of the day and then regroups for reading across grade levels. For example, a reading group may have a combination of fourth, fifth and sixth graders. Effects of the Joplin plan have been positive overall, probably because it reduces within-class grouping, allows teachers more time to provide direct instruction, and reduces the time students must work unsupervised during seatwork (Slavin, 1987b).

4. *Mastery learning:* Slavin suggests that mastery learning can be an effective alternative to homogeneous ability grouping. This teaching approach can also be an effective means of constantly changing teaching and learning decisions to reflect student performance. In mastery learning, whole class instruction precedes a formative test. Then, students with scores above the mastery level begin enrichment activities; those not reaching the stated criterion level receive corrective instruction. Whether implemented as individualized, continuous progress, or another strategy, mastery learning reduces the stigma placed on being grouped with an entire cluster of all low-ability students (Slavin, 1987b, 1988a).

Cooperative Learning

Educators during the 1990s and beyond increasingly will recognize the benefits of students of various abilities working cooperatively. These efforts typically will arise from teams or groups working together to accomplish learning goals. While competition among learners traditionally has been encouraged in American schools, interest in students pursuing learning goals cooperatively can be traced to the early 1900s. The current interest in cooperative learning stems from evidence suggesting that cooperative learning, when properly implemented, has the potential for contributing positively to academic achievement, social skills, self-esteem, and multiethnic relationships. These areas undoubtedly can have positive effects on at-risk learners. In a society becoming increasingly more diverse, all of these dimensions of student growth and well-being will be important. Educators of at-risk students can play a major role in cooperative learning endeavors as they understand and model cooperative strategies, recognize the benefits of cooperative learning, and lead teachers and students toward cooperative learning efforts.

Definition

Cooperative learning involves any one of several organizational structures in which a group of students pursue academic goals through collaborative efforts, work together in small groups, draw on each other's strengths, and assist each other in completing tasks. Learning both academic content and social skills, these students work cooperatively in small heterogenous groups, share responsibility for learning, and develop an appreciation for other's differences (Slavin, 1987a). Effective cooperative learning methods share two common features. First, effective methods have group goals whereby team members work interdependently to earn teacher recognition or other forms of success. Second, methods producing positive results require individual accountability, whereby group success depends on individual contributions and the learning of all members.

Rationale

Research on the effectiveness of cooperative learning revealed positive outcomes in several areas. First, most studies on academic achievement show that high, average, and low achievers gain equally from cooperative learning experiences. Second, research on social skills and gains report consistent findings that students expressed a greater liking for their classmates as a result of working cooperatively. Third, cooperative learning has been found to increase self-esteem because students have more friends and have more positive feelings about their school experiences and academic achievement. Fourth, multiethnic relationships improved because the increased contact between students engages learners in pleasant activities, requires that team members work toward a common goal, and provides feelings of group membership and a greater liking for classmates (Hilke, 1990).

Cooperative Learning Methods

Table 7-1 provides readers with an overview of selected types of cooperative learning methods. It is important to emphasize that educators should select

---

Activity 7-4
Examine Manning's and Lucking's article on cooperating learning strategies (*The Clearing House*, January/February 1991, pp. 152–156) to determine characteristics, advantages, and disadvantages of each. Then mark the ones that may have the most potential for at-risk learners.

---

the cooperative learning strategy that matches at-risk learners' conditions. For example, depending on students' at-risk conditions or needs, the school wanting individual quizzes and team scores might recommend Jigsaw II; however, TGT might be the recommendation for the school wanting to replace quizzes with weekly tournaments. The educator's role in the selection process includes explaining the various cooperative learning types or, better yet, allowing a team to learn cooperatively about cooperative learning strategies and, then, presenting the advantages of each type to other teachers.

Responsible educators who want to plan alternative learning environments for at-risk learners can take several steps:

1. Encourage all professionals responsible for at-risk learners to provide cooperative opportunities.
2. Plan sufficient lead time.
3. Arrange for appropriate in-service activities.
4. Model cooperative learning strategies.
5. Educate parents and families.
6. Teach students the value of cooperation over competition.

Technological Advances

Recent technological advances provide educators with an interesting and motivating means to assist the needs of at-risk students. Learners report word processing programs and computer-assisted mathematics instruction improve attitudes and performance in writing and mathematics, respectively. Also, the use of computers and newer technologies allows educators to match schoolwork with the learning preferences of academically at-risk learners, who require concrete learning activities. Despite the lack of appropriate use of technology in schools, practice, research, and literature suggest that learning activities delivered with a variety of technologies are especially useful and appropriate for minority and disadvantaged students because technology produces positive attitudes toward learning and promoting success for low achievers (Ashbrook, 1984; Baer, 1988; Beebe, 1989; D'Ignazio, 1988; Dowdney, 1987; Hancock, 1992/1993; G. Smith, 1989).

TABLE 7-1   Overview of Selected Cooperative Learning Methods

Method/Proponent	Brief Description/Comments
Learning Together (Johnson & Johnson, 1987, 1989/90)	Emphasizing cooperative effort, Learning Together has five basic elements: positive interdependence (students believe they are responsible for both their learning and the team's); face-to-face interaction (students explain their learning and help others with assignments); individual accountability (students demonstrate mastery of material); social skills (students communicate effectively, build and maintain trust, and resolve conflicts); group processing (groups periodically assess their progress and how to improve effectiveness). Uses four- or five-member heterogeneous teams.
Student Teams-Achievement Divisions (STAD)(Slavin, 1978)	Four student learning teams (mixed in performance levels, sex, and ethnicity); teacher presents lesson, students work in teams and help others master material. Students then take quizzes; cooperative efforts are not allowed on quizzes; team rewards are earned. Applicable to most grades/subjects.
Teams-Games-Tournament (TGT) (DeVries & Slavin, 1978)	Using the same teacher presentation and teamwork as STAD, TGT replaces the quizzes with members of other teams to contribute points to team scores. Competition occurs at tournament tables against others with similar academic records. The winner of each tournament brings six points to her or his team. Low achievers compete with low achievers (a similar arrangement exists for high achievers), which provides all students with an equal opportunity for success. As with STAD, team rewards are earned. Applicable to most grades and subjects.
Jigsaw (Aronson, Blaney, Stephan, Sikes, & Snapp, 1978)	Students are assigned to six-member teams to work on academic material that has been divided into sections. Each member reads a section; then members of different teams meet to become experts. Students return to groups and teach other members about their sections. Students must listen to their teammates to learn other sections.
Jigsaw 2 (Slavin, 1987a)	Students work in four- or five-member teams as in TGT or STAD. Rather than being assigned specific parts, students read a common narrative (e.g., a chapter). Students also receive a topic on which to become an expert. Learners with the same topics meet together as in Jigsaw, and then they teach the material to their original group. Students take individual quizzes.
Team Assisted Individualization (TAI) (Slavin, Leavey, & Madden, 1986)	Uses four-member mixed-ability groups (as with STAD and TGT); differs from STAD and TGT in that it combines cooperative learning and indivi- dualized instruction and is applicable only to mathematics in grades 3 through 6. Learners take a placement test, then proceed at their own pace. Team members check one another's work and help with problems. Without help, students take unit tests that are scored by student monitors. Each week, the teacher evaluates and gives team rewards.

TABLE 7-1 Overview of Selected Cooperative Learning Methods
Continued

Method/Proponent	Brief Description/Comments
Cooperative Integrated Reading Composition (CIRC) (Madden, Slavin, & Stevens, 1986)	Designed to teach reading and writing in upper elementary grades. CIRC assigns students to different reading teams. Teacher works with one team, while other teams engage in cognitive activities: reading, predicting story endings, summarizing stories, writing responses, practicing decoding, and learning vocabulary. Teams follow sequence of teacher instruction, team practice, team preassessments, and quizzes. Quizzes may not be taken until the team feels each student is ready. Team rewards are given.
Group Investigation (Sharan & Sharan, 1989/1990)	Groups are formed according to a common interest in a topic. Students plan research, divide learning assignments among members, synthesize/summarize findings, and present the findings to the entire class.

Source: Manning, M. L., & Lucking, R. (1991). The what, why and how of cooperative learning. *The Clearing House, 64,* 153.

Successful Program: Using Technology to Prevent Pregnancy and AIDS

Lee (1990) tells of Booth Memorial School in Boise, Idaho, which serves as an alternative school for pregnant teenagers and teen parents. The school focuses efforts toward self-esteem, parenting, suicide, women's rights, child abuse, and job-finding strategies. The teenagers at Booth have unique at-risk concerns such as facing legal and medical concerns as well as struggling to keep pace with their academic subjects. The program at Booth incorporates the use of computers and video cameras as well as various other audiovisual equipment. While Booth Memorial statistically has an 80% dropout rate, it graduates more than 90% of its students. The success rate is attributed to its use of technology, which the coordinator feels holds the learners' interest. Mastering of technology, especially computers, increases learners' self-concepts. Also, the school uses video equipment to film role-playing situations such as applying for a job or going to court for a child custody case. Booth bases its programs on the philosophy that keeping students interested requires many different tools and techniques. Career aids and software include *Assessing Employability* (Educational Associates, Chatsworth, California), *Improving Your Self-Concept* (MCE Software, Kalamazoo, Michigan), and *Teenage Parents* (University of Wisconsin at Madison).

Successful Program: Interactive Technology and Algebra

San Marcos High School in San Antonio, Texas, recruited 20 ninth graders for an interactive television (ITV) classroom. The learners came from remedial mathematics classes, where for eight years they had been doing traditional skill work. This ITV program allowed these learners to participate in a curriculum project using full two-way audio and video fiberoptic interactive television. PATH Mathematics (Partnership for Access to Higher Mathematics) formed a partnership with Southwest Texas State University, the San Marcos School District, San Marcos Telephone Company, and various community (families, social agencies, and professional associations) members to improve the mathematical skills of at-risk students. PATH mathematics provides students with a comprehensive, hands-on prealgebra course early in their secondary education so they can complete algebra I, geometry, and algebra II. The program uses the latest interactive communications technology to link the university directly with the high school.

The scope and sequence of PATH focus on using manipulatives and technology coupled with a problem-solving focus in a cooperative setting. PATH's goal is expanding students' knowledge of mathematical concepts and the critical thinking skills necessary to apply the concepts. The PATH program includes a tutoring program; a "Homework Hotline" (Kennedy & Chavkin, 1992/1993, p. 25), social workers and social work interns collaborating with social service agencies; minority and majority businesses, parents, and the university; and parent education workshops (Kennedy & Chavkin, 1992/1993).

A number of successful programs and efforts can be identified:

- IBM and Hazelden Health Promotion Services helps teens see the consequences of drug abuse through their program called TARGET.
- Interactive, Inc., has developed an interactive videodisk for high school students to highlight the consequences of dropping out of school. The consequences of students' choices vary depending on their gender and ethnicity.
- Dialog, Inc., has created an on-line retrieval system for learners that provides access to the most current knowledge in a large number of business, consumer, reference, science, and technology databases.
- "Windows on Science," a videodisk series serving as a teaching tool in grades 1 through 6, provided an alternative to conventional textbooks and illustrates and demonstrates aspects of scientific phenomena that would be difficult to teach using traditional formats.
- The American Broadcasting Company has integrated a large column of news footage with videodisk technology and the Macintosh Hypercard

data organization capability to create a series of interactive packages available for school use (Hancock, 1992/1993).

Special Schooling

Sometimes even the most carefully designed alternative learning environments within schools and classes fail to address the needs of at-risk learners. Teachers not adequately trained or motivated to work with at-risk learners, the negative effects of peer pressure, a lack of relevant materials, and a host of other factors may contribute to the failure of alternative learning environments, within schools and classes, to provide for at-risk learners. Although each at-risk student deserves individual consideration by a group of professionals, these learners might need a learning environment even more different than that customarily provided. For example, these learners might need a separate school—a whole new environment different from what educators normally expect in U.S. schools—such as schools specially designed for at-risk learners that have teachers knowledgeable of and trained in dealing with at-risk students and individual conditions, curriculum tailored to meet the needs of at-risk learners, and alternative means of assessment. This section continues to examine alternative learning environments for at-risk learners.

Types of Special or Alternative Schools

A look at the various schools across the United States designed to address specific at-risk conditions reveals several general types and also reveals that alternative schools exist to address almost any at-risk condition. The first part of this section looks at several representative types and then suggests programs for a number of specific at-risk conditions.

Type 1, *schools focusing on culture,* includes selecting children from a variety of races, cultures, ethnic groups, and socioeconomic classes. These learners study, learn, socialize, and play together for designated parts of the school day. During other parts of the school day, learners have instruction in their own cultural or ethnic group and learn about their cultural heritages such as backgrounds, language, history, and other significant aspects that might influence their lives. Then the learners return to the large group and share cultural learnings and attitudes. Such an arrangement provides at-risk learners with opportunities to better understand others' cultural backgrounds as well as their own.

Type 2, *schools focusing on the learner,* place emphasis on learners as either children or adolescents. Educators recognize the importance of basic skills and other school learning, but the overall welfare of the learner, or more precisely the child or adolescent, is considered more important than content and skills to be learned. Goals include children and adolescents having positive self-concepts, perceiving school as a successful place, being able to deal with difficult situations and events, and using their own interests as a basis for learning.

Type 3, *schools focusing on skills and training,* almost the opposite of type 2, places emphasis on learning and achievement, specifically in the areas of basic skills such as reading, writing, and mathematics. Type 3 is similar to the more conservative view of the schools' roles except for perhaps classes being smaller and the primary focus being more on specific educational needs than on an overall education. The major difference is that the so-called "frills" are not emphasized at the expense of basic skill learning.

Type 4, *schools focusing on the community,* provides for school experiences being derived from the community. For example, school experiences come from "real life" things such as malls, manufacturing companies, courts, social agencies, and other educational resources in the community. Type 4 schools provide at least two important assets. First, parents and other community people, becoming actively involved in school matters, better understand the need for the involvement of the entire community and, second, learners see the relevance of their studies to real life. For example, the learner studying law enforcement procedures can have firsthand experiences working in court situations or perhaps with social service agencies.

Type 5, *schools focusing on specific at-risk conditions,* places major emphasis on a single (or perhaps two) at-risk conditions. Such efforts may include schools designed to address only the needs of pregnant teenagers or teenage mothers, the needs of potential school dropouts, the needs of learners with limited English skills, or the needs of promising students who need an extra boost toward success. These and other programs (and the addresses of their contact persons) designed to address specific at-risk conditions are discussed in more detail in the next section.

Exemplary Programs

While most at-risk programs fall into one of these five school types, their actual focus depends on the at-risk condition being addressed. The rationale for this chapter holds that for a number of reasons (perhaps unknown reasons), some at-risk learners do not respond to "more of the same" or slightly different approaches and, therefore, need alternative learning environments. This section examines several exemplary programs that address the needs of at-risk students who either cannot or do not have the skills to succeed in regular classroom settings. The programs being discussed in this section were selected for their evidence of effectiveness and because they address specific at-risk conditions. It is important to note that while these have been proven successes, many other fine at-risk efforts exist today.

Improving Self-Esteem

The Apollo Program, based on the belief that positive self-esteem is necessary for achievement, works to involve students in the school process and in their learning. This program in Simi Valley, California, provides an alternative learning environment for about 400 students who have not succeeded in traditional high school programs. The major goal of the Apollo Program is to increase self-esteem in the belief that self-esteem leads to academic achievement. Rather than viewing students as problems, this program sees the educational system as the problem, and then tries to involve students in changing the educational system to meet their needs. The program bases efforts on the four A's: attention, acceptance, appreciation, and affection.

Students in the Apollo Program participate in establishing the rules and share in the responsibility of enforcing the rules. Meetings are held throughout the school year for students to express their opinions and input. Teachers in this alternative learning program have more than 300 hours of training in learning styles, group processes, communication skills, classroom management techniques, effective discipline methods, and problem-solving skills. Results of the program include habitually late students being punctual, a decrease in obscene graffiti, students being given help to end drug and alcohol abuse rather than being suspended, and fighting being handled through discussion sessions rather than punishment. Readers who desire additional information should contact Principal, Apollo Continuation School, 3150 School Street, St. Simi Valley, California 93065.

Providing Meaningful and Relevant Work

As previously suggested, for several reasons, schoolwork and related activities, often seem to have little meaning for some at-risk learners. They feel schoolwork does not relate to their life events, to their community, and to their world.

One program, the Media Academy, tries to provide meaningful work and experiences learners can use in the neighborhood and in their personal lives. Actually a school-within-a-school, the Media Academy increases the interest of at-risk African- and Hispanic-American students by providing opportunities to produce school publications. Students take an active part in journalism courses while enrolled in other courses required by the school and state. Members of the Media Academy make up approximately 90% of the staffs that produce the school newspaper, the yearbook, and a Spanish/English newspaper distributed to neighborhood residents. Also, students have regular exposure to production operations in local radio and television stations. The program provides five motivating factors that engage students in their work: competence in the work they do, extrinsic rewards such as field trips, intrinsic rewards such as being a part of something happening, social support, and ownership of the program and its products. For additional information, contact Gregory A. Smith, Project Assistant at the University of Wisconsin–Madison, 1025 West Johnson, Madison, Wisconsin 53705.

The following programs came from *Educational Programs That Work* (Sopris West, Inc., 1992), a publication of The National Diffusion Network. Readers will find more detailed information about this excellent resource in the section at the end of the chapter on "For Additional Information."

Pregnant and Parenting Teens

The major goal of Graduation, Reality, and Dual-Role Skills (GRADS) is to keep pregnant and parenting teens in school, with additional goals of encouraging positive health care practices and helping young parents set occupational goals. GRADS has been approved for all pregnant and parenting teens, male and female, in grades 7 through 12 in urban, suburban, and rural communities. An important feature of the program is the 1300-page *Adolescent Parent Resource Guide*, which provides the practical problems, concepts, and strategies that guide the development of skills in teenage parents. The guide discusses communication and skills necessary for effective decision-making in the teen family. It recognizes the stresses affecting pregnant teens and focuses on management skills required for teen family wellness.

The central themes of the guide and the curriculum (which emphasizes practical reasoning) are the practical problems of the adolescent parent at home, school, and work; the development of knowledge and skills to solve problems in real life; developing economic independence; building self-esteem; considering alternatives; judging consequences; scrutinizing decisions; and taking morally defensible actions. Audiovisuals, textbooks, and supplemental texts are also part of the program. Regular GRADS classes are supplemented by seminars and individual projects. Teachers serve one school or travel among three or four. Teachers also build strong relationships with students through home visits and visits with parents. For additional information, contact Ohio Department of Education, Division of Vocational and Career Education, Room 909, 65 South Front Street, Columbus, Ohio 43266-0308. Phone: (614)466-3046.

Poor Attendance and Low Academic Performance

The DeLaSalle model is a last chance alternative school for high school dropouts unable to be served by any other public or private school. This model has been approved for populations fitting the high school level (grades 9 through 12), with most students between the ages of 14 and 18. The DeLaSalle Education Center is a private not-for-profit agency that has served the greater Kansas City area since 1971. Its goals include increasing school attendance, improving academic skills, and enhancing self-esteem and educational attitudes in students who have dropped out of high school and have no other chance for completing an education.

DeLaSalle employs a variety of programming features and services within a comprehensive model to allow every youngster to be successful. These include a supportive nontraditional school structure, a small student-teacher ratio, individualized learning, student contracting, intensive counseling, vocational skill training, and a diagnostic prescriptive teaching process. These services are designed around a core academic curriculum that can be adapted to any ability or age level because of the individualized focus of the program. For additional information, contact DeLaSalle Education Center, 3740 Forest, Kansas City, Missouri 64109-3200. Phone: (816)561-3312; fax (816)561-6106.

Academically Promising Urban School Student
Public and private school collaboration provides an opportunity for advanced residential study for academically promising urban school students. The program is designed for high school students, grades 10 and 11, who have demonstrated high academic achievement and motivation.

Public and private school collaboration makes connections work. Where public and private schools have not traditionally joined forces, they do so within a collaborative framework. This allows them to apply their finest resources to meet significant needs. It also allows them to gain the support of leading corporations and foundations as well as research institutions and museums as they seek to respond to those needs. A five-week program of advanced residential study is conducted for students from 13 urban school districts. They have been joined by distinguished corporations (from AT&T to Xerox) and noted research institutions (from Brown University to the federal Star Schools Program). Students study topics ranging from advanced astronomy to vectors and matrices. They return to their schools encouraged by their accomplishments. Many other collaborative activities have flowed from this initiative and include programs for students and teachers alike. For additional information, contact Office of Public Private Collaboration, Choate Rosemary Hall, Box 788, 333 Christian Street, Wallingford, Connecticut 06482. Phone: (203)269-7722, ext. 313.

Limited-English-Proficient Learners
Valued Young Program is a cross-age tutoring program designed to reduce dropout rates among seventh- and eighth-grade children who are limited-English-proficient (LEP) and at risk of leaving school. The Valued Youth Program is unique in that tutors work with LEP students at risk of dropping out of school. When placed in a responsible tutoring role and supported in their efforts, tutors gain significant social and economic benefits. The program has three levels that incorporate all the major features of the model—philosophy, instruction, and support.

The philosophical base consists of tenets such as all students can learn; all students, parents, and teachers have a right to participate fully in creating

---

Successful Program: City-As-School

City-As-School (CAS) can be described as follows:

- An independent alternative high school that links students with hundreds of learning experiences throughout the community.
- Students spend up to 30 to 40 hours per week in learning experiences utilizing community resources of a business, civic, cultural, social, or political nature.
- Academic credit is granted for each learning experience successfully completed.
- A structured, student-centered Learning Experience Activity Packet (LEAP) helps to identify and evaluate discrete areas of instruction in each resource.
- Students attend resources for one cycle (nine weeks) or two cycles

and receive credit or no credit rather than letter or numerical grades.

- Specialized, small classes support activities at community resources.
- Weekly seminar groups serve as the forum for discussions of guidance, academic, and social issues.

Several indicators document the effectiveness of CAS:

- Improvement in attendance
- Increase in course completion rate of students
- Better attitude toward schooling, career, and adults
- Evidence derived from school records, pre- and post-test comparison of a control group and use of Likert-scaled instruments.

Adapted from Sopris West, Inc. (1992). *Educational Programs That Work*. Longmont, CO: Author, p. C-1.

and maintaining excellent schools; excellence in schools contributes to individual and collective economic growth, stability, and advancement; and commitment to educational excellence is created by including students, parents, and teachers in setting goals, making decisions, monitoring progress, and evaluating outcomes. The instructional strategy incorporates five major components including classes for tutors; tutoring sessions; field trips; role-modeling; and student recognition. The support strategy involves curriculum, coordination, staff enrichment, family involvement, and evaluation activities. For additional information, contact Intercultural Development Research Association, 5835 Callaghan Road, Suite 350, San Antonio, Texas 78228. Phone: (512)684-8180.

Another program, Early Prevention of School Failure Migrant Program (for Spanish- and English-speaking children), is designed to determine the migrant child's strengths and needs. The goal of the program is to reduce

---

Activity 7-5

Consider the at-risk programs just discussed and list the essential characteristics that seem to underlay all successful programs. For example, are
there similar characteristics for all effective at-risk programs, i.e., do all
(or most) effective programs include an emphasis on basic skills, self-concepts, or parent involvement?

---

the at-risk factor by assessing needs and strengths and developing an appropriate program for each child. The project provides follow-up activities in
kinesthetic, visual, auditory, expressive language, and receptive language
skills. Appropriate program resources and effective teaching materials for
large and small group instruction are available. Also the program has developed three parent components: 1) growth and development, 2) building
school success, and 3) parent involvement in the school and with the child's
educational process. For additional information, contact Project Director,
Peotone School District 207-U; 114 N. Second Street, Peotone, Illinois 60468.
Phone: (708)258-3478.

Considerations for All Special Schools

Educators planning and implementing special schools for at-risk learners
have a responsibility to both at-risk learners and other learners. Specific
guidelines warrant consideration to ensure equity and equal access to all
educational programs. Individual at-risk learners, schools, and communities need to be considered individually; however, the following guidelines
represent a starting point and also show the importance of careful planning
to avoid educational and professional as well as legal problems.

1. At-risk students and their parents have input into the decision regarding attendance at a special school rather than learners being sent or
   assigned to the school because other alternative learning environments
   have not worked.
2. At-risk students have opportunities to socialize with learners of other
   ability and motivation levels and other racial, cultural, and socioeconomic groups rather than experiencing a form of segregation.
3. At-risk students and their parents are not faced with financial burdens
   greater than the regular schools would have imposed.
4. At-risk students and their parents are not given false hopes or claims of
   success that are not realistic or possible.
5. At-risk learners should be considered as individuals rather than as a group
   of homogeneous learners experiencing the same at-risk condition.

6. At-risk learners should have the opportunity to return to other alternative learning environments or to regular classroom settings rather than the special school being considered a "last resort" place to be sent.
7. At-risk learners have programs based on their individual needs and also program dimensions that focus on educational aspects needed by all learners such as an emphasis on basic skills, positive self-concepts, and socialization skills.

Testing and Assessment

Educators have recognized in recent years that testing and assessment have the potential for taking a considerable toll on children and adolescents, both at risk and others. This issue, being heavily debated in the 1990s, will undoubtedly continue to be a concern during the twenty-first century. The consequences of testing may be more serious for at-risk learners who already struggle in a vulnerable position. The challenge for educators is to understand the dangers of testing, especially with at-risk learners, and to take deliberate action to ensure these learners are tested fairly and objectively with *appropriate* testing instruments.

Without doubt, some testing and assessment procedures are fair, measure the intended knowledge or skill, and serve an educationally useful purpose, i.e., some diagnostic tests used to diagnose an individual's strengths and weaknesses are valid. Proponents of tests include their widespread public and professional acceptance, their cost-efficiency in administration and reporting, their usefulness in accountability, their usefulness in placing students in special programs, and their role in the making of curricular decisions (Miller-Jones, 1989).

Arguments against testing include the extent of whether knowledge domains are sufficiently understood to be adequately represented in a sample of items, whether test items are biased toward a particular sociocultural experience, and whether test items are fair (Miller-Jones, 1989). While Miller-Jones was not referring specifically to at-risk learners, important issues are raised: Do tests measure the particular strengths of at-risk learners? Do tests favor more successful, high-achieving students? Are tests available to measure esoteric interests, which may be the only factor keeping at-risk learners in school? Except for the previously mentioned diagnostic tests, the seemingly national obsession with testing has several drawbacks: testing for all the wrong reasons, testing with inappropriate instruments, and mismatching learners and their tests.

Rather than this text advocating a total ban on testing, the authors recommend testing instruments *designed for* at-risk learners. These learners should not be placed in further jeopardy by having their futures determined by instruments that fail to test their strengths. Several points surface when considering testing at-risk learners:

1. Tests should be designed specifically for at-risk learners.
2. Tests should be free of cultural, gender, and social class bias.
3. Tests should be only one factor in determining at-risk learners' strengths and weaknesses.
4. Tests should provide an understanding of the reasoning behind a child's response.
5. Tests should be of a nature that they can be understood by at-risk learners and their families.
6. Tests should take into account that many at-risk learners may have not been successful academically and, therefore, might not be "good" test takers.

Educators of at-risk children and adolescents have a challenge and responsibility to these learners. Both proponents' and critics' arguments deserve to be understood and considered. Then this question should be answered: Do testing instruments measure at-risk learners' strengths in a fair and nonbiased manner? It is unlikely that educators will not have to test at-risk learners (and probably unwise)—testing plays too significant and powerful a role in U.S. schools. Educators need to determine appropriate tests, to remember that even the most carefully designed testing instruments may have their limitations, and to plan educational programs based on the test results as well as other criteria.

Case Study 7-2 shows how educators can considered alternative learning environments for a Native American young adolescent.

Case Study 7-2: Considering Alternative Learning Environments

John C., a 14-year-old Native American boy, is a seventh grader at a reservation school. His school record has been plagued with problems—he has been retained once, and he has low academic achievement, motivation, and self-concept. He was first identified as an at-risk student in the fourth grade when his teachers and counselor began to realize that he was not "keeping up" with the other students. He has demonstrated considerable ability in spatial relationships—he can "see" geometric perspectives and designs that most learners cannot see, yet continues to experience difficulty in all basic skills areas. John's teachers, mostly middle-class African- and Anglo-Americans (only a handful of the teachers at the school are Native American), implemented an educational program they think is appropriate for John. Emphasis is placed on large-group homogeneous instruction, academic achievement, considerable book and content knowledge, and, generally speaking, preparing for the future.

A team of teachers, counselors, school psychologists, and administrators met to plan an individual program designed to help John. At the beginning, it was decided that John would have to be understood—his individual differences, his cultural background, and his various strengths and weaknesses.

Early in the meeting, the team decided that John's previous educational record did not indicate he would benefit from traditional educational experiences. Therefore, the team decided John would need an alternative learning environment that would contribute to his academic achievement and his overall educational development. A beginning agenda for helping John included the following:

1. Understanding his concept of motivation, especially since Native Americans' concept of motivation varies from Anglo-American perceptions. One example will be his teachers' "preparing him for the future," a concept incompatible with Native Americans' emphasis on the present.
2. Providing cooperative learning experiences since Native Americans generally like to work for the betterment of the group and also because Native Americans have responded positively in cooperative learning situations (Little Soldier, 1989).
3. Continuing to place emphasis on basic skills yet also allow practical and hands-on experiences rather than the current emphasis on content knowledge.
4. Providing opportunities for him to build on his intelligence in spatial relationships and to place less emphasis on other subject areas that clearly could not be considered one of his "intelligences."
5. Working on his self-concept (and his cultural identity) in a way that teaches him how to be academically successful.
6. Removing him from homogeneous ability classes (and *all* other learners) to avoid negative consequences on his academic achievement, self-concept, and cultural identity.

The team decided that since John had several problems, the school could take definite steps to help him. The steps would include, first, understanding John's Native American background and his perceptions of success and motivation, and second, providing educational experiences to which he could relate and see a purpose.

Reviewing What You Have Read About Alternative Learning Environments

1. It is important that educators turn to _____ _____ _____ _____ with enthusiasm, as a new hope, and as means of changing practices that have not worked rather than out of frustration or because they feel like they have failed at their profession.

2. Educators often view _____ from middle-class Anglo-American perspectives and expect such school behaviors toward learning and achievement from learners of other cultures and social class backgrounds.

3. _____ _____ , or tailoring learning activities to the students' needs, probably continues to be the most effective means of instructing learners.

4. Beliefs that _____ _____ _____ lowers self-concepts and causes psychological damage among lower ability students can be seen in learners' opinions that being placed in lower ability groups means they are "dumb."

5. Available research suggests that the desirable attitudes and _____ _____ of low-ability children may be seriously impaired when homogeneously grouped.

6. _____ _____ _____ _____ _____ allows learners to remain in heterogeneous groups most of the day and then "regroup" within the class for selected subjects, for example, reading and mathematics.

7. _____ involves any one of several organizational structures in which a group of students pursue academic goals through collaborative efforts, work together in small groups, draw on each other's strengths, and assist each other in completing tasks.

8. _____ , a cross-age tutoring program designed to reduce dropout rates among seventh- and eighth-grade children, is unique in that tutors work with limited-English-proficient students at risk of dropping out of school.

9. The major goal of _____ is to keep pregnant and parenting teens in school, with additional goals of encouraging positive health care practices and helping young parents set occupational goals.

10. The _____ is a last chance alternative school for high school dropouts (grades levels 9 through 12) who are unable to be served by any other public or private school.

11. The _____ , based on the belief that positive self-esteem is necessary for achievement, works to involve students in the school process and in their learning.

12. Cooperative learning has been found to improve _____ _____ because the increased contact between students engages learners in pleasant activities, requires that team members work toward a common goal, and provides feelings of group membership and a greater liking for classmates.

13. Educators planning and implementing _____ for at-risk learners have a responsibility to both at-risk learners and other learners to ensure equity and equal access to all educational programs.

14. One program, _____ , tries to provide meaningful work and experiences that learners can use in the neighborhood and in their personal lives by providing opportunities for at-risk African- and Hispanic-American students to produce school publications.

15. Programs such as Working With Pregnant Teenagers, Helping Drop-outs, and Helping Limited-English-Proficient Learners are examples of _____ .

Answer Key: 1. alternative learning environments; **2.** motivation; **3.** Individualized instruction; **4.** homogeneous ability grouping; **5.** self-concepts; **6.** Regrouping by subject area; **7.** Cooperative learning; **8.** Valued Young Program; **9.** Graduation, Reality, and Dual-Role Skills; **10.** DeLaSalle model; **11.** Apollo Program; **12.** multiethnic relationships; **13.** special schools; **14.** Media Academy; **15.** specific at-risk programs

Summary

This chapter on alternative learning environments does not imply that all traditional teaching approaches have failed and does not suggest that alternative learning environments and strategies will solve all at-risk learners' problems. However, it does take a strong stance that some at-risk learners do not benefit from approaches usually long accepted in elementary, middle, and secondary schools. At-risk learners face equally serious consequences when all students are labeled or categorized as being alike and are provided identical learning experiences. Perceptive educators perceive learners as individuals with a wealth of individual, developmental, and social class differences. The key to at-risk learners' educational as well as other successes will be in educators determining what works for a particular individual rather than overrelying on traditional approaches or providing "more of the same" educational experiences.

For Additional Information on Alternative Learning Environments

Ames, C. A. (1990). Motivation: What teachers need to know. *Teachers College Record, 91,* 407–421. This comprehensive study includes an examination of motivation, how it relates to theory and research, and how it relates to culture and developmental changes.

Blythe, T., & Gardner, H. (1990) A school for all intelligences. *Educational Leadership, 47*(7), 33–36. Blythe and Gardner briefly explain the concept of multiple intelligences and then suggest alternatives to current educational practices in areas such as range of abilities addressed, learning environments, assessment measures, and concepts of learners.

Dunn, R., Beaudry, J. S., & Klavas, A. (1989). Survey of research on learning styles. *Educational Leadership, 46*(6), 50–58. Dunn, Beaudry, and Klavas reviewed a number of research articles on learning styles and concluded that students' achievement increases when teaching methods match learning styles.

Educational programs that work (18th ed.). (1992). Longmont, CO: Sopris West, Inc. This catalogue provides a yearly listing of proven exemplary educational programs and practices and can be purchased from Sopris West Incorporated, 1140 Boston Avenue, Longmont, Colorado 80501. Phone: (303)651-2829.

Gentile, L. M., & McMillan, M. M. (1992). Literacy for students at risk: Developing critical dialogues. *Journal of Reading, 35*(8), 636–641. These authors propose that at-risk learners need to develop literacy skills and provide examples of how critical dialogues can be used with at-risk learners to improve their ability to read, write, and think.

Hancock, V. E. (1992/1993). The at-risk student. *Educational Leadership, 50*(4), 84–85. Hancock briefly reviews the research on technology and provides specific examples of technological projects that provide alternative learning environments.

Hatch, T., & Gardner, H. (1988). New research on intelligence. *Learning, 17*(4), 36–39. Hatch and Gardner provide a description of the various intelligences and how educators can apply the theories.

Manning, M. L., & Lucking, R. (1991). The what, why and how of cooperative learning. *The Clearing House, 64,* 152–156. Cooperative learning could provide an innovative alternative learning strategy for at-risk learners. This article looks at cooperative learning and provides a detailed description of several major types.

Martino, L. R. (1993). A goal setting model for young adolescent at-risk students. *Middle School Journal, 24*(5), 19–22. Martino proposes a goal-setting model for at-risk learners, i.e., the setting of goals and expected levels of attainment. Also, the author provides a detailed discussion on how goals should be selected.

Titus, T. G., Bergandi, T. A., & Shryock, M. (1990). Adolescent learning styles. *Journal of Research and Development in Education, 23*(3), 165–170. These researchers determine adolescent learning styles by comparing male and female students at various grade levels.

Zukowski, A. A. (1993). The systems blueprint. *Momentum, 24*(2), 77–78. Zukowski looks at designing long-range technology plans, time schedules, and practical issues such as wiring.

8

Parents and Families of At-Risk Students

Outline

Overview

Probing Directions

Involving Parents and Families of At-Risk Learners
    The Need for Parental Involvement and Participation
    Rationale for Including Both Immediate and Extended Families
    Reasons Parents and Families Might Resist Teachers' Efforts
    The Need for Collaboration

Parental and Family Involvement
    Understanding Parents and Families of At-Risk Students
    Communication
    Involving Parents and Families as Volunteers
    Advisory Councils and Other Committees

Parent/Teacher Conferences
    Opportunities to Exchange Information
    Suggestions for Working Successfully with Parents of At-Risk Students
    Suggesting Referral Services and Community Organizations

Parent Education
    Concept
    Rationale
    Programs

Reviewing What You Have Read About Parents and Families

Summary

For Additional Information on Parents and Families

Overview

Educators have long recognized the importance of parents in children's and adolescents' education. Whether through involving, conferencing, or educating, efforts to include parents in educational efforts have contributed to learners' academic achievement and school progress. In some cases, however, educators have worked only with parents of middle- and upper-class learners, those learners who either have demonstrated high academic achievement or have the ability to be successful in school efforts.

During the 1990s and into the twenty-first century, two points will continue to become increasingly clear. First, educators serious about addressing the needs of at-risk learners will want to take advantage of the insight and involvement that parents can offer. Second, at-risk learners deserve educators who seek to involve parents, just as educators do with middle- and upper-class learners. Such efforts validate the importance of treating at-risk learners like other learners and also the necessity of involving parents in learners' education. This chapter provides a rationale for involving and conferencing with parents of at-risk learners and suggests ways to involve parents and families in the lives of children and adolescents.

Probing Directions

This chapter on parents and families of at-risk learners does the following:

1. Explains the importance of involving parents and families in the education of at-risk children and adolescents.
2. Explains the importance of including *both* immediate and extended family members in efforts to help at-risk learners.
3. Examines reasons parents and families might resist educators' efforts.
4. Shows how educators can gain a better understanding of parents and families through firsthand contact, surveys, and visiting in homes.
5. Shows how educators can involve parents and families as volunteers and committee members and in other ways.
6. Shows how educators can provide education programs for parents and families that provide valuable information about their son's or daugh-

ter's at-risk condition and also how the school addresses at-risk conditions.

7. Provides an indication of the many referral agencies and community organizations that educators can suggest for parents wanting additional help or resources.

8. Provides readers with additional sources of information on working with the parents and families of at-risk learners.

Involving Parents and Families of At-Risk Learners

The Need for Parental Involvement and Participation

All learners undoubtedly need the benefit of their parents being involved in their education. In fact, educators of at-risk learners have a particular responsibility to involve, seek help from, and, generally speaking, work with parents and families of at-risk learners. Many parents of successful children and adolescents extensively involve themselves in their children's schooling. However, while teachers undoubtedly should praise all parents for their interest and involvement, all too often, teachers do not see parents whose children and adolescents are at risk either academically, behaviorally, or socially.

The benefits of active and positive family-school partnerships can include the following:

- Helps families provide support at home to encourage children and adolescents to succeed in school.
- Identifies and supports family interactions that motivate, aspire, and show the relationship between school achievement and future options.
- Improves the interaction between families and schools to support academic and social achievement and improve the schools.
- Helps parents understand the nature of at-risk conditions and how family-school partnerships can benefit children and adolescents.

Rationale for Including Both Immediate and Extended Families

The authors feel strongly that this chapter should include *families* as well as parents in family-school partnerships. While educators cannot assume at-risk learners are culturally diverse or that cultural diversity itself is an at-risk condition, culturally diverse at-risk learners may have extended family

---

Activity 8-1

Conduct a survey of teachers in three schools—one elementary, one middle, and one secondary school—to determine whether teachers and administrators are serious about parental involvement. For example, schools offer considerable lip service about wanting parental involvement, input, and cooperation, but to what extent do teachers want parents involved? (It might be best to allow teachers and administrators to remain anonymous.)

---

members who play significant roles in children's and adolescents' education. Unlike most Anglo-Americans, many culturally diverse people subscribe to the extended family concept, i.e., grandparents, aunts, and uncles play major parenting roles. Therefore, when working with culturally diverse at-risk learners, educators should expect and actually take the initiative to include extended family members when addressing the needs of at-risk children and adolescents. Also, if the at-risk learner lives only with the mother or father, he or she might spend considerable time with other family members, especially after school or during the weekends. These extended family members may have insight and information to share to which the immediate parent or parents might not be privy.

Reasons Parents and Families Might Resist Teachers' Efforts

Teachers often face a challenge trying to involve parents and families of at-risk learners. For several reasons, parents of at-risk learners may be the last to visit the school, to inquire about student progress, and to volunteer participation. Teachers have been known to wonder why parents visit schools to discuss the progress of the academically successful child and not check with the teacher of the academically unsuccessful child or of one with a behavior problem. Such actions suggest that parents either do not know what to do with the unsuccessful child or do not care. The school may view the parents as not concerned about their own children, uninterested in education, not supportive of academic goals, unwilling to cooperate with school efforts, and guilty of undermining the authority of the schoс (Fox & Forbing, 1992).

Rather than blaming parents for an apparent lack of interest, teachers need to understand several reasons that might be the basis for parents failing to respond to teacher requests for assistance and advice. First, parents themselves may have had unsuccessful school experiences and may still feel uncomfortable handling school matters, especially when they have previously been unsuccessful helping their child or adolescent. Fox and For-bing (1992) maintain that parents may view the school as impersonal and uncaring and unable to understand their problems. They may be intimi-dated by the authoritarian stance of the school and feel educators consider their opinions unimportant. The resulting defenses include withdrawal, lack of interest, and passive resistance. Second, many parents place total responsibility on the school—they feel it is the school's responsibility to teach, to enforce behavior expectations, and to counsel. Third, parents may be among the last to recognize children's at-risk symptoms. Perhaps not recognizing (or being unwilling to admit) at-risk symptoms, parents often do little to help at-risk learners. Fourth, parents and families may not understand at-risk conditions and may consider their children and ado-lescents "dumb," "obstinate," "wild," or just "stubborn." Fifth, some par-ents do not want to admit failure because it casts a negative reflection on the family.

The Need for Collaboration

Constructive collaboration between parents and the school contributes to the overall welfare of the at-risk learner. The groundwork for collaboration may be best achieved by employing a professional facilitator who can con-sider at-risk programs and collaborative efforts in a partial and objective manner. Establishing group identity, mutual trust, and productive commu-nication techniques requires time and long-term commitment. Also, the development of such collaborative relationships will be difficult or impossi-ble if parents perceive that the schools seek to control the so-called collabo-rative group. Therefore, a professional facilitator to help establish a truly collaborative group can be a wise investment to save time and effort and to avoid frustration in the long term. The importance of building a sense of collaboration between parents and schools cannot be overemphasized, espe-cially since this bridge creates a broader support base for both schools and families (Fox & Forbing, 1992).

Case Study 8-1 looks at how several perceptive teachers sought to con-vince parents and families that they could help both their young adolescents as well as the school.

Activity 8-2

Propose a page-long program for involving parents and families in the education of at-risk learners. This plan should include goals, objectives, rationales, methods, resources, time schedules, the specific roles of all participants, and an assessment plan.

Case Study 8-1: Convincing Parents and Families They Can Help

A team of administrators, teachers, and counselors at the New Visions Alternative High School in Norfolk, Virginia, met to decide on strategies for involving parents and families in the education of at-risk learners.

After discussing the low level of parental involvement and participation, the team reached a conclusion: A plan needed to be developed to engage parents and families in the efforts of New Visions Alternative High School (NVAS). The team met on several other occasions to devise a program with stated objectives and goals.

The overall program objective was to reengage parents and families in the education of their at-risk adolescents. Specifically, the plan was designed to (1) make parents and families aware of the goals and activities of NVAS, (2) get parents and families involved in specific school activities, and (3) convince parents and families of the benefits of parent/teacher conferences.

Procedures to address these objectives included the following:

1. Inform parents and families (i.e., letters, telephones, and advertising) that their presence, input, and assistance are needed and requested.
2. Inform parents and families of the purposes and goals of parent/teacher conferences.
3. Inform parents and families that parental involvement and participation have the potential to help their adolescent academically, behaviorally, and socially.
4. Speak firsthand with community organizations such as social service agencies, churches, and clubs to convince parents and families to visit and then consider participating in NVAS.
5. Conduct a parent survey to determine perceptions of strengths, weaknesses, problems, and concerns.
6. Visit, if necessary and after telephoning for permission, parents and families in the home to learn firsthand about learners' immediate and perhaps extended families and also to learn about at-risk learners' home conditions.

One of the team members stated, "During our next session, we need to devise an evaluational plan—a set of procedures to determine whether our objectives have been met and whether we need to change the program procedures."

The committee agreed that the program would be only as good as its evaluation system and that devising evaluation procedures should be the next agenda item.

Parental and Family Involvement

Understanding Parents and Families of At-Risk Students

A prerequisite to planning and implementing effective at-risk programs is for educators to understand parents and families of at-risk learners. Many educators, especially middle-class educators, assume that children and adolescents come from homes like the ones they experienced. In some cases, such assumptions may be valid, but one cannot make such broad assumptions and generalizations. Three major methods of gaining a better understanding of families include firsthand contact, parent surveys, and visiting parents and families in the home.

Firsthand Contact

Educators too often based at-risk programs (as well as other educational efforts) on misperceptions, opinions of other educators, comments on permanent records, and, generally speaking, erroneous assumptions. There is, however, no substitute for firsthand contact with parents and families. Without doubt, considerable and valuable knowledge can be gained from reading books and journals, taking courses, and attending professional conferences. However, although these means can provide considerable insight into at-risk learners and their lives and should be an integral part of educators' learning agenda, firsthand contact continues to be one of the most effective means of gaining an accurate perspective of at-risk learners' families. Firsthand contact has several advantages that other means cannot always provide: learning directly about people and their individual attitudes, values, and concerns. With an enlightened understanding of parents and families and the at-risk learner's home life, it is hoped that educators will be better able to provide appropriate educational experiences.

Parent Surveys

Although there is probably no adequate substitute for firsthand contact with families of at-risk learners, it is possible to gain information through a parent survey. Without doubt, the most effective means would be to use the parent survey in addition to firsthand contact.

The design of a parent survey should include several considerations such as parents' and families' proficiency with English, the likelihood parents will complete and return the survey, whether parents consider questions to be too personal, and the information and accompanying reasons for requesting the information. Generally speaking, parent surveys should be clear and short, require only a brief amount of time to complete, and avoid conveying middle-class perspectives.

Examples of Parent Survey Questions

_____   1. To what extent do you feel educators in your child's or adolescent's school understand and meet the overall needs and concerns of its at-risk population?

_____   2. To what extent do you feel school policies recognize that at-risk children and adolescents differ from the so-called "not at-risk" population?

_____   3. To what extent does the media center (children's and adolescents' books, films, and other visual material) reflect at-risk and other exceptional conditions?

_____   4. To what extent has the school succeeded in employing a faculty and staff (administrators, teachers, special personnel, speech therapists, guidance counselors, psychologists, school nurses) that understand at-risk conditions and are motivated to work with these learners?

_____   5. To what extent do you feel school expectations (competition, motivation, achievements, aspirations) reflect the values and expectations of lower socioeconomic learners?

_____   6. To what extent do you feel extracurricular activities in the school reflect the needs and interests of at-risk children and adolescents?

_____   7. To what extent do you feel teaching methods and strategies (lecture format, small group, cooperative learning, ability grouping) reflect a concern for the educational well-being of at-risk learners?

_____   8. To what extent do you feel the school has provided opportunities to offer opinions, input, advice, and suggestions concerning improvement of the school program, or changing an aspect you would like to see changed?

_____   9. To what extent do you feel your child or adolescent is "progressing" or "succeeding" toward goals that you deem important?

_____   10. To what extent do you feel the school provides information and assistance concerning community agencies and social service organizations?

_____   11. What comments or suggestions do you want to offer concerning your child or adolescent in school?

Adapted from Baruth, L. G., & Manning, M. L. (1992). *Multicultural education of children and adolescents.* Boston: Allyn and Bacon.

These sample questions are not intended to be all inclusive, nor are they designed for a specific at-risk group. Educators with a large percentage of one type of at-risk population might want to design specific questions to pinpoint certain areas.

Visiting Parents and Families in the Home
Visiting in the home may be one of the most effective ways of getting to know learners, their immediate and extended families, and their home environment. Too many middle- or upper-class professionals probably believe that their homes and families are representative of most learners. However, in many cases, especially with lower-class families, what teachers believe to be representative or prototypical might not be the case.

Communication

The importance of effective communication between educators and parents of at-risk learners cannot be overemphasized. As previously conveyed, educators need to understand parents' perceptions of at-risk condition and the school's efforts. Likewise, parents need to understand at-risk conditions and the school's plan for their child or adolescent. Communication can take two major types: Speaking with parents and families in person or on telephone and, second, writing letters to parents. While both have their degrees of effectiveness and their advantages, the most effective method might be both—speaking with parents concerning their at-risk learner and then following up with a written summary of the conversation. While such a summary should not be too formal or legalistic, it can serve to clarify points and as documentation of the meeting.

Whether communicating through speaking directly, telephoning, or writing to parents, educators are responsible for not allowing language or communication differences, verbal or nonverbal, to interfere with overall communication. Several factors warrant additional consideration: First, as mentioned previously, parents' English skills especially in a neighborhood with many culturally diverse families might not allow for effective communication. Second, nonverbal communication might pose a problem. For example, the Anglo-American who looks the Native American in the eye while communicating might be considered rude, while the educator might think a Native American glancing the other way to be a sign of disinterest or irritation (Sanders, 1987). Other examples of problems that can result from nonverbal communication include Asian-American parents and families who are especially sensitive to nonverbal messages and who may construe a teacher's folded arms or other casual gestures as indicative of an indifferent attitude (Chavkin, 1989). Third, parents often do not understand school language and terminology such as continuous progress, ability grouping,

---

Activity 8-3
Reread the comments and suggestions for educators conducting home visits. Then make your own list of the "do's and don'ts" of home visits. Consider cultural, social class, and geographical differences that might affect perceptions (both teachers' and parents') during the home visit.

---

cooperative learning, percentiles, grade levels, grading systems, and any of the many programs that focus specifically on at-risk learners.

Telephoning Parents and Families

Telephoning represents another means of communicating with parents and demonstrates the teacher's personal interest in both the at-risk learner and the parents. Positive telephone contacts can significantly affect a child's school performance; conversely, negative calls can have a negative effect. As with other forms of communication, teachers must use caution when using telephones as a means of communicating with learners. Telephoning provides an excellent means of encouraging parents to attend meetings, conferences, and other school-related events (Shea & Bauer, 1985).

A telephone call from a teacher can be extremely threatening, especially to parents of learners who have a history of school problems or who have propensity toward being at risk. Also, some parents and family members still carry negative baggage from their school days. Some suggestions follow for telephoning parents of at-risk learners:

1. Call before a situation grows so serious that a reasonable solution cannot at least be suggested.
2. Speak in a tone that expresses respect and courtesy, which places parents and families at ease as much as possible.
3. Speak of the learner's accomplishments and strengths prior to discussing a problem to be addressed.
4. Speak in language the parents will understand and avoid educational jargon that might seem threatening or may make parents feel inadequate to handle the situation.
5. Do not leave the parent with a sense of hopelessness and despair.
6. Ask the parents to call or visit the school when problems arise or when they feel a situation deserves to be discussed.

Writing Parents and Families

Educators can also write notes and letters to keep parents informed of children's progress, of administrative and record-keeping problems and concerns, schedule changes, special events, holidays, workshops, field trips, and other items of interest. Effective notes are clear, concise, and positive, and with English-speaking parents and families, may be written in native languages. Unless used systematically, however, notes and letters have limited value in reinforcing the child's academic performance or social/emotional behavior, and are best used as one component of the overall parent/teacher communication (Shea & Bauer, 1985).

Suggestions follow for communicating with parents and families through letters, notes, and other written forms:

1. Be sure the parents' and families' educational levels will allow them to understand the communication.
2. Be sure to include some positive points about the learners to avoid a totally negative communication.
3. Be brief so parents and families will not be overwhelmed or consider the situation hopeless.
4. Provide a telephone number for parents and families to call or an address for parents and families to write and call if questions arise.
5. Write in native languages if parents and families are not proficient in English.

Involving Parents and Families as Volunteers

Getting parents and families to volunteer their services and expertise can reap handsome dividends. The task, however, for educators is greater than simply requesting and convincing a parent to volunteer. There must be a reason for the involvement as well as a consideration of the type of involvement being sought and several essentials that contribute to involvement being successful. Upon establishing effective programs, dividends can include parents sharing special abilities and areas of expertise with at-risk learners, parents and teachers become closer and working together toward common goals, and parents gaining a better understanding of the school's efforts to address the needs of at-risk children and adolescents.

Rationale

Parent volunteers can contribute significantly to the quality of the services offered to learners in the school (Shea & Bauer, 1985). The National School Volunteer Program cited four reasons for using volunteers in the classroom and school:

1. Relieving the professional staff of nonteaching duties.
2. Providing needed services to individual children to supplement the work of the classroom teacher.

3. Enriching the experiences of children beyond that normally available in school.
4. Building a better understanding of school problems among citizens, and stimulating widespread citizen support for public education.

Although parents are the most frequent volunteers, siblings, relatives, older elementary and secondary students, college students, senior citizens, business and professional groups, and other members of the community can volunteer to participate in school activities (Shea & Bauer, 1985).

Although Shea and Bauer (1985) were referring to volunteers working with handicapped children, many of their recommendations and suggestions also apply to other parents and family members who volunteer to assist. Volunteers should participate in a brief preservice training program and an on-the-job training program. Preservice training programs should introduce volunteers to school procedures and expectations, and spell out their roles and functions. This training should emphasize the importance of confidentiality and attendance, and should offer an opportunity to discuss the program with experienced volunteers and to visit with the teacher in the actual classroom setting. On-the-job training is a continuous process in which volunteers learn the specific activities for which they will be responsible (Shea & Bauer, 1985).

Major Types of Parental Involvement
Parental involvement programs can be divided into five basic types, each having different outcomes. Table 8-1 provides a summary of these five types so educators can, first, distinguish between the types and, second, reach more informed decisions concerning which type is the most feasible for the goals they wish to meet.

Essential Considerations for Effective Parental Involvement
The Southwest Educational Development Laboratory (SEDL) identified and described characteristics of promising parental involvement programs. While some of the selected programs were affiliated with organizations such as the National Educational Association or the National School Volunteer Program, others resulted from the efforts of local schools. The programs shared seven essential elements:

1. *Written policies* legitimized the importance of parental involvement and helped frame the context for program activities.
2. *Administrative support* included a main budget for implementing programs, material/product resources, and people with designated responsibilities.
3. Promising *training programs* were initiated for both staff and parents.
4. Promising programs made the *partnership approach* their essence.

5. *Two-way communication* between the home and the school occurred frequently on a regular basis.
6. *Networking* served to identify additional resources and encouraged people to share information, resources, and technical expertise.
7. Regular *evaluation,* during key stages and at the end of the cycle or phase of the program, provided indicators of progress and outcomes (Williams & Chavkin, 1989).

Volunteer Helpers

Volunteers working with at-risk learners might need special instruction and training to introduce volunteers to school procedures and expectations, and to clarify expectations and roles. Volunteers need to understand the at-risk conditions and the characteristics of each; the need to avoid under all circumstances the desire to blame the victim for academic and social problems; the dangers of placing value judgments on at-risk learner behavior (such as "fussing at" students for being sexually active or experimenting with drugs); and the necessity of understanding at-risk programs, their goals, and their methods.

TABLE 8-1   Five Major Types of Parental Involvement Programs

Type 1:	The *basic obligations of parents* refers to the responsibilities of families for ensuring children's health and safety; parenting and child-rearing skills needed to prepare children for school; continual need to supervise, discipline, and guide children at each age level; and the need to build positive home conditions that support school learning and appropriate behavior.
Type 2:	The *basic obligations of schools* refers to the communications from school to home about school programs and children's progress. Schools vary the form and frequency of communications (such as memos, notices, report cards, and conferences) and this greatly affects whether the information about school programs and children's progress can be understood by all parents.
Type 3:	*Parental involvement at school* refers to the parent volunteers who assist teachers, administrators, and children in classrooms or in other areas of the school. It also refers to parents who come to school to support student performances, sports, or other events.
Type 4:	*Parental involvement in learning activities at home* refers to parent-initiated activities, or child-initiated requests for help, and ideas or instructions from teachers to parents that can help parents assist their children at home with learning activities.
Type 5:	*Parental involvement in governance and advocacy* refers to parents' taking decision-making roles in the PTA/PTO, advisory councils, or other committees or groups at the school, district, or state level.

Adapted from Brandt, R. (1989). On parents and schools: A conversation with Joyce Epstein. *Educational Leadership, 47*(2), 24–27.

Successful Program: Family Day Program

The Family Day Program at Daniel Hale Williams School in Gary, Indiana, strengthens ties between educators, families, and students by having a special day that parents come to school with their children to watch films, hear speakers, sing together, and participate in other learning activities. Parents, students, and staff encircle the school and recite the Family Day Rap and sing the school song. Parents and children share their likes and dislikes, suggest ways to improve family interactions, discover each other's uniqueness, and learn to cope with each other (Manning, 1993a).

Advisory Councils and Other Committees

Jennings (1989) suggests that school staff, parents, other community leaders, and students, working together on advisory councils, can create better schools. Essentials for organizing effective councils include (1) cultural and gender diversity on the council, (2) an orientation session to make members' roles and functions clear, and (3) a commitment to work together and to participate in shared decision making. Other advice and suggestions from Jennings (1989) include the following:

1. Educators should show equal respect for all participants, show the importance of their opinion and input, and show appreciation for their involvement.
2. Educators should form a council of 9 to 18 members. Fewer than 9 members can result in too few to represent a range of opinion; more than 18 becomes expensive or unwieldy.
3. Educators should remember that *all* parents want a good education for their children and adolescents.

The inclusion of parents of at-risk learners on advisory councils and other committees means that scholls need to make sure parents of at-risk learners do not feel that at-risk programs shortchange their children or that the school simply does not place adequate emphasis on at-risk children and

---

Activity 8-4
Design an information sheet for parent volunteers that welcomes them to the school and makes school or district rules clear. Include, for example, the need to be conscientious about involvement times and the necessity of confidentiality concerning students' test scores and overall progress.

---

adolescents. Also, an advisory council should have a speaker explain at-risk conditions, the numbers of students in each at-risk category, programs in operation, cost expectations, and how students in at-risk programs socialize.

Parent/Teacher Conferences

The parent/teacher conference presents an opportunity for parents and teachers to exchange information about the child's school and home activities and also provides an occasion to involve parents in planning and implementing their child's educational program. When teachers contact parents to schedule progress report conferences, they should explain the purpose of the conference. In attempting to reduce the parents' anxiety about the conference, teachers might provide parents with a written agenda. Educators should also remember that the purpose of the conference centers on the child and school progress, not on the teacher's or parent's personal, social, emotional, or marital problems. While these issues may affect the learner's overall school progress, educators should direct the focus of the conference toward areas of school functioning (Shea & Bauer, 1985).

The agenda for the parent/teacher conference might include discussion by the teacher and the parent of the learner's test scores or assessment results. Although most parents might benefit from an explanation of the terms normally associated with measurement and evaluation, parents of at-risk learners might need even more detailed information. Test results, usually a concern for parents, may cause strong reactions if the results indicate their child or adolescent is functioning at a lower level than most learners. Educators should ask parents to state their understanding of the information, and make sure parents understand the results and conclusions. Also, teachers should make a sincere effort to alleviate any anxiety expressed by parents over possible misuse of test results (Marion, 1981; Shea & Bauer, 1985).

Opportunities to Exchange Information

At-risk students and their parents and teachers can benefit from effective parent/teacher conferences. Information can be exchanged that contributes to a better understanding by parents and teachers of their children and students, respectively, which will, in turn, allow parents to improve home environments and teachers to improve curricular, organizational, and instructional practices.

Parents, teachers, and learners can provide their own perceptions of strengths and weaknesses and at-risk situations that others might not understand. Parents can provide "home perceptions" of the at-risk students: attitudes toward school, homework habits, leisure time activities, feelings toward teachers and their efforts, and, perhaps, strengths and weaknesses not evident in school. In fact, teachers may be surprised to find that learners who appear at risk at school may not demonstrate these symptoms at home. Likewise, teachers can provide a picture that allows parents to understand teachers' efforts and their child's or adolescent's school attitudes and behaviors. Most parents and teachers have experienced situations where students appear motivated at home yet, for some reason, do not demonstrate these attitudes at school. Last, at times agreed on by both parents and teachers, at-risk learners should be allowed to participate in parent/teacher conferences by providing input, opinion, perspectives, perceptions of strengths and weaknesses, and suggestions concerning how special needs can be met. Conferences between parents and teachers or with at-risk students themselves will be more effective and productive when educators work toward openness, trust, clear communication, and respect for both parents and at-risk learners.

Parents might be reluctant to share information with educators; however, it is the teacher's responsibility to make parents feel comfortable and to want to share ideas and suggestions for improving the education of students. Refining the process of exchanging information will not be an easy task and should include a consideration of the culture, race, socioeconomic levels, and educational levels of the parents.

Suggestions for Working Successfully with Parents of At-Risk Students

What can teachers do to ensure or at least encourage parental involvement and participation in a child's education? The following, while not an exhaustive list, provides representative suggestions. Educators need to consider at-risk learners in their classes, the respective at-risk conditions, the learners' parents and families, and then add suggestions that meet individual situations.

- Encourage parents to accept and understand their child's or adolescent's at-risk condition—this can be difficult yet it is a very crucial and significant step.
- Involve parents in the solution or a written plan to help the at-risk child or adolescent.
- Realize that parents usually see children and adolescents more than school personnel—seek information about learners' habits at home.

- Request parental participation in school activities, both curricular and extracurricular.
- Involve parents and families in the evaluation procedures, explain the results in clear and plain terms, and seek their efforts in the modification of the school's goals and programs.
- Help parents develop realistic expectations for children and adolescents. The drug addicted can be helped; suicidal learners can be helped before they take drastic action; sexually active students can be warned of the serious consequences and encouraged to take precautions; lower achievers can be provided remedial programs. These conditions can be addressed, and parents should make expectations clear yet not place undue stress on the child or adolescent to change attitudes and behavior overnight.

Case Study 8-2 shows how a team of teachers conducted a conference, how they formulated their goals, and how they decided to get more support from the mother and the extended family members.

Case Study 8-2: Planning the Parent/Teacher Conference

Mrs. Miller, the eighth grade team leader, informed other members of the team of an upcoming parent conference. "Ms. Steele and the grandparents are finally coming for a conference," she announced. "I have been working for several months to get them to attend." Immediately, the team began to plan the meeting so Ms. Steele and the grandparents would be at ease or as much at ease as they could be made. The team decided on several "specifics" designed to reduce the stress of the visit and to get their cooperation. These specifics included the following:

1. Ask the visitors whether they wanted coffee or a soft drink.
2. Sit at a round table instead of the teachers being behind the desk.
3. Allow Ms. Steele and the grandparents to talk, to ask questions, and to voice concerns.
4. Avoid asking the whereabouts of Mr. Steele.
5. Avoid educational jargon and terminology that might appear foreign or threatening.
6. Explain the at-risk condition in lay terms, being careful to avoid placing unrealistic expectations on Ms. Steele and the grandparents.

7. Discuss current achievement levels, problems, strengths, and possible routes to addressing weaknesses.
8. Ask for their support, assistance, and cooperation in both their child's education and also the overall school program.
9. Determine strengths (i.e., the grandfather worked as a carpenter for many years) and suggest in a nonthreatening tone specific activities he might do with the students.
10. Invite Ms. Steele and the grandparents back for a PTA meeting, another conferences, or just to visit the school.

Admittedly, the team did not plan in such detail for all conferences, but this one was unique—this was the first time Ms. Steele and the grandparents had been to school and the team wanted to encourage future visits and participation. It was imperative that this first meeting be so successful that Ms. Steele and the grandparents would *want* to visit again.

Suggesting Referral Services and Community Organizations

Sometimes at-risk students' problems are greater than educators and parents can address. In these more acute situations, it is imperative that educators avoid letting parents leave conferences feeling hopeless about their child's or adolescents' future. Instead, responsible educators can be prepared to suggest community organizations and social service agencies that might be prepared to provide assistance. While readers will want to learn about organizations and agencies in their own communities, selected sources of help include area health departments, Tough Love, AIDS information hotlines, urban leagues, departments of social services, area mental health centers, Share Self-Help Support Groups, Big Sister–Big Brother, YMCA and YWCA, Quest International, Planned Parenthood, and crisis pregnancy centers.

Activity 8-5

Make a list of social service agencies, referral services, and community organizations in your community. Include their addresses, telephone numbers, and resources provided. Then prepare a sheet for distribution to parents and families who need assistance the school cannot provide.

Parent Education

Educators working with at-risk children and adolescents sometimes feel parents and family members do not understand at-risk conditions, the problems their children and adolescents face daily, and schools' efforts to address learners' special needs. A carefully planned parent education program often serves as a vehicle to address parents' and family's needs to be better informed about their learner's at-risk conditions and needs.

Concept

The concept of parent education dates back to the 1800s and carries differing definitions and perceptions. A wide array of activities is considered appropriate for parent education programs, ranging from family and cultural transmission of child-rearing values, skills, and techniques to more specific parenting behaviors. Specifically, however, the term "parent education" has evolved to denote "organized activities that have been developed in order to further parents' abilities to raise their children successfully" (Mitzel, 1982).

Rationale

The need for parent education has been well documented. However, although parent education programs have become routine aspects of many early childhood programs, educators of other grades generally have not developed programs designed to teach about at-risk learners' conditions and needs. Early childhood education appears to have made substantial progress in planning and implementing parent education programs and has provided the framework in both theory and practice for other school levels (Manning, 1992).

Programs

Programs are needed that reflect a sound understanding of the parent education concept and of the unique at-risk conditions and symptoms. Parent education programs can include "an opportunity for parents to become active participants in their children's education, to interact with professional adolescent specialists, to receive support from other parents struggling through the same difficult period, and to gain a better understanding of the school and its education problems" (Batsell, 1983).

Two factors document the importance of educating parents of at-risk learners: understanding the specific at-risk condition and understanding schools' efforts to address at-risk conditions. First, parents may fail to recognize at-risk symptoms; may not believe their child would participate in at-risk behaviors; may not understand the consequences of long term at-risk behaviors; and may feel helplessly inadequate to deal with the problem. Parents in such situations need parent education programs designed to convey content about at-risk conditions, to teach skills to deal effectively with their children and adolescents, and to convince parents that learners need love and understanding during these challenging times. Second, parent education programs can show parents the school's role in helping at-risk youngsters. All too often, parents do not realize the extent of the school's efforts—teachers' commitment, specially designed techniques, identification procedures, materials and resources, and alternative approaches to helping at-risk learners.

Educators may purchase packaged programs focusing on specific at-risk conditions. Although such programs have the advantages of requiring less preparatory time and being unlikely to require major revision, they may be specific only to the community for which they were developed.

Successful Program: Restructuring Parent/Teacher Associations

Several indicators suggest that the restructuring of parent/teacher associations (PTAs) can increase parents' influence on the education process. Six key goals identified by the National PTA and designed to restructure PTAs include recognizing that families have changed dramatically; remembering the needs and abilities of members; offering services to attract new members; conducting a variety of activities; writing clear goals; and being sure the PTA supports school goals.

Selected restructured PTAs include the Parent Involvement Program (PIP), Parents In Touch Program, and Family Fair. PIP in New York City includes networks, community groups, and the open school concept for parents. The concept suggests parents can be key choice makers in selecting schools for their children, and parents can be equal partners in parent education and community networks. PIP develops a greater commitment to the family, broadens the definition of parent involvement, and uses a variety of improvement strategies. In Indianapolis, the Parents in Touch Program for minority parents organizes seminars and workshops dealing with topics such as questions and test procedures and effective parent training. The Family Fair is another means of promoting family interaction. A day-long activity with exhibits and activities for parents, the program provides suggestions on how to improve education occurring in the family. The program also seeks to change parents' perceptions that they might not be effectively parenting (Radd, 1993).

Developing a parent education program based on specific family and community needs might prove more effective and might be received more enthusiastically by parents. Regardless of the format selected, an assessment or needs inventory should first be conducted to determine preferred methods and content (Manning, 1992).

Parent education programs can play vital roles in teaching parents about at-risk conditions and the school's agenda to help children and adolescents. Educators preparing parent education programs can conduct a needs assessment, plan and implement sessions and topics, and can serve as resource specialists. Parents who understand their at-risk youngsters and the school's educational efforts will be more supportive of both their youngsters and the school.

Reviewing What You Have Read About Parents and Families

1. Many _____ people subscribe to the extended family concept, i.e., grandparents, aunts, and uncles play major parenting roles.

2. Educators who want to avoid basing at-risk programs on misperceptions, opinions of other educators, comments on permanent records, should seek _____ contact with parents and families.

3. The design of a _____ should include several considerations such as parents' and families' proficiency with English and whether parents consider questions to be too personal.

4. Parent surveys should be clear and short, require only a brief amount of time to complete, and avoid conveying _____ .

5. _____ may be one of the most effective ways of getting to know learners, their immediate and extended families, and their home environment.

6. Whether communicating through speaking directly, telephoning, or writing to parents, educators are responsible for not allowing _____ _____ to interfere with overall communication.

7. _____ in parent/teacher conferences might pose a problem, i.e., the Anglo-American who looks the Native-American in the eye while communicating might be considered rude, or the educator might interpret a Native-American glancing the other way to be a sign of disinterest or irritation.

8. _____ cited reasons for using volunteers in the classroom and school, including relieving the professional staff of nonteaching duties and providing needed services to individual children.

9. Essentials for organizing effective _____ include cultural and gender diversity, an orientation session to make members' roles and functions clear, and a commitment to work together and to participate in shared decision making.

10. The _____ presents an opportunity for parents and teachers to exchange information about the child's school and home activities, and provides an occasion to involve parents in planning and implementing their child's educational program.

11. When at-risk students' problems are greater than educators and parents can address, responsible educators can be prepared to suggest _____ _____ that might be prepared to provide assistance to avoid letting parents feeling hopeless about their child's or adolescent's future.

12. Parent volunteers might need _____ to understand the at-risk conditions and the dangers associated with "fussing at" students for being sexually active or experimenting with drugs.

13. _____ can provide parents with information on at-risk symptoms and conditions and with needed assistance on ways to address at-risk children's and adolescents' unique needs.

14. During parent/teacher conferences educators should avoid _____ _____ that might appear foreign or threatening and rely on more lay terms to explain at-risk conditions.

15. Essential considerations for effective _____ include written policies, administrative support, and training programs.

Answer Key: 1. culturally diverse; **2.** firsthand; **3.** parent survey; **4.** middle-class perspectives; **5.** Home visits; **6.** verbal or nonverbal communication differences; **7.** Nonverbal communication; **8.** The National School Volunteer Program; **9.** advisory councils; **10.** parent/teacher conference; **11.** community organizations and social services agencies; **12.** special instruction and training; **13.** Parent education; **14.** educational jargon and terminology; **15.** parent involvement programs.

Summary

Whether through conferences or actual involvement, parents and families can be assets in the effort to address the needs of at-risk learners, regardless of conditions posing the risk. Parents better understand the nature of at-risk conditions, better understand their child's or adolescent's strengths and weaknesses, and also show support for school's efforts to provide effective at-risk programs. Likewise, equally important to other benefits, learners can see parental concern and support. The effectiveness of at-risk programs will depend significantly on the quantity and quality of parents' and families' efforts and also educators' efforts to ensure parental participation.

For Additional Information on Parents and Families

Bureau for At-Risk Youth, 645 New York Avenue, Huntington, NY 11743. This organization offers help to at-risk adolescents and their parents by providing *For Teens Only* (a series of 24 pamphlets focusing on substance abuse, emotional health, life skills, sexual violence, and assault) and *How to Set Up a Parent Education Center for Your Organization,* which offers a step-by-step outline for establishing a center in schools and churches.

Chavkin, N. F. (1989). Debunking the myth about minority parents. *Education Horizons, 67*(4), 119–123. Chavkin provides credible evidence that minority parents care about their children's education, and also provides a discussion of promising parental involvement programs.

Jennings, W. B. (1989). How to organize successful parent advisory committees. *Educational Leadership, 47*(2), 42–45. Jennings looks at several aspects of parent advisory programs: shared decision making, membership, orientation, constitution, and working together.

Liontos, L. B. (1992). *At-risk families and schools: Becoming partners.* Eugene, OR: ERIC Clearinghouse. This practical report includes information on involvement, barriers, empowerment, support for parents and teachers, and culturally diverse families.

Morrow, R. D. (1989). Southeast-Asian parent involvement: Can it be a reality? *Elementary School Guidance and Counseling, 23,* 289–297. Morrow reports on factors that affect parental involvement, and provides implications for professionals who want to make parental involvement a reality.

NASSP Bulletin 76(543). This April 1992 issue published a number of excellent articles on increasing parental involvement in the schools such as parents and schools working for student success; increasing parental involvement in secondary schools, parent education programs in middle level schools; and involving parents in urban schools.

Williams, D. L., & Chavkin, N. F. (1989). Essential elements of strong parent involvement programs. *Educational Leadership, 47*(2), 18–20. Williams and Chavkin examine successful parental involvement programs in a five-state area and conclude that seven essential elements characterize the programs.

9

Programs and Efforts Addressing School Conditions

Overview

Identifying at-risk conditions and providing alternative instructional practices and learning environments are without doubt prerequisites to addressing the needs of at-risk children and adolescents. Educators can then begin to make decisions concerning whether to adopt at-risk programs already in operation or whether to develop a program based entirely on student needs. To assist readers in deciding how to most effectively address the needs of at-risk learners, this chapter describes selected programs and efforts and also provides listings of the characteristics of effective programs that all successful at-risk programs should incorporate. It is important to note at the outset that the at-risk programs discussed in this chapter are only representative examples of the many effective at-risk programs available today. The programs mentioned in this chapter were selected because of their potential; however, educators will find many other excellent programs when efforts are directed toward addressing the needs of at-risk learners.

Probing Directions

This chapter on at-risk programs and efforts does the following:

1. Encourages educators to provide effective programs for at-risk children and adolescents, either by adopting programs already in operation or developing programs that use the most effective features of existing programs.
2. Explains specific programs that focus on at-risk conditions such as being a lower achiever, being a potential school dropout, being a learner with exceptionalities, and attending urban schools.
3. Explains specific programs that address multiple at-risk conditions or are designed to prevent children and adolescents from becoming at rirsk in more than one area.
4. Lists characteristics of effective at-risk programs, which should be recognized when developing at-risk programs.
5. Suggests special considerations and factors for all at-risk programs and efforts, regardless of the focus or area addressed.
6. Provides a listing of sources of additional information on programs and efforts designed to help at-risk children and adolescents.

Exemplary Practices

Program effectiveness can be significantly enhanced when educators recognize 11 exemplary practices that contribute to the effectiveness of all programs, regardless of their direction or goal. Table 9-1 examines these 11 essentials and suggests one program that exemplifies the practice.

TABLE 9-1 Exemplary Practices of Effective At-Risk Programs

Exemplary Practice	Goal	Program/Brief Description
Comprehensive approach (Price & Swanson, 1990)	Dropout prevention	Focuses on matching learner needs with curriculum and school goals; works toward both academic and personal achievement
Early intervention (Shine-Ring, 1990)	Multiple at-risk conditions	Focuses on early intervention, multidisciplinary, community involvement; needs assessment, provides clear expectations, develop social skills
Diagnostic/prescriptive approaches (Mitchell & Johnson, 1986)	Multiple at-risk conditions	Focuses on diagnosis and remediation; uses staff and five agencies for diagnostic assessments and treatment planning
Individual determination (Swanson, 1989)	Culturally diverse; low socioeconomic status	Focuses on stressing attitudes and environment for success; uses elective high school credit to help underachievers
Promoting self-esteem (Canfield, 1990)	Multiple at-risk conditions	Focuses on responsibility, the positive; uses support groups, identifies strengths and resources; then sets goals and objectives
High expectations (Lewin, 1987)	Disadvantaged	Focuses on high expectations and deadlines for students performing at grade level; stimulating lessons and use of parental and community resources
Social skills (Comer, 1987)	Urban learners	Focuses on team effort to teach social skills *and* academic skills; focuses on skills needed for successful adult living
Appropriate challenges (Clifford, 1990)	Multiple at-risk conditions	Focuses on teaching students to tolerate failure and learn from mistakes; appropriate task levels, motivation, and feedback
Motivation (Alderman, 1990)	Multiple at-risk conditions	Focuses on link between success and motivation; student responsibility for learning
Appropriate materials and expectations (Taff, 1990)	Multiple at-risk conditions	Focuses on teacher and students agreeing on learning materials and expected results
Involving parents and families (Family Day) (Smith, 1988)	Multiple at-risk conditions	Focuses on schools hosting celebration of family and strengthens school pride; includes films, time with children, speakers, and meetings with faculty

---

Activity 9-1
Consider three of the exemplary practices given in Table 9-1 and the at-risk programs selected as an example of each. Name other exemplary practices and programs. Also, list and briefly describe other at-risk programs that exemplify the suggested practices.

At-Risk Programs and Efforts

This chapter looks at programs and efforts to address the various school-related at-risk conditions: lower achievers, school dropouts, exceptionalities, and urban schools. Reaching decisions concerning how to meet most effectively the needs of at-risk children and adolescents must include a consideration of such factors as time and commitment, financial and other resources, geographic locations (i.e., rural or urban), numbers of learners to be served, parental and community participation, and a host of other factors. After reflecting on these programs and seeking additional information if necessary, readers can either adopt these programs or glean the most effective characteristics of each program as they develop their own at-risk programs. Cohen (1989) reminds designers of at-risk programs that implementation rarely follows a neat and orderly path. Beginnings are often confusing and filled with unforeseen problems.

Lower Achievers

Educators at all school levels can verify the concern and frustration of low-achieving students. While low achievement in and of itself can pose serious problems in terms of lost potential, low achievement can also contribute to other at-risk conditions such as a learner becoming a school dropout. For example, as Chapter 2 indicates, a correlation exists between low achievement and a female's tendency to become pregnant during the teenage years (McClelland, 1987). This section provides representative examples of at-risk programs that have focused attention on ways to improve academic achievement.

RAD (Responsibility and Determination)
The principal and assistant principal at San Francisco's Petrero Middle School made a commitment to team teach a group of low-achieving students. Interested students were invited to join the RAD program. The program consisted of one period per day, took the place of one elective, and had the aim of improving academic performance. Classes provided instruction on organizational skills, study tips, tutoring, and work assignments. The

program included after-school transportation and financial support for needy students. To be selected for the RAD program, the students had to agree to an additional set of mandatory rules; convince school officials they should be allowed to join RAD; maintain in excellent condition a special RAD three-ring binder; maintain a daily log of classwork and homework; check themselves into one extra study hall every day; bring a weekly progress report to class each Friday signed by all teachers; receive no referrals for misbehavior; and be present at school except for serious illness (White, 1989).

The results of the RAD program included the following: achievement climbed; other faculty members supported the program's efforts; and other students wanted to join the program. White (1989) summarized the ingredients that made the program work: consistency, requiring solid study habits, getting a sincere commitment from students to do their best, and using the power of the office of the principal to let undernurtured students know the professional staff considered them both special and capable.

Success for All

The philosophy behind the Success for All program holds that learning problems should be addressed early—before problems increase in severity. The program provides immediate, intense intervention and one-on-one tutoring for students falling behind in reading skills. The goal is to have all students reading at grade level by the end of the third grade (ASCD, 1991).

Success for All is built on two essential principles: prevention and immediate intensive intervention. In essence, major learning problems must first be prevented by providing learners with the best available classroom programs and by engaging parents to support school efforts. When learning difficulties appear, corrective interventions must be immediate, intensive, and minimally disruptive to students' progress in the regular program. Basically, students receive help early—before problems increase in severity—so they can continue to profit from regular classroom instruction. Rather than falling further and further behind, Success for All strives to give students the help they need in the basic skills (Madden, Slavin, Karweit, & Livermon, 1989).

The program elements of Success For All include an array of professional and program aspects that contribute to the success of low-achieving learners. First, certified reading tutors replace Chapter 1 and special education personnel and work one on one with students having difficulty. These tutors reduce class size for reading and also identify effective teaching strategies for individuals. Second, the program facilitator works at the school full time to oversee (with the principal) the operation of the Success for All program, helps with the schedule, and visits classes and tutoring sessions. Third, the reading program includes grades 1 through 5 in which students are heterogeneously grouped (about 25 most of the day). Then, students are regrouped according to grade level (about 15 students per level) to allow teachers to teach the whole reading class without using reading groups within the class. Also, this plan reduces the time needed for seatwork and increases direct instruction time. Other program elements include language arts and writing being provided during the homeroom class; assessment occurring every eight weeks; a half-day preschool for eligible students; a full-day kindergarten with no more than 20 children; a family support team; and advisory and steering committees (Slavin, Karweit, & Madden, 1989).

The Success for All program began in 1987–1988 and currently operates in 15 schools, five main sites being in Baltimore. Program results include students achieving, in general, at or above grade level and also, very importantly, students developing an appreciation for reading (ASCD, 1991).

Early Success in Schools

Designed for kindergarten through the third grade, the Early Success in Schools program (Wells, 1990) emphasizes the prevention of early school failure rather than just its remediation. The program focuses on expanding the kindergarten through third-grade curriculum to provide classroom activities that foster children's thinking skills and allow the children to develop more positive attitudes toward themselves and their school work. Readers who want additional information on this early intervention program should contact Hugh Cox, Ph.D., Director, or Carol Swain, Coordinator, P.O. Box 13, Corte Modera, California 94925.

Reading Recovery

Started in Ohio, Reading Recovery is an early intervention program for young children who have experienced difficulty in beginning reading. The program, based on the research of Marie Clay, a New Zealand child psychologist, was initiated in 1985 and has spread to 16 states. Reading Recovery includes a specifically designed set of interventions, procedures for teaching children, recommended materials, a staff development program, and a set of administrative systems that work together to assure continued quality. Usually, within a school site, the program provides the lowest achieving students in the first grade with intensive one-to-one tutoring for 30 minutes each day, in addition to classroom reading instruction. As the child becomes an independent reader and can profit from classroom instruction, the tutoring is discontinued and another child joins the program (Pinnell, 1990).

While the teacher works within a flexible framework and makes decisions, several steps show how the program works:

1. *Familiar rereading:* The child reads several books that he or she has previously read.
2. *Running record analysis:* The child reads yesterday's new book while the teacher records reading behavior using a coding system called a *running record*. The teacher retreats to a neutral role, and the child reads as independently as possible.
3. *Writing a message:* With the teacher's help, the child first composes and then writes a message, usually one or two sentences, which the student reads many times.
4. *Putting together a cut-up sentence:* After writing the message, the teacher quickly writes it on a small sentence strip and then cuts it apart. The child reconstructs the message, which requires searching for visual information and then checking by rereading.
5. *Reading a new book:* The teacher selects a new book, just a bit more challenging for that particular child, and introduces it to the child by looking at the pictures and talking about the story. Then the child reads the story with some teacher help.

Reading Recovery reveals a masterful combination of reading and writing during which the teacher works alongside the child, and through frequent interaction focuses attention on the text, sentence, phrase, word, or letter—whatever is most appropriate. These minute-to-minute interactions are the heart of the process called "teaching for strategies." The program's goal is to support the child's development of the processes that good readers seem to use naturally (Pinnell, 1990).

Case Study 9-1 looks at a teacher's efforts to help a low-achieving learner.

Case Study 9-1: Helping Low Achievers

Mr. Rowe looked at 12-year-old Greg's school records and listed the factors contributing to Greg's being at risk: consistently low achievement test scores, below-average academic achievement, below-average reading skills, poor self-concept, little motivation, and unable to work independently for even moderate periods of time. So many signals pointed to Greg being at risk that he could not ignore them. He wondered what his course of action should be and finally decided that he would be unable to handle all of Greg's problems alone. His first move was to complete the referral forms required by the administration. He also knew he needed to talk with Greg's parents.

The assistant principal to whom Mr. Rowe had sent the referral forms advocated a team approach and scheduled a meeting with

Greg's parents and all the appropriate school professionals. The meeting resulted in a specific plan to help Greg. Over the next few weeks, the assistant principal coordinated the remediation plan and worked out Greg's schedule. The reading resource teacher tested Greg to determine specific reading difficulties. The counselor developed a plan to improve Greg's self-concept. Greg's parents agreed to help him at home and to provide low-level/high-interest reading materials. Mr. Rowe agreed to reinforce and build on the efforts of the resource teacher and counselor.

Greg was fortunate to have a teacher who recognized his propensity toward being at risk. His difficulties were recognized and an appropriate plan developed *before* problems grew more severe.

Distar

Distar (Becker & Carnine, 1980), developed at the University of Oregon, is unusual, even within the range of continuous-progress programs. It provides teachers with very specific scripts to use in teaching reading and mathematics and trains teachers in very specific methods, down to the level of how to use hand signals to elicit student responses and how to call on students. In describing the program, Distar's developers tend to emphasize the sequential, hierarchical curriculum design, direct instruction and rapid pace, and high frequency of student responses (Becker & Carnine, 1980). Teachers work with students in small homogeneous groups, assess learners frequently on their progress, and regroup learners according to assessment results.

Strong evidence supports the effectiveness of Distar for increasing student performance in certain skill areas. Distar has consistently positive effects on the achievement of disadvantaged students. The effects of Distar appear primarily on language and mathematics computations tests, not on such higher order skills as reading comprehension or mathematics problem solving. Recent research on Distar has found that the program's effects can be long lasting. In an inner city New York elementary school, Distar students exceeded control groups in high school graduation; about 55% of the former Distar students graduated, compared to 34% of control students (Meyer, 1984).

Despite the well-documented and widely acknowledged positive effects of Distar, there has also been much criticism of this approach, principally on the basis of its use of scripted lessons and a perceived focus on rote skills rather than higher order, learning-to-learn skills. Many teachers and administrators resist Distar for these reasons. Given this reality, it is important to note that Distar is only one of several successful continuous-progress mod-

> **Activity 9-2**
> Review the literature on at-risk programs and such resources as *Educational Programs That Work* to identify other efforts to address the needs of lower achievers. If you were planning such a program, what three or four "essentials" would you include in the effort?

els, is the only one to use scripted lessons, and is one of only two to emphasize the highly organized, teacher-centered classroom structure that many teachers find offensive (Slavin & Madden, 1989).

Low Achievers: Characteristics of Effective Programs

1. Programs place major emphasis on individualized, small group, and one-on-one instruction.
2. Programs attempt to diagnose problems and provide remediation at an early age before problems increase in severity and lead to other at-risk conditions.
3. Programs place responsibility for improving achievement on the learner as well as educators.
4. Programs adopt a sequential and continuous progress approach.
5. Programs have carefully planned procedures, materials, and evaluational approaches based on the effective teaching research.
6. Programs have provisions for teacher development—knowledge, skills, and attitudes—through formal coursework, in-service opportunities, and other educational ventures.
7. Programs show coordinated commitments and efforts of all educators (including administrators, counselors, and special education specialists), learners, and parents.
8. Programs emphasize basic skills and also address related areas such as study skills, self-concept, and attitudes.

School Dropouts

Several programs and efforts have directed attention toward reducing the school dropout rate. While each takes a different approach, each could be adapted to meet the needs of another school, at-risk situation, or geographical region. Educators can take advantage of the exemplary aspects of these programs as they plan and implement new dropout programs.

Diem (1992) used the case study approach to determine strategies used to assist potential school dropouts. Enrollment in these programs varied by individual according to academic, personal, or behavioral needs. Some students participated in more than one at-risk program at a time. Strategies found by Diem (1992) included the following:

1. *Literacy programs—before-school, after-school, and pull-out*: Before- and after-school programs, usually voluntary in nature, provided tutorial assistance. Students made appointments to receive help with any subject area in which they felt the need for assistance. Teachers also scheduled appointments with students falling behind in class or who might benefit from academic assistance. Pull-out programs included traditional classroom models where educators send students to basic skills specialists to work on particular literacy deficits. These sessions provided students with opportunities to work at one's own pace in a nongrade-oriented environment. Diem's study revealed that students placed in pull-out programs (rather than having the student *choose* to participate) often appeared uncooperative, especially at the beginning of the school year.

2. *Teacher and community mentors:* At-risk students often lack the ability to develop positive interpersonal relationships with teachers, adults, and even peers who may assume the role of an authority figure. To address this tendency, mentor programs included school-based and community/business orientation. School-based mentors were teachers who had agreed to work with one or more at-risk students before, after, or during school. Such mentoring often requires extensive training. The community/business mentoring program involved a wide variety of community and business people who offered their services to help at-risk students. For example, culturally diverse business people often volunteered to help youngsters from their communities stay in school. Both groups used literacy development as a major interpersonal communications component.

3. *School-business partnerships:* These partnerships provide schools with opportunities that otherwise would be unavailable to the schools and their at-risk students. Examples of assistance may include financial assistance, training in motivation, and alternative education experiments.

4. *School counselor programs:* The schools in Diem's Study had an at-risk program coordinator responsible for monitoring, implementing, and evaluating all school-based at-risk activities. Within the schools, specific responsibilities varied, i.e., some schools expected these special counselors to limit activities to data collection and ongoing program maintenance. In others, educators encouraged more creative efforts, i.e., offering various classes and activities as well as seeking external funding for at-risk projects (Diem, 1992).

The PRIDE Center (Positive Responsible Individuals Desiring an Education)
In 1989, San Marcos (Texas) Consolidated Independent School District (SMCISD) began the PRIDE Center, which provided an alternative high

school of choice for dropouts and potential dropouts. The program enables students to begin and complete courses at any time of the year and to follow a self-paced, competency-based curriculum that includes mentoring, counseling and guidance services, tutoring, computer-based instruction, college preparation, career decision making, a positive atmosphere, and high expectations (Chavkin, 1991).

The aim of the coalition formed by SMCISD and the Institute of Social Work at Southwest Texas State University is to provide a forum for collaboration among social agencies, businesses, parents, schools, and a university and to become a model for reducing the dropout rate nationwide. Four interrelated goals include to increase attendance rates, decrease dropout rates, increase graduation rates, and disseminate the project nationally in the third year. To reach the goals, the coalition focuses attention on several key factors: parental involvement, a referral system, utilization of community resources, student self-esteem, a tutoring program, and a mentoring program.

Three key characteristics of the PRIDE Center include its referral system and its links with community resources and agencies. First, the easy-to-use referral system allows initial information to be taken over the telephone; more in-depth information gathering takes place at a later date. The program strives to encourage referrals and to begin work with an at-risk student as quickly as possible. Significant aspects of the program include a computerized tracking system and its social workers who have extensive experience in the community and have identified existing community resources appropriate for at-risk students and their families. Social workers have created links between the school and community resources to fill a variety of needs: nutritional education, legal aid, family planning, child protection services, juvenile detention, psychological services, and drug rehabilitation. Community agencies provided summaries of available services and an appropriate utilization form. Third, the coalition emphasizes multiethnic/school/community collaboration through an advisory council and also through broad input from educators, parents, and community agencies.

I Have a Dream

Eugene Lang, a multimillionaire industrialist, spoke to the sixth-grade graduates in East Harlem in 1981 and offered his "I Have a Dream" pledge. Lang's pledge provided college costs for every student in the class who finished high school. Lacey (1991) described the "I Have a Dream" program, explained the financial commitment to sponsor a class of "Dreamers," suggested the organizational features needed for successful programs, and warned against expecting definitive answers to whether such programs influence the quality of teaching and learning in the schools.

A successful approach to dropout prevention requires the combined efforts of social workers and counselors as well as tutoring and recreational resources. Organization features include a flexible structure that enables staff to respond to situations, revise strategies, and pursue aims over time. In collaboration with the sponsor, the project coordinator arranges for all services in close conjunction with others involved in the "Dream Team" and the "Educational Village." The Dream Team, led by the sponsor and coordinated by the project coordinator, focuses on Dreamers and their families, and consists of the school, the foundation, the community, the sponsor, and the community-based organization. All the individuals and groups work as a part of the Educational Village, which comes from an African proverb which proposes that educating a child takes a whole village. The village consists of the foundation, volunteer agencies, school-business partnerships, municipal agencies, community-based organizations, and the sponsor.

Although such programs undoubtedly help some learners, educators seeking a sponsor for a "I Have a Dream" program should realize that not all learners will be successful. In Lang's program, 34 of the original 61 students enrolled at least part-time in colleges and another nine completed high school. Problems facing students in Lang's class included mobility, teenage pregnancy, and criminal behaviors. In addition, questions defy easy answers: Do Dreamers become more engaged in school and more motivated academically and socially? Does the program result in any attitude or behavioral changes on the part of administrators and teachers? To some degree, the Education Village concept is an idealized concept. Still, programs that adopt these strategies prove beneficial because all participants work together for the students' welfare and to recognize a wider range of possibilities and resources than Dreamers would normally have. Lacey believes the strength of any dropout program lies in its capacity to foster awareness of untapped resources, ripe opportunities, and fresh possibilities in school and in life (Lacey, 1991).

Using Technology to Reduce Dropouts

Believing that dropout programs should speak to the whole person and should incorporate technology, Sunrise Middle School in Ft. Lauderdale, Florida, began a program designed to raise the self-esteem and academic achievement of at-risk students. Lee (1990) explained that the program's coordinator felt that student apathy toward school was the program's biggest challenge. This lack of interest in school often leads to other social problems such as experimenting with drugs. The program tries to convince students to see the importance of learning in the belief that other at-risk conditions will be reduced.

Technology plays a major role in this dropout program. Lee (1990) explained that although software and video equipment are useful in enhancing students' academic skills, they can also be valuable tools in address-

---

Activity 9-3

Check through various media centers, audiovisual collections, and software catalogs and make a list of additional technology and software. Include titles, producers, and descriptions of software for any at-risk conditions. Why do you think software particularly helps at-risk students? If you were preparing a software package for at-risk learners, what essentials would you include?

---

ing the social problems of students in trouble. Once identified as being at risk, students rotate through a computer lab every two weeks to work on specific academic areas in which they need remediation. In the lab, students can work at their own pace in an individualized setting where they receive immediate feedback about their work. Student behavior changes have been evident. Students previously disruptive or apathetic in regular classes show excitement about their work in the computer lab. The program's coordinator believes the changes result from the use of computers that focus on the attention of these learners in a manner that regular classes could not.

In addition to computer software being used to teach basic academic subjects and problem solving, the program also uses programs designed to teach career options: *Discovery* (A.C.T. Discover Center, Hunt Valley, Maryland), *Choices Center* (Florida Department of Education), and *Microzine*, a monthly software series published by Scholastic in Jefferson City, Missouri. Also, filmstrips and videos play a major role in this program designed to help at-risk learners (Lee, 1990).

Another program incorporating technological advances includes Sousa Junior High School in Washington, DC, whose dropout program focuses on improving skills in the core academic subjects. To facilitate students' passing of basic objectives, the program's coordinator incorporates social issues such as teenage sexuality, job skills, and self-esteem. Local guest speakers supplement and enrich class discussions and the use of technology. Videos dealing with specific social problems include *Running Scared* (The Media Guild, San Diego, California), *A Desperate Exit* (Intermedia, Seattle, Washington), *Dropping Out, The Road to Nowhere, Jobs for the '90s,* and *Diploma or Dropout, It's Your Choice* (Alpha Resource Center, Washington, DC) (Lee, 1990).

Effective Continuation Schools

Teeters (1990) tells of California reports that indicate 30% of high school students drop out prior to obtaining a diploma—among low-income youth, the numbers might be even higher. The Yucaipa Joint Unified School District, which has less than a 3% dropout rate, appears to have found an answer to the dropout problem. Students experiencing difficulty at the comprehensive high school transfer to Green Valley High School in an effort to deal with academic and social problems. Success at Green Valley can be measured in several ways: First, the dropout rate for at-risk students remains low; second, students demonstrate consistently high achievement scores; and third, many students continue their education in vocational schools, colleges, and universities.

Green Valley offers an alternative instructional style and instructional medium to better facilitate the education of at-risk learners. Using the philosophy of alternative education, the school holds the same or higher expectations, and often even more expectations than other California high schools. In fact, students at Green Valley take the same proficiency examination as other state high school students and participate in the same academic activities. Potential Green Valley students apply through a formal process and with parental consent. They must appear before the district's transfer board and must show that their academic success depends on this alternative school. Applicants must be at least 16 years old and must demonstrate legitimate efforts to graduate. Once accepted, students attend on a voluntary basis (Teeters, 1990).

Green Valley makes definite rules at the beginning: "no fighting, no drugs or alcohol or paraphernalia involved with drugs or alcohol; no weapons or anything construed as a weapon; no abusive language or actions to other students or teachers; and finally, no smoking" (Teeters, 1990, p. 50). Students know that the violation of rules brings serious disciplinary action. Teachers at Green Valley have an environment based on mutual respect. Educators treat students with the respect due all human beings and the staff expects respect in return (Teeters, 1990).

Educators planning at-risk programs also benefit from knowing Green Valley's public relations program with the community. In the belief that successful continuation schools depend on positive public relations with the community, educators at Green Valley work diligently to change the public's image of alternative programs. Many people think Green Valley and other alternative schools consist of drug addicts, fighters, and criminals. The principal speaks to church and community groups in an attempt to dispel these myths. He explains how Green Valley offers a valuable service to needy students who may have missed extended periods of school, to married teens unable to attend the comprehensive high school, and to students who are married or have to care for infants (Teeters, 1990).

Enterprise High: Helping School Dropouts Become
Self-Supporting Adults

Benedict, Snell, and Miller (1987) described Enterprise High in Macomb County, Michigan, which serves economically disadvantaged 16- to 21-year-old dropouts. The curriculum centers on two issues, both relevant to students eager to leave school: how to earn a living and how to manage life. To accomplish these two areas, the curriculum at Enterprise High has basic academic skills, group problem solving, enterprise, and simulation. Three component parts provide a description of the program: (1) an ungraded, points-based grading system (where success depends on mastery, not time), (2) weekly collaborative professional development opportunities, and (3) democratic involvement in the policy-making and administrative decisions of those having an investment in the program.

Trust, considered to be an integral component of the program, allows students and educators to work together and also creates an emotionally supportive and safe environment that allows students to risk failure. Educators at Enterprise High suspend judgment, cultivate friendship, honestly share feelings, and show feelings of caring (Benedict, Snell, & Miller, 1987).

Benedict, Snell, and Miller (1987) provide several suggestions for educators planning programs such as Enterprise High: develop facilitative trust relationships between teachers and students; engage students in whole, personally meaningful, life-based experiences; provide students with instruction and evaluational systems that allow students sufficient time for mastery; give staff members opportunities for professional development; and give staff and students a democratic voice in policy making and administration.

Case Study 9-2 examines how a high school addressed its dropout problem.

Case Study 9-2: Westside High's Dropout Prevention Program

During their retreat, the administrators and faculty at Westside High School discussed the dropout problem. They readily recognized the growing seriousness of the problem. Numbers had been increasing yearly for a number of reasons: dissatisfaction with school, teenage pregnancy, decisions to seek employment, low academic achievement, and a host of other problems. "We know there is a problem," said Dr. Hill. "Now we need to find possible solutions."

The discussion centered around whether to adopt one of the better known dropout programs or whether to use the best of existing programs and then design their own program. One perceptive educator announced, "Regardless of the program we adopt, trust needs to be a basic tenet—we need to learn to show genuine trust toward students and help them to develop trust in us—no more of the 'we against them mentality.'"

Next, the group decided to design its own program to address the needs of Westside students. "What are our dropouts like?" questioned one member. Comments poured forth such as boys, low academic achievers, the poor, nonparticipators, and learners whose older brothers or sisters had dropped out. The group quickly agreed that a checklist was needed to pinpoint potential dropouts. Likewise, the necessary referral forms would have to be developed. The next session was a brainstorming session during which the group listed the basic tenets of their proposed program: the previously mentioned trust; conscientious attempts to involve parents and families; use of community resources; direct instruction in the basic academic subjects; use of technology; coordination of administrators, teachers, counselors, and other educators; providing potential dropouts with a reason for staying in school; diagnostic and remediation programs; addressing of the previously mentioned at-risk conditions; career information and options . . . the list went on and on.

The group realized their task was complex with no easy answers. Likewise, they realized they had little power to change home and community conditions that contribute to students being at risk of dropping out. However, the group also realized that a coordinated and comprehensive effort had been initiated—this was a first and significant step.

Dropout Prevention: Practical Efforts

Downing and Harrison (1990) maintained that dropout prevention should acknowledge several hurdles and should recognize several practical tactics for keeping learners in school. Hurdles included high school graduation requirements that reflect college entrance requirements, teaching approaches that place a priority on teaching college-bound students, competency examinations that pose major barriers for learners needing diplomas, the mind-set that the good life means a college degree, school rules and policies that aggravate at-risk conditions, and, in some situations, bigotry and racism that result in lower expectations for some students (Downing & Harrison, 1990). Advocating a strategy of "small wins" to the dropout problem, Downing and Harrison suggested several practical tactics: (1) efforts to end the "us against them" attitude and to increase collaboration during which counselors verbally take the side of the student; (2) giving or making sure the student has a reason for staying in school, i.e., bringing in employers to explain different jobs for graduates and nongraduates; (3) early identification procedures in which feeder schools suggest potential dropouts; and (4) offering different levels of diplomas or certificates of completion.

Dropout Prevention: Characteristics of Effective Programs

1. Programs place major emphasis on trust and collaboration between educators, potential dropouts, and parents.
2. Programs focus on involving and coordinating efforts of interested parties: potential dropouts, parents and families, educators, community resources and volunteer agencies, foundations, and school-business partnerships.
3. Programs provide for alternative instructional styles, instructional materials, and learning environments.
4. Programs seek community support (financial and otherwise) through carefully planned public relations efforts designed to explain the goals of dropout prevention and also designed to provide an accurate and objective description of the students being served.
5. Programs provide direct instruction in the core academic subjects.
6. Programs implement an easy-to-use referral system, which allows potential dropouts to be readily identified as being at risk.
7. Programs address the problems often associated with "turf issues" in which people may feel their roles and responsibilities are being infringed upon.
8. Programs provide potential dropouts with specific and relevant reasons for staying in school.
9. Programs address the other various at-risk conditions (i.e., drugs, pregnancy and STDs, or lower academic achievement) that may be contributing to the learners' likelihood of dropping out.
10. Programs have advisory councils, which consist of concerned people who can look at the dropout program from various points of view and can suggest recommendations for improvement and change.

Exceptionalities

Significant efforts such as PL 94-142, the Education for All Handicapped Children Act, have been directed at assisting exceptional learners. While many efforts have been successful, some have failed to meet their potential. In fact, only a few today would say that the needs of exceptional learners have been adequately met. This section looks at several efforts and provides a listing of characteristics of effective programs.

Mainstreaming

A major effort to address the needs of exceptional children and adolescents occurred when Congress passed PL 94-142. Often called the *mainstreaming law*, this law required a free and appropriate education for all children that emphasizes special education and related services. This law no longer allowed exceptional children and adolescents to receive second-class treatment or to be placed in classes or institutions without a thorough diagnosis and treatment plan. In effect, many exceptional children were placed in regular classrooms for either part or all of the school day. While this law has resulted in considerable progress for exceptional learners, some students continue to be at risk and in need of more specialized services and programs.

Project ACTT

ACTT stands for Activating Children Through Technology and is one well-known project using computer-assisted instruction. Efforts include integrating an innovative microcomputer curriculum model into educational programs for young special-needs children. The physical, sensory, and cognitive limitations of many exceptional children do not allow them to manipulate toys or objects. The ACTT project has customized toys, keyboards, switch-operated toys, voice synthesizers, and robots for use by children with physical and sensory handicaps. The following suggestions for the program include providing a color monitor, purchasing a joy stick or game paddle, limiting distractions, setting up a computer activity center, and encouraging independence and cooperation (McCormick, 1990). More information can be obtained by writing Project ACCT, 27 Horrabin Hall, Western Illinois University, Macomb, Illinois 61455.

ACCEPTS

This program, A Curriculum for Children's Effective Peer and Teacher Skills, is a social skills curriculum designed to teach crucial social behavior skills for successful adjustment to the behavioral expectations of mainstream settings. The primary objective of ACCEPTS is to prepare exceptional children in kindergarten through sixth grade to enter and to succeed in less restrictive settings. A related goal is to teach skills that enhance classroom adjustment and contribute to peer acceptance. ACCEPTS includes 28 skills grouped into five major content areas: classroom skills, basic interaction skills, getting along, making friends, and coping skills. The classroom skills area focuses on competencies essential for successful classroom adjustment as defined by teachers (such as listening and following directions). The other four areas focus on skills needed for competent interaction with others.

The ACCEPTS program has direct instruction and utilizes a variety of practice activities during instruction. Instructional formats include one-to-one, small group, or large group presentations. Depending on students' rates of progress, the program can be completed in 5 to 10 weeks. Results have included the teaching of social behavior skills and the changing of the behavior of exceptional children in classroom and playground settings (Cullinan & Epstein, 1990).

Activity 9-4

Visit several special educators in different schools to determine how at-risk programs in special education classrooms differ from programs in regular classrooms. Should at-risk learners be educated in special education classes or regular classes, or do decisions about placement depend on the individual learner?

Project Re-ED

Project Re-ED is a residential treatment situation for exceptional children and adolescents who are experiencing disturbed home situations. Nontraditional treatment staff offer reeducation for the child or adolescent while the disturbed home, school, and other community environments become more supportive of the youngsters on return (Cullinan & Epstein, 1990).

Case Study 9-3 shows how a school initiated a team approach to helping Jill, a nine-year-old with several problems.

Case Study 9-3: Jill—An Exceptional Child

Jill, nine years old, has been diagnosed as having below-average levels of intelligence, a significant hearing loss, and relatively minor articulation problems. Her teacher, the special education teacher, the hearing specialist, the communication disorders specialist, the school psychologist, and the counselor discussed how they could best help Jill. Because she has an older sister who had dropped out of school in the tenth grade, the team wanted to address Jill's at-risk conditions before her problems grew worse. The team decided to devise a plan specifically for Jill. The plan included having her hearing problems and articulation problems addressed by the hearing specialist and the communication disorders specialist, respectively. There might be a correlation between the hearing problem and the articulation problem. The counselor devised a self-concept plan. Rather than focusing only on her exceptionalities, the team decided that in addition to addressing Jill's weaknesses they would build on her strengths. Team members also scheduled two meetings per month to provide each other with feedback and to monitor Jill's progress.

The CLASS Program

The CLASS (Contingencies for Learning Academic and Social Skills) program enables regular classroom teachers to control the aggressive and disruptive behavior of students. The program has several key elements. First, there is a classroom group-oriented contingency. The student earns points for displaying appropriate classroom behavior and following the teacher's rules. The teacher praises the student each time a point is earned. Second, if enough points are earned during the day, the entire class shares a preselected award (i.e., recess). Third, educators make arrangements with the parents to provide a home reward such as extra television time or a treat when the student brings home a satisfactory report card, which occurs only if the student earns a sufficient number of points.

As the CLASS program nears completion, teachers phase out the point system and use praise to maintain students' appropriate behavior. The CLASS program is designed to be completed in about two months. Results indicate that the CLASS program works and can be used with a variety of students with behavior problems. The program has usually been implemented to prevent the need for additional special services (Cullinan & Epstein, 1990).

Exceptionalities: Characteristics of Effective Programs

1. Programs demonstrate an understanding of the legal mandates and a willingness to commit to providing effective educational experiences in the least restrictive environment.
2. Programs make appropriate use of technology designed or modified to meet the needs of exceptional learners.
3. Programs emphasize social skills as well as academic skills and insist on learners learning how to work and socialize cooperatively with teachers and learners in mainstreamed situations.
4. Programs teach acceptable behavior and insist on (as with all students) a "bottom line" for appropriate behavior.
5. Programs employ educators who *want* to work with exceptional children and adolescents and who have the professional background to be effective.
6. Programs involve parents and families in the planning and implementation of educational experiences.

Urban Schools

Without well-planned and deliberate action, the many problems associated with urban schools will probably continue into the twenty-first century. While schools have little control over some problems of urban schools (i.e., poverty and poor housing), other problems (i.e., the low achievement commonly associated with urban schools) can be addressed. This section examines at-risk programs for urban learners and suggests characteristics of effective programs.

Cities in Schools

The Cities in Schools (CIS) program began in 1975 to bring professional help directly to the school site. CIS repositions social service staff in all fields—counseling, health, recreation, financial, legal, and employment—in the schools themselves, making services both more accessible to students and better coordinated. Often the program provides human services to the entire family to keep a child in school.

In each CIS location, representatives from the school, social service agencies, local businesses, and the community form a nonprofit board to raise funds and set policies for the program. These boards form a link between community leaders and the disenfranchised; often they reveal the holes in the delivery system. The program has shown the greatest success in two areas: in improving attendance and decreasing dropout rates, and in improving violent, drug-ridden schools, usually within a year. The CIS model has been replicated in 50 cities, including Atlanta, Houston, and New York City; and many more programs are "in the pipeline" (ASCD, 1991). For additional information, contact Sarah DeCamp, Cities in Schools, 1023 15th Street, NW, Suite 600, Washington, DC 20005.

School-Community Connections

A collaboration between New Haven, Connecticut, schools and their communities shows how a support network for at-risk students can enhance their academic and social success. In 1968, the collaboration began with two elementary schools, and the project gradually evolved. The program consists of a process model in which administrators, parents, teachers, and support staff collaboratively work through three mechanisms: a governance and management group, a mental health or support-staff group, and a parents' group. The goal of the collaborative effort is to create a social climate that helps to close the student development gap, to create an academic program based on achievement data, and to carry out a staff development program based on social and academic goals established at the building level. The coordinating element is the governance and management group, which, with the support of the school staff, develops and carries out a comprehensive building plan to address school social climate, academic performance, and staff development.

One unique feature of the program is that the mental health team shares child development and behavior knowledge, skills, and sensitivity with parents, teachers, and administrators. Then, they apply their development and behavioral knowledge to social and academic program planning and in their interactions with students. This approach provides a preventive element as well as the more traditional treatment mode. Such coordination combines academic, social, cognitive, and affective resources in a manner that can best meet the needs of growing children and also can close the developmental gaps for learners at risk.

The Social Skills Curriculum for Inner City Children integrates the teaching of basic academic subjects, social skills, and art appreciation. Carried out during elective times, the program consists of units focusing on the social and academics skills necessary to be successful adults: politics and government, business and economics, health and nutrition, spiritual and leisure time. This program permits low-income, disproportionately high-risk children to gain the skills that children from better educated and higher income families often gain simply by participating in the activities of families (Comer, 1987).

Project Interface

Begun in 1982, the Interface Institute provides an effective tutorial program for promising African-American urban students who demonstrate potential in mathematics and the sciences. Two groups work together in carefully planned sessions. One group consists of high-potential African-American junior high school students eligible to enroll in college preparatory classes but who are not yet enrolled. The other group consists of college students who aspire to professional careers in mathematics and science. These college students assume responsibility for teaching and tutoring the junior high school students. The program maintains a staff of about 15 college students who work with about 60 to 70 junior high school students. Study groups of 4 to 6 students bridge learning gaps, communicate the content of the course material, and introduce the students to college preparatory work. The program includes the Science Exploration Series, a complete computer lab, the Role Model/Mentor Series, actual scientists demonstrating their work, and the Saturday Field Trip Series. Project Interface has demonstrated its effectiveness on standardized tests, placement in college preparatory classes, and follow-up of college progress and graduates (Wilson, 1989).

Urban Learners: Characteristics of Effective Programs

1. Programs bring professional help—counseling, health, recreation, financial, and legal services—to the school campus so students will have easy access and also will be aware of available services.
2. Programs demonstrate understanding of the plight of many urban students.
3. Programs work to improve attendance and decrease dropout rates.
4. Programs implement school-community connections, which provide a network for at-risk students.
5. Programs provide opportunities to enhance learners' academic and social successes.
6. Programs teach social skills necessary for living and coping in densely populated areas.

7. Programs provide for effective tutorial programs without cost to learners and at convenient times for learners.
8. Programs work to prevent problems as well as address problems when they occur.
9. Programs provide faculty and staff with appropriate in-service opportunities and other educational experiences designed to teach about teaching and dealing with urban learners.

Other Programs and Efforts Addressing Multiple At-Risk Conditions

While this chapter has focused predominantly on programs and efforts designed for specific at-risk conditions, other programs address the needs of at-risk learners in a more general manner. It is important to note that many such fine programs serve children and adolescents and that the selection of these programs does not negate the importance of other effective programs.

Ambassadors (Cahoon, 1989) pairs university students who serve as role models with at-risk students. Students meet weekly to help elementary students with social and academic skills and to develop positive attitudes toward work and self. Goals include improving academic achievement, attendance, problem-solving skills, self-esteem, and also involving parents. Interested readers may contact Peggy Cahoon, Principal, William E. Ferron Elementary School, 4200 Mountain Vista, Las Vegas, Nevada 89121.

Bluemel and Taylor (1990) maintain that the library media center can play a vital role as educators plan programs for at-risk learners. The success of intervention efforts is influenced by research skills (on areas of interest, i.e., the cost of a CD player), involving at-risk students as aides, using media centers for resources related to cultural backgrounds, and using the technological innovations of media centers.

Sternberg, Okagaki, and Jackson (1990) maintained that PIFS (Practical Intelligence for Success) addresses multiple at-risk conditions, considers various types of intelligence (linguistic, spatial, musical, kinesthetic, interpersonal, intrapersonal), and provides practical lessons in areas where students' intelligence lies.

The Learning Support Program offers students counseling in behavior modification, remedial help in basic skills, assistance with regular subjects,

---

Activity 9-5

Many reports suggest that living in an urban area contributes to learners being at risk or makes the conditions worse. But how about rural learners? Rural learners often attend schools that have fewer resources and programs. Are rural learners at risk and, if so, what can be done to address their needs?

time-out rooms to avoid confrontations, and consistent monitoring of performance (Koslofsky, 1991).

Youth Opportunities Unlimited (Goodwin & Flatt, 1991) is a comprehensive academic and work program for 14- and 15-year-old disadvantaged students. The goal is to teach lifetime sports in an attempt to teach the sport itself as well as provide opportunities for learning social skills, physical exercise, motivation, and for working together toward common goals.

Reviewing What You Have Read About Programs and Efforts

1. Designed for kindergarten through the third grade, _____ _____ emphasizes the prevention of school failure rather than just its remediation.

2. At-risk programs for _____ should emphasize early diagnosis and remediation, responsibility and determination, sequential and continuous progress approaches, and an emphasis on basic skills.

3. _____ provides teachers with specific scripts to use in teaching reading and mathematics and trains teachers in specific methods.

4. The _____ program, an early intervention program for young children, provides immediate, intense instruction, and one-on-one tutoring.

5. _____ , an early intervention program for young children experiencing difficulty in reading, is based on the research of Marie Clay and has a specifically designed set of interventions.

6. Software programs such as *Running Scared* and *A Desperate Exit* address problems associated with _____ .

7. _____ , a school dropout program, enables students to begin and complete courses at any time during the year and to follow a self-paced, competency-based curriculum that includes a wide array of services.

8. _____ programs should address other various at-risk conditions such as drugs, teenage pregnancy, and STDs.

9. Significant efforts such as _____ have been directed toward assisting exceptional learners.

10. The _____ program is a social skills curriculum for kindergartners through sixth graders designed to teach critical social behavior skills for successful adjustment prior to being mainstreamed.

11. _____ , is a well-known project using computer-assisted instruction, which integrates an innovative microcomputer curriculum model into educational programs for young special needs learners.

12. _____ is a collaboration between the New Haven, Connecticut, schools and their communities, which shows how a support network for at-risk students can enhance their academic and social success.

13. The _____ project was started in 1975 to bring professional help—such as counseling, health, recreation, financial, legal, and employment—into the schools themselves.

14. _____ addresses multiple at-risk conditions and considers the various types of intelligence such as linguistic, spatial, musical, kinesthetic, interpersonal, and intrapersonal.

15. Begun in 1982, _____ provides an effective tutorial program for promising African-American urban students who demonstrate potential in mathematics and science.

Answer Key: **1.** Early Success in Schools; **2.** low achievers; **3.** Distar; **4.** Success for All; **5.** Reading Recovery; **6.** school dropouts; **7.** PRIDE; **8.** School dropout; **9.** PL 92-142, the Education for All Handicapped Children Act; **10.** ACCEPTS; **11.** Project ACTT, Activating Children Through Technology; **12.** School-Community Connections; **13.** Cities in Schools (CIS); **14.** PIFS (Practical Intelligence for Success); **15.** Project Interface.

Summary

Undoubtedly many effective at-risk programs serve children and adolescents. Some have been developed by institutions, others by individuals or groups. This chapter has focused on representative at-risk programs and has offered suggestions for educators designing their own programs. Whether adopting or designing at-risk programs, it is important to remember that program effectiveness can be enhanced by including several basic essentials, i.e., parent involvement, an emphasis on basic skills, and placing responsibility (yet not blaming the victim) on the learner. Likewise, educators adopting or planning programs can benefit from learning about successful programs currently serving at-risk populations, resources available to educators, and organizations whose purpose it is to serve at-risk populations.

For Additional Information on Programs and Efforts

Brandt, R. S. (1990). *Readings from Educational Leadership—Students at risk*. Alexandria, VA: ASCD. Made up of articles from *Educational Leadership*, this book explores the challenge of working with at-risk youth, what can be done, exemplary programs and practices, dealing with social problems, and working with parents and community agencies.

Center for Research on Effective Schooling for Disadvantaged Students (CDS), The Johns Hopkins University, 3505 North Charles Street, Baltimore, Maryland 21218. The CDS works to determine successful teaching-learning methods for disadvantaged learners and disseminates information to educators.

Council for Exceptional Children (CEC), 1920 Association Drive, Reston, Virginia 22091-1589. CEC works for the overall welfare of exceptional children and provides a journal and other services for educators working with exceptional children.

Kammoun, B. B. (1991). High school dropout programs: Elements for success. *NASSP Bulletin, 75*(538), 9–14. In this case study, Kammoun suggests several key factors that are essential to all successful dropout programs.

Manning, M. L. (1993). Seven essentials of effective at-risk programs. *The Clearing House, 66*, 135–138. As the title implies, this article looks at several essentials of at-risk programs such as addressing self-concept and improving social skills and describes a program exemplifying each essential.

National Dropout Prevention Center, Clemson University, Clemson, South Carolina 29631. This center provides information on school dropouts, suggests checklists to identify potential dropouts, and suggests strategies for reducing the school dropout rates.

Rogus, J. F., & Wildenhaus, C. (1991). Programming for at-risk learners: A preventive approach. *NASSP Bulletin, 75*(538), 1–7. Rogus and Wildenhaus offer a number of ideas for a preventive approach to helping at-risk learners.

Slavin, R. E., Karweit, N. L., & Madden, N. A. (1989). *Effective programs for students at risk.* Boston: Allyn and Bacon. These authors include 12 excellent and well-documented readings on areas such as at-risk students, effective programs, pull-out programs, preschool programs, effective kindergarten programs, and instructional issues.

Slavin, R. E., Madden, N. A., Karweit, N. L., Dolan, L. J., & Wasik, B. A. (1991). Success for all: Ending reading failure from the beginning. *Language Arts, 68*, 404–409. These researchers at the Center for Research on Effective Schooling for Disadvantaged Students at Johns Hopkins University examine the various components of the Success for All model.

Wells, S. E. (1990). *At-risk youth: Identification, programs, and recommendations.* Englewood, CO: Teachers Ideas Press. Wells focused attention on the dropout problem and methods of identifying potential dropouts. Wells also provides an extensive listing of programs and services.

Wilson, A. B. (1989), Theory into practice: An effective program for urban youth. *Educational Horizons, 67*(4), 136–144. Wilson tells of the Interface Institute where tutors work with promising African-American urban students in mathematics and science. Wilson examines such related topics as school environments, high expectations for students, consistent evaluation, administrative support, and cultural strengths.

10

Programs and Efforts Addressing Societal and Personal Conditions

Summary

For Additional Information on Programs and Efforts

Overview

Not all at-risk conditions can be traced to learners' abilities and to school practices. Unfortunately, children's and adolescents' at-risk conditions sometimes result from societal and personal factors. Although the school cannot be expected to eliminate all the problems learners bring to school, educators can identify at-risk characteristics and formulate appropriate educational plans. U.S. society continues to have many people living in poverty, which does not contribute positively to school achievement; the increasing culturally diverse population continues to face problems associated with living in a hostile and often racist society; and children and adolescents experience problems and engage in behaviors that contribute to them being at risk. This chapter looks at at-risk conditions for which society usually does not place blame on the schools yet expects schools to help learners to overcome.

Probing Directions

This chapter on at-risk programs and efforts designed to address societal and personal conditions does the following:

1. Recognizes responsibility for addressing societal and personal conditions that contribute to children's and adolescents' propensity to being at risk.
2. Explains specific programs and efforts designed to address poverty, low socioeconomic conditions, and disadvantaged learners; the growing problems associated with teenage pregnancy and sexually transmitted diseases (STDs); substance abuse; juvenile delinquency; suicidal students; and health-related problems.
3. Lists characteristics of effective at-risk programs, which educators can use as a blueprint for planning and implementing at-risk programs.
4. Encourages all educators to recognize at-risk conditions and also recognize learners' strengths on which educational efforts can be based and built.
5. Lists sources of additional information on at-risk programs currently operating to address the needs of young people.

At-Risk Programs and Efforts: Societal and Personal Conditions

This chapter examines efforts and programs directed at poverty, low socioeconomic conditions, and disadvantaged learners; the growing problems associated with teenage pregnancy and STDs; substance abuse; juvenile delinquency; suicidal students; and health-related problems. As with Chapter 9, this chapter examines representative programs and efforts designed to address these at-risk conditions. Readers can find many other fine programs with documented results or which have the potential for helping at-risk children and adolescents.

Poverty, Lower Socioeconomic Conditions, and Disadvantaged Learners

Living in poverty can drastically affect learners' attitudes toward school as well as their social and academic achievement. While educators might have little influence over learners' actual home conditions, learners living in poverty will benefit when educators understand conditions associated with poverty, understand how poverty affects academic achievement, and know effective means of addressing the social and educational problems of the poor.

National Center for Children in Poverty
The National Center for Children in Poverty (NCCP), established in 1989 to strengthen programs and policies for children and their families who live in poverty, suggests that much can be done to protect poor young children and to help them become productive adults. To provide universal access to child health, the NCCP (1990) offers several recommendations:

- Efforts to expand child care subsidies for poor and low-income families
- Expansion of Head Start and other effective preschool programs to serve all poor children
- Programs for preventing teenage pregnancy and support programs for teenage parents
- Educational and employment opportunities designed to motivate teenagers to postpone parenthood
- High-quality schooling and training for technically demanding occupations
- Coordinated community-based services designed to help poor parents cope effectively with personal problems and parental responsibilities (NCCP, 1990).

Activity 10-1
Contact the National Center for Children in Poverty (Columbia University, 154 Haven Avenue, New York, New York 10032) and request the most current information on children and adolescents living in poverty. We often look to the federal government to provide financial resources and programs, but name several ways educators and community members on the local level can respond to help children and adolescents living in poverty.

Overall, the NCCP (1990) proposes that the needs of socioeconomically disadvantaged learners cannot be solved without addressing the needs of families. In the meantime, however, and in the absence of social and economic programs, educators can better understand the plight of children in poverty and can try to provide teenage pregnancy programs and a higher quality of schooling, and they can work closer with community-based organizations.

Through the Omnibus Budget Reconciliation Act of 1990, PL 101-508, Congress established two new child care programs: Child care for low-income working families in need of such care and otherwise at risk of becoming eligible for Aid for Dependent Children (AFDC) (the At-Risk Child Care Program) and the Child Care and Development Block Grant program. The At-Risk Child Care Program provided child care to low-income working families in an attempt to avoid welfare dependency. States can provide care directly through the use of service contracts, by providing cash or vouchers directly to the family, by reimbursing the family, and by using other arrangements as deemed necessary. The Child Care and Development Block Grant program, provides child care services for low-income families and to increase the availability, affordability, and quality of child care and developmental services (*Federal Register*, 1991).

Accelerated Schools for Disadvantaged Students
Lewin (1987) maintained that the rhetoric of recent state reforms stressed improvement of education for all children yet, in reality, the reform movement neglected educationally disadvantaged students. Two problems surface when considering current reforms. First, current reforms suggest raising standards at the secondary level yet do not provide new resources or strategies to help disadvantaged students meet these higher standards. Second, the current movement assumes that disadvantaged students will not be able to maintain a normal instructional pace, that merely providing remedial services closes the learning gap, and that learners do not need a timetable.

Lewin (1987) proposed a new approach for educating disadvantaged learners, which includes high expectations, deadlines for students performing at grade level, stimulating instructional programs, planning by the educational staff offering the program, and the use of all available parental and community resources. These efforts, however, must be transitional in nature and should close the achievement gap after a period of intervention so students can return to regular instruction. To close the achievement gap as quickly as possible, Lewin (1987) recommended a program for accelerated schools designed as transition schools to bring disadvantaged students up to grade level by the end of the sixth grade. The approach also addresses serious achievement deficits, the single most important cause of school dropouts. Lewin (1987) stated that the goal of the accelerated curriculum is to bring all learners up to grade level rather than to limit interventions for the disadvantaged to pull-out programs.

The Accelerated Schools Program has two features that contribute to its success and should be considered when developing other at-risk programs. First, parents need to be involved and must sign a written agreement that clarifies the obligations of school staff, parents, and students. Also, the school provides opportunities for parents to interact with the school program and to assist their children. Second, the program has an extended school day, which provides rest periods and arts activities and time for independent assignments or homework. Since many latch-key children may be the rule rather than the exception, many parents like the extended school day concept for practical as well as academic reasons (Lewin, 1987).

The Accelerated School Program was piloted at two elementary school in 1986 and currently operates in more than 50 schools. Its success has been reflected in higher test scores, better attendance, and greatly reduced retention rates (ASCD, 1991).

New Directions—Alternative Views to Children in Poverty
Knapp, Turnbull, and Shields (1990) claimed that disadvantaged children are capable of more than is usually required, and for these children to meet

---

Activity 10-2
Write a position paper outlining your opinions of the Accelerated Schools Program. Address such items as high expectations, deadlines for learners performing at grade levels, and using all available parents and community resources. How feasible are Lewin's theories? Should disadvantaged learners be expected to meet high standards? Will Lewin's plan help or hurt disadvantaged learners' chances of academic success?

their potential, educators must adopt practices reflecting higher expectations.

Concerning educators' conceptions of disadvantaged learners, Knapp, Turnbull, and Shields (1990) suggest the following:

- Teachers respect the students' cultural/linguistic backgrounds and communicate this appreciation in a personal manner.
- Academic programs encourage students to draw and build on the experiences they have and, at the same time, expose them to unfamiliar experiences and ways of thinking.
- The assumptions, expectations, and ways of doing things in school are made explicit to disadvantaged students by teachers who explain and model these dimensions of academic learning.

Some of their suggestions for the curriculum follow:

- Focus on meaning and understanding from the beginning, for example, by orienting instruction toward comprehending reading passages, communicating important ideas in written text, or understanding the concepts underlying number facts.
- Balance routine skill learning with novel and complex tasks from the earliest stages of learning.
- Provide a context for skill learning that establishes clear reasons for needing to learn the skills, affords opportunities to apply the skills, and helps students relate one skill to another.
- Influence attitudes and beliefs about the academic content areas, as well as skills and knowledge.
- Eliminate unnecessary redundancy in the curriculum (e.g., repeated instruction in the same mathematics computation skills year after year).

Similarly, the teacher's role in instruction includes the following:

- Teach explicitly the underlying thinking processes along with skills, for example, by modeling the cognitive process involved when interpreting a story problem in mathematics or trying to understand the author's point of view in a piece of literature.
- Encourage students to use each other as learning resources and structure their interaction accordingly, as in many cooperative or team learning arrangements.
- As students become more accustomed to constructing knowledge and applying strategies on their own, gradually turn over responsibility for their learning to them, within sequences or units of instruction and across the school year (Knapp, Turnbull, & Shields, 1990).

Collaborating with Parents

Many disadvantaged children are caught in a culture clash between their home and community environment and the expectations of the school. To address this problem, Comer developed a process to foster good relationships among children, teachers, and parents (ASCD, 1991).

The Comer process rests on three pillars. The first is the school planning and the management team, which includes representatives from the teaching staff, support staff, custodial staff, and parent organization. The team develops a comprehensive school plan that sets goals for academics, staff development, and community relations. Second, the mental health team addresses the climate of the school and individual student and teacher concerns. Third, the parent program promotes the active presence of parents in the school. For example, the school conducts social activities to bring families and school staff together to allow teachers to see their students differently and to help parents gain trust in the school.

The program began with two New Haven, Connecticut schools in 1968; today 165 schools participate, in cities such as Topeka, Kansas; Sarasota, Florida; and Washington, DC. The Rockefeller Foundation supports the program's expansion through partnerships between universities and school districts, videos for training and orientation, and consortia to prepare teachers to work in inner-city environments. The program has resulted in impressive results: improved attendance, lowered dropout rates, and declining adolescent pregnancy. For additional information, contact Yale Child Study Center, 230 S. Frontage Road, New Haven, Connecticut 06510.

Chapter 1 and Other Compensatory Programs

For the past quarter century, programs designed to provide quality education for economically disadvantaged children have received substantial funding. Chapter 1, the major federally funded program for disadvantaged learners, accounts for 20% of the U.S. Department of Education's total budget, or almost four billion dollars per year. Approximately one of every nine school-age children participates in Chapter 1 programs (Anderson & Pellicer, 1990; OERI, 1987a). More than 90% of the school districts receive Chapter 1 funds. The major goal of Chapter 1 programs is to increase the reading and mathematics achievement of low-achieving students within schools and concentrations of students from families of low socioeconomic status (Slavin, 1989).

Compensatory education refers primarily to federal programs targeted toward low-achieving disadvantaged students. Schools receive Chapter 1 funds on the basis of the number of low-income students they serve, but within schools, funds serve students according to educational needs rather than their poverty level. Because of this, and because nonpoor students outnumber poor ones, the majority of students receiving Chapter 1 funds are not themselves from families in poverty (Slavin, 1989).

Five principal models of service delivery used in Chapter 1 programs include pull-out, in-class, add-on, replacement, and schoolwide models. In pull-out (the most overwhelmingly used), students are taken out of regular classroom settings for 30 or 40 minutes of remedial instruction from a certified teacher and in a class of eight or fewer students. In-class models provide for teachers or instructional aides working with eligible children in the classroom. Add-on programs provide service outside the regular classroom (i.e., after-school or summer programs). Replacement models, requiring school districts to provide supplementary funds, place Chapter 1 students in self-contained classes for most or all of their instruction. Schoolwide projects, as the name implies, are used when all students in a high-poverty school benefit from Chapter 1 funds (Slavin, 1989).

Educators can benefit from recognizing Chapter 1 programs using a systematic needs assessment, which sought input from civic clubs, the local Chamber of Commerce, parent groups, and school staff. This needs assessment became the specific objectives around which educators developed the Chapter 1 program (Crawford, 1989).

Other compensatory programs that have addressed the needs of at-risk students include Head Start and Follow Through. Head Start provides instruction for students from age three to school entry. This half-day preschool setting for children from low-income families provides activities designed to enhance socioemotional growth and cognitive growth, and most programs provide health, nutrition, and/or family support services. Follow Through, designed to maintain the successes of students in Head Start, incorporates special services for the early elementary grades. Follow Through became a source of funding for model programs designed to help children of the poor (Slavin, 1989). The Follow Through program, designed to extend educational support from kindergarten to the third grade, did not meet its potential due to budget cuts. In reality, Head Start learners did not benefit from Follow Through dollars (Stein, Leinhardt, & Bickel, 1989).

Case Study 10-1 looks at the consequences of poverty and how a school took action to address the problem.

Case Study 10-1: The Consequences of Poverty

Jason, a 14-year-old, is a seventh grader who has been retained twice. He comes from a home of poverty. His single-parent mother works two part-time jobs, both paying minimum wage and neither providing health insurance. Rent and utilities consume most of the income. Jason "appears" not to be motivated and experiences academic difficulties. Mrs. Jones, Jason's teacher, asked at a unit meeting, "What can we do to help Jason?"

Mr. Smith responded, "Nothing—it is not our problem! We cannot cure all society's ills—his mother is to blame anyway!"

Mrs. Jones spoke calmly and matter of factly: "We cannot blame the victim and Jason suffers from poverty conditions. True, we cannot cure all of society's and Jason's problems, but as professional educators and humanitarians, we have a responsibility to help Jason."

Mr. Smith calmed down and the unit began brainstorming for ways to help Jason. Suggestions included the following:

1. Encourage Jason to accept responsibility for his learning rather than letting poverty become an excuse for failure.
2. Contact Jason's mother to let her know of the school's concern and efforts to help Jason overcome any at-risk conditions resulting from her financial problems.
3. Contact appropriate social service agencies to determine available financial assistance.
4. Seek assistance from all school professionals to pinpoint Jason's learning difficulties and to formulate a specific plan for addressing his weaknesses.
5. Understand that, although Jason does not "appear" to be motivated, he actually may be—definitions and outward appearances of motivation differ.
6. Praise Jason's school successes and build on his strengths.

Ventures in Education

Ventures in Education (VIE), a New York City firm supported by the Macy Foundation, works with 39 schools in four states to raise the achievement and college-bound rate of disadvantaged youth. Two-thirds of the schools' 4100 students are culturally diverse. Of the 1000 graduates at the program schools in the class of 1990, 95% went on to four-year colleges. The program achieves these results with a rigorous academic core curriculum, mandatory homework and reading assignments, and an extended school day. The success of the schools and the VIE project can be attributed to faculties and staffs agreeing to establish academic standards and confidence levels of students. VIE hopes to expand its program to reach 100 more schools, which will serve nearly 40,000 students (ASCD, 1991).

Poverty, Lower Socioeconomic Conditions, and Disadvantaged Learners: Characteristics of Effective Programs

1. Programs place priority on collaboration between students, parents administrators, teachers, counselors, and special education teachers.
2. Programs place emphasis on extracurricular activities (i.e., field trips) as well as on academic instruction.

3. Programs address areas vital to academic achievement such as self-concept, social and personal growth, and health and physical well-being.
4. Programs provide a systematic needs assessment to determine strengths and weaknesses of the at-risk learner.
5. Programs provide more than one type of assessment, i.e., a portfolio approach for assessing student progress—prior, during, and after instruction.
6. Programs should be intellectually stimulating rather than using the same materials and instructional approaches that did not previously work.
7. Programs should demonstrate an understanding of disadvantaged learners and the problems associated with poverty.

Teenage Pregnancy and Sexually Transmitted Diseases

The many problems associated with teenage pregnancy call for educators' conscientious efforts. Whether through preventive efforts or helping teenagers after childbirth, educators are in a prime position to help young people. This section looks at established at-risk programs and also offers suggestions for educators designing their own programs.

Alachua County Continuing Education for Pregnant Teens (ACCEPT)

Wells (1990) explained that the ACCEPT program in Gainesville, Florida, seeks to help students at the middle and high school levels. ACCEPT provides an alternative education program and other services for pregnant teenagers who want to complete middle or high school and want to learn appropriate skills to enable them to raise a child responsibly. The program's educational objectives include the following:

1. Provide an education program that corresponds to Alachua County standard curriculum so that the student may return to her home school on program completion.
2. Offer individual instruction to conform to diverse abilities and grade levels.
3. Provide specialized curriculum in parenting, health, reproduction, sexuality, child health, nutrition, and LaMaze.

The life skills management component includes self-esteem building, career goal setting, life planning, coping skills, and substance abuse prevention. Additional services include day care for infants while parents attend school and work, weekly clinic services provided by a Women's Clinic, breakfast and lunch programs, and bus transportation throughout Alachua County. The on-site infant care allows for an experiential component in child development and parenting skills. For additional information, readers may contact The Loften Center, ACCEPT, 3000 East University Avenue, Gainesville, Florida 32601.

Teenage Parent Center Program

Designed for middle and high schools, the Teenage Parent Center Program in Kansas City, Missouri, has several purposes: to prevent pregnant girls from dropping out of school, to improve the students' educational and job skills, and to help maintain and/or improve the health and welfare of the students during pregnancy, childbirth, and the postpartum time of their lives (Wells, 1990).

Staffed by certified personnel, the center includes a nurse, a counselor, and a part-time social worker. The nurse counsels the student about sex, motherhood, the birth process, family relationships, and child care. She acts as a liaison between the school and the various health agencies involved in the student's health care. The responsibilities of the counselor include providing career, vocational, and college information. The social worker helps link the student with supportive community services.

The academic program consists of all levels of English and mathematics, biology, human sciences, civics, world history, current affairs, art and home economics, and family living. Instruction is mostly on an individualized basis. Community resource persons and agencies enrich the program. The contact person is Dr. Jasper Harris, Director, Division of Special Education and Pupil Services, Kansas City School District, 1211 McGee Street, Kansas City, Missouri 64106.

Teens Learning to Care (TLC)

This high school level program in Oxford, Mississippi, is an alternative high school completion program serving the needs of young parents and expectant parents and their children. High school students who have children or who are pregnant may enroll in TLC. Classes meet Monday through Friday, which allows students to earn up to two and one-half credits per semester. Instruction on pregnancy, child development, parenting, consumer skills, decision making, and career planning supplement traditional academic classes. Adult education counselors and social workers provide group and individual counseling. Nursery and toddler centers provide child care. Families and young fathers may participate in the counseling and support group to assist them in working through problems. TLC provides a supportive atmosphere for the young parent and child. For additional information, contact Program Coordinator, Oxford Community Education, 105 Pontiac Street, Oxford, Mississippi 48051.

Activity 10-3

Take a stand concerning whether schools should address at-risk conditions such as teenage pregnancy, AIDS, and STDs. Are these school, social, or personal problems? If you feel schools should not be responsible, write a position paper outlining your argument. If you feel schools should be responsible, compile a list of several additional at-risk programs and include a description of each (goals, methods, contact person).

Education for Parenting

Scattergood (1990) explains the Education for Parenting program, which strives to make youngsters better parents, *but encourages them to wait to be parents until they grow up.* This nonprofit program seeks to head off teen pregnancy by exposing elementary school children to the demands of child care. Topics examined include pregnancy, child development, and the skills required to be effective parents; however, at the same time, efforts include trying to dispel youthful fantasies and to convince teenagers to defer parenthood to adulthood.

Education for Parenting includes efforts such as monthly classroom visits by parents and infants; curriculum guides and teacher's handbooks dealing with child care costs, infant growth, and time demands; student exercises requiring interviewing parents; and basic skills reinforcement. The program, divided into four K–3 instructional units, provides a more advanced curriculum for students in grades four to eight: Unit 1, Learning About Newborns and Their Parents; Unit 2, Learning About Infants and Their Parents; Unit 3, Learning About Toddlers and Their Parents; and Unit 4, Learning About Caring for Infants. Students who see that living babies needing to be fed, burped, and changed and need constant care can come to realize that having a baby requires emotional maturity and financial security (Scattergood, 1990).

Teenage Pregnancy: Characteristics of Effective Programs

1. Programs promote self-esteem, both as responsible adults and as successful students capable of educational accomplishments during high school and beyond.
2. Programs incorporate technology into instructional programs and rely on the best prepared and most effective computer software.
3. Programs place emphasis on helping rather than blaming the victim for engaging in at-risk behaviors.
4. Programs dispel youthful fantasies of childbearing and childrearing and emphasize realistic perceptions.

5. Programs provide alternative educational programs for pregnant teen-agers who want to continue their education and to learn how to raise children responsibly.
6. Programs utilize community and social agencies to provide a comprehensive package of coordinated services.
7. Programs provide educational experiences in career goal setting, life planning, coping skills, and substance abuse.

Alcohol, Tobacco, and Other Drugs

Use and abuse of alcohol, tobacco, and drugs have been a cause for alarm for many years. Many problems are currently in the spotlight: drinking and driving, lost potential and lost lives due to drugs, and the many health hazards associated with tobacco. Many at-risk programs address the condition and provide insight for educators developing programs.

School Services for Drug-Addicted Children

Kelker (1991) explained in some detail how the All Handicapped Children Act (AHA) did not recognize alcoholism or drug addiction as handicapping conditions. The act, does, however, apply to students with learning disabilities and serious emotional illnesses. If educators suspect a student has a learning disability or an emotional illness in addition to problems associated with addiction, the student should be evaluated, because a chemically dependent student can receive a special education examination. The abuse of drugs does not preclude students from being considered for special education services.

Substance-abusing students without handicapping conditions recognized by AHA may still qualify for a school evaluation under Section 504 of the Rehabilitation Act of 1973. Under this section, drug addiction and alcoholism are recognized as physical impairments, and a chemically dependent student can be considered handicapped under Section 504 because addiction interferes with life activities or academic performance. Services under Section 504 might include academic placement of the student at an appropriate level; counseling to help the student benefit from education; changes in placement to avoid association with negative friends; modification of the school day to allow the student to attend after-school care programs; and design of a longer high school program so students can make up credits lost during drug addiction and treatment (Kelker, 1991).

Illahee Junior High

Started as a response to problems with alcohol, Illahee Junior High School in Federal Way, Washington, has a strong drug education program. Staff training received major consideration since everyone at Illahee needed to be an integral part of the program. Staff members need to feel comfortable dealing with sensitive issues such as identifying students using alcohol and other drugs and also need to know the appropriate action to take. Illahee has received federal, state, and local funds to bring consultants to the school and to send staff to seminars. The Student-Assistance Team provides an organized method of providing help to students. A student experiencing academic difficulties or misbehaving may be referred to the team. It then gathers information on the student by looking at attendance, grades, and discipline records. Teachers may be asked for additional information or perhaps a drug and alcohol assessment will be done by a private counseling group that cooperates with the school. Some Illahee students find themselves learning tae kwon do martial arts at night, thanks to the Student-Assistance Team. Tae kwon do emphasizes self-discipline and self-control.

Creating positive role models is also at the heart of Friends In Cooperation—Friends Inc. Sponsored by counselor Vince Blauser, this student group started with 42 members. Currently it boasts more than 220, one-third of Illahee's enrollment. Open to all students, Friends Inc. members pledge not to smoke, drink, or use other drugs. At twice-monthly evening meetings attended by an average of 150 kids, members participate in discussions that focus on communication and conflict resolution skills, and peer and parent relations. But it's not all serious stuff. There are games and food, too, because Illahee wants students to enjoy being drug free (Hereford, 1993).

Friday Night Live (Drinking and Driving)
This program provides a powerful message to teenagers at risk of driving and drinking. This program in California includes a 15-minute multimedia program characterized by fast-paced action and music levels teenagers like. The program begins with teenagers partying with alcohol; then students see an arrest and see and hear about the effects of alcohol and about the dangers of drinking and driving. Fellow students and mothers and fathers of victims appear on the stage to give powerful testimonials that provide teenagers with convincing stories of the dangers of driving and drinking. Next, a student leader, the president of Students Against Drunk Driving, and the leader of the area's Friday Night Live chapter address the students and ask them to sign a pledge to avoid drinking and driving. Parents and families become involved when they sign pledge cards. Students also agree to participate in campaigns during the year to persuade peers to party safely (Watson, 1988).

Skills for Growing
Resnik (1988) believes: quick fixes to the drug problem will not work; program success requires parent and family involvement; effective prevention takes time; successful drug education programs assume positive and

constructive approaches; and, for school-based programs, prevention programming requires effective teaching efforts. Skills for Growing, a joint effort of Lion's Club International and Quest International, targets grades K through 5.

The Quest model advocates an environment that provides opportunities for young people to engage in positive social behavior; communicates clear expectations that young people will behave in responsible ways; provides feeling of warmth, safety, and caring; and provides appropriate reinforcement and support. Positive social behaviors, the principal outcomes of Quest's program, can be divided into four categories: self-discipline, responsibility, good judgment, and the ability to get along with others.

Skills for Adolescence
Another joint effort of Lion's Club International and Quest International focuses on middle and junior high schools and addresses a broad array of at-risk conditions, including drug education, behavior, cognition, and personal relations. Seven broad goals of the Skills for Adolescence program follow:

1. Understand the changes of adolescence.
2. Build self-confidence and communication skills.
3. Understand and manage feelings.
4. Improve friendships and resist negative peer pressure.
5. Strengthen family relationships.
6. Make wise and healthy decisions, especially with regard to alcohol and drug use.
7. Set goals for successful and healthy living (O'Connor, 1991).

The program considers the role of parents to be crucial and recognizes the importance of parental involvement. It incorporates a number of approaches designed to establish an effective, ongoing relationship with parents. Efforts to involve parents and families include meetings focusing on improving the self-confidence of the child, improving communication skills, solving family conflicts with love and limits, and talking to one's child about drugs. Activities in parent meetings help build children's self-confidence, help parents review and practice effective listening, show parents the importance of communication skills, give parents facts about drugs and drug use, help parents understand the Skills for Adolescence program, and provide parents with opportunities to meet with other parents (Resnik, 1988).

New Holstein Student Assistance Program
The New Holstein (Wisconsin) School District established a need for intervention regarding the problems of alcohol and other drug abuse by students

or by a family member. Designed for elementary, middle, and high school students, program goals include decreasing alcohol-related problems, increasing student knowledge of alcohol and drugs, and increasing community awareness of the program. The program seeks to identify and refer students and provides resources necessary to assist at-risk conditions.

The New Holstein Student Assistance Program benefits students by developing a core group of faculty, staff, parents, and community members who have received intensive alcohol and other drug education, thereby enabling them to provide the leadership to coordinate the program. Student groups (use/abuse, support, and after-care) aid students in dealing with the situation. Results have included a decrease in alcohol- and drug-related problems in school, a decrease in absenteeism, an improvement in grades, and a decrease in school suspension (Wells, 1990). For additional information, contact Joseph Wieser, School Districts of New Holstein, 2226 Park Avenue, New Holstein, Wisconsin 53061.

Case Study 10-2 examines how a high school addressed its students' alcohol abuse.

Case Study 10-2: Addressing Alcohol Abuse Among Teenagers

Public High School 161 knew the alcohol problem needed to be addressed as evidenced by beer cans on the school grounds, one teenager arrested for driving under the influence, several alcohol-related wrecks, alcohol found in one locker, and several indicators that drinking had occurred during the school day. When one faculty member stated, "It might be too late; those students began drinking in the middle school," the faculty decided to ask the middle school educators whether they wanted to engage in a joint effort. Perceiving that they had more and more students at risk, the middle school educators agreed to join the effort.

First, the goals had to be established. The schools started with identifying at-risk students, expanding knowledge of alcohol and its effects, explaining the dangers of alcohol use and abuse, explaining the dangers of drinking and driving, and convincing students of the dangers of peer pressure.

Students were taught effective communication and listening skills, the medical and legal aspects of alcohol, alternatives to or strategies to avoid alcohol, and the importance of designating a driver when drinking was occurring. While victims would be asked to share their experiences, the effort would be directed more toward knowledge, understanding, and common-sense approaches rather than the use of scare tactics.

It was decided that the effort would include all school personnel—administrators, teachers, counselors, nurses, and others—and that specific roles would be delineated for each participant. Resource people from the community would include medical personnel, law enforcement officers, addiction counselors, and parents of victims. The program would also work to get parent support and involvement in all phrases of the program.

The middle school and high school felt their program was off to a good start—now, they would have to assess the program and its results on a regular basis and make changes as needed.

Gateway Alive

Gateway Alive (Wells, 1990) is a group of high school students against drug and alcohol abuse. They believe that education about substance abuse and prevention is the best means to help students say "no" to drugs and alcohol. The Gateway program chooses students based on personal interest, teacher recommendations, and a personal interview. Members visit middle schools to discuss drug abuse, sponsor "Awareness Day," and distribute materials imprinted with "Gateway Alive Says No to Drugs and Alcohol." Through films, speakers, group discussions, and various workshops activities, students learn about themselves and how to relate better to others. Students learn and practice refusal skills. The program stresses drug and alcohol prevention, decision-making skills, assertiveness training, dealing with stress and grief, and self-image improvement. Additional information may be obtained by contacting Marcia Krett, Counselor, Gateway High School, 1300 South Sable Boulevard, Aurora, Colorado 80012.

Tobacco Cessation Programs

The dangers of using tobacco are evident: Cigarette smoking was predicted to cause more than 157,000 deaths in 1991; lung cancer now kills more smokers than heart disease; and smoking plays a major role in cancers of the mouth, esophagus, pancreas, larynx, bladder, and kidney. In fact, the risk of dying from lung cancer has doubled in the past three decades for male smokers and increased four times for female smokers (Cancer from smoking . . . , 1991).

The Springfield, Massachusetts, organization STAT (Stop Teenage Addiction to Tobacco) focuses attention on preventing teenagers from starting to smoke. The organizers claim tobacco companies induce about 3000 new minors to smoke each day with advertising targeted at young people. The organizers call for boycotts, guerilla tactics, and even civil disobedience to keep cigarettes from teenagers (Anti-smokers plan . . . , 1991).

While this program has placed major emphasis on cigarette smoking, schools should also focus attention on smokeless tobacco, which can lead to teeth decay, gum disease, and a number of oral cancers. Totten (1988) maintained that tobacco cessation programs should be school based. School efforts include the Fairfax (Virginia) School Board banning tobacco use on school grounds, a California law banning student use of tobacco products on all school campuses, and the National School Boards Association's project called "Tobacco-Free Young America by the Year 2000." School-based cessation efforts also include setting more stringent penalties for tobacco use, learning about effective school practices, changing attitudes by means other than scare tactics, and expanding knowledge of health and the importance of healthful choices.

Seven tips follow for setting up a drug-education program:

1. Recognize that some students may be using drugs and then do an assessment or anonymous survey to gauge the extent of the problem.
2. Formulate a written policy that prohibits use of tobacco, alcohol, or other drugs on campus, and state the consequences for breaking those rules.
3. Train staff in types of drugs, signs of drug use, and ways to help drug users.
4. Educate students about different types of drugs and their physical and psychological effects; also teach conflict-resolution skills and ways of coping with peer pressure.
5. Involve parents in key roles in the program and educate them about types of drugs and how to help their children resist pressures.
6. Reach out to local businesses, churches, hospitals, and civic groups to help educate the community about drug use and to enlist broad support for the program.
7. Find ways for drug-free students to act as positive role models for peers (Hereford, 1993, p. 18).

Alcohol, Tobacco, and Other Drugs: Characteristics of Effective Programs

1. Programs avoid scare tactics and quick fixes to convince children and adolescents of the dangers of substance abuse.
2. Programs emphasize the school's role and the provision of school services.
3. Programs utilize media (i.e., loud music) to which at-risk learners can relate.
4. Programs involve parents in the identification of problems and the planning and implementing of programs.

5. Programs emphasize and provide positive and constructive experiences designed to build self-esteem.
6. Programs teach clear communication between program participants and also between children and their parents.
7. Programs provide educational opportunities concerning alcohol, tobacco, and other drugs.

Juvenile Delinquency and Criminal Behaviors

Juvenile delinquency and criminal behaviors present a number of problems for schools: vandalism, gangs, students who are afraid to attend school—just to name a few. Concluding that ignoring the problem does not work, some schools have taken an active stance to combat criminal behaviors. This section examines programs and efforts that have been successful.

Police Liaison Program

This program, designed for at-risk students in elementary, middle, and high schools, consists of police officers serving as a liaison between the schools and the police department. These police officers also teach, counsel, train, and advise concerning the legal penalties for certain at-risk and illegal activities. Liaisons also investigate students and adults who are with other students and adults committing violations against students (Wells, 1990). For more information, contact Green Bay School District, 200 South Broadway, P.O. Box 1387, Green Bay, Wisconsin 54305.

Police Athletic League

A program similar to the Green Bay program, yet developed only for the middle school level, involves the Oakland (California) Police Department and the Oakland Unified Schools. These two organizations have established a cooperative program at Madison Middle School aimed at designing activities for students after school, on weekends, and in summer as a means of engaging students. Police personnel volunteer their time to design and run activities such as weightlifting, basketball, and special interest groups after school and on weekends. The officers run a camp for students in the summer (Wells, 1990). The contact person is Sam Holton, Oakland Police Department, P.O. Box 24376, Oakland, California 94623.

The Safe Campus Program

Most students attending Granada Hills High School in San Fernando, California, do not participate in gangs. In essence, all students are at risk when gang activity influences their lives by victimizing them and generally making them fear for their safety. At Granada Hills, school officials identified more than 30 different gangs on campus—gangs that were often struggling for power. The Granada Hills Safe Campus Program evolved over several years and adopted the goal of creating a safe environment so as to instill a sense that all students have a right to attend school despite rivalries and to encourage students to consider the school as neutral territory.

Program efforts included understanding the nature of gangs and the evidence of gang activity, setting the standards and a dress code, starting a counseling program, and offering tutoring to improve grades and to increase literacy skills. Results have included a safe campus for all, some students have discovered a way out of the gangs, faculty and student awareness has increased, and graffiti has been photographed (for gang identification) and removed and perpetrators have been identified and prosecuted (Rattay & Lewis, 1990). Readers wanting additional information should contact Kathleen Rattay, Granada Hills High School, San Fernando, California.

C.I.T.Y.

C.I.T.Y., or Comprehensive Intervention for Troubled Youth, recognizes the negatives of expulsion resulting from behavior problems. The C.I.T.Y. program focuses efforts in several directions:

1. Tutoring
2. Counseling, depending on the infraction
3. Professional counseling, if deemed appropriate
4. Community support
5. Volunteer services in settings where confidence and esteem can be developed
6. Participation in activities that had the potential for long-term involvement.

The C.I.T.Y. program requires parents to sign a document indicating several agreed-on terms: the program is voluntary, course credit would not be automatically awarded, educators have permission to make referrals to appropriate agencies, educators have the right to share student ability information with referral agencies, and transportation is not provided. While the C.I.T.Y. program has had numerous successes, looking at the program's problems may help other educators when planning programs. Common problems included the lack of required mandated participation, limited personnel at both the social and educational levels, limited agency and human service organizations in various areas of the city, and the lack of a tailored agenda designed to meet the unique academic, personal, and social needs of at-risk students (Dumaree, 1991).

Safe Schools in Portland

The Portland, Oregon, public schools adopted a "get-tough" approach to protect student and staff members from violence resulting from drugs and gangs. To show its commitment to safe schools, the district called a news conference to announce its "get-tough" response to gang activity and gang violence. The district immediately pledged to protect students and staff members by employing additional campus monitors; pursuing and expanding existing policies on searching students, lockers, and school grounds for weapons and drugs; expelling any students possessing weapons; removing all graffiti from school buildings; prohibiting any clothing or adornments worn to identify gang membership; and empowering campus monitors to ask anyone without identification to leave school property. The district's broad-based approach also included gang-awareness training sessions for staff members, gang-awareness lessons for students, neighborhood workshops, and cooperation with local police and juvenile court authorities. The rationale behind this tough policy included gaining control of gang activity in the city's schools and letting the community know gangs did not control the schools (Prophet, 1990). For additional information, contact Matthew Prophet, Superintendent, Portland Public Schools, Portland, Oregon.

ADAPT

ADAPT, a treatment program for juvenile delinquents, combines behavioral skill training, supportive network development, and involvement in prosocial activities for youths reentering the community from state correctional facilities. Project ADAPT creates conditions for bonding once incarcerated youths return to the community by enhancing their opportunities, skills, and rewards for prosocial behavior. To help in reaching this goal, ADAPT addresses seven areas: consequential thinking, self-control, avoiding trouble, social networking, coping with authority, problem solving, and relapse coping. ADAPT has two phases: the Reentry Preparation Phase (three months while still in the institution) and the Aftercare Phase (six months post institution). The Reentry Preparation Phase includes the areas just mentioned, while the Aftercare Phase includes homework placement, school/work, and prosocial activities and relationships (Haggerty, Wells, Jensen, Catalano, & Hawkins, 1989). The contact person for ADAPT is J. David Hawkins, Director, Social Development Research Group, University of Washington, School of Social Work, 4101 15th Avenue, NE, JH-30, Seattle, Washington 98195.

Mark Twain Middle School

Mark Twain Middle School in San Antonio, Texas, with the help of nearby Trinity University, instituted an innovative program to address the needs of its most seriously at-risk students. Twain's worst discipline problems were removed from their regular classes to become a part of a school-within-a-school arrangement where they received intensive, individualized instruction from a cluster of four core program teachers. The program included a part-time counselor and a special after-school component to offer additional support and motivation for the students considered most at risk. Twenty-five students considered by their teachers to be most affectively and cognitively at risk met in grade-specific groups twice a week to receive tutoring and group counseling and to engage in games and other motivational techniques. Big Bothers, Big Sisters, and undergraduate volunteers from Trinity University served as additional sounding boards for student problems. Graduate students at Trinity charted patterns in grades, attendance, and tardiness for the students participating in the program (Cohen, 1989).

Combating Gang Activities: Other Directions

McEroy (1990) maintained that some measures to combat gang activities have failed and some have even made matters worse. Practices that have not worked include "get-tough" law enforcement measures, increased police presence on school grounds, strong suspension programs, attempts to suppress gang involvement, and refusals to confront gangs. McEroy's alternatives includes creating opportunities for gang members to transfer allegiance and loyalties to more acceptable groups, involvement in other extracurricular activities that provide success beyond the classroom, peer-assisted programs where select students receive guidance and training in helping peers, and gaining access to gangs by having storefront schools on their own turf (McEroy, 1990).

Juvenile Delinquency and Criminal Behaviors: Characteristics of Effective Programs

1. Programs involve law enforcement officers working cooperatively with school officials, community leaders, and social service agencies.
2. Programs provide for law enforcement officers teaching, counseling, and advising students about illegal activities and also providing opportunities to participate in athletic events and other school functions.
3. Programs incorporate the use of technology and developmentally appropriate computer software to make at-risk students aware of appropriate and inappropriate behaviors.
4. Programs emphasize social skills as well as academic skills.
5. Programs employ educators who want to work with children and adolescents and who have appropriate professional backgrounds.
6. Programs involve parents and families in planning and implementing appropriate awareness and preventive experiences.

Activity 10-4

Plan an at-risk program designed to address gang activity. Be sure your plan includes identification procedures, a statement concerning the importance of physically and psychologically safe learning environments, objectivity, specific at-risk conditions to be addressed, possible materials and resources, and program assessment methods.

Suicides

The pain and sorrow associated with suicides give educators sufficient reason to identify and help potentially suicidal students. After identifying a potentially suicidal student, professionals must take rapid action to help the student. Also, after a suicide has occurred, schools have to take appropriate action to help students deal with their feelings and the loss.

A Team Approach to Intervention

Adopting a team approach to suicide intervention is the most promising innovation in suicide prevention. Team programs originated from drug intervention teams and special education placement teams. Rather than working with only a few students, concerned educators use a school-based team approach to include all children and adolescents who need help. The use of a team approach allows combined expertise and a vigorous approach to identify potential suicidal students, to intervene, and to remediate at-risk conditions.

Each school district can have a suicide intervention team consisting of the principal, classroom teachers, and special service teachers such as the school psychologist, counselor, nurse, and social worker. The group meets on a regular basis to plan strategies and to make intervention decisions. The classroom teacher who makes the referral becomes an essential member of the team with regard to the potential suicide.

The intervention team serves several vital functions: takes advantage of local resources, determines which steps should be taken, recommends various types of group or individual counseling, and recommends curriculum-based strategies that focus on awareness, communication, decision making, and personal alternatives. The team also participates in implementing the process, monitoring results, revising strategies, and providing long-term follow-up (Seibel & Murray, 1988). For more information about the team approach, contact Maxine Seibel, Director of Guidance, Tuscarawas Valley Local Schools, Box 92, Zoarville, Ohio 44656.

Impact Program, S.O.S., and Y.E.A.H.
These programs, designed for middle school and high school students, include prevention and intervention components, suicide crisis team, Students Offering Support (S.O.S.) groups, peer counseling, Youth Excited About Helping (Y.E.A.H.) groups, and a core team of trained faculty members. Program objectives include the following:

- Heighten awareness about chemical dependency, suicide intervention, and family problems.
- Respond to impact of suicides on schools.
- Clarify the role of the school personnel.
- Offer practical skills for school professionals in the identification, intervention, and referral of chemically dependent students, students depressed or suicidal, and students not experiencing success in the educational setting.
- Propose effective school programming and successful implementation of the concepts mentioned here.

Upon completion and submission of a student referral form to the Impact Counselor, a member of the Impact Team assumes the role of Core Team leader and contacts all of the student's teachers to determine at-risk behaviors. Depending on the behaviors related and the information gathered, a variety of options is considered. These options include student contact, parent contact, counselor referral, S.O.S. referral, or assessment referral with parental permission to a treatment program. The Core Team leader keeps in contact with the referring person and submits a final report to all involved (Wells, 1990). For more information, contact Donna Stefanic, Counselor, Hinkley High School, 1250 Chambers Road, Aurora, Colorado 80011.

Suicide Prevention Program
The specialized suicide prevention curriculum of Fairfax County, Virginia, (Lee, 1990), stresses sensitizing school staff members so they can identify troubled youth and intervene quickly and effectively. The program makes use of lunchtime discussion groups, led by a social worker, that cover a range of topics from self-esteem to bereavement. Audiovisuals play a major role in this program and supplement and reinforce discussion groups. Videos used include *Fragile Times* and *Tackling Tough Stuff* (Extension Service of the University of Minnesota), *Too Sad to Live* (Massachusetts Committee on Children and Youth, Boston), *Teen Suicide* (ABC Notes Series), *Amy and the Angel* (Learning Corporation of America), *Teens Choose Life* (Sunburst), and *The Crime Teens Never Forget* (Films, Inc. Wilmette, Illinois).

The Fairfax program sensitizes staff members to identify troubled students and to consult area experts such as social workers and psychologists.

After using the audiovisuals, trained professionals include in the "human factor" (Lee, 1990, p. 50) by discussing students' feelings and emotions. The program also provides an opportunity for students to feel that some caring person is concerned about them who is available when they want to talk and who can tell them where to go for help (Lee, 1990).

Suicidal Prevention: Characteristics of Effective Programs

1. Programs use a team approach of administrators, teachers, school psychologists, school counselors, special education personnel, school nurses, and social service personnel to provide a coordinated approach and a wide array of services.
2. Programs utilize local resources and community agencies when students need referral services.
3. Programs provide for effective counseling (individual, small and large groups) by professionals trained to work with at-risk students.
4. Programs provide for a heightened awareness about chemical dependency and other life-threatening behaviors.
5. Programs provide for appropriate referral forms and systems designed to obtain professional help as efficiently and as quickly as possible.
6. Programs use carefully selected technological innovations to meet program objectives.
7. Programs sensitize administrators, faculty, and staff members to identify troubled students and to rely on professionals such as social workers and psychologists.

Health

The national emphasis on health and health-related concerns has undoubtedly spread into the schools. More and more communities expect schools to respond to learners' health needs and also to provide services previously the responsibility of families or community organizations. While some controversy has surrounded the role of schools in health-related areas, it appears fairly certain that the schools will continue to accept these responsibilities during the 1990s and beyond.

School-Based Social and Health Services
According to Dryfoos (1991), an increasingly popular belief holds that schools should become a center for a wide range of psychological, health, social, recreational, and treatment services. School-based health service programs can take several directions: comprehensive health clinics, school-based mental health clinics, student assistance counselors, and after-school recreation and services.

Comprehensive health clinics are operated on school premises by health and youth services agencies. Health clinics in elementary schools and school-employed medical personnel have been around for years; however, these clinics function to address drugs, sex, violence, abuse, depression, and stress. Primarily found in urban high schools, these programs provide an array of medical and social services, including general physical examinations, emergency care, lab tests, immunizations, counseling, and referral. Sometimes referred to as "sex clinics," less than a fourth of the visits are for family planning and only 12% provide contraceptives on site.

School-based mental health clinics result from community health agencies trying to supplement the work of school services by bringing school psychologists and social workers into the schools. Unfortunately, inadequate financial resources have plagued such problems. One program consists of a former band room, renovated into a youth center with recreational facilities such as ping-pong and pool, snack bars, quiet games, and reading corners. Several full-time psychologists and social workers provide intensive counseling and treatment services as well as group counseling and employment services.

The third approach, student assistance counselors, consists of professionals and specialized staff members and is based on a successful approach industry used to address the problem of employee alcohol abuse. Outside agencies employ and train social workers to assist students with at-risk problems and situations. Counselors offer individual and group counseling, expedite referrals for drug intervention, work with families, and train staff in the identification of problems.

Fourth, after-school recreation and services, often found in suburban communities, have community programs, adult education, extracurricular sports, and little theater and musical programs. One such center in New York City serves young people ages 12 to 21 and offers tutoring, recreation, creative arts, and sports. The program provides counseling, sex education and family planning, health screening, referral, high school equivalency examinations, and bilingual classes (Dryfoos, 1991).

Comprehensive School Health

A comprehensive school program suggests a broad spectrum of activities and services that meet the health needs of students and perhaps their families. A wide range of cognitive, affective, and skill-development opportunities contribute to overall competence with respect to health. Curricula include physical, mental, social, and emotional health and address such matters as disease prevention, diet, exercise, stress reduction, alcohol and drug abuse, growth and development, sexuality, human relationships, and smoking. These comprehensive health approaches include a close working relationship between school and community and include coalitions of interested parents and community and business leaders who share a commitment to improve school and its health programs. Concrete steps for school health programs include securing adoption of a comprehensive K–12 curricular approach to school health education, providing staff development for educators at all levels, and recognizing the school as an accepted provider of basic primary health care services (DeFriese, Crossland, MacPhail-Wilcox, & Sowers, 1991).

Growing Healthy

Developed during a 13-year period of active school and community involvement, Growing Healthy integrates substance prevention studies with standard student health classes. The curriculum was formulated by the American Lung Association in 1974, financed by the Centers for Disease Control in 1975, and shaped by a series of formative evaluations; it has been adopted in 696 school districts in 41 states. The results of Growing Healthy include a reduced percentage of students who use alcohol on a regular basis, an expression of stronger beliefs from students that they would not drink alcohol as adults, a reduced percentage of students trying drugs, an expression of stronger beliefs from students that they would not use drugs as adults, and a reduced percentage of students smoked tobacco products on a regular basis.

Anchored to a standard scope-and-sequence chart for a K–7 health education curriculum, Growing Healthy is implemented through a teacher training program provided by the National Center for Health Education. The program provides classroom-tested curricular materials for each grade level, with each level building on the preceding year's curriculum. An added benefit of this sequential process is that an integrated set of health care goals pervades the thinking of school staff (Moore, 1988). To obtain more information on Growing Healthy, contact the community office of the American Lung Association or the National Center for Health Education, 30 E. 29th St., New York, New York 10016.

Activity 10-5

Survey a number of schools to determine their responses to healthful living. In other words, do schools "practice what they preach"? Do schools convey the dangers of tobacco, yet provide teachers with a place to smoke? Is healthful nutrition emphasized, yet students provided vending machines with cookies, candies, and soft drinks? Do physical education programs provide proper opportunities for exercise? Also, determine what programs are available to address the needs of at-risk learners.

Health Programs: Characteristics of Effective Programs

1. Programs provide provisions for early intervention and identification of problems.
2. Programs emphasize the importance of basic skills and of increasing academic achievement.
3. Programs emphasize a healthy and positive school environment.
4. Programs place emphasis on meeting with and involving parents in efforts to help learners.
5. Programs recognize the importance of peers and involve peers in the actual program whenever possible.
6. Programs provide for life-planning curricula, experimental education, and volunteer or paid jobs in community agencies in an attempt to make at-risk students aware of opportunities.
7. Programs provide social and life skills to prepare at-risk youth for living and working outside the school setting.

Adapted from Dryfoos, J. G. (1991). School-based social and health services for at-risk students. *Urban Education, 26*(1), 118–137.

Case Study 10-3 shows how a middle school took deliberate action to change students' dietary habits.

Case Study 10-3: A Middle School Takes a Stand on Healthful Dietary Choices

Andrews Middle School, located in an upper-class suburban setting, draws its students from three similar elementary schools. The administration and faculty were astonished at the amount of food thrown away each day and also the number of snacks and soft drinks purchased from the school's vending machines.

The menus met all district guidelines and were well balanced, and most students purchased lunches, yet they threw most or all away. Then, after lunch, they either snacked from the vending machines or from their lockers. While the educators respected the students' access to choice, the administrators and faculty decided to meet with the district nutritionist and lunch supervisor to discuss healthful choices. During the meeting, other issues were raised: Shouldn't students be allowed to make their own choices? Wouldn't students eat better in the cafeteria if the vending machines were removed? But didn't the vending machine provide a sizable source of revenue?

After much discussion, the committee made several somewhat controversial decisions. First, the vending machines would be removed from the school grounds. Second, developmentally appropriate lessons on nutrition and healthful choices would be integrated into science and mathematics classes. Third, Andrews Middle School would offer students healthful choices. While previous choices had been the prescribed lunch or snacks, students in the future would have a choice of lunches—for example, a typical lunch might be the main buffet of meat and vegetables or a fruit and salad bar. Another choice might be a main buffet of spaghetti, vegetable, bread, and dessert or tuna salad or combo sandwiches or a fruit and salad bar.

One committee member summarized the situation with "I feel pretty good about this—now students will have a choice and also a nutritional lunch!"

Reviewing What You Have Read About Programs and Efforts

1. Recommendations offered by the _____ for helping at-risk children in poverty included expansion of Head Start and other preschool programs, programs for preventing teenage pregnancy, and coordinated community-based programs.

2. The _____ program proposes that disadvantaged children are capable of more than is usually required and should be expected to reach higher levels of achievement.

3. _____ programs such as Chapter 1, Head Start, and Follow Through refer primarily to federal programs targeted toward low-achieving and disadvantaged students.

4. _____ suggests collaborating with parents of at-risk learners to promote good relationships among children, teachers, and parents.

5. _____ strives to raise the achievement and college-bound rate of disadvantaged youth by providing a rigorous academic core curriculum, mandatory homework and reading assignments, and an extended school day.

6. _____ wants youngsters to be better parents (but when they grow up) and seeks to head off teen pregnancy by exposing elementary school age children to the demands of child care.

7. _____ , or Comprehensive Intervention for Troubled Youth, recognizes the negatives of expulsion resulting from behavior problems and focuses on tutoring, both school and professional counseling, community support, and youth volunteering services.

8. Students abusing substances who do not appear to have a handicapping condition recognized by the All Handicapped Children Act may still qualify under _____ .

9. _____ and _____ programs are joint efforts of the Lion's Club and Quest International and focus on areas such as self-esteem and drug prevention.

10. Designed for elementary, middle, and secondary schools, the _____ _____ seeks to decrease alcohol-related problems in school and to increase students' knowledge of alcohol and drugs.

11. _____ provides a powerful message to teenagers at risk of driving and drinking and includes a 15-minute multimedia program of fast-paced action and high music levels.

12. _____ , an independent researcher and respected author, suggested that schools should become a center for a wide range of psychological, social, recreational, and treatment services.

13. The _____ program provides an alternative education program and other services for pregnant teenagers who want to finish their education and learn to raise their children responsibly.

14. _____ began a drug education program that provided staff training for all school professionals and also student-assistance teams to help students.

15. The goals of the _____ are to prevent pregnant girls from dropping out of school, to improve students' educational and job skills, and to help teenagers during pregnancy and childbirth.

Answer Key: 1. National Center for Children in Poverty (NCCP); **2.** New Directions—Alternative Views to Children in Poverty; **3.** Compensatory; **4.** Comer; **5.** Ventures in Education (VIE); **6.** Education for Parenting; **7.** C.I.T.Y.; **8.** Section 504 of the Rehabilitation Act of 1973; **9.** Skills for Growing, Skills for Adolescence; **10.** New Holstein Student Assistance Program; **11.** Friday Night Live; **12.** Dryfoos; **13.** ACCEPT; **14.** Illahee Junior High; **15.** Teenage Parent Center Program.

Summary

Educators planning and implementing at-risk programs designed to address social and personal conditions can look to the programs selected for discussion in this chapter or can develop programs that meet the specific needs of a particular school or community. Whichever approach educators choose, the prerequisite decision must be made to address at-risk conditions that do not result from school practices, yet have a definite impact on academic achievement and overall student development. Such a decision to address at-risk conditions shows a commitment to learners and to the education profession.

For Additional Information on Programs and Efforts

Araki, C. T., & Takeshita, C. (1991). Students helping students: Dispute management in the schools. *NASSP Bulletin, 75*(538), 31–37. Disputes at school often lead to students becoming at risk. These authors discuss a dispute management plan that can lessen problems yet also respect students' rights.

Barish, S. (1991). Responding to adolescent suicide: A multi-faceted plan. *NASSP Bulletin, 75*(538), 98–103. Barish discusses the tragedy of adolescent suicide and suggests a school's response plan to avoid additional pain and suffering.

Brandt, R. S. (1990). *Readings from Educational Leadership—Students at risk.* Alexandria, VA: ASCD. Made up of articles from *Educational Leadership,* this book explores the challenge of working with at-risk youth, what can be done, exemplary programs and practices, dealing with social problems, and working with parents and community agencies.

Cohen, R. M. (1989). Learning from failure: Finding the formula for success in one middle school at-risk program. *American Secondary Education, 18*(1), 13–16. Cohen describes an at-risk program but also provides a candid look at the "mistakes" made in the first year of the program—very helpful reading for educators designing and implementing programs.

Dryfoos, J. (1991). School-based social and health services for at-risk students. *Urban Education, 26*(1), 118–127. Dryfoos, a skilled writer and advocate for children, looks at who at-risk children are, what works for at-risk learners, effective communitywide programs, and examples of school-based social and health services.

Educational Leadership (December 1992/January 1993). This issue of *Educational Leadership* focused on the school's role in addressing at-risk conditions such as inequities, reading problems, behavior problems, AIDS, and crack-affected learners.

Fox, C. L., & Forbing, S. E. (1992). *Creating drug-free schools and communities.* New York: Harper Collins. Fox and Forbing provide a useful and comprehensive examination of drugs in the schools, identification of drugs and their effects, major drugs being used, solutions to the problem, and working with parents and families.

Hispanic Policy Development Project, Suite 310, 1001 Connecticut Avenue, NW, Washington, DC 20036. This organization monitors the progress of Hispanic youth and offers suggestions for closing social, educational, and economic gaps.

Horton, L. (1992). *Developing an effective drug education program.* (fastback 332). Bloomington, IN: Phi Delta Kappa. Horton looks at warning signs of drug and alcohol use and ways to design effective drug education programs.

Indian Youth of America, 609 Badgerow Building, P.O. Box 2786, Souix City, Iowa 51106. This Native American organization sponsors cultural enrichment projects, summer camps, and a resource center in its attempts to improve the lives of Native American children and adolescents.

Lee, M. L. (1990). Educators & programs reaching out to at-risk youth. *Media and Methods, 26*(3), 12–15, 50. Lee describes several programs designed to address such at-risk conditions as dropouts, AIDS, teenage pregnancies, and potential suicides. The use of technology becomes clear as Lee provides detailed listings of audiovisuals and computer software.

Middle School Journal (May 1993). This issue of the *Middle School Journal* featured several articles on at-risk learners and focused on such topics as the school's role in raising expectations and setting goals.

National Black Child Development Institute, 1463 Rhode Island Ave., NW, Washington, DC 20005. This organization is dedicated to improving the quality of life of African-American children and adolescents and focuses on issues such as health, child welfare, education, and child care.

National Center for Children in Poverty (NCCP), Columbia University, 154 Haven Avenue, New York, New York 10032. NCCP works to strengthen government and social policies for children and their families who live in poverty in the United States.

Southeast Asia Center, 1124–1128 W. Ainslie, Chicago, Illinois 60640. The Southeast Asia Center provides for the independence and well-being of Lao, Hmong, Cambodian, Vietnamese, and Chinese people.

Tonks, D. (1992/1993). Can you save your students' lives? Educating to prevent AIDS. *Educational Leadership, 50*(4), 48–51. Tonks urges educators to commit to six important goals in an attempt to preview AIDS.

Wright, W. J. (1991/1992). The endangered black male child. *Educational Leadership, 49*(4), 14–16. Wright explains the plight of the African-American male child and suggests a program designed to help these children.

Epilogue

Prospects for the Twenty-First Century

Outline

Indications Suggesting a Brighter Future

The Future: A Time for Responsive Action

Indications Suggesting a Brighter Future

At least five indicators suggest that at-risk children and adolescents will have their educational needs met during the 1990s and the twenty-first century. Needless to say, however, at-risk learners' educational experiences will depend significantly on the commitment educators bring to the task. Likewise, as with educating all learners, the success of educational efforts varies and depends on whether educators genuinely care about learners and commit to work toward learners being successful. Similarly, at-risk learners sometimes experience remarkable success when financial resources do not allow innovative programs yet when educators strive daily to provide at-risk learners with the most effective educational experiences possible. Therefore, readers are encouraged to remember that the five indicators can improve learners' chances of success only when educators demonstrate genuine concern for at-risk children and adolescents.

Indication 1: Recognition of At-Risk Learners

The first indication comes from the fact that at-risk learners and their need for appropriate educational experiences are increasingly being recognized in educational practice, in scholarly journals and books, and in teacher education curricula. Not many years ago, the term "at risk" was not widely recognized and was virtually unknown in some educational circles. Now, journals donate many pages and occasionally entire theme issues, books address these students' needs, and programs are being planned and implemented. It is true that recognition does not always result in concrete action; however, the number of at-risk programs and efforts in operation today provide a clear indication that educators' recognition is a step toward genuine commitment.

Indication 2: Recognition of the Importance of Prevention

The second indication is the emphasis on prevention. Efforts are focusing toward early detection and remediation of at-risk learners' conditions. Rather than identifying problems and conditions in the middle or secondary school years when remediation efforts may be too late, the current emphasis focuses on preventing at-risk conditions and problems. For example, preventive efforts include early diagnosis of learning problems, substance abuse programs beginning in the elementary grades, developmentally appropriate sex education for elementary-age children, and detailed instruments to spot potential school dropouts. Contemporary emphases include prevention and early intervention. Previously, when at-risk conditions were detected, it was too late for educators to take substantive action—the learner was already addicted to drugs or alcohol, the adolescent girl was already pregnant, STDs had claimed another victim, and the boy who was older than his peers had already dropped out of school.

The emphasis on prevention can have dual effects, both positive for at-risk learners. First, educators may be able to identify at-risk symptoms before conditions grow more serious so that programs can be directed toward addressing individual at-risk needs. Second, efforts directed toward identifying problems and conditions may also have the potential for preventing problems. Likewise, the extra time provided learners, questions about individual needs, working with parents, and coordination of professionals' efforts all can show children and adolescents that educators are concerned with the learner's present and future welfare. Nearly all educators can think of at least one teacher who significantly affected their lives and contributed to the person they are today. Educators working to prevent at-risk conditions may, consciously or unconsciously, offer a statement or convey a nonverbal message that may have a long-lasting and positive effect on learners.

Indication 3: Recognition of At-Risk Learners' Need for Alternative Learning Environments

Studies focusing on how children and adolescents learn and research on effective teaching have contributed to educators' understanding of the methods and procedures that are especially useful with at-risk learners. Positive outcomes have occurred and will continue to result when educators recognize and accept that many at-risk learners need alternative learning environments:

- Identification of testing and assessment procedures that recognize at-risk learners' strengths rather than focusing only on weaknesses and shortcomings.
- Utilization of individualized methods that reflect development levels and specific at-risk conditions.
- Recognition of learning styles and how educators can address individual styles.
- Understanding the concept of multiple intelligences and the need to recognize that intelligence can exist in more than one form.
- Adoption of hands-on methods and the need for practicality rather than just theoretical learnings.
- Adoption of cooperative learning methods where learners learn together rather than compete with each other.

The challenge for educators will be to first recognize that at-risk learners might not respond to traditional teaching approaches. The second step will be to consider each individual at-risk learner to determine what will work with that particular child or adolescent. This indication is of paramount significance because it recognizes that "more of the same" is not appropriate. For example, giving the at-risk learner more drill, more worksheets, and more homework may not be the answer. If previous efforts to educate the at-risk learner have failed, it is unlikely that continuing with the same curricular approaches and instructional methods will produce positive results.

Indication 4: Recognition of the Benefits of Coordinated Efforts

Educators have recognized the benefits of coordinated efforts by classroom educators, special service personnel, social service agencies, and parents. Regardless of degree of concern and extent of training, educators cannot be expected to be experts in all areas. A teacher might have considerable expertise in working with learners experiencing academic difficulties, a counselor may work miracles with sexually active adolescent girls, and a teacher at an alternative school might be able to understand and change delinquent behaviors. Most educators can remember adults who were capable of making significant changes in children's and adolescents' lives.

Educators' special strengths and the increasing recognition that collaboration works have shown educators the need to work together to help at-risk learners. Cooperation and collaboration seem to be essentials for the education profession during the twenty-first century. Scholarly literature, in-service workshops, and at-risk programs ring with words such as "cooperation," "collaboration," "coordinated efforts," and "team approaches." A clear rationale for collaboration exists: Education professionals can benefit from others' expertise, special talents, and strengths when working together. An individual teacher cannot provide the resources and expertise that two or more professionals working together can provide.

Efforts toward coordinating efforts hold considerable potential for helping at-risk learners. First, as previously mentioned, at-risk learners benefit from the expertise of more than one professional, and also educators can call on social service agencies and the various government organizations to complement services provided by educators, counselors, and other school personnel. Second, at-risk learners can see obvious evidence that more than one professional is working to lessen the effects of the at-risk condition. Third, at-risk learners can see their parents and families involved in the coordinated effort—involved and caring parents and families can offer significant contributions at home and can reinforce educators' efforts. Fourth, as previously mentioned, at-risk learners can benefit from professionals in social services agencies who can provide various resources and complementary services.

Although at-risk learners will undoubtedly benefit from coordinated efforts, expectations for success must be kept in perspective. Some conditions—poverty, drug addiction, problems associated with urban living, and AIDS—take a heavy toll and often outweigh even the most coordinated efforts.

Indication 5: Recognition of the Need for Teachers To Be Trained To Work with At-Risk Learners

For decades, teacher education institutions prepared teachers to work with average or slightly above average learners. The assumption evidently held that educators could modify curricular approaches, instructional techniques, and the teaching-learning environment to accommodate the needs of slower and faster learners. Realistically speaking, however, this assumption did not always become reality. Faster and brighter learners sat bored while slower students were frustrated and fell further behind. Students either became at risk due to school practices or, if already at risk, they found school practices did little to address their at-risk needs.

Recent state and national teacher-accreditation agencies have prescribed stricter and more specific standards for students preparing to teach:

- More field experiences, especially with at-risk children and adolescents
- Specific course work (either a course focusing on at-risk learners or content experiences integrated into two or more courses)
- One or more diagnostic/remediation courses in which students learn to diagnose problems and plan remediation procedures
- Survey courses examining the various exceptionalities and at-risk conditions
- Methods and content courses to address the nature and needs of at-risk learners.

What, then do all these changes in teacher education mean for at-risk learners? Basically, teachers are better prepared to work with at-risk learners. Teachers know characteristics or symptoms that indicate a propensity toward being at risk, have had firsthand experiences working with learners who need special attention, and better understand the need to provide developmentally and educationally appropriate experiences for at-risk learners.

In closing, the prospects for at-risk children and adolescents are improving. Recognition, teachers better prepared to help at-risk learners, and coordinated beliefs contribute to the educational achievement and overall development of at-risk learners. Once again, it is important to bring reality into the education of at-risk learners—efforts and programs will reflect commitment from educators.

The Future: A Time for Responsive Action

The increasing likelihood that educators will teach at-risk learners underscores the need for trained professionals who understand at-risk learners and conditions and who provide appropriate teaching-learning experiences. While at-risk conditions continue to jeopardize the future of many children and adolescents, many programs and efforts provide evidence of progress. However, there is also a sense of urgency—lower achievers, AIDS, STDs, teenage pregnancy, learning problems, health conditions, and a host of other conditions suggest that immediate action is needed to improve the lives and education of at-risk learners. Action taken now has the potential for success, whereas failure to respond or a mediocre response will result in more students being at risk and students already at risk receiving little help of a substantive nature.

Increasing numbers of educators are recognizing the need to address at-risk learners' individual needs. Continued advances in understanding at-risk conditions and also in how to provide appropriate teaching-learning experiences for at-risk learners suggest a brighter future for children and adolescents in need. The authors hope during the 1990s and twenty-first century that the needs and problems of at-risk children and adolescents will be met with unqualified success.

The success of the responsive action taken to address the needs of at-risk learners will depend on educators' efforts to do the following:

1. Increase emphasis on at-risk conditions and address the needs of at-risk children and adolescents.
2. Increase use of diagnostic assessment instruments to determine specific at-risk conditions.
3. Increase recognition of parents and extended families and their role in helping at-risk learners.
4. Change views of "success"—success does not necessarily mean a college degree.
5. Recognize the need for alternative learning methods and environments.
6. Increase attention to at-risk learners and their conditions in scholarly journals and the professional literature.
7. Encourage teacher education accrediting organizations to place more emphasis on identifying and working with at-risk learners.

The current efforts and trends discussed in *At-Risk Students* indicate a bright future for at-risk children and adolescents. Educators' knowledge of conditions and programs and their professional commitment to help all learners can empower at-risk children and adolescents to achieve academically and to seek control of health- or life-threatening behaviors. While the major responsibility rests with educators, at-risk students also need to make a commitment to work with educators and parents and to work toward empowering themselves to deal effectively with life and academic activities. Professionals, parents, and at-risk learners working together can have a forceful impact toward helping at-risk learners lead successful, productive, and healthful lives. Such goals and, eventually, accomplishments will prove fruitful for both learners and the nation.

Appendix

Resources

Overview

Educators working with at-risk children and adolescents can benefit from a number of resources available from foundations, corporations, professional associations and organizations, government initiatives, etc. The likelihood of providing appropriate educational experiences for at-risk learners can be greatly enhanced when educators seek help both within school systems and also from these types of groups. This appendix examines many of these groups, provides addresses and telephone numbers when available, and provides titles and descriptions of selected resources. The selection of these organizations and resources does not negate the many other organizations disseminating excellent information. Also, although the authors have tried to provide a comprehensive listing of organizations, this list should be considered a beginning point. Readers are encouraged to continue to collect organization names and addresses and to plan a systematic means of collecting and evaluating resources.

Foundations, Corporations, and Professional Associations

A number of foundations, corporations, and professional associations provide resources that contribute to improving the lives of youth either by complementing schools' efforts or by providing financial resources, expertise, or materials to plan, implement, and sustain educational programs.

These organizations come in many forms: professional associations, philanthropic organizations, special interest groups, and research centers. To prevent delays and misdirected inquiries, it is important for educators of at-risk children and adolescents to pinpoint several aspects prior to contacting organizations.

1. *The age range,* i.e., will the target group of at-risk learners be children, young adolescents, or adolescents?
2. *The at-risk condition,* i.e., are at-risk conditions academic, drug related, health related, financial or some other condition?
3. *The assistance requested,* i.e., do educators need overall financial support, financing for a specific program, materials, and other resources, or experts or consultants in particular fields?

The following request letter provides educators with points to remember when requesting materials. While the importance of providing all of the needed information cannot be overemphasized, perceptive educators readily recognize the need to address their students' at-risk conditions; therefore, some modification in the sample request letter might be in order.

NEW HOPE ALTERNATIVE SCHOOL

① 1718 North Street

Washington, DC 20001

(the date)

② (the organization)
(the address)

③ Dear Dr. Smith:

④ New Hope Alternative School is planning and designing educational experiences for 23 academically at-risk 10- to 14-year-olds. Our students need ⑤ resource materials in reading and mathematics written on or about the third- or fourth-grade level. We will appreciate any information or resources you may offer.

Thank you for your assistance and for any materials you have to offer.

Sincerely,

Suggestions:

(1) Use school stationery to show credibility.

(2) Choose an organization that sources indicate has the specific resources needed.

(3) Use a specific name if possible.

(4) Identify the specific at-risk condition being addressed and number of students in the program.

(5) Identify, if possible, specific materials being requested.

The remainder of this appendix suggests various organizations that provide resources and also describes some of the publications and services they provide.

Carnegie Council on Adolescent Development, Carnegie Foundation, 2400 N. Street NW, 6th Floor, Washington, DC 20037; (202)429-7979.

The Carnegie Council on Adolescent Development produced *Turning Points: Preparing American Youth for the 21st Century,* which examined a number of at-risk conditions and suggested possible educational strategies to reduce the impact of at-risk conditions. For example, *Turning Points* looked at at-risk conditions such as cigarette, alcohol, and drug use; sexual activity at specific ages; poverty and discrimination; and academic under-achievement. The report examines the financial costs of these at-risk conditions and suggests that definitive statistics are not available on the numbers of youth at risk of unhealthy and unproductive lives.

Children's Defense Fund (CDF), 25 E Street NW, Washington, DC 20001; (202)628-8787.

The Children's Defense Fund is a nonprofit research and advocacy organization that exists to provide a strong and effective voice for the children of America, who cannot vote, lobby, or speak for themselves. Particular attention is given to the needs of poor, minority, and disabled children. The goal is to educate the nation about the needs of children and encourage preventive investment in children before they get sick, drop out

---

Activity A-1

Consider the many foundations, corporations, and associations mentioned in this appendix. Then choose a particular at-risk condition and make a list of possible foundations, corporations, and associations to contact. Use the sample letter provided for resources and assistance.

of school, suffer family breakdown, or get into trouble. CDF is supported by corporate and foundation grants and by individual donations. CDF provides several catalogs per year that describe publications such as research reports, advocate guides, clearinghouse summaries, and various posters in both English and Spanish. Examples of specific publications follow:

- *Outside the Dream: Child Poverty in America* (1991). This stirring photo essay documents the day-to-day survival struggles and the incredible strength and courage of America's poor children.
- *The Adolescent and Young Adult Fact Book* (1991). This publication provides a comprehensive reference on America's adolescent and young adult population: family income, education of parents, where youths live, family types, health status, mortality, causes of death, school enrollment, educational attainment, sexual activity, childbearing, drug and alcohol use, crime and victimization.
- *The State of America's Children* (1992). CDF's annual report on the status of America's children and the developments and trends shaping their condition. Fact sheets are included on children's status in each of the states, as well as chapters covering family income, maternal and child health, childcare and early childhood education, and children and adolescents in crisis.
- *The Health of America's Children* (1991). This CDF publication provides an annual assessment of maternal and child health and presents comprehensive data on infant mortality, low birthweight, prenatal care, births to teens, and key health objectives for the year 2000.

These four titles provide only a glimpse at the many, high-quality publications produced and disseminated by the Children's Defense Fund. Other CDF publications include *Welcome the Child: A Child Advocacy Guide for Churches* (1991), *Falling by the Wayside: Children in Rural America* (1992), *When I Dream* (a 13-minute VHS video), and *An Advocate's Guide to Fundraising* (1990). Another fine publication, *Making the Middle Grades Work*, provides a detailed look at the problems and at-risk conditions plaguing 14- to 19-year-olds and provides a blueprint for teaching young adolescents effectively. A particularly interesting feature of *Making the Middle Grades Work* is a listing of individual states and their provision of special state resources for at-risk youth in grades 5 through 8.

Activity A-2
Contact the Children's Defense Fund for a catalog of services, publications, and posters. Make a list of CDF publications that might assist in addressing at-risk programs in your school.

Case Study A-1 looks at how Teacher Team A decided on a strategy for contacting organizations to determine available materials.

Case Study A-1: A Teacher Team Requests Materials

At the recommendation of the principal, Teacher Team A met to plan a strategy for requesting resources for at-risk classes. Several frustrations led to this recommendation: cutbacks in financial allocations, a realization that additional programs or resources were needed, a general dissatisfaction with current programs, and a motivation to restructure programs to address the needs of at-risk learners.

The team decided to plan a strategy before actually contacting organizations. Their agenda included the following steps:

1. Decide on age at-risk learner is to be helped.
2. Pinpoint the at-risk condition to be addressed.
3. Decide on materials or resources to be sought and a rationale for each.
4. Match resources to actual needs of at-risk learners.
5. Write requests on school letterhead to demonstrate the legitimacy of the request.
6. Learn the details of writing grants so organizations could readily ascertain whether at-risk projects fall into their guidelines and are worthy of funding.
7. Decide on a time to have all requests made so materials and resources could be either integrated into the curriculum or could become the basis for future programs.

The decision was reached to first learn about the available materials and resources. One teacher suggested that additional funding not be requested until program objectives and implementation plans were firmly in place. Once the team studied written materials and decided how best to utilize available resources, then financial funding, if necessary, could be sought from an appropriate organization.

"Who should we include in this effort to obtain resources?" a teacher asked.

Suggestions from the group included other teachers and resource professionals in the schools, parents and community people who might have contacts, a consultant from the local university, school administrators, and specialists from the school district office. With these ideas, the team decided to invite a number of these types of people to participate in a brainstorming effort. Such a team approach and the wealth of resources available had the potential for addressing the needs of at-risk learners and, generally speaking, improving learners' chances of academic and social success.

Education Writers Association (EWA), 1001 Connecticut Avenue NW, Washington, DC 20036; (202)492-9680.

With funding support from the Edna McConnell Clark Foundation, EWA publishes *High Strides* five times per year. *High Strides* focuses primarily on urban middle grades and directs attention to at-risk conditions such as self-concept, violence and its alternatives, ability grouping or tracking, making schools safe for learners, and dropout programs. A major plus of *High Strides* is its efforts to include timely and urgent topics and also the inclusion of actual descriptions (program titles, addresses, telephone numbers) for programs that address the needs of urban at-risk youth.

Lilly Endowment, Inc., P.O. Box 88068, Indianapolis, IN 46208; (317)924-5471.

The Lilly Endowment seeks to improve the lives of school-age youth in three areas: religion, education, and community. Primarily focusing on the concerns of Indianapolis and Indiana, the Lilly Endowment occasionally widens its scope to a more national level. Lilly's Education and Youth Committee focuses attention on elementary and secondary schools, youth, and higher education. An annual report details the work of the committee and also lists the names and addresses of the grants rewarded. For example, the 1991 annual report examined the maturing of middle schools and detailed the efforts of specific schools such as John Marshall Junior High School, Indianapolis, Indiana; Eggers Junior High, Hammond, Indiana; and West Side Junior High, Chicago, Illinois. It also reported on "Guiding Stars," a program designed to inspire youth to be successful academically. The program, Future Academic Scholars Track or FAST, is guided by a team of counselors and teachers, coupled with support from parents and community members. The academic component of FAST blends presentations about self-esteem with the rich culture of African-American students. Results boost participants' beliefs in their skills, their aspirations, and themselves.

The Edna McConnell Clark Foundation, 250 Park Avenue, Room 900, New York, NY 10017; (292)986-7050.

The Clark Foundation has at least five purposes and activities. Programs are presently narrowly defined and directed: 1) Reduce unnecessary removal of children from troubled families; 2) improve the educational opportunities of disadvantaged young people by designing intervention programs for the middle school years; 3) seek a more effective criminal justice system by establishing constitutional conditions in adult and juvenile correctional institutions, encouraging community-based sanctions for adults as alternatives to incarceration, and helping to dismantle large state training schools in favor of community-based programs for juveniles; 4) reducing the debilitating and deadly burden of illness in the poorest countries of the developing world through a targeted research program aimed at controlling the tropical diseases schistosomiasis, trachoma, and onchocerciasis; and 5) seeking to assist families in New York City to move out of emergency shelters and hotels into permanent housing. The foundation also maintains a small program of special projects that focuses primarily on projects serving the poor and disadvantaged outside the established program areas.

The foundation's interests include child welfare, crime and law enforcement, law and justice, family services, medical research, youth, schistosomiasis, disadvantaged, homeless, ophthalmology, mathematics, secondary education. Types of support include consulting services, continuing support, research, seed money technical assistance, and special projects. Publications include an annual report, informational brochures (including application guidelines), grants list, and occasional reports.

Professional Organizations

Various professional organizations demonstrate their commitment to help at-risk children and adolescents by publishing journal articles, monographs, and conducting workshops. Several prominent organizations, their addresses, and telephone numbers are listed next.

Association for Childhood Education International (ACEI), 11501 Georgia Avenue, Suite 315, Wheaton, MD 20902-4110; (301)942-2443

ACEI is a professional association that publishes *Childhood Education* five times per year and addresses childhood issues and the education and well-being of children from infancy to early adolescence. The association provides informative position papers on topics such as testing and assessment and other crucial issues affecting the lives of children and young adolescents.

Association for Supervision and Curriculum Development (ASCD), 125 N. West Street, Alexandria, VA 22314; (703)549-9110.

ASCD publishes books and journal readings on a wide variety of topics, including at-risk children and adolescents. Readers will find helpful *Readings from Educational Leadership: Students at Risk* (1990). Another excellent resource produced by ASCD includes *Effective Schools for Children At-Risk,* a

---

Activity A-3
Write a professional organization of your choice for information on at-risk learners. Perhaps join the association most appropriate for the at-risk condition you are addressing.

video featuring experts such as Robert Slavin and James Comer. The video provides a vivid description of effective schools and creates scenes from inner-city elementary schools.

National Middle School Association (NMSA), 4807 Evanswood Drive, Columbus, OH 43229; (614)848-8211.

NMSA publishes materials on at-risk students and conducts "at-risk" workshops nationwide. Focusing mainly on young adolescents or 10- to 14-year-olds, NMSA recognizes and advocates equal access for all learners to all school programs—academic and otherwise. The *Middle School Journal*, published five times per year, contains articles on suicide, AIDS, low achievement, and other at-risk conditions. Specific publications or efforts that interest educators of at-risk learners include monographs looking at learner development, the changing family, organizational practices, and guidance functions.

National Association of Secondary School Principals (NASSP), 1904 Association Drive, Reston, VA 22091; (703)860-0200.

The NASSP publishes the *NASSP Bulletin* nine times per year. Focused primarily toward secondary school learners, the *NASSP Bulletin* examines a wide variety of at-risk conditions and programs such as adolescent suicide, school dropout programs, and other adolescent-related issues.

Phi Delta Kappa (PDK), Eighth and Union, P. O. Box 789, Bloomington, IN 47402; (812)339-1156.

Phi Delta Kappa publishes the *Kappan,* which focuses on general issues as well as occasional at-risk articles. Likewise, PDK publishes a variety of Fastbacks, small but in-depth publications on a wide array of educational issues and topics. Examples of Fastbacks focusing on at-risk learners and conditions include:

Fastback 197—Effective Programs for Marginal High School Students
Fastback 217—Adolescent Alcohol Abuse
Fastback 234—Teenage Suicide: What Can the Schools Do?
Fastback 242—High School Dropouts: Causes, Consequences, and Cure
Fastback 265—AIDS Education: Curriculum and Health Policy
Fastback 315—Student Obesity: What Can Schools Do?
Fastback 321—Street Gangs and the Schools: A Blueprint for Intervention
Fastback 332—Developing Effective Drug Education Programs

While these titles provide educators of at-risk learners with representative titles, PDK has more than 300 titles from which to choose. Approximately 10 new Fastback titles are published each year.

Other valuable information can be obtained from Phi Delta Kappa's *Research Bulletin,* a publication of the Center for Evaluation, Development,

> **Activity A-4**
> Prepare a bibliography of books, journals, and other publications pub-
> lished by at least two professional associations. Also, make a list of
> workshops and special sessions designed to interest educators of at-risk
> learners.

and Research. The *Research Bulletin* (December 1991) provides a detailed
examination of "hate crimes" by focusing on the characteristics of hate
crimes, the recent increase, the causes, and the crucial role of schools. Information concerning the *Research Bulletin* can be obtained by writing Phi Delta
Kappa at the address provided.

National Association of Elementary School Principals (NAEP), 1615 Duke
Street, Alexandria, VA 22314; (703)684-3345.

Founded in 1921, the NAEP consists of a number of professional educators such as principals, assistant principals, and supervisors and works to
improve the quality of leadership among elementary and middle school
principals. This association publishes *Principal* five times per year as well as
a number of other books, handbooks, and pamphlets.

Research and Resource Centers

Some universities have research centers that provide resources such as materials, workshop speakers, and consultants. While not all centers focus on
specific at-risk conditions, most have materials or other resources that provide information to help educators of at-risk learners. This appendix cannot
provide an exhaustive list; however, representative centers are listed.

Center for At-Risk Youth, Education Hall 318, College of Education, Oregon State University, Corvallis, OR 97331-3502.

The Center for At-Risk Youth provides various publications on helping
and addressing the needs of at-risk youth.

National Center on Effective Secondary Schools (NCESS), School of Education, Wisconsin Center for Educational Research, University of Wisconsin–Madison, 1025 W. Johnson Street, Madison, WI 53706.

The NCESS conducts research on how secondary schools can use their
resources to enhance student engagement in order to boost the achievement
of all learners. Its studies deal with higher order thinking in the curriculum,
programs for at-risk students, and many learning opportunities occurring in
secondary schools.

Center for Research on Elementary and Middle Schools (CREMS), The Johns Hopkins University, 3505 North Charles Street, Baltimore, MD 21218.

The mission of the CREMS is to produce useful information about how elementary and middle schools can foster growth in students' learning and development, to develop practical methods for improving effectiveness of elementary and middle schools based on existing and new research findings, and to develop and evaluate specific strategies to help schools implement effective research-based school and classroom practices.

The center conducts research in three areas—elementary schools, middle schools, and school improvement—and provides information on a wide array of topics such as effective schools, cooperative learning, behavior management techniques, and school organizational practices, just to name a few examples.

Governmental Initiatives

The many branches of the U.S. government disseminate a multitude of materials and resources. Since a listing of organizations and their respective resources would be far too lengthy to list here, readers interested in governmental publication should consult the *Washington Information Directory* described at the end of the chapter in the "For Additional Information on Resources" section. Examples of publications focusing directly on at-risk learners include *Adolescent Health* (1991). *Vol. 1: Summary and Policy Options.* Published by the Office of Technology Assessment (OTA), an arm of Congress, *Adolescent Health* provides readers with a comprehensive examination of adolescents and the problems they face. Representative topics examined include adolescents' health conditions, possible causes and preventative measures, the federal government's role, legal access to health care, and all the at-risk conditions mentioned in this text. The document can be obtained from the Superintendent of Documents, U.S. Government Printing Office, Washington, DC 20402-9325.

The OTA also publishes monthly reports, called *OTA Report Brief*, that provide information on at-risk conditions and other impediments to children's school success. For example, the April 1991 issue addresses barriers to health care, looks at preventive measures, and suggests strategies for improving U.S. adolescents' access to appropriate health services. *OTA Briefs* and other OTA publications can be obtained by writing the Congress of the United States, Office of Technology Assessment, Washington, DC 20510-8025; (202)224-8996.

Once resources are obtained, educators need to evaluate materials to determine their "worth", their overall quality, and the degree of scholarly thought that preparers invested in the preparation of the materials. Case

Study A-2 looks at Teacher Team A's efforts to devise a checklist for evaluating materials and resources.

Case Study A-2: Evaluating Resources

Teacher Team A directed their requests for resources in two major directions: 1) organizations providing the team with resources designed to promote understanding of at-risk conditions and 2) organizations such as corporations who could provide actual materials for at-risk learners to use. The team decided that some resources were more useful and, generally speaking, "better" than other resources. Therefore, the team needed an agreed-on evaluation process to determine the feasibility of materials. Work began on checklists designed to evaluate materials designed for both learners and educators. The group agreed on the necessity of a detailed evaluation; however, evaluative criteria could be placed in four overall groups: objectives, accuracy, appropriateness, and feasibility.

First, the team planned evaluational criteria for resources designed for educators' use.

1. Are resources appropriate for the respective at-risk population?
2. Are claims reasonable and do they emphasize the point that at-risk programs take time and conscientious effort?
3. Do resources show an understanding of at-risk conditions and recognition of and respect for both gender and cultural diversity?
4. Can resources be appropriately coordinated with existing resources?
5. Do resources complement the existing curriculum?
6. Do the resources have clear and identifiable objectives?
7. Are resources free without hidden costs such as lengthy procedures and postage?
8. Does the process of obtaining the resources make the practice unfeasible?
9. Can the resources be utilized in more than one learning situation?
10. Can resources be used by more than one learner at a time?

Next, the team planned a checklist for evaluating resources actually used by learners:

1. Do the resources promote a brand or a social cause?
2. Do the resources show alternative views of crucial issues?

3. Do all resources present well-written grammar, spelling, and sentence structure?
4. Do resources provide sufficient and appropriate instructions designed for at-risk learners?
5. Do resources provide realistic experiences with which at-risk learners can relate?
6. Do the glossy paper and colorful pictures become more important than the content or skills to be learned?
7. Do resources moralize about at-risk conditions such as sexual activity or drug abuse?
8. Do resources present situations from at-risk learners' perspectives?

Teacher Team A realized that these checklists represented only a beginning. Resources would be evaluated on arrival and the checklists further changed and refined to provide a fair and comprehensive evaluation of resources received.

Resources: Drug Prevention and Education Programs

Southeast Regional Center for Drug-Free Schools and Communities, Spencerian Office Plaza, University of Louisville, Louisville, KY 40292.
    Established in 1987 under a cooperative agreement with the U.S. Department of Education and located at the University of Louisville, this center works with 12 Southern states in the development of drug prevention programs. The *Southeast Sun* is published quarterly and addresses issues related to preventing alcohol, tobacco, and drug use and helping students who are addicted.

Indiana University, College of Education, Bloomington, IN 47405
    A computer-based support system has been developed at Indiana University to assist teachers and administrators with creating effective drug prevention programs. With the DIADS (Drug Information, Assessment, and Decisions for Schools) system, computer users can access information about drugs; a database with exemplary drug abuse prevention programs that include curriculum, peer, student assistance, parent, and community programs; an assessment plan to weigh the effectiveness of a current drug prevention program; and a step-by-step action plan that enables teachers to implement drug prevention programming in their schools.

University of West Florida, College of Education, Pensacola, FL 32504

This university has piloted a sequence of three modules on drug prevention in its professional education sequence during undergraduates' junior and senior years. The modules were developed at Pensacola Junior College through the federally funded Drug-Free Schools and Community Project. The first module, "Drug Education Awareness: A Psychological Perspective for Beginning Teachers," presents classification of drugs according to effects and ways to identify users. The second module, "A Sociological Perspective," reviews the history of drug use, the legal attempts at control, and factors contributing to drug use. The third module is selected from three areas (elementary, secondary, or special education), according to the focus of a student's program. These modules address the problems of defining and monitoring school policy and introducing drug prevention education across the curriculum.

Iowa State University, College of Education, Ames, IA 50011

This university developed the "Rural Iowa Early Intervention Initiative: Drug Prevention Training for School Personnel." The project provides in-service training to middle school personnel and community members to enable them to create school/community partnerships for the screening, intervention, and referral of students; to organize peer tutoring groups for at-risk middle school students; and to learn the necessary skills to address drug prevention for middle school youths.

Southern Illinois University at Carbondale, College of Education, Carbondale, IL 62901

An unusual drug abuse prevention program at this university targets children aged three through eight years old for special attention. Funded by the Illinois attorney general's office, the program curriculum includes five core "hands-on" activities and a parental involvement component, and also incorporates information from the Office of Substance Abuse Prevention and the U.S. Department of Education. (Member institutions strive . . . , 1992).

National Federation of Parents for Drug-Free Youth, 8730 Georgia Avenue, Suite 200, Silver Springs, MD 20910; (301)585-KIDS (in Maryland), (800)554-KIDS (elsewhere)

This national organization offers information on preventing drug and alcohol abuse, influences legislation, and acts as a clearinghouse for printed material and media. With a networker in every state, the federation can provide information on local parent groups and technical assistance in organizing youth and parent groups.

Parents Against Drugs (PAD), 70 Maxome Avenue, Willowdale, Ontario, Canada M2M 3K1; (416)225-6604

PAD offers a network of services in Canada: support groups led by trained parents, a peer counseling program, a crisis telephone line for parents, public forums and presentations, and a drug awareness workshop for educators and police officers.

Parents' Resource Institute for Drug Education, Inc. (PRIDE), PRIDE Canada, Suite 111, Thorvaldson Building, College of Pharmacy, University of Saskatchewan, Saskatoon, Saskatchewan Canada S7N 0W0; (800)667-3747 and PRIDE, Inc. (United States), 100 Edgewood Avenue, Suite 1002, Atlanta, GA 30303; (800)241-7946

Both groups aim at increasing public awareness of drug abuse and offer extensive resources for parents and teachers, including national conferences and research studies, a newsletter, speakers, training sessions, and a toll-free hotline in each country.

National Clearinghouse for Alcohol and Drug Information, P.O. Box 2345, Rockville, MD 20852; (301)468-2600

A service offered by the Office for Substance Abuse Prevention of the Alcohol, Drug Abuse, and Mental Health Administration, Department of Health and Human Services. Single copies of a wide variety of publications are available free of charge.

Educators can call 1-800-788-2800 and immediately access any of seven federal clearinghouse and information centers focusing on alcohol and other drugs. The Office of National Drug Control Policy (in cooperation with the Department of Health and Human Services, the Department of Justice, the Department of Housing and Urban Development, and the U.S. Department of Education) established the Federal Drug, Alcohol and Crime Clearinghouse Network. By dialing 1-800-788-2800, a caller can receive information and resource material from the following federal services (New phone number accesses . . . , 1992):

- The National Clearinghouse for Alcohol and Drug Information, Department of Health and Human Services, Office of Substance Abuse Prevention
- Drugs and Crime Data Center, Department of Justice
- Drug Abuse Information and Referral Hotline, Department of Health and Human Services
- Detailed information on development and implementation of drug-free workplace programs (Drug-Free Workplace Helpline, Department of Health and Human Services)
- The most current information available on national and community-based programs on prevention and control of drug abuse in public and

assisted housing (Drug Information Strategy Clearinghouse, Department of Housing and Urban Development)

- Up-to-date information on AIDS, drug abuse, and drug abuse prevention (National AIDS Clearinghouse, Department of Health and Human Services)
- Comprehensive information on criminal justice issues on the national and international level (National Criminal Justice Reference Service, Department of Justice)

Resources: Violence and "Hate Crimes" Organizations

American-Arab Anti-Discrimination Committee
4201 Connecticut Avenue NW, Suite 500
Washington, DC 20008; (202)244-2990

American Jewish Committee
Institute of Human Relations
165 East 56th Street
New York, New York 10022; (213)751-4000

Anti-Defamation League of B'nai B'rith
6505 Wilshire Boulevard, Suite 814
Los Angeles, California 90048; (213)655-8205

Center for Democratic Renewal
P.O. Box 50469
Atlanta, Georgia 30302; (404)221-0025

Committee Against Anti-Asian Violence
Tompkins Square Station
P.O. Box 20756
New York, New York 10009; (718)857-7419

County of Los Angeles
Commission on Human Relations
320 W. Temple Street, Suite 1184
Los Angeles, California 90012; (213)974-7611

Interagency Gang Task Force
500 W. Temple Street #343
Los Angeles, California 90012; (213)378-5945

Intercultural Communication Institute
8835 S.W. Canyon Lane, Suite 238
Portland, Oregon 97225; (503)297-4622

Klanwatch Project
Southern Poverty Law Center
400 Washington Avenue
Montgomery, Alabama 36104; (205)264-0286

Resources: Families, Health, Cultural Diversity, and Drug Education

Canadian Home and School and Parent-Teacher Federation, 323 Chapel Street, Ottawa, Ontario, Canada, K1N 7Z2; (613)234-7292
This organizations promotes public education programs on drug use and abuse and has identified smoking prevention as a priority.

Parents in Touch and Methods for Achieving Parent Partnerships, Indianapolis Public Schools, 901 North Carrollton, Indianapolis, IN 40202; (317)266-4134 or (800)232-MAPP
This group sponsors many activities to improve home-school collaboration, including Dial-a-Teacher (a homework hotline), a Parent Focus series to encourage home-based activities, and Parent Line (phone access to more than 150 tapes on education and social problem topics).

Families in Action, 3845 North Druid Hills Road, Suite 300, Decatur, GA 30033; (404)325-5799
Families in Action publishes *How to Form a Families in Action Group,* operates a drug information center, and distributes a newsletter with drug information.

Hispanic Policy Development Project, 1001 Connecticut Avenue NW, Suite 310, Washington, DC 20036; (202)822-8414
This organization focuses on the needs, concerns, and development of young Hispanics and provides impressive documents that illustrate the problems and challenges facing Hispanic-Americans.

National Black Child Development Institute, 1463 Rhode Island Avenue NW, Washington, DC 20005; (202)387-1281
This organization's 33 affiliates throughout the United States focus on improving child care, child welfare, education, and health and offer leadership training for adults through an annual conference and workshop. The institute has a number of publications available and will send information packets on request.

National Clearinghouse for Bilingual Education, 11501 Georgia Avenue, Wheaton, MD 20902; (800)647-0123
This is the largest clearinghouse in the United States for bilingual and bicultural educational materials. Among its publications are affective materials geared to parents' needs and a bimonthly newsletter. The organization

disseminates information over the phone, through the mail, and electronically.

National Council of La Raza, 20 F Street NW, Washington, DC 20001; (202)628-9600

The National Council of La Raza provides technical assistance and materials on Hispanic education issues, including parent involvement in schools. It has also developed five curriculum models that involve community-based education.

Resources: Missing and Exploited Children

National Center for Missing and Exploited Children, 2101 Wilson Boulevard, Suite 550, Arlington, VA 22201; (703)235-3900

This national center works with parents and law enforcement officials to locate missing and exploited children.

Toll-Free Numbers

State Law Enforcement Division Missing Persons Information Center	1-800-322-4453
National Center for Missing and Exploited Children	1-800-843-5678
Runaway Hotline	1-800-231-6946
National Runaway Switchboard	1-800-621-4000
Covenant House (Runaways)	1-800-999-9999
Parents Anonymous Hotline	1-800-421-0353
FBI National Child Abuse Hotline	1-800-422-4453
FBI Hotline	1-800-327-8529

Organizations Working to Improve Youths' Lives and Overall Welfare

Activity A-5
Review the sources provided in the section "For Additional Information on Resources" such as the *Foundation Directory*. Write for information concerning application procedures, types of programs and projects funded, and examples of previously funded at-risk programs.

Selected Major National Youth Organizations

Junior Achievement, Inc., One Education Way, Colorado Springs, CO 80906; (719)540-8000

Junior Achievement's At-Risk Program teaches students how the American economic system works and how education contributes to successful participation in the economy. Called The Economics of Staying in School (ESIS), the program appeals to middle-grade students and educators and consists of six activities designed to examine why peers drop out of school and the personal and social effects of withdrawing from school. Other themes include Facing the Issues, Exploring Careers, and Helping Others Say No.

This section was adapted from Hechinger, F. M. (1992). *Fateful choices: Healthy youth for the 21st century.* New York: Carnegie Council on Adolescent Development.

ASPIRA, 1112 16th Street NW, Suite 340, Washington, DC 20036; (202)835-3600

ASPIRA encourages and supports Hispanic young people in the pursuit of education. One of its initiatives, the National Health Careers Program, seeks to increase the number of Hispanic youth graduating from medical and other health professional schools. ASPIRA serves 13,000 students per year and offers the following services: recruitment, counseling, financial assistance, workshops on career choice and applications, health fairs, conferences, trips to schools, and student counseling.

Boy Scouts of America (BSA), 1325 Walnut Hill Lane, P.O. Box 152079, Irving, TX 75015; (214)580-2000

BSA stresses the development of mental and physical fitness and outdoor skills. One requirement of becoming a First Class Scout is physical fitness. Badges earned by Cub Scouts include safety and swimming.

Boys and Girls Clubs of America: Boys Club, 771 1st Avenue, New York, NY 10017; (212)351-5900. **Girls Club,** 30 East 33rd Street, New York, NY 10016; (212)689-3700

These organizations have health and physical fitness among its core programs. National programs that are health related include Smart Moves, an initiative to prevent substance abuse and early sexual involvement. A demonstration project currently active in 33 clubs is aimed at gang prevention and intervention. The organization also sponsors national sports programs.

National Coalition of Hispanic Health and Human Services Organizations, 1030 15th Street NW, Suite 1053, Washington, DC 20005; (202)371-2100

This coalition was founded by mental health professionals to improve community-based mental health services for Hispanics. In 1978, the organization expanded to include health and human service organizations and professionals. Members currently include community-based health and mental health organizations, social service providers, practitioners and officials in the fields of public health, nursing, social work, psychology, and youth services, and research programs and educational institutions. Its programs include health research, health promotion, and disease prevention and the education and training of health-care providers. Existing demonstration projects include AIDS education, alcohol and drug prevention, gang and drug abuse prevention, and inhalant abuse prevention.

Girl Scouts of the USA (GSA), 830 3rd Avenue, New York, NY 10022; (203)940-7500

GSA stresses personal well-being and fitness. Activities focus on physical and mental health including nutrition and exercise, interpersonal relationships, the home, safety, work and leisure, and consumer awareness. The organization publishes a series of booklets called *Contemporary Issues,* which addresses current topics including preventing teenage pregnancy, growing up female, preventing youth suicide, preventing child abuse, and preventing substance abuse.

National Network of Runaway and Youth Services, 1030 15th Street NW, Suite 1053, Washington, DC 20005; (202)371-2100

This network of approximately 900 organizations serves runaway, homeless, and other at-risk children. Basically, these organizations offer safe shelter and counseling to young people. Two national programs are 1) Youth-Reaching-Youth, a peer counseling program that discourages drug abuse, and 2) an AIDS prevention program called Safe Choices.

National Urban League, 500 E. 62nd Street, New York, NY 10021; (212)310-9000

The league has national programs that address adolescent pregnancy prevention and parenting, teaching adolescent male responsibility as a component, as well as drug, tobacco, and alcohol prevention, through a project called Time to Be Me: Looking at My Future.

YMCA of the USA, Commerce Building, Suite 111, 8200 Humboldt Avenue, Bloomington, MN 55430; (612)885-0273

This organization is dedicated to healthy minds, bodies, and spirits. A number of sports programs are in operation; however, improving personal health is the organization's main priority.

YWCA of the USA, 726 Broadway, New York, NY 10003; (212)614-2700

The YWCA promotes health, sports participation, and fitness for women and girls. Health care is a main priority. Specific topics addressed include health instruction, teen pregnancy prevention, family life education, self-esteem enhancement, parenting, and nutrition.

For Additional Information on Resources

Corporate 500: The Directory of Corporate Philanthropy. (1975 with irregular updates). This directory provides 1- to 2-page summaries of the top 500 corporations in the United States. Each entry provides address, telephone number, name of any associated foundation, areas of interest, eligibility requirements, policy statement, financial profile, and information on the application process. The directory is also indexed by areas of interest, eligible activities, geographical location, and names of corporate personnel and grant recipients.

The Foundation Center Source Book. (1975). The *Foundation Center* seeks to relate the needs of fund seekers to the activities of foundations and to assist foundations in making their programs known to a wider public. Fund seekers will find the essential data needed to determine if proposals fall within the scope of programs. Foundations are listed alphabetically with the following information: 1) descriptive and fiscal data; 2) statement of policy, programs, and application procedures; and 3) a listing of recent grants illustrating current programs.

Washington Information Directory. (1975/1976 with annual updates), Congressional Quarterly, Inc. Subject chapters list executive agencies, congressional committees, and private organizations as information sources. Each entry provides address, telephone number, director, and brief description of agency. This handbook provides detailed appendixes that include information on executive agencies, religious organizations, state and local officials, and regional federal information sources.

Research Centers Directory. (1960 with biennial updates). Gale Publications. First called *Directory of University Research Bureaus and Institutes,* the *Research Centers Directory* provides a guide to university-related and other nonprofit research organizations established on a permanent basis and carrying on continuing research programs in a number of areas, including education.

Government Research Centers Directory. (1960 with biennial updates). Gale Publications. This guide to U.S. government research and development centers, institutes, and laboratories focuses attention on a number of areas, including education. The publication is indexed by name, keyword, acronym, and government organization.

Encyclopedia of Associations. (1956 with annual updates). This five-volume series includes v. 1, National Organizations of the United States; v. 2, Geographical and Executive Index; v. 3, New Associations and Projects; v. 4, International Organizations; and v. 5, Research Activities and Funding Programs. This comprehensive listing with descriptions of associations is grouped according to the categories mentioned in the subtitle, with an alphabetical and keyword index.

References

Adcock, A. G., Nagy, S., & Simpson, J. A. (1991). Selected risk factors in adolescent suicide attempts. *Adolescence, 26*, 817–828.

Alderman, M. K. (1990). Motivation for at-risk students. *Educational Leadership, 48*(1), 27–30.

Allen, H. A., Splittgerber, F., & Manning, M. L. (1993). *Teaching and learning in the middle level school.* Columbus, OH: Merrill.

Ames, C. A. (1990). Motivation: What teachers need to know. *Teachers College Record, 91*, 407–421.

Anderson, L. W., & Pellicer, L. O. (1990). Synthesis of research on compensatory and remedial education. *Educational Leadership, 48*(1), 10–16.

Anti-smokers plan tough tactics to discourage teenagers. (1991, August 23). *The State* (Columbia, SC), p. 9A.

Araki, C. T., & Takeshita, C. (1991). Students helping students: Dispute management in the schools. *NASSP Bulletin, 75*(538), 31–37.

Arnold, J. (1991). The revolution in middle school organization. *Momentum, 22*(2), 20–25.

Aronson, E., Blaney, N., Stephan, C., Sikes, J., & Snapp, M. (1978). *The Jigsaw classroom.* Beverly Hills, CA: Sage.

ASCD. (1991, June). *Accelerating learning*, unnumbered, Alexandria, VA: Author.

Ashbrook, B. (1984). What will we do for the poor, disadvantaged, and computer illiterate? *Instructional Innovator, 29*(3), 22–23.

Atwater, E. (1988). *Adolescence.* Englewood Cliffs, NJ: Prentice-Hall.

Axelson, J. A. (1985). *Counseling and development in a multicultural society.* Monterey, CA: Brooks/Cole.

Baer, V. (1988). Computers as composition tools. *Journal of Computer-Based Instruction, 15*(4), 144–148.

Balch, P. M. (1989). Reducing twenty-first century student dropout rates. *The Clearing House, 63*(4), 170–171.

Banks, J. A. (1987). *Teaching strategies for the ethnic studies* (4th ed.). Boston: Allyn and Bacon.

Barber, L. W., & McClellan, M. C. (1987). Looking at America's dropouts: Who are they? *Phi Delta Kappan, 69,* 264–267.

Barish, S. (1991). Responding to adolescent suicide: A multifaceted plan. *NASSP Bulletin, 75*(538), 98–103.

Barth, R. P., Middleton, K., & Wagman, E. (1989). A skill building approach to preventing teenage pregnancy. *Theory Into Practice, 28*(3), 183–190.

Baruth, L. G., & Manning, M. L. (1992). *Multicultural education of children and adolescents.* Boston: Allyn and Bacon.

Baruth, L. G., & Manning, M. L. (1991). *Multicultural counseling and psychotherapy: A lifespan perspective.* Columbus, OH: Merrill.

Batsell, G. (1983). Parent education—A planned program pays off. *Middle School Journal, 15,* 10–11.

Beck, A. T., Ward, S. H., Mendelson, M., Mock, J., & Erbaugh, J. (1961). *Archives of General Psychiatry, 4,* 561–571.

Becker, W. C., & Carnine, D. (1980). Direct instruction: An effective instruction for educational intervention with the disadvantaged and low performers. In B. J. Lahey and A. E. Kazdin (Eds.), *Advances in child psychology* (pp. 429–473). New York: Plenum.

Beebe, F. (1989). Cooperative learning and self-esteem on the staff of the "Junior Lynx." *The Computing Teacher, 17*(3), 8–11.

Bell, L. C. (1986). Learning styles in the middle school classroom: Why and how. *Middle School Journal, 18*(1), 18–19.

Benedict, R. R., Snell, R., & Miller, D. (1987). Enterprise high: Helping school dropouts become self-supporting adults. *Educational Leadership, 44*(6), 75–78.

Bergman, J.L., & Schuder, T. (1992/1993). Teaching at-risk students to read strategically. *Educational Leadership, 50*(4), 19–23.

Berliner, D. (1986). Does ability grouping cause more problems than it solves? *Instructor, 94*(8), 14–15.

Biehler, R. F., & Snowman, J. (1990). *Psychology as applied to teaching* (6th ed.). Boston: Houghton-Mifflin.

Bluemel, N. L., & Taylor, R. H. (1990). Library media center: Oasis for the at-risk. *Media and Methods, 26*(3), 14–15.

Blythe, T., & Gardner, H. (1990). A school for all intelligences. *Educational Leadership, 47*(7), 33–36.

Bodinger-deUriarte, C. (1991, December). Hate crime: The rise of hate crime on school campus. *Research Bulletin* (no. 10), 1–6.

Boykin, A. W. (1982). Task variability and the performance of black and white school children. *Journal of Black Studies, 12,* 469–485.

Brandt, R. S. (Ed.). (1990). *Readings from Educational Leadership: Students at risk.* Alexandria, VA: ASCD.

Brodkin, A. D. (1990, November/December). The shy child's many faces. *Instructor, 100,* 14–15.

Brophy, J. (1987). Synthesis of research on strategies for motivating students to learn. *Educational Leadership, 45*(2), 40–48.

Brophy, J., & Good, T. L. (1986). Teacher behavior and student achievement. In M. C. Wittrock (Ed.), *Handbook of research on teaching* (3rd ed., pp. 328–375). New York: Macmillan.

Brown, A. J. (1993). Developing leadership among urban youth. *Momentum, 24*(2), 46–50.

Buie, J. (1987). Teen pregnancy: It's time for the schools to tackle the problem. *Phi Delta Kappan, 68*, 737–740.

Cahoon, P. (1989). Ambassadors: Models for at-risk students. *Educational Leadership, 46*(5), 64.

California State Department of Education. (1987). *Caught in the middle.* Sacramento, CA: Author.

Cancer from smoking to kill 157,226 in '91, report says. (1991, August 22). *The State* (Columbia, SC), p. 9A.

Canfield, J. (1990). Improving students' self-esteem. *Educational Leadership, 48*(1), 48–50.

Carnegie Council on Adolescent Development. (1992). *Fateful choices: Healthy youth for the 21st century.* Washington, DC: Author.

Carnegie Council on Adolescent Development. (1989). *Turning points: Preparing American youth for the 21st century.* Washington, DC: Author.

Chafel, J. A. (1990). Needed: A legislative agenda for children at risk. *Childhood Education, 66*, 241–242.

Charles, C. M. (1992). *Building classroom discipline.* White Plains, NY: Longman.

Chavkin, N. F. (1991). Community collaboration gives dropouts a choice. *The Education Digest, 56*(7), 17–19.

Chavkin, N. F. (1989). Debunking the myth about minority parents. *Educational Horizons, 67*(4), 119–123.

Checklist for identifying the potential dropout. (October 1986). *California Curriculum News Report.* Sacramento: California State Department of Education.

Children's Defense Fund. (1992). *The state of America's children.* Washington, DC: Author.

Children's Defense Fund. (1991). *Child poverty in America.* Washington, DC: Author.

Children's Defense Fund. (1988). *Making the middle grades work.* Washington, DC: Author.

Christensen, E. W. (1989). Counseling Puerto Ricans: Some cultural considerations. In D. R. Atkinson, G. Morten, & D. W. Sue (Eds.), *Counseling American minorities* (3rd ed., pp. 205–212). Dubuque, IA: William C. Brown.

Clark-Johnson, G. (1988). Black children. *Teaching Exceptional Children, 20*, 46–47.

Clifford, M. M. (1990). Students need challenge, not easy answers. *Educational Leadership, 48*(1), 22–26.

Closing the gap for U.S. Hispanic youth. (1988). Report from the 1988 Aspen Institute Conference on Hispanic Americans and the Business Community. Washington, DC: The Hispanic Policy Development Project.

Cohen, R. M. (1989). Learning from failure: Finding the formula for success in one middle school at-risk program. *American Secondary Education, 18*(1), 13–16.

Colten, M. E., & Gore, S. (Eds.). (1991). *Adolescent stress: Causes and consequences.* New York: Aldine De Gruyter.

Comer, J. P. (1987). New Haven's school-community connection. *Educational Leadership, 44*(6), 13–16.

Cornett, C. E. (1983). *What you should know about teaching and learning styles* (Fastback 191). Bloomington, IN: Phi Delta Kappa.

Crawford, J. (1989). Instructional activities related to achievement gain in Chapter 1 classes. In R. E. Slavin, N. L. Karweit, & N. A. Madden (Eds.) *Effective programs for students at risk* (pp. 264–290). Boston: Allyn and Bacon.

Crist, K. (1991). Restoring opportunity for dropouts. *Equity and Excellence, 25*(1), 36–39.

Cullinan, D., & Epstein, M. H. (1990). Behavior disorders. In N. G. Haring & L. McCormick (Eds.), *Exceptional children and youth* (pp. 153–191). Columbus, OH: Merrill.

Davis, A. K., Weener, J. M., & Shute, R. E. (1977). Positive peer influence: School-based intervention. *Health Education, 8,* 20–21.

Dawson, M. M. (1987). Beyond ability grouping: A review of the effectiveness of ability grouping and its alternatives. *School Psychology Review, 16,* 348–369.

DeFriese, G. H., Crossland, C. L., MacPhail-Wilcox, B., & Sowers, J. G. (1991). Comprehensive school health. *The Educational Digest, 56*(7), 42–45.

DeVries, D. L., & Slavin, R. E. (1978). Teams-Games-Tournaments (TGT): Review of ten classroom experiments. *Journal of Research and Development in Education, 12,* 28–38.

Dewey, J. (1956). *The child and the curriculum and the school and society* (combined edition). Chicago: University of Chicago Press.

Diem, R. A. (1992). Dealing with the tip of the iceberg: School responses to at risk behaviors. *The High School Journal, 75*(2), 119–125.

D'Ignazio, F. (1988). Bringing the 1990s to the classroom of today. *Phi Delta Kappan, 70*(1), 26–27.

Dowdney, D. (1987). Computers can reconnect potential dropouts. *The School Administrator, 44*(8), 12–15.

Downing, J., & Harrison, T. C. (1990). Dropout prevention: A practical solution. *The School Counselor, 38,* 67–74.

Dropout Prevention Survey. (May 1985). Pontiac, MI: Oakland County Schools.

Dryfoos, J. (1991). School-based social and health services for at-risk students. *Urban Education, 26*(1), 118–127.

Dumaree, R. M. (1991). Project C.I.T.Y. (Comprehensive Intervention for Troubled Youth). *American Secondary Education, 19*(2), 21–26.

Dunn, R., Beaudry, J. S., & Klavas, A. (1989). Survey of research on learning styles. *Educational Leadership, 46*(6), 50–58.

Dunn, R. S., & Dunn, K. J. (1979). Learning styles/teaching styles: Should they . . . can they . . . be matched? *Educational Leadership, 36*(4), 238–244.

Dunn, R. S., Dunn, K., & Price, G. E. (1986). *Learning style inventory manual.* Lawrence, KS. Price systems.

Edelman, M. W. (1989). Defending America's children. *Educational Leadership, 46,* 77–80.

Elam, S. M., Rose, L. D., & Gallup, A. M. (1992). The 24th annual Gallup Poll of the public's attitudes toward the public schools. *Phi Delta Kappan, 74,* 41–53.

Elkind, D. (1993). Whatever happened to childhood? *Momentum, 24*(2), 18–19.

Elkind, D. (1981). *The hurried child.* Reading, MA: Addison-Wesley.

Elliot, I. (1992). A blueprint for tomorrow. *Teaching K–8, 23*(3), 34–38.

Ellis, A. K., Mackey, J. A., & Glenn, A. D. (1988). *The school curriculum.* Boston: Allyn and Bacon.

Epstein, M. H., & Cullinan, D. (1986). Depression in children. *Journal of School Health, 56*(1), 10–12.

Exline, J. (1993). Children in crisis in the classroom. *Momentum, 24*(2), 12–16.

Federal Register. (1991, June 25). Aid to families with dependent children at-risk child care program, p. 29,054.

Fitzgerald, J. (1990). Students at risk: Are secondary teachers able to identify potential school dropouts? *Education, 111*(2), 226–229.

Fitzpatrick, J. P. (1987). *Puerto Rican Americans: The meaning of migration to the mainland* (2nd ed.). Englewood Cliffs, NJ: Prentice-Hall.

Fox, C. L., & Forbing, S. E. (1992). *Creating drug-free schools and communities.* New York: Harper Collins.

Gamoran, A. (1986). Instruction and institutional effects of ability grouping. *Sociology of Education, 59,* 185–198.

Gardner, H. (1987a). Developing the spectrum of human intelligence. *Harvard Education Review, 57,* 187–193.

Gardner, H. (1987b). An individual-centered curriculum. *In The schools we've got, the schools we need.* Washington, DC: Council of Chief State School Officers and The American Association of Teacher Education.

Gentile, L. M., & McMillan, M. M. (1992). Literacy for students at risk: Developing critical dialogues. *Journal of Reading, 35*(8), 636–641.

George, P. S. (1993). Tracking and ability grouping: Ten tentative truths. *Middle School Journal, 24*(4), 17–24.

Gollnick, D. M., & Chinn, P. L. (1990). *Multicultural education in a pluralistic society.* Columbus, OH: Merrill.

Goodwin, J., & Flatt, D. (1991). Teaching lifetime sports to at-risk students. *Journal of Physical Education, Recreation, and Dance, 65*(5), 26–27.

Grant, L., & Rotenberg, J. (1986). The social enchantment of ability differences: Teacher-student interactions in first- and second-grade reading groups. *The Elementary School Journal, 87,* 29–49.

Greenbaum, S., & Turner, B. (Eds.). (1989). *Safe schools overview: NSSC resource paper.* Malibu, CA: U.S. Department of Justice, U.S. Department of Education and Pepperdine University.

Haggerty, K. P., Wells, E. A., Jensen, J. M., Catalano, R. F., & Hawkins, J. D. (1989). Delinquents and drug use: A model program for community reintegration. *Adolescence, 24,* 439–453.

Hahn, A. (1987). Reaching out to America's dropouts: What to do? *Phi Delta Kappan, 69,* 256–263.

Hall, E. T. (1981). *Beyond culture.* Garden City, NY: Anchor.

Hancock, V. E. (1992/1993). The at-risk student. *Educational Leadership, 50*(4), 84–85.

Haring, N. G., & McCormick, L. (1990). *Exceptional children and youth* (5th ed.). Columbus, OH: Merrill.

Harp, B. (1989). What do we know about ability grouping? *The Reading Teacher, 42,* 430–431.

Hatch, T., & Gardner, H. (1988). New research on intelligence. *Learning88, 17*(4), 36–39.

Hereford, N. J. (1993, April). Saying no to drugs. *Middle Years,* 14–18.

Hiebert, E. (1983). An examination of ability grouping for reading instruction. *Reading Research Quarterly, 18,* 213–255.

Hilke, E. V. (1990). *Cooperative learning.* (Fastback 299). Bloomington, IN: Phi Delta Kappa.

Horton, L. (1992). *Developing effective drug education program.* (Fastback 332). Bloomington, IN: Phi Delta Kappa.

Hranitz, J. R., & Eddowes, E. A. (1990). Violence: A crisis in homes and schools. *Childhood Education, 67,* 4–7.

Irvine, M. (1992). The Summerbridge program for at-risk middle schoolers. *The Education Digest, 58*(2), 20–23.

Jarolimek, J., & Foster, C. D. (1989). *Teaching and learning in the elementary school.* New York: Macmillan.

Jennings, W. B. (1989). How to organize successful parental involvement advisory committees. *Educational Leadership, 47*(2), 42–45.

Johnson, D. W., & Johnson, R. (1989/1990). Social skills for successful group work. *Educational Leadership, 47*(4), 29–33.

Johnson, D. W., & Johnson, R. (1987). *Learning together and alone: Cooperative, competitive and individualistic learning.* Englewood Cliffs, NJ: Prentice-Hall.

Johnston, L. D., O'Malley, P. M., & Bachman, J. G. (1986). *Drug use among American high school students, college students, and other young adults.* Washington, DC: National Institute on Drug Abuse.

Joyce, B. R. (1988). Training research and preservice teacher education: A reconsideration. *Journal of Teacher Education, 39*(5), 32–43.

Kammoun, B. B. (1991). High school dropout programs: Elements for success. *NASSP Bulletin, 75*(538), 9–14.

Keefe, J. W. (1990). Learning style: Where are we going? *Momentum, 21*(1), 44–48.

Keefe, J. W. (1987). *Learning style: Theory and practice.* Reston, VA: NASSP.

Keefe, J. W., & Monk, J. S. (1986). *Learning style profile examiner's manual.* Reston, VA: NASSP.

Kelker, K. A. (1991). Acquiring school services for drug-addicted children. *The Education Digest, 56*(7), 46–48.

Kennedy, P. A., & Chavkin, N. F. (1992/1993). Interactive technology brings technology to all. *Educational Leadership, 50*(4), 24–27.

Kenny, A. M. (1987). Teen pregnancy: An issue for schools. *Phi Delta Kappan, 68*(10), 728–736.

Knapp, M. S., & Shields, P. M. (1990). Reconceiving instruction for the disadvantaged. *Phi Delta Kappan, 72,* 753–758.

Knapp, M. S., Turnbull, B. J., & Shields, P. M. (1990). New directions for educating the children of poverty. *Educational Leadership, 48*(1), 4–8.

Koslofsky, N. (1991). A learning support program for at-risk students. *NASSP Bulletin, 75*(534), 104–106.

Kostelnik, M. J., Stein, L. C., Whiren, A. P., & Soderman, A. K. (1988). *Guiding children's social development*. Cincinnati, OH: Brooks/Cole.

Kovacs, M. (1981). Rating scales to assess depression in school-aged children. *Acta Paedopsychiatrica, 48,* 305–315.

Kuhns, T. (1992). *Creative at-risk education*. Paper presented at the meeting of the National Middle School Association, San Antonio, TX.

Lacey, R. A. (1991). "I have a dream" for dropout prevention. *The Education Digest, 56*(7), 20–23.

Landers, S. (1989). Homelessness hinders academic performance. *APA Monitor, 20*(11), 5.

Lee, M. L. (1990). Educators & programs reaching out to at-risk youth. *Media and Methods, 26*(3), 12–15, 50.

Lee, S. (1992). *Project KARE (Keeping at-risk enrolled)*. Paper presented at the meeting of the South Carolina Middle School Association, Myrtle Beach, SC.

Lewin, H. M. (1987). Accelerated schools for disadvantaged students. *Educational Leadership, 44*(6), 19–21.

Linn, R. L., & Dunbar, S. B. (1990). The nation's report card goes home: Good news and bad about trends in achievement. *Phi Delta Kappan, 72,* 127–133.

Liontos, L. B. (1993). *At-risk families and schools: Becoming partners*. Eugene, OR: ERIC Clearinghouse on Education Management.

Little Soldier, L. (1989). Cooperative learning and the Native-American student. *Phi Delta Kappan, 71,* 161–163.

Living with 10–15 year olds: A parent education curriculum. (1982). Carrboro, NC: The Center for Early Adolescence.

Lonner, W. J., & Ibrahim, F. A. (1989). Assessment in cross-cultural counseling. In P. B. Pedersen, J. G. Draguns, J. Lonner, & J. E. Trimble (Eds.), *Counseling across cultures* (3rd ed., pp. 299-333). Honolulu: University of Hawaii Press.

Lum, D. (1986). *Social work practice and people of color: A process-stage approach*. Monterey, CA: Brooks/Cole.

Madden, N. A., Slavin, R. E., Karweit, N. L., & Livermon, B. J. (1989). Restructuring the urban elementary school. *Educational Leadership, 46*(5), 14–18.

Madden, N. A., Slavin, R. E., Stevens, R. J. (1986). *Cooperative integrated reading and composition: Teacher's manual*. Baltimore, MD: The Johns Hopkins University, Center for Research on Elementary and Middle Schools.

Maggi, B. (1991, Fall). One-on-one: Adopting middle level at-risk students. *Schools in the Middle,* 12–13.

Manning, G., & Manning, M. (1981). Assaults on childhood. *Childhood Education, 58,* 85–87.

Manning, M. L. (1993a). Seven essentials of at-risk programs. *The Clearing House, 66,* 135–138.

Manning, M. L. (1993b). Making equal access a middle school priority. *Focus on Later Childhood/Early Adolescence* (ACEI), *5,* 1–2.

Manning, M. L. (1993c). *Developmentally appropriate middle level schools*. Wheaton, MD: ACEI.

Manning, M.L. (1992). Parent education programs at the middle level. *NASSP Bulletin, 76,* 24–28.

Manning, M. L., & Allen, M. G. (1987). Social development in early adolescence: Implications for middle school educators. *Childhood Education, 63,* 172–176.

Manning, M. L., & Baruth, L. G. (1991). Appreciating cultural diversity in the classroom. *Kappa Delta Pi Record, 27*(4), 104–107.

Manning, M. L., & Lucking, R. (1990). Ability grouping: Realities and alternatives. *Childhood Education, 66,* 254–258.

Manning, M. L., & Lucking, R. (1991). The what, why and how of cooperative learning. *The Clearing House, 64,* 152–156.

Martinet, K. (1993). Youth gangs: A spreading problem. *Momentum, 24*(2), 68–72.

Martino, L.R. (1993). A goal setting model for young adolescent at-risk students. *Middle School Journal, 24*(5), 19–22.

Marion, R. (1981). *Educators, parents and exceptional children.* Rockville, MD: Aspen Systems.

Marion, R. (1979). Minority parent involvement in the IEP process: A systematic model approach. *Teaching Exceptional Children, 10*(4), 1–15.

Mason, D. A. (1993). An advocate for at-risk young adolescents: Tim Madrid and the junior academy. *Middle School Journal, 24*(3), 62–66.

McCarty, R. J. (1993). Adolescent suicide: A ministerial response. *Momentum, 24*(2), 61–65.

McClelland, M. C. (1987). Teenage pregnancy. *Phi Delta Kappan, 68,* 789–792.

McCormick, L. (1990). Communication disorders. In N. G. Haring, & L. McCormick (Eds.), *Exceptional children and youth* (pp. 327–363). Columbus, OH: Merrill.

McDonald, N., & Wright, E. (1987). MOP: A strategy for dropout prevention. *The Clearing House, 61,* 367–368.

McEroy, A. (1990). Combating gang activities in schools. *The Education Digest, 55*(2), 30–34.

McGeady, M. R. (1993). The runaways. *Momentum, 24*(2), 33–35.

McLaughlin, T. F., & Vacha, E. F. (1992). The at-risk student: A proposal for action. *Journal of Instructional Psychology, 19*(1), 66–67.

McWhirter, B. T., & McWhirter, J.J. (1990). University survival strategies and the learning disabled student. *Academic Therapy, 25*(3), 345–351.

Member institutions strive for drug free schools and youth. (1992, May 11). *AACTE Briefs, 13*(10), 1.

Mercer, C. D. (1990). Learning disabilities. In N. G. Haring, & L. McCormick (Eds.), *Exceptional children and youth* (pp. 109–151). Columbus, OH: Merrill.

Metz, E. D. (1993). The camouflaged at-risk student: White and wealthy. *Momentum, 24*(2), 40–44.

Meyer, L. A. (1984). Long-term academic effects of the direct instruction Project Follow Through. *Elementary School Journal, 84,* 380–394.

Miller-Jones, D. (1989). Culture and testing. *American Psychologist, 44,* 360–366.

Mirandé, A. (1986). Adolescence and Chicano families. In G. K. Leigh & G. W. Peterson (Eds.). *Adolescents in families* (pp. 433–455). Cincinnati, OH: Southwestern.

Mitchell, S. T., & Johnson, P. H. (1986). Richmond's response to students at risk. *Educational Leadership, 43*(5), 62–64.

Mitzel, H. E. (1982). Parent education. *Encyclopedia of Educational Research* (5th ed., vol. 3, pp. 1379–1382). New York: The Free Press.

Moore, D. D. (1988). Growing healthy: An effective substance abuse program. *Educational Leadership, 45*(6), 13.

More bad news on the achievement front: Students are falling short in mathematics. (1991). *The American School Board Journal, 178*(7), 4–5.

Morgan, D. P., & Jensen, W. R. (1988). *Teaching behavioral disordered students.* Columbus, OH: Merrill.

Morganthau, T., et al. (1992, March 9). It's not just New York. *Newsweek,* pp. 25–29.

Morrow, R. D. (1989). Southeast-Asian parent involvement: Can it become a reality? *Elementary School Guidance and Counseling, 23,* 289–297.

Morse, S. (1990). The nonschooled immigrant child. *Thrust, 19*(4), 36–38.

Muha, D. G., & Cole, C. (1991). Dropout prevention and group counseling: A review of the literature. *The High School Journal, 74*(2), 76–79.

Murphy, J. A. (1988). Improving the achievement of minority students. *Educational Leadership, 46*(2), 41–42.

Myers, C. B., & Myers, L. K. (1990). *An introduction to teaching and schools.* Fort Worth, TX: Holt, Rinehart, and Winston.

Nardini, M. L., & Antes, R. L. (1991). What strategies are effective with at-risk students? *NASSP Bulletin, 75*(538), 67–72.

NASSP. (1979). *Student learning styles—diagnosing and prescribing programs.* Reston, VA: Author.

National Center for Children in Poverty (NCCP). (1990). *Five million children: A statistical profile of our poorest young citizens.* New York: Author.

National Catholic Education Association. (1993). Confronting the risks. *Momentum, 24*(2), 4.

New telephone number accesses all federal alcohol and drug clearinghouses. (1992). *Southeast Sun* (Southeast Regional Center for Drug-Free Schools and Communities), *2*(3), 7.

Nicholson, G., Stephens, R., Elder, R., & Leavitt, V. (1985). Safe schools: You can't do it alone. *Phi Delta Kappan, 66,* 491–496.

Noddings, N. (1991/1992). The gender issue. *Educational Leadership, 49*(4), 65–70.

Nordland, R. (1992, March 9). Deadly lessons. *Newsweek,* pp. 22–24.

O'Connor, J. R. (1991). Skills for adolescence: A middle school guidance program. *American Secondary Education, 19*(2), 26–27.

Office of Educational Research and Improvement. (1987a). *The current operation of the Chapter 1 program.* Washington, DC: OERI.

Office of Educational Research and Improvement. (1987b). *Dealing with dropouts: The urban superintendents' call to action.* Washington, DC: U.S. Government Printing Office.

Office of Technology Assessment. (1991). *Adolescent health.* U.S. Congress, Washington, DC: OTA Publication Office.

Ogden, E. H., & Germinario, V. (1988). *The at-risk student: Answers for educators.* Lancaster, PA: Technomic.

Orbach, I. (1986). The "insolvable problem" as a determinant in the dynamics of suicidal behavior in children. *American Journal of Psychotherapy, 40,* 511–520.

Ornstein, A. C., & Levine, D. U. (1993). *Foundations of Education* (5th ed.). Boston: Houghton-Mifflin.

Pecaut, L. S. (1991). Why can't Johnny learn? *Principal, 70*(4), 29–30.

Peck, P. (1989). The child at risk: Closing in on success. *Instructor, 98*(6), 30–32.

Phi Delta Kappa. (1993). *Growing up is risky business, and schools are not to blame.* Bloomington, IN: Author.

Pigford, A. B. (1992). Solving the at-risk problem: Healthy schools can make the difference. *The Clearing House, 65,* 156–158.

Pinkney, A. (1975). *Black Americans.* Englewood Cliffs, NJ: Prentice-Hall.

Pinnell, G. S. (1990). Success for low achievers through Reading Recovery. *Educational Leadership, 48*(1), 17–21.

Pollard, D. S. (1989). Reducing the impact of racism on students. *Educational Leadership, 47,* 73–75.

Ponterotto, J. G., Pace, T. M., & Kavan, M. G. (1989). A counselor's guide to the assessment of depression. *Journal of Counseling and Development, 67,* 301–309.

Porter, A. C., & Brophy, J. (1988). Synthesis of research on good teaching: Insights from the work of the Institute of Research on Teaching. *Educational Leadership, 45*(8), 74–85.

Postman, N. (1983). The disappearing child. *Educational Leadership, 40,* 10–17.

Price, T., & Swanson, K. (1990). Reaching and teaching the whole student: A comprehensive approach for at-risk students. *Thrust, 19*(4), 13–16.

Prophet, M. (1990). Safe schools in Portland. *The American School Board Journal, 177*(10), 28–30.

Purkey, W. W. (1970). *Self-concept and school achievement.* Englewood Cliffs, NJ: Prentice-Hall.

Purkey, W. W., & Novak, J. M. (1984). *Inviting school success.* Belmont, CA: Wadsworth.

Radd, T. (1993). Restructuring parent teacher organizations to increase parental influence on the education process. *Elementary School Guidance and Counseling, 27,* 280–287.

Rattay, K., & Lewis, J. (1990). Gangs and the school: A plan for action. *Thrust, 19*(4), 17–22.

Reed, S., & Sautter, R. C. (1990). Children of poverty: The status of 12 million young Americans. *Phi Delta Kappan, 71*(10), K1–K12.

Resnik, H. (1988). Putting it all together: Quest's skills for growing program. *Elementary School Guidance and Counseling, 23,* 93–98.

Riccio, L. L. (1985). Facts and issues about ability grouping. *Contemporary Education, 57,* 26–30.

Richardson, E. H. (1981). Cultural and historical perspectives in counseling Indians. In D. W. Sue (Ed.), *Counseling the culturally different* (pp. 216–255). New York: John Wiley.

Rodriguez, H. R. (1993). Every child can learn. *Momentum, 24*(2), 51–52.

Rogus, J. F., & Wildenhaus, C. (1991). Programming for at-risk learners: A preventative approach. *NASSP Bulletin, 75*(538), 1–7.

Rudd, D. C. (1991, November 1). School's always out for 10% of city kids. *Chicago Tribune,* pp. 1,16.

Ruff, T.P. (1993). Middle school students at-risk: What do we do with the most vulnerable children in American education? *Middle School Journal, 24*(5), 10–12.

Salholz, E. et al. (1992, March 9). How to keep kids safe. *Newsweek,* p. 30.

Sanders, D. (1987). Cultural conflicts: An important factor in the academic failures of American Indian students. *Journal of Multicultural Counseling and Development, 15,* 81–90.

Santrock, J. W. (1990). *Adolescence* (4th ed.). Dubuque, IA: William C. Brown.

Sarafino, E., & Armstrong, J. (1986). *Child and adolescent development.* New York: West.

Scales, P. C. (1991). *A portrait of young adolescents in the 1990s: Implications for promoting healthy growth and development.* Chapel Hill, NC: Center for Early Adolescence.

Scattergood, S. P. (1990). A taste of parenthood. *The American School Board Journal, 177*(10), 24–25.

Seibel, M., & Murray, J. N. (1988). Early prevention of suicide. *Educational Leadership, 45*(6), 48–51.

Seifert, K. L., & Hoffnung, R. J. (1991). *Child and adolescent development* (2nd ed.). Boston: Houghton-Mifflin.

Sendor, B. (1989). Root out racial bias in student placement. *American School Board Journal, 176*(3), 24–25.

Sharan, Y., & Sharan, S. (1989/1990). Group investigation expands cooperative learning. *Educational Leadership, 47*(4), 17–21.

Shea, T. M., & Bauer, A. M. (1985). *Parents and teachers of exceptional children: A handbook for involvement.* Boston: Allyn and Bacon.

Shepherd, G. D., & Ragan, W. B. (1992). *Modern elementary curriculum.* New York: Harcourt, Brace, & Jovanovich.

Shine-Ring, A. (1990). Developing effective early intervention programs. *Thrust, 19*(4), 39–41.

Slavin, R. E. (1989). Students at risk of school failure: The problem and its dimensions. In R. E. Slavin, N. L. Karweit, & N. A. Madden (Eds.), *Effective programs for students at-risk* (pp. 3–19). Boston: Allyn and Bacon.

Slavin, R. E. (1988a). Cooperative learning and student achievement. *Educational Leadership, 47*(4), 31–33.

Slavin, R. E. (1988b). Synthesis of research on grouping in elementary and secondary schools. *Educational Leadership, 46*(1), 67–77.

Slavin, R. E. (1987a). Ability grouping and student achievement in elementary schools: A best-evidence synthesis. *Review of Educational Research, 57,* 293–336.

Slavin, R. E. (1987b). Grouping for instruction in the elementary school. *Educational Psychologist, 22,* 109–127.

Slavin, R. E. (1978). Student teams and achievement divisions. *Journal of Educational Research, 12,* 39–49.

Slavin, R. E., Karweit, N. L., Madden, N. A. (1989). *Effective programs for students at-risk.* Boston: Allyn and Bacon.

Slavin, R. E., Leavey, M. B., Madden, N. A. (1986). *Team accelerated instruction - mathematics.* Watertown, MA: Mastery Education Corporation.

Slavin, R. E., & Madden, N. A. (1989). Effective classroom programs for students at risk. In R. E. Slavin, N. L. Karweit, & N. A. Madden (Eds.), *Effective programs for students at-risk* (pp. 23–51). Boston: Allyn and Bacon.

Slavin, R. E., Madden, N. A., & Karweit, N. L. (1989). Effective programs for students at risk: Conclusions for practice and policy. In R. E. Slavin, N. L. Karweit, & N. A. Madden (Eds.), *Effective programs for students at-risk* (pp. 355–372). Boston: Allyn and Bacon.

Smith, E. J. (1981). Cultural and historical perspectives in counseling Blacks. In D. W. Sue (Ed.), *Counseling the culturally different* (pp. 141–185). New York: John Wiley.

Smith, G. (1989). The media academy: Engaging students in meaningful work. *Educational Leadership, 46*(5), 38–39.

Smith, V. G. (1988). Family day: An investment in our future. *Educational Leadership, 45*(8), 56.

Sopris West, Inc. (1992). *Educational programs that work* (18th ed.). Longmont, CO: Author.

Stein, M. K., Leinhardt, G., & Bickel, W. (1989). Instructional issues for teaching students at risk. In R. E. Slavin, N. L. Karweit, & N. A. Madden (Eds.), *Effective programs for students at-risk* (pp. 145–194). Boston: Allyn and Bacon.

Sternberg, R. J., Okagaki, L., & Jackson, A. S. (1990). Practical intelligence for success in school. *Educational Leadership, 48*(1), 35–39.

Stewart, W. J. (1990). Learning-style-appropriate instruction: Planning, implementing, evaluating. *The Clearing House, 63*, 371–374.

Strother, D. B. (1986). Suicide among the young. *Phi Delta Kappan, 67*, 756–759.

Sue, D. W. (1981). *Counseling the culturally different.* New York: John Wiley.

Sue, D. W., & Sue, S. (1983). Counseling Chinese-Americans. In D. W. Atkinson, G. Morten, & D. W. Sue (Eds.), *Counseling American minorities: A cross-cultural perspective* (2nd ed.) (pp. 97–106). Dubuque, IA: William C. Brown.

Swanson, M. C. (1989). Advancement via individual determination: Project AVID. *Educational Leadership, 46*(5), 63–64.

Taff, T. G. (1990). Success for the unsuccessful. *Educational Leadership, 48*(1), 71–72.

Taylor, R., & Reeves, J. (1993). More is better: Raising expectations for students at-risk. *Middle School Journal, 24*(5), 13–18.

Teeters, P. B. (1990). Effective continuation schools: A cure for the dropout rate. *Thrust, 19*(4), 48–51.

Theriot, R., & Bruce, B. (1988). Teenage pregnancy: A family life curriculum. *Childhood Education, 64*, 276–279.

Thompson, C. L., & Rudolph, L. B. (1988). *Counseling children* (2nd ed.). Monterey, CA: Brooks/Cole.

Thornburg, K. R., Hoffman, S., & Remeika, C. (1991). Youth at risk: Society at risk. *The Elementary School Journal, 91*, 199–208.

Titus, T. G., Bergandi, T. A., & Shryock, M. (1990). Adolescent learning styles. *Journal of Research and Development in Education, 23*(3), 165–170.

Today's gangs cross cultural and geographical bounds. (1992). *The Education Digest, 57*(9), 8–10.

Tonks, D. (1992/1993). Can you save your students' lives? Educating to prevent AIDS. *Educational Leadership, 50*(4), 48–51.

Totten, S. (1988). The myriad dangers of tobacco use: Ignorance is anything but bliss. *Educational Leadership, 45*(6), 28–31.

Turning points: Preparing American youth for the 21st century. (1989). Washington, DC: Carnegie Council on Adolescent Development.

U.S. Bureau of the Census. (1992). *Statistical abstracts of the United States: 1991* (112th ed.). Washington, DC: U.S. Government Printing Office.

U.S. Bureau of the Census. (1991). *Statistical abstracts of the United States: 1991* (111th ed.). Washington, DC: U.S. Government Printing Office.

U.S. Bureau of the Census. (1990). *Statistical abstracts of the United States: 1990* (110th ed.). Washington, DC: U.S. Government Printing Office.

U.S. Department of Education. (1990). *A profile of the American eight grader.* Washington, DC: Author.

Vander Zanden, J. W. (1989). *Human development* (4th ed.). New York: Alfred A. Knopf.

Viadero, D. (1989, October 25). Drug-exposed children pose special problems. *Education Week,* pp. 1, 10–11.

Wager, B. R. (1992/1993). No more suspensions: Creating a shared ethical culture. *Educational Leadership, 50*(4), 34–37.

Walberg, H. J. (1988). Synthesis of research on time and learning. *Educational Leadership, 45*(6), 76–85.

Walker, K. (1991). All students are at-risk. *NASSP Bulletin, 75*(539), 112.

Walters, J. M., & Gardner, H. (1985). The development and education of intelligences. In F. R. Link (Ed.), *Essays on the Intellect* (pp. 1–21). Alexandria, VA: ASCD.

Watson, D. (1988). The greatest risk of all. *Educational Leadership, 45*(6), 16–17.

Watson, D. L., Northcutt, L., & Rydell, L. (1989). Teaching bilingual students successfully. *Educational Leadership, 46*(5), 59–61.

Wax, M. L. (1971). *American Indians: Unity and diversity.* Englewood Cliffs, NJ: Prentice-Hall.

Wells, S. E. (1990). *At-risk youth: Identification, programs and recommendations.* Englewood, CO: Teachers Ideas Press.

White, P. D. (1989). Reaching at-risk students: One principal's solution. *Thrust, 19*(1), 45–46.

Williams, D. L., & Chavkin, N. F. (1989). Essential elements of strong parent involvement programs. *Educational Leadership, 47*(2), 18–20.

Wilson, A. B. (1989). Theory into practice: An effective program for urban youth. *Educational Horizons, 67*(4), 136–144.

Wilson, B. J., & Schmits, D. W. (1978). What's new in ability grouping? *Phi Delta Kappan, 60,* 535–536.

Winn, M. (1983). *Children without childhood.* New York: Pantheon Books.

Wolf, J. S. (1990). The gifted and talented. In N. G. Haring, & L. McCormick (Eds.), *Exceptional children and youth* (pp. 447–489). Columbus, OH: Merrill.

Wright, W. J. (1991/1992). The endangered black male child. *Educational Leadership, 49*(4), 14–16.

Wylie, V. L. (1992). The risk in being average. *Middle School Journal, 23*(4), 33–35.

Young adolescents at risk. (1993). *High Strides, 5*(1), 2.

Zukowski, A. A. (1993). The systems blueprint. *Momentum, 24*(2), 77–78.

Name Index

Subject Index